OLIVER CROMWELL
Painting by R. Walker, National Portrait Gallery.

[*front.*

CARLYLE

ON

CROMWELL AND OTHERS

(1837—48)

BY

DAVID ALEC WILSON

LONDON

KEGAN PAUL, TRENCH, TRUBNER & CO., LTD.

NEW YORK: E. P. DUTTON & CO.

1925

3983

Printed in Great Britain by Stephen Austin & Sons, Ltd., Hertford.

PREFACE

THE acknowledgments, etc., in the Prefaces to *Carlyle till Marriage* and *Carlyle to " The French Revolution "* apply to this volume also, and need not be repeated here. In this as in the preceding volumes, footnotes are omitted which relate to the books about Carlyle, biography, letters, etc., published by J. A. Froude, C. E. Norton, and A. Carlyle. The *Guide to Carlyle* of A. Ralli supplies clues to students seeking to trace anything here which is based on what is in these books. The original of the portrait of Mrs. Carlyle published here belonged to John Sterling and is now in the Carlyle House, Cheyne Row. For help in correcting proofs, I have to thank my friends John Henry Alexander, James Tennant and Samuel Scott.

Francis Espinasse is only one of many who have helped me and died before the work appeared. I saw him in the Charterhouse in his old age, and foretold to him the use here made of his *Literary Recollections*. He was a fine specimen of the Victorian journalist, who did indeed live by his trade, but hardly thought of his wages, living as if it were a matter-of-course in the true spirit of the highest human ideals,—monks, dervishes, and other " sons-of-god ", apostles, prophets, and sages.

DAVID ALEC WILSON.

Ayr, 1925.

NOTICE.—*Free permission is given to publish translations of this book.*

v

CONTENTS

BOOK XI

LECTURING (1837-40)

BOOK XV

LOOKING ROUND (1846–47)

I

HOW HE BEGAN

(1837)

CARLYLE was in need of wages, and the only offer he had was for lecturing in America. In March he was writing, " My mother too may perhaps go to America, and the whole set of us, root and branch! Far older emigrants than she have gone." A letter to his brother, Dr. John, in Rome, reveals his feelings :—

' The beggarly economical part of this existence on earth seems to me the more beggarly the longer I look at it ; the existence itself the more tragical, sublime. Not a hair of our heads but was given to us by a God.

' My chief pity is for Jane. She hoped much of me ; had great faith in me ; and has endured much beside me, not murmuring at it. I feel as if I had to swim both for her deliverance and my own. Better health will be granted me ; better days for us both.

' It is my fixed hope at present either to go to Scotland or to Italy next summer, stick in hand. If any offer occur to detain me here, it shall be well ; if none, it shall be almost better. This is what I meant by being balanced.'

He compared himself to Teufelsdröckh, taking a stick and going to " roam the earth " like a tramp, but in declining Miss Wilson's invitation to visit her brother and her at Tunbridge, he put it more prettily [1] :—

' I love England and hope to see it all some day. One of my darling day dreams is that of wandering over the whole world on foot. One feels as if, communing with the dumb old rocks, man's babblement and madness all left fairly in the rear, it would be well with one ! '

It was at dinner at the Wilsons' that he used to meet Spedding, Maurice, and Sir James alias " Mother-country "

[1] *Nineteenth Century Mag.*, 1921, May, pp. 802–4.

Stephen, the head clerk of the Colonial Office. Mrs. Carlyle
was often there, and was grateful for Miss Wilson's
affectionate reluctance to see the Cheyne Row household
broken up, and Carlyle abroad in search of an audience.
Miss Martineau was emphasizing his good prospects in
America ; but agreed there was also hope at home. So she
and Miss Wilson decided to act together, Mr. Wilson and
Henry Taylor helping them. They began by getting the
consent of Carlyle to deliver six lectures on German literature
in London next season ; and then they offered him to the
Royal Institution. It had no vacancy. When they reported
this to Carlyle, " there's nothing in that," said he. " Forty
or fifty human beings wanting to hear about German
literature, and one human being ready to tell them somewhat about it : this is the soul and body of the business ;
we get house-room anywhere we want and are independent
of all the Institutes in the world ! "

They snatched at the saying and hired Willis's Room,
" where the Almack balls are held, a painted and gilded
saloon, with long sofas for benches." By March, 1837, the
tickets were printed and being sold at a shop, a guinea for
the six lectures, on Mondays and Fridays from three to
four, beginning on the first of May. " Society," including
Brougham, took tickets enough to give him a net profit
of about £135, which made his house safe for another year.

The lecturer had nothing to do but meet his audience,[2]
which was fortunate, for he did not finish the proofs of
" The French Revolution " till 27-4-37, when he wrote
to Mill : " There remain two days in which to prepare for
that sublime course of lectures." Faithful to Scotch
tradition which despises paper, he said from the first, " I
mean to *speak* the lectures."

' One of his lady admirers,' wrote Mrs. Carlyle to her
uncle in March, ' was saying the other day that the grand
danger to be feared for him was that he should commence
with " Gentlemen and Ladies ", instead of " Ladies and
Gentlemen ", which would ruin him at the very outset.
He vows, however, that he will say neither the one thing
nor the other, and I believe him very secure on that side.
Indeed, I should as soon look to see gold pieces or penny
loaves drop out of his mouth, as to hear from it any such
humdrum unrepublican-like commonplace.'

[2] Besides *T. C. Letters, etc.*, see Miss Martineau's *Autobiography*, I,
pp. 382-3. Also the *Corr. of Abraham Hayward*, I, pp. 58-9, etc.

For fear of a breakdown, Mrs. Carlyle did not venture to the first lecture, which was reported and criticized at length in the *Spectator* (6-5-37) :—

There was ' a very crowded and yet a select audience of both sexes. Mr. Carlyle may be deficient in the mere mechanism of oratory ; but this minor defect is far more than counterbalanced by his perfect mastery of his subject, the originality of his manner, the perspicuity of his language, his simple but genuine eloquence, and his vigorous grasp of a large and difficult question. The most important branch of the first lecture was a history and character of the German people. They have, in fact, never been subdued ; and have been themselves by far the greatest conquerors in the world. The first mention of the Germans in history dates three hundred years before Christ. A merchant of the Greek colony of Marseilles sailed up the Elbe and described the progenitors of Luther, of Shakespeare and Milton, and Newton, Watt and Washington, as a quiet, respectable, and inoffensive people ; a singular character enough for barbarians, and which distinguishes the race at once, and in its very origin.

' The next mention is under the name of Cimbri and Teutoni, 102 B.C. Mr. Carlyle gave a most spirited and accurate description of Tacitus, who wrote in his study at Rome pleasant and respectable gossip, but neither critical nor accurate.

' The grand characteristic of the Teutonic intellect was expressed by the word *valour* ; by which, of course, he meant not mere animal courage, but that cool, dogged, onward, indomitable perseverance by which alone great things are ultimately achieved. His examples of individual cases were Kepler and his calculations, Milton and his *Paradise Lost.* Of national examples, he gave the conquest of England, the settlement of America by the conquerors of England— the conquest of India and the colonization of Australia. . . It is pretty clear that, in progress of time, they must either occupy or hold rule over the greater portion of the earth. But the influence of the Germans has been by no means confined to the examples we have given. The French, the Spaniards and Italians seem to owe all that is masculine and durable in their character to the Gothic race. We are not quite sure, indeed, but that the breed has been in some cases even improved by crossing and transplanting—as in the instances of the English and Americans and the French.

. . . We can, indeed, set no bounds to the progress of those who have invented, and what is better than inventing, who are capable of using, the printing-press, the steam-engine, firearms, the compass, and representative government.

' After what we have already said of Mr. Carlyle, it is almost superfluous to add that we heartily wish all success to his ingenious, instructive and interesting prelections.'

" Prelections," wrote the reporter, meaning lectures read, as if he had been busy on his notebook and never doubted that such a discourse was written. Many a bet was staked in the next few years on whether Carlyle lectured extempore, and many an argument spoken and even printed on both sides of that question ; but there is no question now—the lectures were all *spoken*. He made little use of notes, and never failed to send away the audience feeling that they had received the value of their money. That was what he said he wanted to do.

When he came home from the first lecture he had unusual gold in his pocket, and gave a sovereign each to his wife and her mother, who was visiting them. Mrs. Welsh bought a parasol with hers as a souvenir, and they both attended the rest of the lectures.

II

THE FIRST COURSE

(1837)

THE lectures followed the prospectus, from the Nibelungen Lied to the poets and novelists of the day. The number of hearers steadily increased. There was never any chairman.

When Mrs. Carlyle heard of his nervous misery at starting, or stage-fright, she mixed a little brandy and water for him to drink then and he gratefully obeyed, but it seemed to make no difference. Once, when she was worried by the sight of his " agony of incipiency ", Miss Wilson whispered to her, " Never mind him, my dear. People like it. The more of that, the better does the lecture prove." Which sounded harsh, but was true, she discovered.

There was more excuse for stage-fright than usual. He had little in common with any fashionable crowd, however " select ". It was a time of " crisis " and unemployment, taxes on food and famine, when some of the " working-classes " were killing their children in desperation. Whereby Carlyle was so heated with sympathy that he had to make an effort to be patient with his own good angel, Harriet Martineau herself, whose glory was to popularize the shibboleths of current " economy ". The ' good Harriet ' could be forgiven, but not the " hard-faced " gentry atop, the Broughams and Lyndhursts. To " speak " six lectures on German literature to an audience drawn from such ruling classes was what Carlyle had to do. It would have been trying to an orator by habit and trade ; and he had seldom spoken in public in his life before.

" My pleasure was a good deal spoiled," wrote the ' good Harriet ', " by his unconcealable nervousness. Yellow as a guinea, with downcast eyes (and) broken speech at the beginning, and fingers which nervously picked at the desk before him, he could not for a moment be supposed to enjoy his own effort. The merits of Carlyle's discourses were,

7

however, so great that he might probably have gone on year after year till this time (1855)." But, as she said,[1] while the lecturing lasted, he " scarcely slept and grew more dyspeptic and nervous every day ".

The women attending the lectures rather liked his obvious modesty, and agreed in admiring his good looks, particularly praising his " florid complexion and large blue eyes ".[2]

[1] *Autobiography of H. Martineau*, I, pp. 382-3.
[2] Told to D. A. W. by a lady, without permission to give her name.

III

JEFFREY, &c., ON THE HISTORY

(1837)

IN the middle of May (16–5–37) a copy of the History reached Jeffrey in Edinburgh, and he wrote on the next day but one (18–5–37) :—

'MY DEAR CARLYLE,—

'A thousand thanks for your book of the F. Revolution. It would have been very welcome to me (whatever its quality had been), as indicating a return of that old kindness, which I had feared you were withdrawing from me. But it certainly gives me greater pleasure, as it is a work which I feel assured will do you more honour and bring you into more notice than anything you have hitherto produced. It is a book, written most emphatically in your own manner, and yet likely to be very generally read, and which cannot be read anywhere, without leaving the impression that the author (whatever else may be thought of him) is a man of genius and originality, and capable of still greater things than he has done even here. It is no doubt a very strange piece of work, and is really, as Coleridge I think said of something else, like reading a story by flashes of lightning ! It is beyond all question the most *poetical* history that the world has ever seen, and the most moral also, tho perhaps not the fullest of wisdom. The descriptions are the finest things in it, and next, the sentiments, especially those of a soft, indulgent and relenting character, which are generally full of truth and beauty, [N.B.—The next nine words are inserted above the line, as if written afterwards.] and it *must* be owned outnumber all the *others*. Your ratiocinations (as those of poets are apt to be) are less satisfactory, and not very intelligible.'

He went into details, remarking : 'I have neglected my judicial duties to get thro' so much of it,' and concluding :—

'And my fair cousin ! I hope she does not mean to

9

disclaim me. I think of her often, with the greatest regard.
God bless you, my dear Carlyle. I shall never think of you
but with kindness, and shall always rejoice most sincerely in
all your good fortune. Ever very faithfully yours,

'FR. JEFFREY.'

Both Carlyle and his wife responded; and after this
Jeffrey never missed a chance of seeing them in London,
nor Carlyle of seeing him in Edinburgh. Whenever they met
bystanders felt superfluous.

Another presentation copy sent to Edinburgh was to
Sir William Hamilton, who is said to have read the three
volumes at a sitting of thirteen hours, from 3 p.m. to 4 a.m. ;
whereas Crabb Robinson declared it "should be called
rhapsodies—not a history. And provided I take only small
doses, and not too frequently, it is not merely agreeable,
but fascinating. It is just the book one should buy, to muse
over and spell, rather than read through. He who will give
himself the trouble will be rewarded by admirable matter.
Wordsworth is intolerant. Southey both reads Carlyle and
extols him".[1]

[1] *Diary, Rems., and Corr. of H. C. Robinson*, ed. by Dr. T. Sadler,
1869, III, p. 171.

IV

WORDSWORTH AND SOUTHEY, &c.

CRABB ROBINSON'S report was true. Wordsworth could only curse what Carlyle had written ; but his sonnet against the history had none of the cant about its being unintelligible. It seemed to him only too plain.

> " Portentous change ! When History can appear
> As the cool Advocate of foul device . . . . .
> Hath it not long been said the wrath of Man
> Works not the righteousness of God ? Oh bend,
> Bend, ye Perverse ! to judgments from on High,"

and so on, in a style becoming a respectable official dealing in stamps and a biographer of Peter Bell. Southey did better —he praised the " Pindaric History " to Taylor,[1] adding that he would probably " read it six times over ", and wrote to his friend Wynn [2] that Carlyle's was " a book like which there was nothing in our language before, nor is likely to be again ". When Southey came to town Taylor re-introduced Carlyle, to whom this second meeting was a treat that lingered in his memory for the rest of his life. Southey was the first man " of eminence " who cordially agreed with his way of thinking. It was a great " surprise " to find such a one, a Tory too, so " full of sympathy, assent, and recognition ". They talked at large about " the huge event itself ", which Southey had " dwelt with ever since his youth, and tended to interpret exactly as I—the suicidal explosion of an old wicked world, too wicked, false and impious for living longer ;—and seemed gratified, and as if grateful, that a strong voice had at last expressed that meaning."

They saw as much of each other as possible after this, and Southey called at Cheyne Row. He was about 63, and tho he knew it not, was soon to die.

---

[1] In the *Nineteenth Century Mag.*, June, 1881, pp. 1013–14.
[2] The Hon. C. W. W. Wynn, *Letters of Robert Southey*, IV, p. 509.

When Carlyle recalled the candidate at Bristol whose speech was only, " I say ditto to Mr. Burke," Southey eagerly added, " Hah ! I myself heard that ! " He had been a boy in Bristol at the time. He repeated in a mocking tone some verses about a Member of Parliament moving to abolish Death and the Devil, and another to change the obliquity of the Ecliptic.

Southey spoke of Shelley with sorrow and aversion. Carlyle said : " A haggard existence that of his ! " Southey paused, and said earnestly : " It *is* a haggard existence."

Many years ago Southey had cited the Jerusalem mob's election of Barabbas over Christ as characteristic of democracy. At the time Carlyle had dissented strongly ; but after finishing the *French Revolution* he was beginning to reconsider the point.

' The last time I saw Southey was on an evening at Taylor's, nobody there but myself. We sat on the sofa together ; our talk was long and earnest ; topic ultimately the usual one, steady approach of democracy, with revolution (probably *explosive*), and a *finis* incomputable to man— steady decay of all morality, political, social, individual, this once noble England getting more and more ignoble and untrue in every fibre of it. Our perfect consent ' made ' the dialogue copious and pleasant.'

Carlyle suddenly broke off and rose as a signal he must go. Southey stood up and chimed in cheerfully with the quotation : " It is not, and it cannot come to, good." As they shook hands he invited Carlyle to come to Cumberland "to see the Lakes again", and called after him as he passed beyond the door of the room : " Let us know beforehand that the rites of hospitality—"

" Ah, yes, thanks, thanks ! " cried the other from outside, and so departed, and they saw each other no more.

Henry Taylor has explained that Carlyle was reasonable in despairing now of such " recognition by others " as would enable him to live by writing, and without disclosing a name, he reveals some confidential inner history.[1]

' At a time when he was sadly struggling for the means of subsistence, I was in communication on the subject of literary pensions with the one of our statesmen now gone to their rest who was the most distinguished for his love of

literature, whilst his feelings of benevolence certainly exceeded what most of our public men have time for. I ventured to propose that a pension should be offered to Carlyle, and the answer was that a man who wrote such a style as that *ought* to starve.'

Which was partly cant, of course. There was a great deal more than the style of Carlyle objectionable to his lordship.

' Carlyle did not know of the proposal at the time, nor did it ever come to his knowledge, nor would it perhaps have met with his approval. But the reception given to it is significant of what was thought of him by most men of high cultivation in the orthodox and classical school of literature. No vagrant or gipsy could have had to break his way through more boundaries.

' " The world was not his friend, nor the world's law." '

V

" SUCCESS " BEGINNING

(1837)

THO Fraser did not advertise enough to please Jeffrey, he was soon reporting that the " French Revolution " was " moving, moving " towards a second edition. In the middle of June Carlyle had gone to Scotsbrig, and from there he was writing to Sterling in July to say he was enjoying the silence. The music of the Middlebie brook beside him was sweeter than any opera : " I look on the sapphire of St. Bees Head and the Solway mirror from the gable window ; I ride to the top of *Blaweary* (a hill near by), and see all round from Ettrick Pen to Helvellyn, from Tyndale and Northumberland to Cairnsmuir and Ayrshire : *voir c'est avoir* (to see is to have) : a brave old Earth after all—in which I am content to acquiesce and hold my peace. It is what we ought to do. One night, late, I rode through the village where I was born. The old ' Kirkyard Tree ', a huge old gnarled ash, was rustling itself softly against the great Twilight in the north ; a star or two looked out ; and the old graves were all there, and my Father's and my Sister's : and God was above us all. I really have no words to speak."

On a sunny Monday morning early in August, Betty Smeal coming from the Ecclefechan Post Office handed him newspapers, one of which was the *Times* with Thackeray's review of his history. His brothers, Alick and James, who were with him made him sit down under the shade of the hedge and beech-trees and " read it all over to them ". He felt obliged to Thackeray ; but moralized to Mill (10–8–37) that he would like to get the book swept out of his head. " I look upon the curse of all curses that man bears in this world to be self-conceit : it is ineradicable. The Mythus of Lucifer is one of the wisest ever conceived."

Perhaps it was self-conscious modesty that made him in that letter anticipate he might come to agree with Mill about Logic, which he had defined as the " Art of telling

14

other men *what* you believe ".   He had been encouraging
Mill to persevere in writing a book about it, on the general
ground that one should "write on the thing he knows about".
He confessed he had found logical methods misleading
altogether, and learned in that way " hardly any truth
that I set much store by.   Nevertheless, I am curious to
hear what *you* say they should be ".

When he came home in the middle of September
Mrs. Carlyle was hiding behind the outer door to give him a
joyful surprise, and began telling good news before he
took off his hat.   And what she said was true.   He soon found
he was growing " famous ", which made him remember
how at Scotsbrig he had enjoyed Pickwick more than a
good history.   " It is worth noting," he moralized in his
journal, " how loth we are to read great works ; how much
more willingly we cross our legs, back to candle, feet to fire,
over some Pickwick or other lowest trash of that nature.
The reason is we are very indolent, very wearied and forlorn,
and read oftenest that we may forget ourselves.   Consider
what popularity in that case must mean."

What his wife was saying was : " Oh, it has had a great
success, dear ! "   And he was fain to believe it, for it meant
he might continue to make a living by writing ; but the only
editor soliciting an article from him was Mill, who wrote
from Brighton for one on Scott, and came himself to beg
it about 9–11–37.   Carlyle undertook it, and while doing it
can be seen in Crabb Robinson's Reminiscences : [1]

' November 25th, 1837.   I dined with a very superior
man, a hard-headed Scotchman, Craufurd.   Thomas Carlyle
was there [and] excited strong disgust [in me] by his
outrageous declamation in favour of the negro slavery of
the Americans . . . a natural and just aristocracy—that of
race indicated by colour.   He hoped this slavery would last
for ever . . . He was personally civil to me, which I coldly
noticed.   I resolved to be no longer acquainted with him.'

The essay on Scott was finished on 6–12–37.   Carlyle
had refused to do an obituary article for Fraser when Scott
died ; but Lockhart's many volumes now provided the stores
of knowledge which he always needed, as his mason father
needed durable stones.   His description was too good a

---

[1] *The London Mercury Mag.*, October, 1922, p. 610.

likeness to please admirers at the time, but exactly what the Radicals wanted.

The best indication of his " success " was an offer from Fraser for the republication in London of his Collected Essays or *Miscellanies* and *Sartor*. He turned to Miss Martineau as business adviser, " a very shrewd creature," he wrote to his brother John (12–12–37), and added about fame :—

' The liveliest image of Hell-on-Earth that I can form to myself is that of a creature blown up by popular wind. Let me break stones on the highway rather, and be in my own heart at peace ! I do feel a peace not dependent on other men or outward things but on myself : God be thanked for it, and make it grow ! '

Meanwhile his books were being reprinted in America. Dr. Lebaron Russell and others were arranging that. They were taking the risk and the trouble and leaving him all the profit.

HARRIET MARTINEAU
Drawing by G. Richmond, National Portrait Gallery.

[face p. 16

BOOK XI

LECTURING

(1837–40)

CONTENTS

LIST OF ILLUSTRATIONS

VI

CARLYLE AND THE PRINTERS

' IN 1837,' wrote Harriet Martineau,[1] ' he came to me to ask how he should manage, if he accepted a proposal from Fraser to publish his pieces as a collection of " Miscellanies ". After discussing the money part of the business, I begged him to let me undertake the proof-correcting. He nearly agreed to let me do this, but afterwards changed his mind. The reason for my offer was that the sight of his proofs had more than once alarmed me— so irresolute, as well as fastidious, did he seem to be as to the expression of his plainest thoughts. Almost every other word was altered ; and revise followed upon revise. I saw at once that this way of proceeding must be very harassing to him ; and also that the profits must be cut off to a most serious degree by this absurdly expensive method of printing. I told him that it would turn out so.

' As might be expected, the printing went on very slowly. One day, while in my study, I heard a prodigious sound of laughter on the stairs ; and in came Carlyle, laughing loud. As soon as he could, he told me what it was about. He had been to the [printing-] office [at Charing Cross] to urge on the printer : and the man said, " Why, Sir, you really are so very hard upon us with your corrections ! They take so much time, you see ! " After some remonstrance, Carlyle observed that he had been accustomed to this sort of thing, that he had got works printed in Scotland, and—" Yes, indeed, Sir," interrupted the printer, " We are aware of that. We have a man here from Edinburgh ; and when he took up a bit of your copy he dropped it as if he had burnt his fingers, and cried out, ' Lord have mercy ; have you got that man to print for ? Lord knows when we shall get done—with all his corrections ! ' " '

The master-printer here quoted may have been the same Mr. Robson who soon after this, if not already, did all the

---

[1] *H. M.'s Autobiography*, I, pp. 384–6.

printing for Carlyle, and continued to do it for many years. Carlyle always stipulated that Robson was to do his printing, and explained to his mother : " They say he is a little dearer. Well, I answer, ought he not ; being considerably better ? A better man ought to be had in respect, and by all methods encouraged wherever we fall in with him." No doubt, but paying more is seldom the best method. " Cheap and nasty " was a proverb he often quoted. " Dear and nasty " is worse. The right thing is " cheap and good ". It might have been better for Robson to charge less ; but maybe he was merely trying to recoup the loss of time on corrections.[2] Reshaping the text while at press was a habit Carlyle caught from Jeffrey, and natural for a rich and busy lawyer and politician editing in haste ; but not suitable for a writer who had to live on a share of the profits of publishing.

[2] Apropos Carlyle there was published a detailed account of Robson's business history, which D. A. W. read about 1900 ; but it is not at hand, and the memory cannot be trusted farther.

VII

HARRIET MARTINEAU

IN 1837 the first of Miss Martineau's two books on America appeared, and Carlyle discussed her in a letter to Emerson :—

' I have read it for the good authoress's sake, whom I love much. A genuine little Poetess, buckramed, swathed like a mummy into Socinian and Political-Economy formulas ; and yet verily alive in the midst of that ! . . . I admire this lady's integrity, sincerity ; her quick, sharp discernment to the depth it goes ; her love also is great ; nay, in fact, it is too great ; the host of illustrious obscure mortals whom she produces on you, of Preachers, Pamphleteers, Antislavers, Able Editors, and other Atlases bearing (unknown to us) the world on their shoulder, is absolutely more than enough.'

With what he said to herself about her books on America she was well content, for she wrote in 1855 [1] :—

' Some of the wisest of my friends at home—and especially I remember Sydney Smith and Carlyle—gently offered their criticism of my more abstract American book in the pleasant form of praise of the more concrete one, the *Retrospect of Western Travel.* Readers liked my second book best who, like Carlyle, wisely desire us to see what we can, and tell what we see, without spinning out of ourselves systems and final causes. Carlyle wrote me that he had rather read of Webster's cavernous eyes and arm under his coat-tail, than all the political speculation that a cut-and-dried system could suggest.'

' She was much in the world,' wrote Carlyle, ' we little or hardly at all ; and her frank friendly countenance, eager

---

[1] *Autobiography of Harriet Martineau*, II, pp. 105–6 ; and III, p. 219.

for practical help had it been possible, was obliging and agreeable in the circumstances, and gratefully acknowledged by us. She was practically very good. I remember her coming down, on the sudden when it struck her, to demand dinner from us ; and dining pleasantly, with praise of the frugal terms. Her Soirees were frequent and crowded ; and we, for sake of the notabilities or notorieties wandering about there, were willing to attend. Gradually learning how *in*significant such notabilities nearly all were.'

Here are a few jottings from Harriet's journal [2] :—

' Thursday, 21st September, 1837.—We had company in the evening. Carlyle was in fine spirits. He made a great laugh at the scientific people. He calls them quacks and what not. I wish he had more sympathy and less cynicism. He has a terrible deal of the spirit of contempt.

' Tuesday, 26th September, 1837.—To the Carlyles. John Sterling there. A young man next door to death, they say, but if he lives a few years sure to be eminent ; so wise, so cheerful, so benignant ! I wish Carlyle would learn somewhat from him, for his views are deplorably dismal, and very unreasonable. He [Carlyle] does not pretend to care whether there is another life to compensate [when I insisted on knowing whether he believed in immortality]. I asked him what was his idea of good, if he is sure all is well, but the best men miserable. He says he can give no clearer reply than that it is found in the New Testament—" The Worship of Sorrow ".'

Which was surely a wise reply to the ' good Harriet ' then. She was a strange mixture of simplicity and sense. She seriously told Carlyle, not meaning fun at all, that she " *had* once "—only once !—" met a man who seemed not to believe fully in immortality ", and she " retailed at bound-less length " what he said.

When Carlyle tried to support his " Worship of Sorrow " by referring her to the New Testament, he received a surprising answer : " I think Jesus Christ lived one of the most joyous lives." This took his breath away. He went home and wrote it down. He seems to have said nothing at the time. He used to avoid argument and not struggle for the last word ; but may have been remembering this as well as Harriet's facility in writing when he said what the editor of her papers reports without a date :—

[2] Ibid., III, pp. 81, 192-4, 205, 209, 218.

' She was, Mr. Carlyle used to say, an instance, and the only one he knew, of clear activity being compatible with happiness. He could not talk before her, he added, about every effort being painful and all labour sorrow. " You are," he said to herself, " like a Lapland witch on her broomstick, going up and down as you will. Other people, without broomsticks, drop down, and cannot come up when they would ; and that's the difference between them and you." '

She used to talk of *writing* being such a *pleasure* to her.[3] Assuredly it was not her work that bothered her. What made her break down in the course of years, and end by leaving London altogether, was her mother nagging her to change into " a larger house in a better street ", befitting better than the modest house they had the superior " society " they now were " moving in ".[4]

Her journal dates some unpremeditated visits and dinners such as Carlyle remembered with pleasure :—

' (Wednesday, 13–12–37).—Walked to Chelsea to dine with the Carlyles. Found her looking pretty in a black velvet high dress and blonde collar. She and I had a nice feminine gossip for two hours before dinner, about divers domestic doings of literary people, which seem really almost to justify the scandal with which literary life is assailed. The Carlyles are true sensible people, who know what domestic life ought to be.

' Saturday, 20–1–38.—The sun shone. Dressed and set out for Chelsea. Walked it within three-quarters of an hour. Mrs. Carlyle looked like a lady abbess ; black velvet cap with lappets, white scarf and rosary. Very elegant creature.

' Sunday, 21–1–38.—Leigh Hunt tells Carlyle that his troubles will cease at five and forty ; that men reconcile themselves, and grow quiet at that age. Let me not wait for forty-five, but reconcile myself daily and hourly to all but my own curable faults.'

Miss Martineau thought Cheyne Row unhealthy because too " close to the river ", and rejoiced when their lease ran out, and " Carlyle ", as his wife told her, " went forth with three maps of Great Britain and two of the world in his

---

[3] *J. W. Carlyle : Letters to her Family*, by L. Huxley, p. 164.
[4] *Autobiography of H. M.*, I, pp. 248–51, 268–9.

pocket, to explore the area within twenty miles of London."
But they stayed where they were. Miss Martineau added :—

' I like the house for no other reason than that I spent
many pleasant evenings in it . . . I have seen Carlyle's face
under all aspects, from the deepest gloom to the most reckless
or most genial mirth ; and it seemed to me that each mood
would make a totally different portrait. The sympathetic
is by far the finest, in my eyes. His excess of sympathy has
been, I believe, the master-pain of his life. He does not know
what to do with it, and with its bitterness ; and savageness
is, in my opinion, a mere expression of his intolerable
sympathy with the suffering. But to those who understand,
his eyes, his shy manner, his changing colour, his sigh, and
the constitutional pudeur which renders him silent about
everything he feels the most deeply, his wild speech and
abrupt manner are perfectly intelligible.

' I have felt to the depths of my heart what his sympathy
was in my days of success and prosperity and apparent
happiness without drawback ; and again in sickness, pain,
and hopelessness of being ever at ease again : I have
observed the same strength of feeling towards all manner of
sufferers ; and I am confident that Carlyle's affections are
too much for him, and the real cause of the " ferocity " with
which he charges himself and astonishes others.'

Till 1839, as long as she lived in London, the ' good
Harriet ' saw much of the Carlyles, and on both sides the
friendship grew and grew till she went away to live at
Tynemouth. They went there to comfort her when she was
sick. Then in the slow course of years their mutual regard
serenely subsided into silent goodwill and latent affection.
There never was unpleasantness. In 1866 he wrote of her :—

' She had a sharp eye, an imperturbable self-possession,
and in all things a swiftness of positive decision, which,
joined to her evident loyalty of *intention*, and her frank,
guileless, easy ways, we both liked. Her very considerable
talent would have made her a quite shining Matron of some
big Female Establishment, but was totally inadequate to
grapple with deep spiritual and social questions.'

This is praise and intended for praise. Carlyle esteemed
more highly than his contemporaries the talents which he
attributed to her.

VIII

THE "ONYX RING" REPORTER

(1837–8)

THE *Onyx Ring* was written by John Sterling at Madeira this winter (1837–8), and contains a description of conversation,[1] which many said was like Carlyle's.

' To the few people he ever sees, he talks quaintly and vigorously, I sometimes think, wildly ; but all he says has a strong stamp upon it, and never could pass from hand to hand without notice. After having heard him, some of his phrases keep ringing in one's ears, as if he had sent a goblin trumpeter to haunt one with the sound for days and nights after. But I have always felt that he has more in his mind than comes out in the expression ; and, odd as his talk is, I should hardly call it affected or conceited.'

The most concrete item is this advice to a leader of working men who came to inquire about a certain candidate for Parliament :—

' *Meddle with no political parties. Their maxims and enterprises are all utterly worthless. Those who flatter you do it only to cheat you.* Have nothing to do with pretensions.'

Writing to Sterling at Christmas, Carlyle defended Goethe thus :—

' Was there a great intellect ever heard tell of without first a true and great Heart to begin with ? Never ; think it not. Worse *blasphemy* I could not readily utter. Nay, look into your own heart, and consider ! The Devil's name is *Darkness*, and that only ; *Eigendünkel* (self-conceit or presumption). Fear no seeing man, therefore ; know that *he* is of Heaven, whoever else be not ; that the Arch-Enemy, as I say, is the Arch-stupid : I call this my Fortieth Church Article—which absorbs into it, and covers up in silence, all the other Thirty-nine.'

---

[1] John Sterling's *Onyx Ring*, pp. 520 and 269-72.

23

IX

LECTURING TO CONTINUE

(1838)

CARLYLE was reading the old Chinese psalms this winter in a German translation, and praised them. He said to Allan Cunningham about the New Year's Day that the increase of age made one quieter. This would be apropos a favourite New Year Greeting, learned from Edward Irving long ago, " *May the worst of our years be past !* "

" A man never gets healthy till he is five-and-forty," said Allan who was 54 ; and Leigh Hunt, who was also 54, agreed with him. Carlyle " could not deny " this was " rare news " for a confirmed dyspeptic.

It seemed plain he would either have to leave London or lecture there again, but he remarked in a letter to Emerson : " If I had the smallest competence of money to get ' food and warmth ' with, I would shake the mud of London from my feet, and go and bury myself in some green place, and never print any syllable more. Perhaps it is better as it is."

One of London's attractions to him now was Covent Garden Theatre. The manager, Macready, sent him a free pass this winter, and he went about once a week to see a play of Shakespeare or anything notable, and wrote to his brother that he saw in Macready " sincerity [and] really a kind of genius ; I hope to know the man personally yet ".

They soon were friends for life. When Macready went to America he had a letter of introduction from Carlyle to Emerson, and when Macready was not present Carlyle was heard to speak of him more than once : " Look there, Mr. Macready in Covent Garden puts our Bishops in their Cathedrals to shame. He *has* faith in what is true ; in the Victory of Truth even among the multitude ; they, none—unless Truth have four thousand five hundred a year in its pocket, the Bishop of London says it has no chance for Victory ! " [1] Which seems to be his humorous interpretation

---

[1] Vaguely reported by sundry ; but the very words made sure by a letter from T. C. to Macready, 24–12–41, sold by Messrs. Christie in June, 1907, and printed in the *Glasgow Herald*, etc., 18–6–07.

of an episcopal speech. Many bishops had only £4,500 a
year, and the Bishop of London, who had £10,000 himself,
had expressed the general feeling of the profession in saying
£4,500 *at least* should be provided for the bishop in a new
diocese about to be arranged. In short, £4,500 should be the
Bishops' trade union minimum.

On Thursday (1–2–38), Carlyle had laid aside his Dante
and was writing to his brother John in Italy, when
Miss Martineau was ushered in like a good fairy, " with ear-
trumpet, muff, and cloak," and sat talking to them for an
hour and a half in "her deft Unitarian-Poetic way", and
settled before she departed that he was to lecture again, and
twelve times this season instead of six.

Resuming his letter, he told his brother the news, and went
on :—

' Jane sits by me, reading *Fraser's Magazine*; sends love.
Enjoy your beautiful Italian spring. Bring as many beautiful
pictures home with you in your head as you can. In your
head ; that is the only place where you can *possess* them ;
and truly I find they are a great possession there ;
much more delightful than when one is acquiring them.'

In a few weeks Miss Martineau, Miss Wilson, and
Erasmus Darwin—" a tall and very courteous gentleman of
the old school," and already one of Carlyle's most " intimate
friends " [2]—these three together had hired a regular lecture-
room in Edward Street, Portman Square, and nothing
remained but to settle the subject. " The French
Revolution," Henry Taylor advised. " Too ticklish for
lecturing," was Carlyle's opinion. " German again," said
the others. He inclined to a series of literary characters,
Homer, Virgil, and so on, to Voltaire and the rest ; and
Taylor suggested for that a title he agreed to : " On the
History of Literature, or the Successive Periods of European
Culture."

" Dicky " Milnes objected ironically to such " a confined
subject " ; but the title fitted the lectures, which were to
range from Homer to Hume and Richter. Charles Buller
had brought Milnes to the house in 1836, and so started one
of the pleasantest of Carlyle's friendships. They had love for
Goethe in common. Milnes was among the rich by birth.

[2] *Literary Recollections*, by F. Espinasse, pp. 230 and 231.

He was already in Parliament, while under 29, and starting
on the political stump ; but nothing ever interrupted his
intimacy with Carlyle, who was often at his parties.[3]

Charles Buller was conspicuous at this time. He also was
in politics, and had been in Canada last year as Chief
Secretary to Lord Durham, against whose settlement of the
Rebellion there Brougham had been bawling his loudest in
the Lords. Durham was defeated in the London Parliament
in his absence, and came home in weak health. He was
dying, but his " Report ", which was mostly written by
Buller, and Mill's defence of it and him in his January
Review, prevailed over Brougham ; and Durham's successor
carried out his policy, giving Canada Home Rule, and making
" famous " the " Report " which justified it.

Durham and Buller were sincere radicals. Brougham
was merely seeking to discredit Durham. Society
grinned approval when Milnes went about repeating what
his friend Carlyle was saying : " Brougham's tongue seems
to be a mere wooden clapper pulled up and down by anybody,
and to have nothing of a reasonable member about it." [4]

The main occupation of Carlyle this winter and spring
was reading at large with the lectures in mind. The Semites
had their Bible and Koran, the Hindus and the Chinese
other Scriptures old and good. Carlyle's opinion was that
there had been books made in Europe equal to any, and he
meant to make that plain.

[3] R. M. Milnes, by Wemyss Reid, I, pp. 171–2, etc.
[4] Ibid., II, p. 481.

X

AMONG THE SAINTS IN LONDON

EARLY in 1838 may be the date of Carlyle's intimacy with Thomas Erskine of Linlathen near Dundee, a rich Scotch laird of Lawyer-lineage, who had taken to religion seriously, and from writing successful books to defend the faith was known as " Evidence Erskine ". Having more economical elbow-room than his friend Maurice, he thought so freely that Dr. Chalmers and others, especially after he became intimate with Carlyle, were afraid he might outgrow the Bible altogether, which he never did. His faith was as spontaneous as Carlyle's, but more old-fashioned, and here is how he used to put the " all-important question " of " authority " [1] :—

' Do you believe that twice two are four because Mr. Cocker or some one else has told you so, and Mr. Cocker is such a very wise man that he must be right ? Or do you know that twice two are actually four, and feel much obliged to Mr. Cocker for having at first pointed it out to you ? If the first, you believe principles because they are delivered to you ; if the second, because they are true.'

Maurice could agree to this and Carlyle chuckled, but imagine the face and feelings of Pusey or Newman on hearing their holy of holies so exposed ! No wonder Erskine and Carlyle drew together at once, and ever more so the longer they lived.

The Rev. Alexander Scott was another " Saint " then public, who resorted much to Carlyle and used to dine with Erskine. " He has a good laugh in him," said Carlyle to his brother, but " Not instructive to me " was all he could be induced to say of Scott's sermons. It was when people tried to drag Carlyle into theology that they could quickly

---

[1] *F. D. Maurice*, by his son Frederick M., I, p. 453.

discover one side of the gospel of silence. We are left guessing the creed of the Mr. Wedgwood and his wife who brought most of the religious people into his circle. They were friends of Erasmus Darwin, whose brother Charles was shortly to marry Wedgwood's sister. Charles himself occasionally met Carlyle at his brother's house. " One must always like Thomas," he wrote to Emma Wedgwood, because Erasmus had told him Carlyle said Emma " was one of the nicest girls he had ever seen." [2] Of her brother Wedgwood, to explain the liking of Carlyle for him, it should be told that in 1837 he resigned his well-paid appointment as police magistrate, after holding it for six years, because he had been slowly convinced that the administration of oaths was contrary to the Gospel. In less than two years he was consoled by an appointment as Registrar of cabs, but that was unexpected.

John Sterling's friend Dunn, the Irish clergyman who refused a bishopric, came with Erskine one evening this year and commenced a friendship which death ended soon. It was he who was described by Maurice in a letter to Trench as " the most finely formed Christian man that I have ever seen ", altho he cautiously adds, " at one time there may have been a secret vein of Arianism in his mind, or, at least, a tendency that way." You never can tell !

" On the whole," Carlyle said to his brother John, " I take up with my old love for the Saints. No class of persons can be found in this country with as much humanity in them ; nay, with as much tolerance as the better sort of them have. The tolerance of others is but doubt and indifference ; touch the thing they do believe in and value, their own self-conceit, and they are rattlesnakes then."

The saints who visited him did not clash with his other friends. As he wrote to his brother John (9–3–38), " Cavaignac and Erskine met one night ; and beautiful to see, fell in love with one another," the earnest atheist and the earnest Christian !

Carlyle delighted in good company of any kind, and many an indigestion and sleepless night he suffered for the sake of it ; but the self-sufficiency of the right sort of man never left him. He remarked to his brother in the letter last quoted : " What company is *so good* as reading Thucydides,

[2] *A Century of Family Letters*, II, p. 13, and also I, pp. 242–3, 257–8, 285–6, and II, pp. 32–4 ; and also *Life and Letters of Charles Darwin*, I, pp. 77–8.

Dante, or Johannes von Müller " (the historian of Switzer-land) ?   " A mixture of both is needful, but the solitary evenings are the best."

In letters to Mill a few weeks later he said what he thought about Niebuhr and Michelet.

' Niebuhr disappoints me : vain jargon of cognoscente scholarcraft ; and for result darkness visible.   I have not found one tolerable idea that is Niebuhr's exclusively, and not the general property of Germany as well.   Michelet is a handy little man, and not without vivacity, nay ideas—especially in the first volume.'   Which was high praise for a modern writer, if we remember the northern idiom of the double negative and also that Carlyle was trying both by the highest standards.

XI

" JENNY KISSED ME "

(1838)

LEIGH HUNT was prospering and writing freely now, but during an influenza epidemic he was ill for some weeks. There were many deaths, and Mrs. Carlyle was anxious about him. This being told him when he suddenly recovered, he went himself to be the bearer of his good news. When Mrs. Carlyle beheld him unexpectedly enter, she jumped up and kissed him ; and that was what inspired his verse in the *Monthly Chronicle* this year. The secret need not be kept any longer.[1] " I never heard of Mrs. Carlyle kissing any other man," said one of her later favourites, " not even me," he concluded with a sigh.

> " Jenny kissed me when we met,
>   Jumping from the chair she sat in ;
> Time, you thief, who love to get
>   Sweets into your list, put that in :
> Say I'm weary, say I'm sad,
>   Say that health and wealth have missed me,
> Say I'm growing old, but add,
>   Jenny kissed me."

This is as neat as anything in Horace, and next to Abou Ben Adhem, the best of Hunt's verses.

---

[1] *Life of Leigh Hunt*, by C. Monkhouse, p. 200, for date, 1838. These details were told D. A. W., with leave to tell them here, by Sir C. Gavan Duffy, who had them direct from the parties.

XII

LECTURES ON EUROPEAN LITERATURE [1]
(1838)

THE first lecture was on Friday, 27–4–38. He started punctually at 3 p.m., but often went beyond the stipulated hour, to the general satisfaction. His wife wrote to his sister (1–5–38) :—

' His nerves were stiffer than last year. I took one glimpse at him when he came on the stage, and to be sure he was as white as a pocket-handkerchief, but he made no gasping and spluttering, as I found him doing last year. By-and-by he recovered all that " bonny red in his cheeks " which Miss Corson cf Craigenputtock so highly admired ; and having a very fine light from above shining down on him he really looked a surprisingly beautiful man. His Lecture was to my taste better than any last year (tho he himself thinks, forsooth, that there was not enough of *fire* in it) ; and he delivered it very gracefully ; that is to say, without any air of thinking about his delivery, which is the best grace of any.'

In a letter to her cousin in Liverpool she described the audience as " more than fair in quantity ; and in quality it is unsurpassable ; there are women so beautiful and intelligent that they look like emanations from the moon ; and men whose faces are histories in which one may read with ever new interest ".

The lecturer began with the Greeks, whose " fiery impetuosity " made them like the French, and he matched the worst horrors of the Revolution from Thucydides.[2] While accepting Wolff's denial of the single authorship of Homer, and correctly anticipating the later discoveries of excavators—" Homer already betokens a high state of

---

[1] T. C. Anstey's report is published as a book edited by R. P. Karkaria, 1902 ; Bombay.
[2] *Thucydides*, III, 79–83, and IV, 46–8.

civilization "—he showed the beauty of the old Epics, whose heroes seemed to live again.

' See Agamennon when he swears by " rivers and all objects, stars ", etc., and calls on them to witness his oath. He does not say what they *are*, but he feels that he himself is a Mysterious Existence, standing by the side of them— Mysterious Existences.'

He maintained that the authors of Homer believed they were telling the truth and not fictions, and even quoted Herodotus to show sincerity in the oracles. He found the keynote of Greek thinking and not of their tragedies only in the belief in Destiny, " the Unchangeable." Their great achievement was repelling the Persians.

' Themistocles was one of the greatest men in the world. Had it not been for him the Persians would have conquered Greece.'

The stolid and arrogant Romans were easier to understand; they muddled through like the English, with thrift for their principal virtue.

' I cannot join in the lamentations over the downfall of the Republic. It had been but a constant struggling scramble for prey, and it was well to end it.'

The most significant, and the greatest of Roman writers, was Tacitus, who " stood like a colossus at the edge of a dark night ".

Leigh Hunt was writing about the lectures in the style of a friendly chorus of an old Greek play. He deplored the praise given to the Romans for so mean a virtue as thrift ; and the very next Sunday (13–5–38) came in sore affliction to Carlyle, and was immediately comforted by a loan of two sovereigns. By that time he was not thinking of Romans. As he leaned against the mantelpiece that evening, the talk was of the latest (Friday) lecture on the Middle Ages. Was Carlyle really serious in putting Peter the Hermit, who believed what he said, above Demosthenes, who confessed his art of persuasion was mere play-acting ? Demosthenes was the standard model of orators, but Hunt had a soul above humbug, and could be pleased with the preference given to Peter, tho he had no patience with " thrift ".

In discussing the " Cid " of the Spaniards, Carlyle had
to mention Mahomet, and said : " I must say that I regard
this man as no impostor at all." The surprise to be seen on
every face at this may have been what made him afterwards
return to Mahomet in 1840 ; but on this occasion he had to
stick to Spanish Literature, and the keynote of his lecture
about it was, " There are only these three, Cervantes,
Calderon, and Lope ; and Cervantes is far above the two
others," thus agreeing with Hazlitt and differing from the
German critics. He spoke of their " forced taste ".
Goethe joked with difficulty, and had no · use for Don
Quixote.

T. C. Anstey is to-day the most important of all the hearers
of the lectures, for his shorthand notes supplied the best
record of Carlyle's extempore talk. He was a young man
then (22), and reading for the bar. He had been turned
into a Roman Catholic by the Oxford Movement, and is said
to have led after him the Quaker, Lucas, who founded the
Tablet paper. He now wrote an article on Carlyle for the
Dublin Review ; and when he heard that Mrs. Carlyle
had started copying the book of his lecture notes, he
insisted on doing it for her, saying, " I will copy it for
you ; it will be a pleasure to me to write them all a
second time."

He " rhapsodized " about her husband, so that she
reported he was " the individual most agog " about *Sartor*.
He said to her once, " The Jesuits are enchanted with all
they find in Carlyle," which shows how discreetly the
Jesuits talked to converts like Anstey. It may have
been on sight of her surprise at this that Erasmus Darwin
asked her :

" After all, what the deuce is Carlyle's religion, or has he
any ? "

She shook her head and assured him, " I know no more
than yourself."

The question was fair. The lecturer behaved to his
audience as he did to his mother, tabooing theology
altogether and minimizing the risk of offence, like another
Confucius. Such had been his method ever since he began
to write. As Lowell has remarked of the *Montaigne* which
he wrote for the Encyclopedia, " There is not a word as to
his religious scepticism." Nevertheless, if the Jesuits read
Anstey's notes their delight would have been a " forced
taste ". He exposed the Jesuits by name, and praised Luther

as the champion of a Reformation still in progress and first
asserter of the right of consulting one's own conscience.
He did, indeed, glorify Belief, the backbone of humanity,
but he was more explicit than usual in saying : " *It is not
doctrines, it is sincerity of heart which constitutes the whole
merit of Belief.*" It would perhaps have been better if he
had simply said sincerity and avoided the word Belief.

While he tabooed the shibboleths of controversy, and
quoted with approval Dante's story of Virgil rebuking him
for heeding two sinners quarrelling in Hell, he talked of
Christianity as coolly as Lucian of Jupiter and Co., and with
the same disinterested curiosity. He said it reached its
greatest height in the eleventh century, when Hildebrand
made the Kaiser come to Canossa and the Crusades began.

' I have repeatedly alluded,' he said, ' to the necessity of
change in doctrine, the impossibility of any creed being
perpetual, any theory which man's small mind may form
of this great universe being complete, tho he should study
to all eternity the immensity of which he is a fraction. Any
opinion he may form will only satisfy him for a time ; it
expands itself daily ; for progression is the law of every
man ; if he be a fool even, it is inevitable.'

He said "Shakespeare's intellect was far greater than that
of any other man that had given an account of himself by
writing books ". John Knox was named as a kind of counter-
part of Shakespeare, and his history of the Scottish
Reformation praised above " any other ".

To De Vere, in Ireland, Milnes reported [3] :—

' Carlyle's lectures have been, perhaps, more interesting
than anything else. There he stands, simple as a child, and
his happy thought dances on his lips and in his eyes, and
takes word and goes away, and he bids it God speed, whatever it be.'

This is precious as perhaps the best glimpse of Carlyle at
work putting words together. Nothing can be more
misleading than much in his diary, wherein he wrote for
his own behoof, and did not need to tell himself the pleasure
he had in composition.

[3] *R. M. Milnes*, by T. Wemyss Reid, I, p. 220.

XIII

INTERLUDES

(1838)

CRABB ROBINSON had a treat recorded in his diary on Tuesday, 22–5–38, the day after the seventh lecture, which was on the Reformation.[1]

' A delightful breakfast with Milnes—a party of eight, among whom were Rogers, Carlyle, who made himself very pleasant indeed, Moore and Landor. Talleyrand's recent death and the poet Blake were the subjects. Tom Moore had never heard of Blake.'

What Moore wrote in his diary was that Robinson and Carlyle talked " a good deal about German authors ", but he felt he had not " lost much " by not knowing these. Carlyle dined that night at old John Marshall's in Grosvenor Street in pleasant company, which included an old acquaintance, Empson, who was soon to marry the only daughter of Jeffrey.

Less pleasant because less harmonious was a dinner party at the Wilsons', where Sterling was babbly and argumentative and Maurice was eager to debate theology, which Carlyle was bound to taboo as the Wilsons were earnestly orthodox. Let the son and biographer of Maurice be the witness, saying [2] :—

' [In 1838] Carlyle was an important element in life to my father. They met in society not infrequently ; always more or less antagonistically. Up to a certain point they agreed exceedingly well : Carlyle always anxious to avoid

---

[1] *Diary, Rems., and Corr., of H. Crabb Robinson,* III, p. 150.
[2] *F. D. Maurice,* by his son, Frederick M., I, pp. 250–1.

35

the points of difference, my father never able to leave them alone.'

What was worrying Maurice was his anxiety for Sterling, who was facing an early death and yet was being drawn by Carlyle's influence away from Christ. This was the year of the Sterling Club, to which Maurice and Carlyle both belonged, as well as John Mill and "Dicky" Milnes, Bingham Baring and M. Rio, etc. The beautiful candour of Maurice reveals a mixture of feelings. " I have the greatest reverence for Carlyle," he was heard to say, " but I am sure he thinks me a sham."

The fact was that it was now about twenty years since Carlyle had seen for himself that theology was as incredible as astrology, and ceased to be interested in it. Whatever he was to Maurice, Maurice was little to him. For the rest of his life Carlyle had abundance of society, his only care was not to have too much lest it might interfere with his work. Affection, indeed, he craved; he could never get enough of it ; and in debating with his wife whether they should remain in London, he was most easily closured by the argument that London was the likeliest place for him to find congenial company. One of the sorrows of the prosperous years now passing was that Mill, who had been the first to press this upon him, and was one of the best friends he had found in London, was now withdrawing himself, and their walks together were becoming few, for no reason Carlyle could discover. The secret was revealed in Mill's autobiography [3] :—

' We never approached much nearer to each other's modes of thought than we were in the first years of our acquaintance. I did not, however, deem myself a competent judge of Carlyle. I felt that he was a poet, and that I was not ; that he was a man of intuition, which I was not ; and that as such he not only saw many things long before me, which I could only, when they were pointed out to me, hobble after and prove, but that it was highly probable he could see many things which were not visible to me even after they were pointed out. I knew that I could not see round him, and could never be certain that I saw over him ; and *I never presumed to judge him until he was interpreted to me by one greatly the superior of us both,*' [Mrs. Taylor, who

[3] *Autobiography of J. S. Mill*, p. 176.

became Mrs. Mill, and] '*who was more a poet than he, and more a thinker than I, whose own mind and nature included his, and infinitely more*'.

As Grote said of his epitaph upon her, only Mill's reputation could survive the like of this.[4] The humour is delicious, but quite unintended ; and Nature's jokes are always the best.

[4] W. L. Courtney's *J. S. Mill*, p. 114.

XIV

THE ELEGANT GEORGE TICKNOR, &c.

(1838)

THE elegant George Ticknor was an American four years older than Carlyle and rich enough to please himself for occupation.[1] He was now finishing a second spell of three or four years in the best society of Europe, in the intervals of which, 1819 to 1835, he had been a Harvard Professor of French and Spanish, etc. He had lately been collecting materials for his monumental *History of Spanish Literature*, when not interviewing ; but is most likely to be remembered by the happy accident that he was sitting with Byron when a man brought in the news of Waterloo, and Byron exclaimed, " I am damned sorry for it," and added after a pause, " I didn't know but I might live to see Lord Castlereagh's head on a pole, but I suppose I shan't now."

Ticknor had interviewed De Staël and Goethe, La Fayette and Talleyrand, Tieck and Chateaubriand, Wordsworth and Southey. Carlyle was nothing more to him than " an obscure writer for the Reviews ". But at the time of the lectures he was in London on his way home—to Boston, of course— and wrote in his journal :—

' June 1. After all I found time to make a visit to Carlyle, and to hear one of his lectures. He is rather a small, spare, ugly Scotchman '—

Which makes one fear that the reporter had heard of Carlyle's disrespectful opinion of most Spanish Literature and had his eyes bewitched by irritation. He continued :—

' with a strong accent, which I should think he takes no pains to mitigate. His manners are plain and simple, but

---

[1] *Life, Lets., and Journals of George Ticknor*, Boston, 1876, I, pp. 60, 137, 259, 262–3 ; and II, pp. 59, 180–1.

not polished, and his conversation much of the same sort. He is now lecturing for subsistence to about a hundred persons, who pay him, I believe, two guineas each.'

Carlyle made no secret of his reason for lecturing—namely, " for subsistence," the phrase may be his own, and may explain the disesteem of Ticknor.

' To-day he spoke—as I think he commonly does—without notes, and therefore as nearly extempore as a man can who prepares carefully, as it was plain he had done. His course is on Modern Literature '—European, rather—'and his subject to-day was that of the eighteenth century ; in which he contrasted Johnson and Voltaire very well, and gave a good character of Swift. He was impressive, I think, tho such lecturing could not well be very popular ; and in some parts, if he were not poetical he was picturesque. He was nowhere obscure, nor were his sentences artificially constructed, tho some of them, no doubt, savoured of his peculiar manner.'

Exit Ticknor,—to compile his "monumental" history, and never suspect how it was that he had been led to call on Carlyle. A few years after this Carlyle "told me quite good-humouredly", says a credible reporter,[2] " of a little practical joke which Milnes played on him."

' He received one day a visit from an American, who had been floating about rather extensively in London society. The visitor, who was homeward bound, stayed an unconscionable time. At last, when he was about to depart, he said that he could not return to the States without paying a farewell visit to Carlyle, who, Milnes had told him, " was talking of him yesterday for two hours." Carlyle had indeed been speaking of him for a considerable period, but it was to denounce him as a bore of the first magnitude.'

[2] *Literary Recollections*, by F. Espinasse, p. 78.

XV

CONCLUSIONS

(1838)

IN the same lecture which vindicated Swift as " by far
the greatest man of that time ", Carlyle said what
John Sterling could not away with, that silence was better
than speech. He meant nothing new.

' I admire that inscription, " Speech is silvern, silence is
golden." It is impossible to prove faith or morality by speech
at all. Logic pretends to force belief, and yet there is no such
constraint possible. Logic can do no more than define to
others what you believe. In mathematics, where things are
called by authorized designations, there alone is it final.
But try, " Virtue is Utility." In every different mind there
will be a different meaning of the words *Virtue* and *Utility*.
In spite of early training I never do see sorites of Logic
hanging together but I conclude that it is going to end in
some miserable delusion.'

He praised Pope, whom it was then the fashion to
depreciate unduly, saying he " was one of the finest heads
ever known, full of deep sayings " ; and he was wonderfully
tender to Dryden, " a man of immense intellect," who
subsided into formalism [1] for a living and did imitations of
French plays. But " his poverty was the cause, not his
will ".
" A formalist," [1] he said, was " a man whose soul was
no longer in contact with anything he got to delineate "
so that he was " for ever thinking of the effect he was to
produce " ; and Addison was a rare instance of a " formal
man doing great things ".

It was the intellect of Dryden he reverenced. There was
no mincing of words about " that most disgraceful class of
people—King Charles' people " ; and in the next lecture
(eleventh, 8-6-38) he ventured on the ticklish topic of the

---

[1] Misspelt *Formulism* and *Formulist* in the reports.

French Revolution, saying what he thought of it with such
acceptance that he was soon deciding to take Taylor's advice
so far as to lecture on European Revolutions next year,
if he lectured at all.

Philosophers to-day say ditto to his account of Hume.
When these lectures appeared in print in 1892, some daring
originalities of 1838 were commonplace ; of which perhaps
this is the best :—

'It is very strange to contrast Hume with Dante, five
centuries from one another, two of the greatest minds.
Dante saw a solemn law in the universe, pointing out his
destiny, with an awful and beautiful certainty, and he held
to it. Hume could see nothing in the universe but confusion,
and he was certain of nothing but his own existence ; *yet he
had instincts which were infinitely more true than the logical
part of him ; and so he kept himself quiet in the middle of it
all, and did no harm to anyone. For as to his books, he believed
that they were true, and therefore to publish them he was bound—
he was bound to do what seemed right to him ; he had no other
business for his intellect than this ; and moreover, as I have
observed, in publishing them he did an useful service for
humanity.'* [2]

This was far better than any of the apologists' replies to
the infidel Hume ; for thus was the nature of duty,
instinctive and infinite, proved from the behaviour of
Hume himself at the expense of his logic. It is one of the
neatest arguments in the history of philosophy.

His main point, however, was that scepticism as an abiding
state of mind was mental disease. He insisted that the
scepticism affected the orthodox and extended to everything
else as well as religion, being produced by that system of
trying to make out a theory on every subject.

'It is good, doubtless, that there should always be some
theory formed, with a view to the apprehension of its subject
[or] for facility of arrangement. But there is a wide difference
between a theory of this kind and a theory by which we
profess to account for it and give the reasons for its being
there at all. Let a man take, for example, the pebble that lies
under his feet. He knows that it is a stone, broken out of

[2] Italics added.

rocks old as the creation ; but what that pebble *is*, he knows not—he knows nothing at all about that. This system of making a theory about everything was what we can call an enchanted state of mind. Everything was placed upon the single table of logic ; one could hardly go anywhere without meeting some portentous theory or other.

' Even the very centre of all was brought to that level— Morals. There was a theory of virtue and vice, duty and the contrary of that. This will come to be thought one day an extraordinary sort of procedure. When I think of this it seems to me more and more that morality is the very centre of the existence of man ; that there is nothing for a man but that which it is his duty to do ; it is the life, the harmonious existence of any man, the good that is in him. No man can know how to account for it ; it is the very essence and existence of himself.

' Besides morality, everything else was in the same state. All was brought down to a system of cause and effect, of one thing pushing another thing on, by certain laws of physics—gravitation—a visible material kind of shoving. A dim, huge, immeasurable steam-engine they had made of this world.'

In short, he derided the French philosophers as pitilessly as ever they derided the mediæval scholastics, and he concluded by the praise of Goethe, Schiller, and Richter, with a candid admission about *Wilhelm Meister* :—

' There is even no positive recognition of a God, but only of a stubborn force ; really a kind of heathen thing.'

Such emphasis of expression had a savour of the northern pulpit in it ; and he was equally emphatic in cursing as " the most fatal thing in men " that " self-conceit " which " never existed but for the ruin of a man ". In the same vein he concluded the last lecture of the course (11–6–38) with his favourite quotation from Richter : " Thou, Eternal Providence, wilt cause the day to dawn," followed by an expression of thanks to his audience which sounded like a benediction, ending " God be with you all ! " to the pious Papist reporter Anstey. A candid biographer has to confess that Carlyle seems to have said *good*, not God.

He wrote to his mother next day (12–6–38) :—

'The lectures went on better and better, and grew at last quite a flaming affair. I had people *greeting* yesterday. I was quite as pleased that we *ended* then and did not make any further racket about it. I have too great evidence in poor Edward Irving's case what a racket comes to at last, and want, for my share, to have nothing at all to do with such things. My audience was supposed to be the best, for rank, beauty and intelligence, ever collected in London. I had bonnie braw dames, Ladies this, Ladies that, tho I dared not look at them lest they should put me out. I had old men of fourscore ; men middle-aged, with fine steel-grey beards ; young men of the universities, of the law profession, all sitting quite mum there, and the Annandale voice gollying at them. Very strange to consider. They proposed giving me a dinner, some of them, but I declined it.'

Which was a very English conclusion. "Our net product is just about £260," he told his mother (21–6–38), in sending her £5, as he often did when money came in. Later this year when the first £50 arrived from America out of the French Revolution profits, in sending her another five pound note he quoted, "The kitlin (kitten) ought to bring the auld cat a mouse." His wife being economical they were now safe for more than a year, and she made up her mind they would stay in London. She never had any patience with his proposals to quit it.

XVI

AMPLIFICATIONS

NOBODY did more to drag Carlyle into " society " than
" Dicky " Milnes,[1] who brought all sorts of men to
meet him, and went riding with him often, beginning this
summer. As a Boswell or reporter of the talk of Carlyle
he is next after Anstey. His notes are seldom dated either
in time or place. They are spread vaguely over many years
from now and were made for Milnes' own benefit and not
for publication, which is only a reason the more for faith
in them.

Here are two that might have fallen in this summer
(1838) :—

' French books have most dancing-dog thought about
them ; ours are like the quiet intelligent meditation of an
elephant or a horse.

' The French are great indeed as cooks of everything,
whether an idea or a lump of meat ; they will make something palatable of the poorest notion and the barest bone.'

Carlyle was addicted to riding hard, whenever he had a
chance. It was good for his liver, and he liked it. Here is
something likely to have been said before Milnes was aware
of that, perhaps this summer, and when the only other ears
within hearing were their horses' :—

' Your horse is going such a pace as if it was following the
funeral of the British Constitution.'

No date is likelier for remarks that seem like amplifications
of debatable parts of the lectures. Milnes had been one of
those who subscribed to make the publishers sure of selling
300 copies of *Sartor*, which came out as a book this summer.
He had dabbled in theology, too, and been in danger of
being carried away by the " Oxford Movement " to Rome.
He was intimate enough to ask confidential questions which
might not be put in public, and drew out much upon religion.

[1] *R. M. Milnes*, by T. Wemyss Reid, I, pp. 187, 193, 223-9, 435-8 ;
and II, pp. 478-81.

Sterling complained of " preaching silence through a trumpet ". Carlyle said :—

' A school for public speaking ! I wish we had a school for private thought ! I know no guilt like that of incontinent speech. How long Christ was silent before he spoke, and how little he then said ! '

This would give a fine opening for what Milnes had to tell of Rome and the religious art of Italy. Carlyle said :—

' I would rather have one real glimpse of the young Jew face of Christ than see all the Raphael's in the world.

' *Some day or other, people will look on our Christianity much as we look on Paganism.*

' Purgatory, a sort of gentleman's waiting-room till the train comes by.

' Some people are trying to get up a worship within a dark crypt roofed over with the fragments of a fallen church.

' These are busy days for religion. Puseyism puts on its beaver and walks abroad ; the old kirk shakes herself and gets up, ashamed to have lain so long among the pots.'

[Probably in reply to Milne's best defence, he said :—]

' Puseyism is a very nice Claude picture, but it won't do to drive a plough into it and work it. That's the worst ; you can't raise food out of a Claude ' [or picture of a landscape], ' and a man hungry for religion will find little comfort in Puseyism.

' We must make people feel that Heaven and Hell are not places for drinking sweet wine, or being broiled alive some distance off, but they are here before us and within us, in the street, and at the fireside.

' *Voltaire's " Ecrasez l'Infâme " had more religious earnestness in it than all the religions of nowadays put together.*

' This Puseyism in the church reminds me of our graziers, who always come to Dumfries market in a new pair of boots when they are hard-up and likely to get into quod. This Puseyism is the new boots of the Church of England.

' If Christ were to come to London now he would not be crucified. Oh, no ! He would be lionized, asked out to dinner to hear the strange things he had got to say, and the " bettermost people " would wonder that a man who could be so sensible on some points should be so foolish on others : would wish he were a little more practical, and so on.'

[Suppose the visitor from another world were Beëlzebub.]

' If Beëlzebub were to appear in England, he would receive a letter from the Secretary of the Manchester Athenæum, as Eugene Sue did, requesting the honour of his interesting company, and venturing to hope for an address.'

According to other reporters, Carlyle said that if Christ came to London, Milnes would ask him to breakfast, and next day all the Clubs would be talking of the " good things " Christ had said.

By " Morality " Carlyle did not mean conventionality or custom only, explaining to Milnes :—

' A man may have a very true morality of his own, tho he seems to go crashing through etiquettes and ten commandments, and such like.' The right sort of " Morality " is good conscience in practice.

XVII

ALISON REPORTS TABLE-TALK

(1838)

AT a dinner given by Milnes, Carlyle was seen by Archibald Alison, the handsome, whiskered and curly-haired Sheriff of Lanarkshire—about three years his senior—and a contented-Tory man of the world, articulating the gentlemanly view of the French Revolution in a *History of Europe* in many volumes that were profitable and famous then—to the bitter disappointment of " Quarterly " Croker, who had intended to do the same. Disraeli described it as " Mr. Wordy's History of the Late War in twenty volumes, a capital work, which proves that Providence was on the side of the Tories." Nothing Alison ever wrote was better than his notes of this dinner.[1]

' The party consisted of Mr. Hallam, the historian, Mr. Carlyle, Professor Whewell, Mr. W. E. Gladstone, and others. Hallam and Whewell were the greatest inter-locutors, and they had a hard struggle for the precedency. Their talk was always able, and often instructive ; but the constant straining after effect soon became tiresome, and led to the too frequent sacrifice of truth or sense to antithesis or point.

' Carlyle said less, but what he did remark was striking. Speaking of Queen Victoria, who had shortly before ascended the throne, he observed : " Poor Queen ! She is much to be pitied. She is at an age when she would hardly be trusted with the choosing of a bonnet, and she is called to a task from which an archangel might have shrunk."

' Again, the conversation having turned on Goethe, and someone having expressed surprise that he did not, like Körner, take an active part in the war of deliverance which was shaking the world around him, Carlyle remarked : " It is *not* surprising he did not do so ; you might as well

[1] *Autobiography of Sir Archibald Alison, Bart.*, Vol. I, p. 413.

expect the moon to descend from the heavens and take her place among the common street lamps." '

This might be about the time of the Coronation, but it was not the Coronation that was keeping Alison in London. A Parliamentary Committee required his evidence on riots arising out of what they called " the cotton-spinners' conspiracy ". Tho bad harvests and corn-taxes had doubled the cost of food, trades unions to keep up wages were illegal, and Alison would doubtless tell the company as much as Hallam and Whewell would allow. But that would be little. Few heeded the rabble. Macaulay was going about telling what struck him after absence in India : " The Radicals are clearly extinct, reduced to Grote and his wife." [2] Carlyle was now trying in vain to persuade Mill to take an article from him " On the Working Classes " ; but Mill said " I dare not ".

Whewell was a big red-faced fellow, who was noticed puffing, choked with indignation, at Carlyle's lectures, and was heard to say : " The man is doing the greatest mischief." [3] He was nicknamed " the harmonious blacksmith " ; and tho admiring Cambridge promoted him this year, his hostility did Carlyle more good than harm. As Venables cruelly remarked, " Whewell's humbug and imbecility reciprocally limit each other," [4] which may be one of the reasons why the good Harriet Martineau was occasionally saddened in " At Homes " to overhear her favourite Carlyle disrespectful of what passed for science in Cambridge and fashionable circles.

[2] *Greville Memoirs*, Part II, p. 112.
[3] *F. D. Maurice*, by his son, F. Maurice, I, p. 280.
[4] *R. M. Milnes*, by T. Wemyss Reid, II, p. 482.

XVIII

CARLYLE MEETS MACAULAY

(1838)

MACAULAY had returned from India with an "independence" this summer, and delighted editor Napier with the surprising news [1] (14-6-38) that he preferred literature to politics, but he could not write an article immediately,—

'Breakfasts every morning, dinners every evening, and calls all day prevent me from making any regular exertion.'

One of the breakfasts was at Rogers'. Carlyle was also there, as well as Milnes, whose biographer tells the story [2]:—

'Macaulay, overflowing with the stores of knowledge which had been accumulating during his sojourn in India, seized the first opportunity that presented itself, and having once obtained the ear of the company, never allowed it to escape even for a moment until the party was at an end. Greatly dissatisfied at the issue of a morning from which he had expected so much' (or hoping to hear something worth repeating), 'Milnes followed Carlyle into the street. "I am so sorry," he said, "that Macaulay would talk so much and prevent our hearing a single word from you." Carlyle turned round and held up his hands in astonishment. "What!" he said, "was that the Right Honourable Tom? I had no idea that it was the Right Honourable Tom. Ah, well, I understand the Right Honourable Tom now."'

Milnes had the pleasure of writing in his notebook a saying by Carlyle : "Macaulay is well for a while, but one wouldn't *live* under Niagara."

---

[1] *Correspondence of MacVey Napier*, pp. 255–8, and *Lord Macaulay*, by G. O. Trevelyan, Chap. VII.
[2] *R. M. Milnes*, by T. Wemyss Reid, I, pp. 190–1; and II, p. 478.

E

XIX

" AT THE TURNING OF A NEW LEAF "

(1838–9)

IN July Mrs. Carlyle persuaded him to give sittings to Laurence for another portrait, which was given to his mother. In August he went by steamer to Leith and Kirkcaldy, and stayed there two weeks in the house of John Fergus, who worked in flax and whose sister had lately been with them in London and was now his hostess. He rode about with Fergus or alone, and swam daily in the sea, and found Kirkcaldy "melodiously interesting". He took tea with the widow of his friend Provost Swan, whose son Patrick, his old pupil, was a man now, and came to see him at the house of Fergus.

He crossed to Edinburgh with Fergus, but found his many friends there out of town. However, a card he left reached Jeffrey, who wrote appointing another day. He went to town again accordingly, and first received a letter from his wife and " retired with it and a cigar " to Calton Hill, where he " had all Edinburgh and the Firth in clear sunshine at my feet ", and felt happy for once.

Jeffrey was ready for him at half-past two, and they had so much to say to each other that it was settled he would not return to Kirkcaldy till next day, and they adjourned to Craigcrook together, as in old times, Jeffrey on a pony and he walking alongside. The Empsons were there, and Mrs. Jeffrey, and at dinner and in the evening the talking continued "immense", but it was about Dickens and other authors and philosophy, and what Carlyle called " clatter "—" we seemed to have made up our minds not to contradict each other ; but it was at the expense of saying nothing intimate." Next morning, Jeffrey drove him to the ferry across the Forth, and so he returned to Kirkcaldy. Going thence to Scotsbrig, he went by Hawick on the Teviot, as his wife desired him to visit her old friend Bess Stodart, now living at Hawick. Bess had inherited money when her uncle died, and taken the Rev. David Aitken for a husband. After a

few days in their house, Carlyle crossed the hills and made
Scotsbrig his headquarters for nearly eight weeks. One of the
newly printed *Sartors* had been sent to an acquaintance,
Alexander Currie, who thus reported with glee after many
years a talk with him [1] :—

'Said he to me—" What do you think of the book I
sent you, Sandy ? " And I said, " Well, Tom, I didn't
understand it ava'." He answered, " I didn't think you
would, Sandy, but keep it—some of your family may think
much of it by-and-bye." And so,' he concluded, ' I kept it,
and am glad I did.'

Returning home in October, he spent a night in the
house of his youngest sister at Manchester,—

' At five in the morning all was as still as sleep and darkness. At half-past five all went off like an enormous mill-
race or ocean-tide. The Boom-m-m, far and wide. It was
the mills that were all starting then, and creishy (greasy)
drudges by the million taking post there. I have heard few
sounds more impressive to me in the mood I was in.'

It was more than a year since Varnhagen von Ense sent
him volumes of Memoirs,[2] and a review of them was the first
job after he returned : an article worth reading, were it only
for the sight of Richter at home, and Wagram battle, and
Napoleon's levee at the Tuileries. This was done for Mill's
London and Westminster. Mill had gone abroad this winter,
leaving his Review in charge of John Robertson, " a burly
Aberdeen Scotchman of seven-and-twenty." Carlyle
enjoyed his hearty laugh and found him amusing—" full of
laughter, vanity, pepticity, and hope." Apparently it was
he who had applied for " something for the October number,"
and when he got it, suggested Cromwell next.
Carlyle agreed at once, for Cromwell was on the lines
of his next set of lectures, which were to be on " The Revolutions of Modern Europe " ; but presently Robertson wrote
to tell him not to go on—" I mean to do Cromwell myself."

---

[1] Told D. A. W. in 1902 by Mr. Anderson, a builder at Annan, who heard
it from A. Currie himself one day at dinner at Annan. In 1902
Mr. Anderson was 90 years old.
[2] See *Letters of T. C.*, printed by Longmans, Green & Co., in 1892,
under the title *Last Words of T. C.*, pp. 196–200.

Which made Carlyle very angry, and in his journal he wrote what shows how much he needed to be continually repressing his own—self-confidence, let us call it.

' Have nothing to do with fools. They are a fatal species. Nay, Robertson, withal, is fifteen years younger than I. To be "edited" by him and by Mill and the Benthamic formula ! Oh heavens ? It is worse than Algiers and Negro Guiana. Nothing short of death should drive a white man to it.'

He dismissed the thought of an essay for the Review, and went on reading about Cromwell and his times. It was relevant to the impending lectures, and interesting in itself. He had meditated a book upon it in 1822, and reading all around it then had discovered that none of the accepted explanations of Cromwell explained him. By the middle of February, he was writing to John : " I find it far inferior in interest to my French subject. But, on the whole, I want to get acquainted with England—a great secret to me always hitherto—and I may as well begin here as else-where." Writing to Mill on 23–3–39, he said the same, and before long received on loan from Mill, a " huge hamper " of books on the Cromwell Period. In respect of books, he found himself worse off in London than he had been in Edinburgh in 1822. "A promising young barrister," Douglas Heath, who used to call upon him, arranged for books to be lent him in portmanteaufuls from Cambridge ; but he felt called to think of others also, and saw a use for the social opportunities he seemed to be neglecting, and so began to agitate for a Public Library. James Spedding joined him in removing the reluctance of Milnes to help, and Milnes when won was a host in himself. Hallam and Rogers approved, and Sir James Clark, a fashionable doctor, was zealous. Society became interested, and some " official Lords ". Carlyle supplied a good argument for it to the *Examiner*.[3] By March he was printing a prospectus and sending his mother a copy.

Mrs. Welsh was then on a visit to them, and to please his mother, his wife gave a soiree in their plebeian dwelling, successful enough, but it was the last. About the same time,

[3] 27–1–39, pp. 52–3, and reprinted in *Carlyle and the London Library*, by Frederic Harrison, 1907, pp. 8–11. See also pp. 6, 7, etc.

he was at a dinner at Bath House, Lord Ashburton's, where Lady Harriet Baring was the hostess, the wife of Ashburton's son, Bingham Baring. The German Bunsen was there " with red face large as the shield of Fingal ", and a flood of words. " The lady hardly hid from him that she feared he was a bore." Charles Buller had made her curious about Carlyle, whom she kept talking to her for an hour. Carlyle reported that Taylor was right in calling her " belle laide ", or plain but pleasant, a " clever devil ". " Not beautiful " in face, all witnesses agree, but stately, a " fine figure of a woman ", so to speak, and at once a favourite of Carlyle, who declared her " the most like a dame of quality of all that I have yet seen ", full of wit and spirit and mirth.

By this time £100 more had come from America for the French Revolution, making £150 in all. He was to lecture in summer again ; and in short had less cause to worry about ways and means than had ever been possible yet since he came to London. So on 12–3–39 he wrote to his brother John :—

' I am reading many books, in a languid way, about Cromwell and his time, but any work on this matter seems yet at a great distance from me. The truth is, I have arrived at the turning of a new leaf, and right thankful am I that Heaven enables me to pause a little, and I willingly follow the monition or permission of Heaven. From my boyhood upwards I have been like a creature breathlessly " climbing a soaped pole " ; ruin and the bottomless abyss beneath me, and the pole quite slippery soaped. But now I have got to a kind of notch on the same, and do purpose, by Heaven's blessing, to take my breath a moment there before adventuring further. If I live, I shall probably have further to go ; if not—we can do either way.'

He wrote to Emerson this winter to the same effect, declaring he rejoiced in laziness for a season, and moralizing on his fellows as a saint might, tho a saint in the pulpit would express it differently :—

' A sad case it is, and a frequent one in my circle, to be entirely cherubic, all face and wings. " Mes enfants," said a French gentleman to the cherubs in the picture, " Mes enfants, asseyez-vous ? " [Do you ever sit, my children ?] " Monseigneur," they answer, " il n'y a pas de quoi ! " [We've nothing to sit with, sir.] '

XX

M. RIO MAKES DISCOVERIES

(1839)

THE next Boswell was A. F. Rio, one of the " lions " of
1838–9. He had been an apprentice priest at Vannes
in 1815, and joined in the royalist rising. Son and grandson
of men who had died in the wars, he had himself been
dedicated by mother and grandmother to the priesthood,
because they thought it safe, and it had attracted him
because he felt pious and saw heroes in the persecuted
priests. The dreary drivel of classrooms makes young men
of the right sort ever ready to quit them. So in 1815 Rio
and the rest stampeded to the field to fight Napoleon, and
did materially help his enemies by detaining in the west of
France an army of his which might have enabled him to
win Waterloo.[1]

In that campaign the like of Rio, the Chouans and the
Vendéans, resembled sunshine on a dunghill. Rio was older
now, and had desisted from adoring Bourbons. Milnes and
Rogers took care that he saw and was seen by " everybody ",
—Hallam and Macaulay, Brougham and Bulwer, Wordsworth and Landor, Sheil and Disraeli, and many another,
such as W. E. Gladstone, with whom he was intimate to
the extent of joining in prayers. He sought the portrait of
Burke, whose blarney he still believed, and wondered to
find hardly anybody but Macaulay agree with him.

At the instigation of Milnes, Mrs. Norton set him talking
about 1815, and decided to make a poem of his story at
once, and brought him to her sisters, Lady Seymour and
Lady Dufferin. Milnes himself declared he would poetize
about it too, and so did Landor and Kenyon, Tom Moore
and Wordsworth, who patronizingly spoke of their
" children's crusade ". Campbell sniffed, and told him
" There are not four true believers in the Commons, nor any
more in the Lords ". Another disappointment was Moore,

---

[1] *Life of Napoleon*, by J. H. Rose, II, p. 449.

54

who was neither the poet nor the catholic he had hoped to find him.

He thought Sheil the best talker in London, and on 10–2–39 was pleased to hear him answering Charles Buller well at the dinner table. Said Buller, " The Roman Catholics adore images and practice polytheism." Sheil retorted, " The English cannot be accused of worshipping many Gods— they worship only one, and that is Mammon." If Rio repeated this to Carlyle, as he may have done, the witty Sheil may deserve the credit of suggesting the famous chapter " Gospel of Mammonism " in *Past and Present.*[2]

Rio had heard and admired Macaulay when he esteemed Sheil supreme. At Rogers' breakfast table he witnessed an hour's tournament between Hallam and Macaulay :—

' It was who would say most words in a given time—their volubility was frightful. Both had prodigious memories, and a loose glibness equally prodigious. Macaulay has the conceited trick of breaking off if only part of the audience are listening to him, and he will walk to the other end of the room, talking all the time. He was too much for Hallam, apparently. His mind is quick, but has no tendency either to soar or to dive, its motions being only horizontal. He has sparkling eyes, and an opener face than Hallam's, which is an intellectual face too, with a sarcastic turn in the upper lip, but there's a hard muscle like a dyke across the middle of Hallam's face which breaks a ripple from either direction, so that a smile from the eyes never reaches the lips, nor one from the lips the eyes.' [3]

M. Rio was delighted to be " all eyes and ears ", but Rogers the host was exasperated by the racket between Macaulay and Hallam. They rattled away for an hour or so about navies and uniforms, policemen and codes of civil law ; but Rogers would not submit to be bored, and succeeded at last in turning the talk to matters more human and interesting. The attentive Rio noted that Hallam was intermediate between Lord Mahon, a Tory, and Macaulay,

[2] Book III, Chapter II, of *Past and Present.* See also *Epilogue a l'art Chrétien*, by A. F. Rio, II, p. 343. M. Rio is a little loose in dates, his days of the week not always corresponding to numbers given ; but he does seem to have jotted down conversations immediately, as he claims to have done, and that is what matters.

[3] *Epilogue, etc.*, by A. F. Rio, II, pp. 330–2 ; and the quotations following are from pp. 332–40.

who was heterodox in religion. Macaulay would have been surprised, perhaps, if he had known that Rio went home and wrote that all these three historians were Conservatives of different shades :—

'But there is a fourth point of view,' continued Rio, 'which is that of a party numerous and earnest enough to frighten the prudent. This school is not new. The head of it (in 1839) was the Scotchman, Carlyle, the historian whose indulgent picture of the worst phase of the French Revolution seemed intended to give his readers a taste in advance of what they would feel when the same principles were applied to themselves. He was then unknown in France; but during my first stay in London his work fell into my hands, and its effect upon me was to prevent any wish to make his acquaintance. I could not help admiring the great artist in him; but I was nauseated by his readiness to pardon crimes which he imputed to I don't know what blind fate, which carried on the criminals in spite of themselves and almost unknown to themselves. My wrath boiled over when I read the page where it is said that " there is no period to be met with in which the general Twenty-five Millions of France suffered *less* than in this period which they name Reign of Terror ". This whimsical opinion was an insult to the victims, and filled me with a hatred to Carlyle which seemed to me unalterable, and which never would have been altered if I had not met him.'

As he was an intimate of Milnes', he could not escape meeting Carlyle; and then, said he :—

'Imagine my amazement to find him, instead of a republican *savage*, such as I expected, a friendly and pleasant man of the right sort. In spite of his rough Scotch accent, he was visibly open to feelings very different from any which the history I had read let me anticipate. The closer we came to the living issues of religion or politics, the more I wondered to find myself agreeing with him; for people had told me he was a violent partisan of the most subversive doctrines, and the unconcealed friend of men who proclaimed them with the utmost boldness. I soon discovered for myself the truth of the latter imputation. Without any hint of what to expect, he had me dining at his house in the company of Godefroi Cavaignac first of all, and then the appalling Mazzini himself.'

There was a slip of memory here, for at the time (7–4–39), Mrs. Carlyle wrote to Miss Welsh, her cousin in Liverpool, who had been visiting them :—

' The very next evening [after you went away] came the French Catholic Rio that Carlyle had described to us as such a striking man. He pleased me much. He is a sort of French John Sterling ; if possible, even more voluble and transparent ; and his Catholicism sits on him just about as lightly as John's Church-of-Englandism sits on him.'

This was well said. Milnes called Rio " the graceful and pious historian of Christian Art", but admitted he was " a Christian in politics and an Artist in religion". [4] Mrs. Carlyle goes on :—

' I happened to ask him if he knew Cavaignac : " Ah, who does *not* know Cavaignac by name ? But I, you know, am a victim of *his* party, as *he* is a victim of Louis Philippe. Does Cavaignac come here ? "
' " Yes, we have known him long."
' " Good gracious ! How strange it would be for us to meet in the same room ! How I should like it ! "
' " Well," I said, " he is to dine here on Monday."
' " I will come ; good gracious, it will be so strange " ; and he seemed amazingly charmed with his prospect.
' Not so Carlyle, who began, before he was well out at the door : " Mercy, Jane, are you distracted ? What *can* you do with these two men ? " etc., etc. I assured him it would go off without bloodshed, and began to think of my *dinner*.'

[In short, she added a beefsteak pie to the leg of mutton, in spite of which, she sadly continues :—]

' The dinner could hardly be called a "successful one". Rio appeared on the scene at half-past three, as if he could not have enough of it. Latrade came as the clock struck four. But Cavaignac—Alas ! Two of his friends were on

---

[4] *Monographs by R. M. Milnes*, Lord Houghton, pp. 46, 48.

terms about blowing each other's brains out, and Cavaignac was gone to bring them to reason ; and not till they were brought to reason would he arrive to eat his dinner.

' Mrs. Macready and Macready's sister, calling, helped to pass the time of waiting, and an hour and half after the dinner had been all ready we proceeded to eat it—Rio, Latrade, and we. And when it was just going off the table cold Cavaignac came, his hands full of papers and his head full of the Devil knows what ; but not one reasonable word would he speak the whole night. Rio said nothing to his dispraise, but I am sure he thought in his own mind—" Good gracious ! I had better never be in the same room with him again ! "

' Rio has been three times last week, and comes again to-night.'

To her mother-in-law, Mrs. Carlyle wrote that M. Rio ' has been flying about us at a prodigious rate. He told us all about how he went to confession, etc., etc., and how he had been demoralized at one period, and was recovered by the spectacle of a holy procession. He seems a very excellent man in his own way, but one cannot quite enter into his ecstasies about white shirts and wax tapers and all that sort of thing '.

Rio's report goes on :—

' Carlyle had made Mazzini read in advance my book on Christian poetry ; but did not let him know till the end of dinner that he was face-to-face with the author—which might have given a queer turn to the talk. But everything passed off politely, thanks to my chapter on Savonarola, which had already led an Italian republican to translate the book. At every new visit it seemed to me that the political ideals of Carlyle were wider and wider apart from those of Mazzini, and so the more encouraging to me. *The point upon which they differed the most, at any rate in my presence, was the right of resistance to everything which could possibly appear to offend the holy dominion of the conscience.*[5] *Carlyle knew every detail of my exploits in 1815, and was as pleased with me as if I had been fighting for a republic.* He took a wicked pleasure in bringing out the chivalrous side

---

[5] Mazzini's *Essays* corroborate M. Rio here.

of our juvenile prowess before one who was always system-
atically running down whatever looked like a religious war.'

These notes bring out the essential difference between
Carlyle and Mazzini. Both agreed in detesting, like Byron,
the existing governments as what St. Augustine called
" organized rascality " ; but Mazzini was seeking what was
called " collective freedom " and saw no harm in repressing
minorities, however conscientious. He believed in Italy
domineering the world, for its good, of course, as Thiers
believed in France doing so, and Macaulay in England, and
Bernhardi in Germany, and so on. Carlyle stood with
Confucius for the freedom of the private conscience, and the
duty of resisting tyrannical force. This was the feeling which
was now enabling him to sympathize with Cromwell and his
Independents, and to explain Cromwell at last. More than
he supposed, he was the spiritual son of Voltaire, as well as
of Goethe. He did not want men to be " good Europeans "
only, still less to be merely good Frenchmen or Italians, good
Germans or Englishmen. Like Voltaire—and Oliver Cromwell—he would have them be good men ; and he did his
best to show them how. M. Rio explains this in his own
way :—

' The fact was that Carlyle was more of an idealist than
most of those who shared his political opinions, and his
wife seemed made to cherish and develop idealism in him.
Several times, returning home after an evening with this
interesting couple, I could not resist writing down in my
diary what remained in my mind of our mutual confidences.
                              ' *Easter Sunday*, 1839.
' Last night I went to call upon Carlyle in his Chelsea
retreat, and came home with my heart genuinely touched by
the warmth of his welcome and the faith in me which he
showed. His Scotch accent did not bother me so much as
last year. As for his wife, the expression of her features
is the best imaginable. I was received by her when I went
in, as her husband had not come back from his walk. She
entertained me with delicious details of how they had lived
two alone together for six years in the country, in Dumfriesshire, immediately after their marriage. Our conversation
grew so real and friendly that I very much regretted an
engagement to spend the evening elsewhere, which alone
prevented me from staying for hours with this interesting

couple, with whom I had so much in common. When at last I had to go, it was like leaving Elysium for the Limbos.

' What hampered my intercourse with Carlyle was that he seldom visited the houses I frequented, and his habit of staying at home put narrow limits on his relations with politicians and men of letters.

' Some days after the Easter call, the Carlyles invited me to dine with them, and here is what I wrote when I came home that night :—

Monday, 1st April (1839).

' Spent with Carlyle three hours which seemed very short. Cavaignac was there, and this time Carlyle told him plainly, without preparation, that I was a Chouan of 1815, whereat the savage republican, instead of frowning at me, paid me the most unexpected compliments upon the energy and pride of the Breton character. Cavaignac's voice is one that would be very powerful when touched by passion. His chest would then be like a drum. There is something of the lion in his face and aspect, noble and serene when not excited, but awful when he is roused. But he was much less interesting to me than Carlyle and his wife, with both of whom I am delighted more and more. I don't know a man in London whose talk is so genial as Carlyle's. I wish I could recall verbatim the fine things he told me about Goethe and the painter Hogarth, whom he thinks a man of genius.

' Idealism is part of Carlyle's nature. It can be traced in all his writings, and I found it in almost all his conversations. The one I had with him on the evening of 8-4-39 shows this best. Here is what I wrote on reaching home: Monday night. I want to fix my impressions of this evening with Carlyle while they are fresh. I have just spent four hours with him, and assuredly they are among the best I've had in London. We sifted several great subjects to the bottom, the Crusades, Dante, the French Revolution, and *the future of religion in Europe, which last he views more hopefully than I can, because of his faith in human progress and the indestructibility of Christianity.* To this I objected the decline of the highest of the Christian virtues, humility, and that did trouble him a little, and all the more because of the importance he attaches to that virtue. He admits that it was better understood and more practised in the middle ages than at any other time.

' He has the liveliest admiration for the Crusades and for Peter the Hermit, whom he contrasted humorously with

Demosthenes. Demosthenes perfected his orations to such
a point that they were felt to smell of the lamp, and he
practised delivery on the shore with pebbles in his mouth,
and bequeathed to us as the golden rule for eloquence,
" Play-acting, play-acting, and always play-acting." Peter,
on the other hand, came out from his cloister with no preparation for the part he was to play but fasting and prayer, and
instead of the method of the eloquent Greek, he preached,
in a very different way, " Faith, faith, and always faith."
Demosthenes had to behold his eloquence defeated and
Philip the master of Greece, whereas Peter led Europe
marching behind him, and delivered the Holy Land.'

Carlyle was fond of contrasting Demosthenes and Peter
the Hermit ; but so far as the reporters go, he never was
answered as he might have been. The voluble Greek was
less sincere than poor Peter, but both were wrong and failed
in the long run. Peter believed what was not true. His
fellow-believers won many a victory and took Jerusalem ;
but they died in heaps, like the lemming rats of Norway
rushing to the sea, and their two-hundred-years' war ended
in utter defeat. The benefit that western Europe got from
the Crusades might have been got in a tenth of the time
without any violence. The true moral of the history is the
folly of offensive fighting. But M. Rio did not think of that.
He agreed as everybody must, that Peter was better than
Demosthenes, and continued :—

' I was equally struck by a parallel Carlyle drew between
Milton's Satan and Goethe's Mephistopheles. The Devil
in Milton is a magnificent personage, the most interesting
in the poem, one who would have admirers if he appeared in
public among us ; but in Faust he is what he ought to be,
supremely disgusting!'—Poor Devil, but only a nightmare!
' Carlyle has a better estimate of Dante than Landor has.
He puts Dante above Milton ; and says the portrait of
Dante makes him look like a soul imprisoned in ice. The
Divine Comedy is, in his eyes, a magnificent crystallization of
Catholicism, more glorious and lasting than its finest Gothic
cathedrals. He seems to like the Purgatory best, declaring
that " no other poet ever went so far and with such fellow-
feeling into the bowels of humanity, no other ever gripped
his subject so tightly ".
' In several ways there is a likeness between Dante and

Carlyle himself ; for he too walks in the world like a soul in torment ; gifted with every possible sensibility to suffering. He has no patience with those who want to make life a holiday and a succession of delights. Every hour of his existence he feels that life is a struggle, and he spurns whoever stops him to prattle about the pleasures of a world which presses so heavily on every worthy mind.

' His description of the impression made upon him by the sight of his native village and the sound of the bells he had heard in babyhood was poetical ; and when I was trying to tell how I was affected in similar circumstances, I could not but admire his kindness in finishing my thought for me. I told him my playmates were sturdy sailors to-day, with never a care about the changes which had exhausted my spirit. " Quite so," said he, " They are healthy, tangible beings, and you—you were wandering among them like a ghost."
' I did not venture to ask either of them about the truth of the romantic story told about their marriage, that her mother had opposed it, and that he had been a tutor in her father's house. The difference between them, in manners and appearance, and particularly in accent, suggests a difference in class. But when the conversation becomes alive, this man with the rugged face and plebeian accent seems to grow into a giant, and shows that he belongs to the very first quality of nature's noblemen.'

For emphasis, Rio breaks into English here, and this last sentence may be transcribed as he wrote it :—

' Mais quand la conversation s'anime, cet homme à la physionomie si rude, à la pronunciation si plébéienne, grandit comme un géant et prouve qu'il appartient *to the very first quality of nature's noblemen.*'

XXI

D'ORSAY

(1839)

A VERY different Frenchman from Rio, Count D'Orsay, an artist and a leader of society, came to Cheyne Row on 31–3–39, in an equipage which Mrs. Carlyle told her cousin was " all resplendent with sky-blue and silver, like a piece of the Coronation Procession ", and " rushed through the street " with " the sound of a whirlwind ", and stopped at their door " with a prancing of steeds and footmen thunder ". It brought two visitors, one already familiar, a red-haired young journalist, Henry Chorley, Dilke's " man-of-all-work " for the Athenæum, and an adherent of Lady Blessington,[1] and now all in a twitter, his very jaw shaking. The other was Lady Blessington's young man, the great dandy, Count D'Orsay, over six feet, and " built like a tower ", Carlyle wrote to his brother, " with floods of dark auburn hair, with a beauty, with an adornment unsurpassable in this planet ! " Mrs. Carlyle was more explicit to her cousin : " sky-blue satin cravat, yards of gold chain, white French gloves, light drab great-coat lined with velvet of the same colour, invisible inexpressibles, skin-coloured, and fitting like a glove, etc., etc."

She enjoyed the contrast of " Carlyle in his grey plaid suit and his tub chair, looking blankly at the Prince of Dandies ; and the Prince of Dandies on an opposite chair, all resplendent as a diamond beetle, looking blandly at *him* ".

D'Orsay had been called by Byron in 1823 [2] " one of the few specimens I have seen of our ideal of a Frenchman *before* the Revolution ". His mother was German, his father one of Napoleon's men, and he was a Paris-bred painter and sculptor, " Bonapartist," but glad to get into a Bourbon regiment till the rich and foolish Lord Blessington took him into his service as a kind of gentleman-courier, ultimately

[1] *Henry F. Chorley*, by H. G. Hewlett, I, pp. 173–93, etc.
[2] T. Moore's *Life and Works of Byron*, Vol. VI, pp. 13–25.

son-in-law.   D'Orsay's young wife soon had to buy a
separation dearly,—poor woman! He much preferred her
step-mother, especially as a widow with £2,000 a year, and
by this time, 1839, doubling that income by her pen—a
popular oracle in petticoats. D'Orsay made money too, but
squandered it and much of the lady's also.

On this visit he alluded to Carlyle's " fine epic ", and said
the Madame Crawford, in whose house Marie Antoinette
hid her Varennes coach, was his mother's cousin. Looking
at Shelley's bust, he said he did not like it—" It is one of
those faces who weesh to swallow their chins ! " He
departed hoping that Carlyle would call and " see
Lady Blessington ", which duly happened soon. It was at
their dinner-table that Carlyle met Savage Landor in a few
weeks, and on the same evening D'Orsay " drew a fine
portrait " of him, " dashed off in some twenty minutes "
in the drawing-room ; " really very like " said everybody.
But Carlyle excused himself from other " eight-o'clock
dinners " there, explaining to his brother, " I did not fall
in love with Countess Blessington," tho he admitted, " she
is smart, good-humoured, blandishing—an *elderly* ' wild
Irish girl ' ! " She was fifty now, and her faithful D'Orsay,
servant cavalier, only 38. As a fashionable fictioneer and
editing a *Book of Beauty*, she could not refuse herself the
luxury of such a fine model of a man, in whose eyes, maybe,
she still was, as when Byron saw her in 1823 at Genoa, a
modern Venus.

Lady Blessington and her D'Orsay continued to decorate
London nine or ten years longer before they had to go to
Paris to avoid their creditors, but they saw little more of
Carlyle, tho always friendly when they met. " They have a
fine library," was his common conclusion when describing
them, to which his wife retorted, " You value your
acquaintances by their libraries, and say, or should say,
' Such an one is a valuable man, a man of 3,000 volumes.' "

From a drawing made after dinner in Lady Blessington's Drawing Room, by Count D'Orsay, in 1839. This Signature is from an Agreement dated 17-5-42, for the publication of *Heroes*, and first printed in a fine article in the Strand Magazine by J. Holt Schooling on *The Hand-writing of Thomas Carlyle from 1809 to 1875*.

[face p. 64.

XXII

COPYRIGHT

(1839)

A BILL was pending in charge of Serjeant Talfourd, to extend the legal limits of copyright beyond 28 years. Southey and Wordsworth, Sheriff Alison and Co. were eagerly pushing it, and Talfourd wanted Carlyle to help by a petition in his own name. He had misgivings, protesting to John Forster (27–2–39) : [1]

' Neither my age, my position nor pretensions could authorize such a step on my part. Ridicule, it seems to me, and the general inquiry, who *is* this pretentious " single person ? " would be the too probable result.' So he counsels Talfourd to stand by Wordsworth and the like, adding : ' I heard an official person, the other night, speaking with a kind of awe, and tone of solemnity, of " having seen the petition of William Wordsworth ". It is better **to keep by** that, and " say ditto to Mr. Burke ", is it not ? '

The others persisting in a contrary opinion, he wrote for Talfourd and Forster the now famous petition which appeared in the *Examiner*, 7–4–39, and was persuasive in its simplicity and candour. One of his arguments was new to lawyers, but felt to carry weight :—

' That all useful labour is worthy of recompense ; that all honest labour is worthy of the chance of recompense ; that *the giving and assuring to each man what recompense his labour has actually merited may be said to be the business of all Legislation, Polity, Government, and Social Arrangement whatsoever among men.'* [2]

---

[1] Unpublished letter.   [2] Italics added.

Another original touch was to intimate that it was stealing to reprint freely after the expiry of the legal term of copyright, as if the author's right were a holy thing. Carlyle had studied law, and would hardly need to be told that copyright was a legal fiction, a temporary artificial monopoly, restricting the natural rights of men to copy freely and dispose for their own benefit of copies they make. The need to recompense the author's work is the one just reason for allowing a little copyright ; and the best of his article was his ungenteel avowal that he was in need of wages for his work. Crabb Robinson sent a copy to Wordsworth, who in reply "could not but praise it highly", concluding, " And as for the style it is well calculated to startle dull men into attention." And the good-natured Crabb Robinson jotted down, " I repeated this to Mrs. Carlyle." [3]

Next year, in sending prospectuses for his proposed London Library to John Sterling, Carlyle declared : ' If we consider it, every human being has, by the nature of the case, a *right* to hear what other wise human beings have spoken to him. It is one of the rights of men ; a very cruel injustice if you deny it to a man ! '

This was not rhetoric. The doctrine is in Sartor, and was the basis of his arguments for general education. But if it is true, then what becomes of holy copyright ? Carlyle would have laughed at the question. The whole of the rickety structure of English Law, then undergoing many alterations and repairs, mostly sham repairs by whitewash, was an elaborate sanctification of the gospel of grab, possession and prescription, and implying a denial of the right to work. It was with good reason that clever lawyers said nothing about the logic of his argument on copyright. It was not a time to let out to a hungry people a trade secret like that.

[3] " Diary, etc., of H. Crabb Robinson " in *London Mercury*, October, 1922, p. 611.

XXIII

" REVOLUTIONS OF MODERN EUROPE "

(1839)

THIS year's lectures were like last year's in Portman
Square, but there were six, not twelve, beginning
1–5–39, on "The Revolutions of Modern Europe". His
audiences were better than ever, " the whole street blocked "
with fine carriages in attendance. In taking stock of the
crowd once, his wife saw Mrs. Edward Irving in her widow's
weeds, and thought kindly of what her feelings must be.
Repeatedly she heard all around exclamations of admiration—" Splendid ! " " Devilish fine ! " " Most true ! "
Another thing the delighted wife remarked, that tho the
English love fine architecture " passionately ", they tolerated
his defence of Knox, and surprised him agreeably with a
cordial burst of applause. They found his candour irresistible,
for, as Leigh Hunt wrote in the *Examiner*,[1] while " he said
what he could for the Scottish Kirk ", he admitted that
" Puritanism would have made this world ' a planet all over
brambles '." Nevertheless, big Bunsen, the Prussian diplomat
and Tory, who enjoyed the lectures himself, may have been
guessing rightly when he wrote to his wife [2] that most of the
audience were " sadly startled " by what they heard.
Leigh Hunt tells us :—

' In describing the " lie " which the Papal tyranny had
become (and which, by implication, all other churches
become when obviously worldly—a formidable and *felt*
deduction), he said it had come to be " one of the most
melancholy spectacles ". None but hypocrites and formalists
have any longer anything to do with such an anomaly.
Good men get out of it. It is quite a secondary kind of man

[1] Quoted in many places, e.g. *Life of T. Carlyle*, by R. H. Shepherd,
I, pp. 197–214.
[2] *Memoir of Baron Bunsen*, by his widow, 1868, I, pp. 520–5.

that gets at the head of it. If the world be a lie, and everything present and future a juggle, then *that* may be a truth,
but not otherwise. There is nothing more to be said of it.
It must be altered, " *a thing like that*." The effect of hearty
convictions like these, uttered in such simple truthful words,
and with the flavour of a Scottish accent (as if some Puritan
had come to life again, liberalized), can be duly appreciated
only by those who see it. Every manly face among the
audience seemed to knit its lips out of a severity of sympathy
whether it would or no ; and all the pretty church-and-state
bonnets seemed to thrill through all their ribbons.'

But even Hunt could not approve what he said of Cromwell,
who practised the Puritanism which Knox had preached.
" In what did *he* succeed, except in making himself for a
short time an unhappy prince ? " demanded Hunt. If
Charles was a liar, was not Cromwell the same ? The
vindication of the Commonwealth was the greatest strain
upon the indulgence of his hearers. It does not appear that
what the lecturer said was different in substance from what
he said again next year ; but the date is interesting. It
finishes the claim that John Robertson of the *London and
Westminster* was the first vindicator of Cromwell, for his
article did not appear till October. When by-and-by
Carlyle was asked his opinion of Robertson's article, he said,
" I never read his trash." His wife remarked, " I thought it
very beautiful." [3]
In the next or fourth lecture, " English Restoration,
Europe till 1789, Voltaire and Arkwright," there was an
up-to-date surprise. " Never shall we forget," wrote Hunt,
" what Mr. Carlyle said of the melancholy spectacle of a
human being willing to labour but forced to starve—' a
thing not endurable, or which ought not to be endurable, to
human eyes ' ; and such a calamity as does not occur to
a beast of the field."
The fifth lecture was on the French Revolution, and
he felt at the end " like a man that had been robbing hen-
roosts ", inasmuch as his " audience, mainly Tory, could not
be expected to sympathize ". He felt bilious, too. So the
day before the last lecture he hired a swift horse and
galloped to Harrow and back, and went " in a kind of rage "
to the lecture room next day, and letting himself go upon

[3] *Literary Recollections*, by F. Espinasse, pp. 127–8.

Sansculottism, he kindled his audience so that his wife was made happy by hearing: " He's a glorious fellow," " I love the fellow's very faults," " A fine, wild, chaotic chap," and " so on over the whole room ". He ended half an hour later than usual, with " universal decisive applause ".

This seems to have been on Saturday (18–5–39). On Monday he was writing to Lockhart, the Editor of the Tory *Quarterly Review* (20–5–39) [4] :—

' DEAR SIR,—

' It will probably seem surprising that I of all persons should propose writing for you in the *Quarterly Review*. Neither do I propose it for a series of times, nor altogether definitely even for one first time. For one first time, however, I find it worth while to consult you.

' I have, and have had for many years ' [ten or twenty, he told Sterling], ' a word to speak *on the condition of the lower classes* in this country. My notions on this subject differ intensely from those of the speculating Radicals, intensely from those of the Whigs ; it seems to me the better class of the Conservatives are, on the whole, the persons to whom it were hopefullest, and in many ways fittest, to address myself . . .'

They had a meeting accordingly somewhere in " the Piccadilly region ", and their cordial conference lasted for hours, the two Scots agreeing beyond expectation. Lockhart told him there was no need to hurry—" the Autumn is the time for things requiring thought " from readers of the *Quarterly*. An article on the " Condition of the Poor " was what they contemplated. Lockhart sent him books next day, and in search of statistics and details he was soon in correspondence with Chadwick, factotum of the Poor Law Commissioners, and chief expert on the factory children, etc.

He had been consulted this year by Thomas Ballantyne, an editor in Lancashire, once a " poor Paisley weaver ", and meditating now an autobiography, which Carlyle admitted was " the most universally interesting of all things, if well done ". He quoted Cellini, and bade Ballantyne remember his early days : " Life in Paisley, in the workshops, at the firesides of the poor. Let a man ' stand always by his own

---

[4] *J. G. Lockhart*, by A. Lang, II, pp. 226–8.

order ', I say ! It is the oldest order of all ; and derives *its* patent, as a great member of it said, ' direct from Almighty God.' " The quotation was from Burns. It was in the spirit of Burns, and not like a new-fledged " gentleman of the Press ", a climber-upward, " scorning the base degrees by which he did ascend," that Carlyle was now preparing to teach the English gentry the " Condition of the Poor ". There had been frost and snow when he was lecturing in May, and sheer starvation was spreading from Ireland to England and Scotland. The people perishing of hunger were swarming from county to county, attacking only hotels as yet, impelled like the migrating birds by empty stomachs.

In his journal last year Emerson had noted that Carlyle's is " the most creditable poverty I know of " ; [5] but so far as his own wants were concerned Carlyle was easily satisfied ; and the glory of his wife is that she did not worry him. The lectures of 1839 brought nearly £200, and a few hundreds more in sight from his books made him turn his thoughts away from that.

Thus it was that he gave only a passing thought to Emerson's invitations to lecture in America this fall. Arthur Buller, fresh from there, corroborated American visitors in saying he would soon make a few thousands, a fortune to him, if he would only write a set of lectures and go round on the stump delivering them. A Professor Lardner from London was doing so, and Carlyle felt he could do it easily. The sight of Anstey's notebook last year may have helped to make him feel confident. But the " Condition of the Poor ", the thought of thousands of willing workers at home made to starve in idleness, or worried into starvation wages, weighed upon him like a nightmare ; and he did not think about himself when he felt called to deliver them from the darkness.

The King of Hanover might tell Humboldt at table with royal rudeness and bucolic wit, " There are two kinds of persons always to be had to any amount for money, the whores and the quill-folk " [federvieh, with a double meaning, poultry and quill-drivers, including writers by trade]. [6] But the writer by trade at Cheyne Row was not to be hired.

---

[5] Emerson's *Journals*, IV, p. 446, dated 9–5–38.
[6] *Monographs by R. M. Milnes*, Lord Houghton, p. 28.

XXIV

CHARTISM, &c.

(1839)

THERE was much to read and inquire about before writing on the working classes. His first employment after the lectures was the new edition of his history, requiring corrections. The *Vengeur* story was put right, and an article sufficient to satisfy even the French with the evidence was sent to Fraser in June.

About the same time old John Marshall, the linen manufacturer from Leeds, was talking to him in his quiet, sensible, low-voiced way, and gave the talk a personal turn, persuading him to accept a present of a horse to ride. " My son William will be *glad* to take it off your hands through winter ; and in summer it will help your health, you *know* ! " Mrs. Carlyle bade him take it. " It's like buying a *laying hen,*" she said, " and giving it to some deserving person. Accept it, dear ! " The mare which William Marshall brought himself accordingly was named " Citoyenne ", French for a female " citizen ", and un-expectedly did more than help the rider's health. He told John Sterling this year : " I never knew what a most lovely country of its sort this London region is. Green, frondent, fertile, entirely subdued to man. The beauty of some of the sun-glimpses I have come upon are things to be enjoyed. I am also greatly delighted with the country people working on the roads, etc., down to the very children ; and rejoice to call such people my kindred."

As he presently noted in his journal : " Green lanes, swift riding, and solitude, how much more delightful ! " than paying calls, as he used to do in the afternoons, for an object to his walks. Then he told Sterling about the gift of the horse and how William Marshall was to pretend to " borrow " it for the winter, the time when it would suit him to " be rid of it " ; and moralized : " Kindness is frequent in this world, if we reckon upward from zero (as

were fair), not downwards from infinity." Which means—
the Sartor gospel.

His wife was delighted to do all the society calls for him.
He met the American Senator Webster at breakfast with
Milnes (18-6-39) and heard him drawl about "our
republican institutions", and so on. His brother, Dr. John
Carlyle, wanted him to visit Germany and was ready to pay
the expense ; but their mother appealed to Tom to come
north " while thy mother is still there ". So John sent money
to their farmer-brothers to buy a horse and gig for their
mother and Tom to drive about in, and Carlyle went north
with his wife in the beginning of July.

Besides *Wilhelm Meister*, which was about to be reprinted,
he was reading Poor Law reports there and meditating an
intended " article on the working people ", and watching
curiously a Chartist meeting in Ecclefechan itself (26-7-39).
Returning in September he thus described the new sensation
of a journey in a railway train from Preston (13-9-39) :—

' The whirl through the confused darkness on those steam
wings was one of the strangest things I have experienced—
hissing and dashing on, one knew not whither. We saw the
gleam of towns in the distance—unknown towns. We went
over the tops of houses—one town or village I saw clearly,
with its chimney heads vainly stretching up towards us—
under the stars ; not under the clouds, but among them.
Out of one vehicle into another, snorting, roaring we flew ;
the likest thing to a Faust's flight on the Devil's mantle ;
or as if some huge steam night-bird had flung you on its
back and was sweeping through unknown space with you,
most probably towards London.'

After finishing a preface to the *Meister* and other such
work, he flung himself with all his heart upon what he
decided to call *Chartism*, and did it in four or five weeks.
Miss Wilson was one of the few who were favoured with a
reading of it, and Carlyle admired how she said nothing to
himself, and praised it to others. Lockhart had it for a
week, in the latter half of November, and praised it, but
said, " I dare not " print it in the *Quarterly*. Carlyle
told him his decision was " what it should have been "
and what he expected.[1] Mill was giving up his ownership

[1] *J. G. Lockhart*, by A. Lang, II, pp. 228-9.

of the *London and Westminster,* wherein a bold eulogy of
Carlyle by John Sterling had just appeared, which made
Carlyle happy and grateful. Mill was now unexpectedly
willing to print *Chartism* in the last number he was to edit,
as " a kind of final shout, that he might sink like the
[mythical] *Vengeur* with a broadside at the water's edge ".
But it may be he had not done more than glance at it when
he said so. His Review was plainly not the place for a work
which expressly attacked Parliamentary Radicals as good-
for-nothings. Fraser brought it out as a 5s. book near the
end of the year, and it had a rapid sale, which delighted the
heart of the bookseller.

It was a wonderful work to have been written in a month;
but it had simmered long in his mind, and the weeks of
writing were like the hour when the molten metal flows out
from the furnace. It was what he said in June it would
have to be, an " utterance of *principles,* grounded on facts
which all may see ", and not an argument from statistics,
" tho I ought to know these, too," he admitted ; and he had
studied all the printed matter available, and candidly
explains : " A judicious man looks at statistics not to get
knowledge, but to save himself from having ignorance
foisted on him ". But one appalling fact he extricated from
surrounding trifles as " pregnant " and " astonishing " :—

' Ireland has near seven millions of working people, the
third unit of whom, it appears by Statistic Science, has not
for thirty weeks each year as many third-rate potatoes as
will suffice him . . . A government and guidance of white
European men which has issued in perennial hunger of
potatoes to the third man extant—ought to drop a veil over
its face and walk out of court under conduct of proper
officers, saying no word ; expecting now of a surety sentence
either to change or die.'

In burning words he told the shameful tale of English
oppression degrading the Irish national character, and ending
now in crowds of starving Irish that " darken all our towns "
and bring down wages in England towards the level of
potatoes and salt. " England is guilty towards Ireland ;
and reaps the fruit of fifteen generations of wrong-doing.
Alas ! that it should, on both sides, be poor toiling men that
pay the smart for unruly Striguls, Henrys, MacDermots,
and O'Donoghues ! "

He laid down plainly right principles new in Europe, tho as old as Confucius in the east, and in particular the right of workers to get work and be treated justly. " It is the feeling of *injustice* that is insupportable to men." He was speaking for the people as Burns might have done. The beautiful poem of Burns, " Man was made to mourn," was tenderly referred to and its meaning explained : " A man willing to work, and unable to find work, is perhaps the saddest sight that Fortune's inequality exhibits under this sun." In short, he raised the " Condition of England Question ", which was first mentioned here, and after 85 years is more alive than ever. Are the idlers or the workers to prevail in England ? That is the question.

It seems an open question still to superficial or sophisticated simpletons, but the right principles Carlyle laid down are so sure that any teacher of economics who questions them writes himself down as incompetent. Explaining the " *half*-truth " in the Poor Law Amendment Act, he said :—

' Any law, however well meant, which has become a bounty on unthrift, idleness, bastardy, and beer-drinking, must be put an end to. In all ways it needs to be proclaimed aloud that for the idle man there is no place in this England. He that will not work according to his faculty, let him perish according to his necessity : there is no law juster than that . . .

' That this law of " No work no recompense " should first of all be enforced on the *manual* worker was natural. Let it be enforced there and rigidly made good. It behoves to be enforced everywhere and rigidly made good—alas, not by such simple methods as " refusal of out-door relief ", but by far other and costlier ones . . . Work is the mission of man on this Earth. A day is ever struggling forward when he who has no work to do, by whatever name he may be named, will not find it good to show himself in our quarter of the Solar System. Let the honest working man rejoice that such Law, the first of Nature, has been made good on him ; and hope that, by and by, all else will be made good. It is the beginning of all.'

Chartism was anon., and conventional critics who had to find fault showed unusual sagacity in saying that " however good it may be in itself, it is a flagrant imitation of Carlyle ". *Chartism* was *Sartor* and the gist of his history

put into plain English, with many matters of fact and only
a few figures of speech, simple, but sometimes very beautiful,
like this often-quoted description of how the steam engine
coming into use was changing ways of working right and
left :—

'The huge demon of Mechanism smokes and thunders,
panting at his great task, in all sections of English land ;
changing his *shape* like a very Proteus ; and infallibly, at
every change of shape, *oversetting* whole multitudes of
workmen, and as if with the waving of his shadow from afar,
hurling them asunder, this way and that, in their crowded
march and course of work or traffic ; so that the wisest no
longer knows his whereabouts.'

Invectives against the " Dantean Hell " of gin made this
book an event to Temperance reformers, and it is a date for
the Labour Party, too. The rights of workers had never been
put so well before ; and his insistence on the urgent need
for both emigration and general education was admitted to
be reasonable even by a Tory critic.[2] But " Girondin
Radicals, Donothing Aristocrat Conservatives, and un-
believing Dilettante Whigs " were all appalled by the tone
of it, scoffing at routine. The Law of England to conform
to the Law of Nature ! ! ! " Whosoever is not working must
be begging or stealing ! ! ! " What then about Prescription ?
And the holy Gospel of Grab, enshrined in the Law of
England ?   Flat " Communism " the Dogberries of the
day agreed to call it, after they had had time to discuss
it and hear what society said, but that took a year or two.
Communism and Socialism were supposed to be the same.
    Such plain-dealing about current economics need not
prevent school-book editors now from using Chapter VIII,
" New Eras." It has curiously vivid passages, such as one
describing in a few sentences the Manchester he saw some
months before, " sublime as a Niagara, or more so " ; and
with almost Shakespearean felicity it gives in a dozen pages
the gist of the whole of the history of England, the best of
what a heap of Hallams could tell in tons of volumes.

[2] G. S. Venables in the *British and Foreign Quarterly*, 1841, p. 316, etc.

XXV

JOSEPH NEUBERG, &c.

(1839)

A LETTER to Mill (2–10–39) reveals that a Professor Nichol was sounding Carlyle through Mill about an approaching vacancy. Was he still willing to become Professor of Moral Philosophy at St. Andrews? That was the question. There was unconscious self-revelation in his reply that he *might* take it if it were offered him, " with expressed or implied liberty to do it as he conscientiously, having regard to all the circumstances of the thing, best could. Would deliberate and decide in 24 hours. But the contingency of the whole matter, the necessity of making application, solicitation, etc., etc., form an altogether conclusive weight in the negative scale ; and I decide at once that I will not become a *candidate* in that sense." He received the option on his own unusual terms when the vacancy had to be filled some years later.

He wrote many letters with a running pen, enough to fill fifty volumes, and from among them here is one worth quoting because the addressee became his greatest helper in the writing of Frederick. It was in December, 1839, that Joseph Neuberg, a merchant at Nottingham, joined with two ladies in sending him a message and a present, thus acknowledged (21–12–39) :—

' My dear Sir,—
      ' Will you accept a hasty word of thanks for your two beautiful lithographs and friendly message . . . I find you are an enthusiastic man, as indeed most of my best friends have a tendency to be ; and that you praise me very enthusiastically. Under penalty, a most severe penalty, of seeing myself changed into an enchanted " Bottom the Weaver " (with ears long, and hairy to the scratch !), I must not believe a word of what you or my two fair Nottingham Titanias so enthusiastically say ; except,

76

indeed, that you do really love me, and this I will, most literally and with all thankfulness, believe. Is not this, too, good news ; the best of news ? This, and the like of this, as our Goethe's Theresa says, "first make the waste empty world into a peopled garden for one ! " . . . The lithographs are beautiful. The Artist has ideas in his head, and surely one of the daintiest hands that ever Artist had. Would he were near you ! He might then send me some portrait. . . . Yours with brotherly thanks,

' T. CARLYLE.' [1]

Neuberg continued to admire what Carlyle wrote ; and attended his lectures in London the following year.[2] But moved instinctively by the right sort of feeling, forgetting himself entirely, he remained at a distance. It was altogether by Emerson's doing that the "enthusiastic" Neuberg was by and by made personally known to Carlyle.

---

[1] Unpublished letter.
[2] Told by J. Neuberg to F. Althaus in 1866 ; and by J. Althaus in *Unsere Zeit*, Leipzig, 1881 (VI).

XXVI

THE CHAPTER WANTING IN CHARTISM

(1840)

THE proofs of *Chartism* done, those of his essays being reprinted became the work in hand, and he read at large about the Norse and the Arabs, Mahomet and Cromwell, etc., while continuing to agitate for a public library. He made full use of the Press, and becoming acquainted with W. D. Christie, a young journalist called to the Bar this year, was assisted by him as a zealous volunteer secretary in respect of the Library.

On New Year's Day (1-1-40) he had written to a sister that he was glad the *Morning Chronicle* scribes accounted him a Tory—" Heaven send the Tory Party abundance of *such* Tories ! " But when the Lancashire editor, Thomas Ballantyne, sent him a book " on the Statistics of the Corn-laws ", and said a chapter upon that was wanting in *Chartism*, he answered (24-1-40), that it was left out intentionally for many reasons :—

' The abrogation of the Corn Laws seems to be the cause of the Middle Classes and manufacturing Capitalists still *more* than that of the Lower Classes, and *has* found a voice, and talks very loud without help of mine, while the great cause I was speaking for, the soul of all justifiable Radicalism as I think, and of which this other is but an outpost and preliminary, continues dumb, able to express itself only in groans and convulsions, and does need a spokesman. The present Radical Members and Agitators have filled me with a deep conviction that in them is no hope ; that, for the cause of the Poor, one must leave them and their battles out of view, and address the rational and just men of England. Abolition of the Corn Law is as sure to my mind as six o'clock is when five has struck.

' The Corn Law I reckon the most brazen-faced injustice and also the blindest fatuity we have to suffer. The

Aristocracy, unhappy mortals, [are] doing no work, leaving the imperatively necessary work without so much as a thought that they are to do it ; pocketing at the same time huge wages (all the land of England) for the work as if it *were done*, and clamouring withal for an overplus produced by obstruction, confusion, sin, suffering and starvation ! They see not that before many years go the question will be not " shall we pay such no-workers an over-plus produced by starvation ? " But " shall we pay them anything at all ? " I find that on the whole there are *more* important questions than the Corn Law, important as that is.'

He had more than he wanted of " dinners, routs, callers, confusions ", and spoke as freely as he wrote, so that by 11–2–40 he was able to tell his mother : " The people are beginning to discover (wise men as they are !) that I am not a Tory. Ah, no ; but one of the deepest tho perhaps the quietest of all the Radicals."

His occasional thoughts in February about the summer lectures were crystallizing in March into a decision to lecture " On the Heroic ", and preach that hero-worship never ceases ; and by that time he had fixed on three of his models : Odin, Mahomet, and Cromwell.

XXVII

IN FASHIONABLE SOCIETY

(1840)

FASHIONABLE society was the natural habitat of the variegated man of letters, Bulwer Lytton. Tennyson said he was a " Bandbox ", when they were cursing each other ; but it might be better to say, the English D'Orsay, with the literary luck of a Lady Blessington. Like her he was making thousands a year by writing, but gave himself no airs on that account when he met Carlyle this season at the dinner-table of the Stanleys in Dover Street : " He is decidedly human," wrote Carlyle, " with afflicted-looking large protrusive eyes ; his appearance, adding the long nose and open mouth, the dandiacal apparel, weak padded figure, and adventitious renown, is *tragic-gawky*. Poor fellow, he has his own battle to fight, like us all. He and I agreed wonderfully well in the touch-and-go fashion ; he seemed desirous to engrush (ingratiate) himself rather than otherwise."

Which was creditable to " poor Bulwer ". The mockery of his *Pelham* in *Sartor* (III and X) would be in the minds of both, tho Carlyle was not likely to know that " poor Bulwer " had betrayed his sufferings by altering the text.

This was a Sunday dinner (23–2–40), with Charles Buller of the party, and Fonblanque of the *Examiner*. Another dinner there a few weeks later was even more memorable. The guest of the evening was the old Whig, Lord Holland, who was on the edge of the grave—he died this year ; and even more notable nowadays, tho little heeded then, was Charles Dickens, a young man beginning life.

' And,' as Carlyle told his brother (17–3–40), ' for soiree upstairs, Morpeth, Lansdowne, French Guizot, etc. He is a fine little fellow—Boz, I think,' meaning Charles Dickens. ' Clear blue, intelligent eyes, eyebrows that he arches amazingly, large protrusive rather loose mouth, a face of most extreme *mobility*, which he shuttles about—eyebrows, eyes, mouth, and all—in a very singular manner while speaking. Surmount this with a loose coil of common-coloured hair, and set it on a small compact figure, very small, and dressed *à la D'Orsay* rather than well—this is Pickwick. For the rest a quiet, shrewd-looking, little fellow, who seems to guess pretty well what he is and what others are. Lady Holland is a brown-skinned, silent, sad, concentrated, proud old dame. Notable word she spake none—sate like one wont to be obeyed and entertained.'

"A personal liking for Charles Dickens" was soon remarked in Carlyle, who said often that Dickens was "the only man of my time" whose writings have genuine cheerfulness. Of this particular evening what he remembered best, he said afterwards,[1] was "the little bob" which he was tickled to see Dickens give, when being introduced to old Holland, as if intimating he did not feel specially honoured.

In 1840 Thackeray had not yet "arrived", as they said then—he was still scrambling up, so to speak. His *Catherine*, a novel to show what criminals are, had just finished appearing in *Fraser*, and he was proudly telling his mother,[2] "The judges stand up for me. Carlyle says it is wonderful."

What made the praise of Carlyle delightful was that Thackeray had seen what few suspected yet, the significance of his new line of literary criticism. In advising his mother last year to read Carlyle's *Miscellanies*, Thackeray had written [3]:—

' A nobler [book] does not live in our language, I am sure, and [meaning, nor] one that will have such an effect on our ways of thought and prejudices. *Criticism has been a party matter with us till now, and literature is a poor political lacquey. Please God we shall begin ere long to love art for art's sake. It is Carlyle who has worked more than any other to give it its independence.*' [4]

Which helps to explain why Carlyle was never at Holland House. There was an instinctive aversion between him and

---

[1] *Literary Recollections*, by F. Espinasse, p. 215.
[2] Volume IV of the Biographical Edition of the *Works of Thackeray*.
[3] *Memoirs*, by A. Thackeray Ritchie, p. 140.
[4] Italics added.

Lady Holland, who was watching him, as he was watching her, and " always questioning her Dr. Allen " whenever he said anything : " What was that ? What was that ? " She felt unable to fathom him, could see he was not laying himself out to entertain the company, but talking as the spirit moved him, as independent as if he were a " man of property ". She decided he was not worth catching for her parties. He felt as if she were " a kind of hungry ' ornamented witch ', looking over at me with merely carnivorous views ". It is likely both were right.

Perhaps she may have been one of the Society folks described by M. Rio as frightened at Carlyle's " subversive doctrines ", and at his being " the unconcealed friend of men who proclaimed them with the utmost boldness ", especially of Godefroi Cavaignac and Mazzini. February, 1840, by the way, is the date of the only letter from Carlyle to Godefroi Cavaignac discovered among the Cavaignac family papers, when search was made there recently.[5] The concluding words of it are interesting now as a clue to the drift of many confidential talks whereof no record remains.—

'My dear Cavaignac, : : . I wish I heard of the first volume of your book being *at press* ! Wise words are better than the sharpest shots, and *carry* infinitely farther. Good be with you, my friend. Come and see us the first hour you have. Yours ever truly, T. Carlyle.'

[5] Communicated to D. A. W. by Prof. A. Koszul, Professor of English Literature at the University of Strasbourg, at whose instance search was made among the Cavaignac family papers by his friend and colleague, Prof. Cavaignac, grand-nephew of Godefroi Cavaignac.

XXVIII

" HEROES "

(1840)

" IT was a narrow turn of the balance," said Carlyle at the time, that he did not decline to lecture this year. It was not till the first week in April that he finally decided.[1] He hoped that this would be the last time, and so it was. He began to write down the lectures in advance, with passing thoughts of going to America in the fall with lectures ready written and " flaming about over two hemispheres with them (too like a Cagliostroccio) "; and, after making a few thousands, buying " an annuity, whereon to retire into some hut by the seashore, and there lie quiet till my hour come ". In fashionable London, at this time of rioting and rick-burning, starvation and waste, he felt like a fish out of water.

In the meantime, as success on the platform depended on his health, he was riding Citoyenne every afternoon ; and as soon as he was in the swing of preparation declined invitations in general, to avoid offence. " Daily," he wrote to his brother (19–4–40), " I *splash* down (as fast as my pen will go) some kind of paragraph on some point or other that has become salient and visible ; something that I might say. I can clip the paragraphs out, and string them together any way I like. I shall be the better able to *speak* of the things written of even in this way. It seems the best I can do."

It had long been common in both France and England to use the word heroes for the men of blood barbarians admire ; but the " Heroes " of Carlyle were what Voltaire called " great men ", not one of them a man of the " happy warrior " type or self-assertive self-shover, except only Napoleon, and he too had started well, but been seduced by " success ".

One or two forenoons had to be given to seeing people about the London Library ; but in general young Christie

---

[1] *Nineteenth Century Mag.*, May, 1921, p. 807.

saved him from that and came in the evenings to report and
consult. They were issuing thousands of prospectuses and
getting help from many newspapers.

The lectures were on Tuesdays and Fridays, 5 to 22–5–40,
and the audiences larger and better than ever, increasing
to the end. Lady Byron, the runaway wife and legal widow
of the poet, was present and making notes.[2] There were
bishops and divines doing ditto, attracted perhaps by the
mention of " The Hero as Divinity ". After the first lecture,
Carlyle reported to his mother that the people seemed
content, but " I was not in good trim. I had awoke at
half-past four " in the morning, which means too little
sleep for one who goes to bed late. The Reverend Trench
(not yet archbishop), writing to beg the Reverend Wilberforce (not yet a bishop) " to string a few of Carlyle's choicest
pearls and send them to us " at a distance, said he heard
that the first lecture " notwithstanding the many delightful
things in it, was partially a failure ; as they always are
unless he works himself up into a true Berserkr fury, which
on that occasion he failed to do." [3] Yet Joseph Neuberg
from Nottingham, attending the lecture, was incited by it
to some fine original research in Norse mythology.

The second lecture made ample amends. It was on
Mahomet. He made a great sensation by insisting that
Mahomet was a great and good man and a true prophet,
and that it was nonsense to say his religion was false because
it propagated itself by the sword. " Nature herself is umpire
and can do no wrong," was assumed like a maxim in Euclid.
The abundant laughter and applause on the day of delivery
was ratified on reflection and debate. The lecture was voted
his best. " It gave great satisfaction," wrote Crabb Robinson
in his diary, after a pleasant chat with Milnes and
Mrs. Gaskell.[4] " Animated and vehement," admitted F. D.
Maurice reluctantly,[5] for the lecturer did not dissemble
indifference as complete as Mahomet's to " those miserable
Syrian sects, with their vain janglings about Homoiousion
and Homoousion ".[6] It was a great revelation, the first

---

[2] *Rems. of Mrs. De Morgan,* pp. 226–7.
[3] *R. C. Trench, Archbishop, Letters and Memorials,* I, p. 248.
[4] *Diary of H. C. Robinson,* III, p. 187.
[5] *Life of F. D. Maurice,* I, p. 282, etc.
[6] The statement of Froude that Carlyle admitted that Christianity
was at stake in the controversy of Homoi-ousion *versus* Homo-ousion is
incredible. Froude was fond of saying so, and Carlyle did not always
contradict him, sometimes only yawned.

thorough-going defence of Mahomet from the fictions which had hidden him to European eyes for over a thousand years ; and it was not only the first, it finished the argument. It is a masterpiece of historical portraiture. The world of Islam deems it the gem of English literature, and nobody of sense disputes the truth of it now.

The actor Macready was one of the audience that first heard it, and wrote in his diary that he had been " charmed, carried away ". Only a conviction of truth could give " such fervour and eloquence ", was the private opinion of the best actor in London, who happened to be also one of the best men there.[7]

The only unpleasant trifle was that Mill interrupted him by standing up and crying " No ",[8] when he was saying " Benthamee Utility, virtue by Profit and Loss ", etc., was a " beggarlier and falser view of Man and his destinies " than Mahomet's, whose Heaven and Hell and Day of Judgment were " a rude shadow of that grand spiritual fact—the Infinite Nature of Duty ", making the difference between right and wrong like that between life and death, Heaven and Hell. " The one must in nowise be done, the other in nowise left undone."

The lecturer went on as if he had not heard, but in the fifth lecture, eleven days later, on " The Hero as Man of Letters ", he explained his view of Bentham's " steam-engine Utilitarianism ", adhering to what he had said— " without offence against the man Jeremy Bentham ", who was " comparatively worthy of praise ". It was not an apology, but a polite explanation, and enough to " save the face " of the headlong Mill.

It is likely to have been the third lecture (12–5–40), on the Hero as Poet, Dante and Shakespeare, which he concluded in a way that caused great amusement and tickled young ladies present so much that they used to entertain their friends by " imitating him very funnily ".[9] After his hour was over he went and looked at his notes and said :—

' I find I have been talking to you all for one hour and twenty minutes, and not said *one word* of what is down

[7] Macready's *Reminiscences*, edited by Sir F. Pollock, II, p. 160.
[8] *Life of Carlyle*, by R. Garnett, p. 171.
[9] *Corr. of Henry Taylor*, by E. Dowden, pp. 400–1.

on this sheet of paper, the subject matter of our lecture
to-day. I ask your indulgence, tho you have good right not
to give it to me ; so Good Morning.'

A contemporary journalist, who did not share Leigh
Hunt's admiration of his " noble homeliness ", felt bound
to say " a few words as to Mr. Carlyle's manner as a
lecturer " [10] :—

' In so far as his mere manner is concerned, I can scarcely
bestow on him a word of commendation. There is something
in his manner which, if I may use a rather quaint term, must
seem very uncouth to London audiences of the most
respectable class, accustomed as they are to the polished
deportment which is usually exhibited in Willis's or the
Hanover Rooms. When he enters and proceeds to the sort
of rostrum whence he delivers his lecture, he is received with
applause ; but he [in short, takes no] more notice of it than
if he were altogether unconscious of it. Having ascended
his desk, he gives a hearty rub to his hands, and plunges
at once into his subject [with] the same seeming want of
respect for his audience. He is not prodigal of gesture
with his arms or body ; but there is something in his eye
which, etc.' ; . . . [Sometimes] ' you can almost fancy that
you see his inmost soul in his face.'

This reporter was particularly scandalized by the Scotch
accent, which irritated him the more because he was himself
a Scot, and had taken pains to correct his own.

On the day of the third lecture (12-5-40), James Fraser
called at Seeley's in Fleet Street, and in waiting for
Mr. Seeley, went up to one of the young men, Daniel
MacMillan, and gossiped about Carlyle. The young Daniel,
who lived to be a big man in his trade, had lately laid
Sartor to heart, and told Fraser of his feelings towards
Carlyle, confessing : " I should very much like to see him." [11]

Fraser was far from well—indeed, he had to die next year,
tho he did not know it ; and listening kindly to the young
man's enthusiasm, remarked : " If you choose to come to
my place in Regent Street I will lend you my ticket to go

[10] *Portraits of Public Characters*, by James Grant, II, p. 152, and
quoted in *Thomas Carlyle*, by H. J. Nicoll, pp. 93–6, and also in R. H.
Shepherd's *T. Carlyle*, I, pp. 215–17.
[11] *Life of Daniel MacMillan*, by T. Hughes, pp. 70, 89, 91–6, 115–16.

to to-day's lecture, as I cannot go myself." Which MacMillan was able to do. He described it in a letter :—

' He lectures without notes of any kind, having thrown aside the piece of paper like a visiting card which he used to bring with him. He is very far from being a fluent speaker. Sometimes he rises into eloquence and gets applauded ; sometimes he comes to a dead stand for want of a word, quietly looking in the face of his audience till he finds the word ; sometimes he leaves his sentence in a quite unfinished state, and passes on to something else. E.g. speaking of the difference between Dante's time and ours, he said : " Our highest has become unattainably high. The apex," here he came to a dead stop for three or four moments, and at last, not being able to complete his sentence, he goes on to say " Our universe has everywhere expanded itself," etc., etc. He rarely moves his hands from the sides of his desk. When he does it is to rub his two forefingers across his forehead, just above his eyebrows. He always said his best things after one or two of these rubs.

' His whole appearance and manner is exceedingly simple. I never saw any one so completely free from anything like pretension. His accent and pronunciation is very broad Scotch, much more so, I think, than Dr. Chalmers'. His dress is plain and simple enough, but no way remarkable.

' It was a great treat to get a sight of such an audience. I never saw so many fine faces. True aristocrats, according to my radical notion of an aristocrat. There must be a great satisfaction to a thinker uttering his thoughts to such listeners. The number, as near as one could guess, was about three hundred. From the lecture-room down to Portman Square was quite lined with carriages.

' From what I saw of his lecturing, I should not think that he is very likely to rap the desk with his fists or anything of that sort.'

Macmillan missed the funny conclusion, having to hurry back to his shop a little before the end.

The fourth lecture, on the Hero as Priest, Luther and Knox, was voted " very good ". Carlyle was always fond of quoting what Luther said when refusing to recant at Worms : " It is neither safe nor prudent to do anything against conscience. So here I stand and can do nothing else—God help me ! " On this occasion he declared that scene " the greatest moment in modern history. English

Puritanism, England and its Parliaments, Americas, etc., French Revolution, etc., the germ of it all lay there. Had Luther done other it had all been otherwise. Luther did what every man lies under the sacred duty to do without counting costs, answered a falsehood when it questioned him, Dost thou believe me ? No ! "

The fifth lecture (19-5-40)—on the Man of Letters, Johnson, Rousseau, Burns—was the first which Caroline Fox attended, a bright young Quaker lady, introduced to Mrs. Carlyle that day by the sister of Mill. She wrote in her diary [12] :—

' Carlyle soon appeared, and looked as if he felt a well-dressed London audience scarcely the arena for him to figure in as a popular lecturer. He is a tall, robust-looking man ; rugged simplicity and indomitable strength are in his face, and such a glow of genius in it—not always smouldering there, but flashing from his beautiful grey eyes, from the remoteness of their deep setting under that massive brow. His manner is very quiet, but he speaks like one tremendously convinced of what he utters, and who had much—very much—in him that was quite unutterable, quite unfit to be uttered to the uninitiated ear ; and when the Englishman's sense of beauty or truth exhibited itself in vociferous cheers he would impatiently, almost contemptuously, wave his hand, as if that were not the kind of homage which Truth demanded. He began in a rather low and nervous voice, with a broad Scotch accent, but it [the voice] soon grew firm.'

Another stranger in the audience fated to become a personal friend was Edward FitzGerald, who by-and-by declared these lectures the best of Carlyle's books, and said the lecturer " looked very handsome then, with his black hair, fine Eyes, *and a sort of crucified Expression* ".[13]

Alexander MacMillan, the brother of Daniel, was at the fifth lecture and said " he was very much applauded several times ", and ended " very abruptly, and left his hearers laughing at a quotation from John Paul "[11] [Richter]. It was a pat quotation, with a double meaning few suspected. He had been explaining how people coming idly to look at Burns had bothered him—' the lion-hunters were the ruin and death of Burns.

---

[12] *Caroline Fox, Her Letters and Journals*, I, p. 182, etc., and p. 188.
[13] *Letters of E. F.* (1894), MacMillan, II, p. 191.   Italics added.

' They hindered his industry. He could not get his Lionism forgotten, honestly as he was disposed to do so. It is tragical to think of ! These men came but to *see* him ; it was out of no sympathy with him, nor no hatred to him. They came to get a little amusement : they got their amusement ; and the hero's life went for it !

' Richter says in the Island of Sumatra [14] there is a kind of Light-chafers, large Fire-flies, which people stick upon spits, and illuminate the ways with at night. Persons of condition can thus travel with a pleasant radiance which they much admire. Great honour to the Fire-flies. But—'

No wonder the audience laughed at the humorous metaphor, comparing the poet to such a fire-fly ; but eight days before then (11–5–40) he had been writing to the Editor Ballantyne in Lancashire, and saying lecturing hurt his health so much that he hoped this would be the last of it.

' Four times spitted on the spear's point like a Surinam [14] *fire-fly* to give light to the fashionable classes ; this is enough of times ! I shall be right thankful to get through it without disgrace, and cease shining in that manner.'

Caroline Fox's version [12] of the *spoken* lecture runs on : " He then told us he had more than occupied our time, and rushed downstairs."

The last lecture was on the Hero as King—a misnomer due to a mistake in etymology. Everywhere in Europe Kings were once elected, and Carlyle approved the Roman method of appointing a Dictator in an emergency. So he shared the mistake of supposing the word King originally meant one who knows and can do things, coming from the root of " can " and " ken "—like the word " know ". It is now agreed the root is " kin ", and etymologically like its common meaning in Europe for centuries, a *hereditary* chief ruler, such as Byron derided and in *Sartor* Carlyle has mocked. Nobody at the lecture mistook his meaning, for the " Kings " he selected for honour were Cromwell and Napoleon, and he said the French Revolution was " the third and final act of Protestantism ; the explosive, confused return of mankind to Reality and Fact, now that they were perishing of Semblance and Sham ".

[14] Surinam or Guiana was right, not the island of Sumatra. In lecturing Carlyle spoke vaguely of Indians, naming neither Sumatra nor Surinam, according to Caroline Fox. The quotation in the text is from the lecture as published.

Once more he championed Cromwell out-and-out, but spoke candidly and not like a partisan. He admitted Napoleon lied in his bulletins, and became a Charlatan when he set up Popery as a kind of vaccination against the Smallpox of Christianity, and, allying himself to "the old false feudalities", tried to start a dynasty—the very actions which had pleased the Tories ; but the audience was carried away again, and applauded warmly. In short, the conclusion was a fitting climax to the course. He praised their tolerance and thanked them, ending—" Good be with you all."

" I am glad to see, Carlyle, that you have adopted my theory of Cromwell," said John Robertson to him heartily, having followed him into the retiring-room after it was over. " Didn't know, sir, that you *had* a theory of Cromwell," was the answer, as Robertson himself reported " without much resentment," [15] having a sense of humour.

There is no certain knowledge of who received the dozen or two of lecture tickets Carlyle gave away for every course. James Fraser would get one, and Mrs. Edward Irving, and maybe Robertson himself ; but the only certainty is reported by Daniel MacMillan, who wrote to a friend (4–6–40) that one was sent to William Hone, a veteran of sixty now, and poor, but one of the best " men of letters " in England. It was he who in 1817 had been prosecuted for " impious and profane libel " because he published political satires illustrated by Cruikshank but " very offensive " to the Prince Regent. He defended himself well ; and three London juries acquitted him amid applause, in spite of the misdirections of judges.[16] He was not well enough to avail himself of Carlyle's kindness, MacMillan tells us, " till the last lecture, when a friend took him up in a coach " and introduced him after it. " Carlyle said he was very glad to see him ; that he used to see Hone's books in his father's house twenty years ago, and so had known him long tho he had never had the pleasure of speaking to him before."

Speaking of his audience by-and-by [17] Carlyle remarked " that their attention was keenest when he touched on the career and personal character of the man of whom he

[15] *Memories of London in the Forties*, by David Masson, p. 12.
[16] Campbell's *Chief Justices*, IV, pp. 284–6. F. W. Hackwood's *William Hone*, Chapters VIII to XI. Miss Martineau's *Thirty Years' Peace*, I, pp. 160–71, etc.
[17] *Literary Recollections*, by F. Espinasse, p. 210.

happened to be speaking, and flagged when he went off into disquisition or literary criticism ".

One of the best notices of the lectures was in the Roman Catholic *Tablet*, which Carlyle sent to his mother, saying Lucas, the editor of it, originally a Quaker, had told him, " *You* have converted me! " to Popery! Other people said Anstey did that ; but Lucas said " *You* did it ! " Which made Carlyle tell the story of an old Italian gentleman who was unable to spring up on his saddle. He prayed for help to Saint Antony, and tried again, and—went over on the other side, exclaiming : " You're *too* good, this time, Saint Antony ! "

He told Emerson that he sometimes felt he could learn to speak in the course of time.

' The beautiful people listened with boundless tolerance, eager attention. I meant to tell them, among other things, that man was still alive, Nature not dead or like to die ; that all true men continued true to this hour—Odin himself true, and the Grand Lama of Thibet himself not wholly a lie. The lecture on Mahomet astonished my worthy friends beyond measure. It seems then that this Mahomet was not a Quack ? Not a bit of him ! That he is a better Christian, with his " bastard Christianity ", than the most of us shovel-hatted ? I guess than almost any of you ! Not so much as Oliver Cromwell would I allow to have been a Quack. All quacks I asserted to be Nothing, *chaff* that would not grow ; my poor Mahomet " was wheat with barn sweepings ". Nature had tolerantly hidden the barn sweepings ; and as to the *wheat*, behold she had said Yes to it, and it was growing !

' I was gratified to see how the rudest *speech* of a man's heart goes into men's hearts.

' In the fire of the moment I had all but decided on setting out for America this autumn, and preaching far and wide like a very lion there. Quit your paper formulas, my brethren—equivalent to old wooden idols, *un*divine as they : in the name of God, understand that you are alive, and that God is alive ! Did the upholsterer make this Universe ? Were you created by the tailor ? I tell you, and conjure you to believe me literally, No, a thousand times No ! Thus did I mean to preach on " Heroes, Hero-worship, and the Heroic " in America too. Alas ! the fire of

determination died away again ; all that I did resolve upon
was to write these lectures down and in *some* way promulgate
them farther.'

Which occupied him every morning till 3–9–40, with few
interruptions, about three months' work altogether. He had
a reporter's record of what he had said, and the paper
whereon he had written what he had decided in advance
that he might say, and he told his sister he was rewriting the
whole of them now " as they might have been and should
have been and wished to be delivered to the people ". And
that was how the book on Heroes came into being and was
published next year.

He felt tired when he finished writing the lectures, and
decided to go nowhere. He rested at home and read at
random, indulging his favourite " daydream " of a " cottage
by the seashore ". He felt at times like an Irishman he saw
one hot day lying prostrate in the Green Park under the
shade of a tree. " Look at the Irishman yonder," said Carlyle
to his wife, as they went along Piccadilly, " in what a depth
of sleep, as if you had poured him out of a jug."

XXIX

CARLYLE AND VOLTAIRE ON MAHOMET AND CROMWELL

THE book on Heroes, etc., was called by Sterling " a sublime book, the best . . . I know in English prose ". It has been found excellent for schools and colleges,[1] and it figures in many a list of the " Best Fifty ", etc., books ; but much that has been written and said about it requires correction. Thus it is a mistake to impute his " doctrines " to Fichte or any other modern. Even Voltaire had articulated Hero-Worship in remarking apropos Don Henry of Portugal : " Almost everything great in history has been done by the genius and character of an individual, acting in spite of the crowd, or leading it after him." In short, the " Gospel " of Carlyle was in the Bible and the good old literature of Greece and Rome, India and China. The essence of Carlyle's " originality " was sincerity and out-spokenness.

The description of Mahomet was at once an addition to European knowledge, and also " confirmation strong " of the main " novelty " in the lecturer's doctrine, the righteousness of Nature, implying that reality and not sham was the condition of success for men and institutions. It is curious to consider how commonplace that " novelty ", which was really as old as civilization, has become to us in the sixty years that followed. It was the best of his teaching, and helps to make his histories a great advance upon Voltaire and Gibbon and Co. It was almost a commonplace in Asia, but Carlyle did not know that.

As for Mahomet, there had been a suspicion in Europe since before the Reformation that he was not the impostor the clergy said. The difficulty was to make sure. In symposiums at Erfurt the youths who were to write in their

[1] There is an edition well edited by Professor MacMechan, published by the Athenæum Press, Boston, and much used in America.

maturity the famous " Letters of Obscure Men ", heard
Canon Muth or Mutianus praising the Koran, in spite of
its teetotalism.[2]

When Voltaire was summing up the history of our " Middle
Ages ",[3] he denied the delusion that the Muslim creed
depended on the sword ; but in his play-writing tradition
was too strong for him, and he made Mahomet an impostor
still, which Napoleon used to say was unfair ("injuste "). In
the same way Goethe in his prime designed to show Mahomet
" a prophet sincerely convinced of the truth of his message,
and inflamed with a disinterested desire to give his countrymen a purer religion ". He ended by merely translating the
play Voltaire had written, and staging it with Schiller's
approval.[4] So it was left to Carlyle to go beyond his masters
and reveal to our astonished eyes the prophet of the Muslims
as a real good man.

What seems to have put him on the track of this great
discovery was not any of the previous surmises, but the right
principle that Nature can do no wrong, and is the same in
morals as in materials. Chance is only a name for our
ignorance. By this time it was plain that the " religion "
Mahomet taught was a great advance, like Buddhism a
millennium before him and the intellectual revival in Europe
eight hundred years later. It followed that such a great
result as the rise of the Muslims must have had some
adequate cause, and could not be explained by human
trickery. Men can bully or humbug each other, but not
Nature. This led Carlyle to study candidly the evidence.
The Koran and other documents were accessible in
translations, and that was how he was able to verify the
truth and hold the mirror up to Nature better than Voltaire
himself by the very method of Voltaire, the appeal to facts.

There was a great deal more than method in common
between them, and a Plutarch at leisure might draw an
amusing parallel. They both preferred the country to the
town, and both were happily henpecked, and so on. In
one essential they were really alike—they wrote in perfect
indifference to money. Voltaire had made plenty in other
ways, and Carlyle had the sense to be easily content with the
little he was able to earn.

[2] See the 1909 edition of *Epistolæ Obscurorum Virorum* and pp. LVII–
LIX of the introduction of F. G. Stokes.
[3] In the last chapter of his *Essai sur les Moeurs*.
[4] P. Hume Brown's *Life of Goethe*, pp. 181-4; and Bielschowsky's
Goethe, I, pp. 246-7, and II, p. 411.

Freethinkers both, and disbelieving the magic inspiration of the Bible, they differed in their attitude to professional Christians because they had to deal with different churches. In France Voltaire beheld a domineering church, unclean, unjust and cruel, and he made war upon it as " l'infâme ", the abominable thing. In Scotland Carlyle saw Christianity at its best, like a fine flower of freedom, the soul of a people, identical almost with idealism and righteousness ; and far from suffering by it, he was happy enough to meet much kindness from the pious, who were often among the best of his friends. Thus all his prejudices and native pugnacity were enlisted on their side, and he concluded against inspiration with real reluctance, and cordially coincided with many contemporaries in feeling averse to any avoidable speech about it.

Thus it was that in writing and lecturing he dwelt upon what to believe, and said little about what to disbelieve. We have to remember that his chosen religious hero was Luther, and that Luther lived to regret he had spoken out so much, declaring he had thought men better than they were.

In spite of such reasons for reticence, Carlyle was in the course of time exasperated by the hocus-pocus party in the Church of England, a faint and far-off mimicry of the rascaldom which provoked Voltaire. He said it was needful to make an " Exodus from Houndsditch ", an exit from their old clothes' shops, and in private talk and public writings scoffed at them and their shibboleths in a way that hurt them more than controversy would have done, and made them his bitterest enemies—which pleased him well. He loathed the Jesuitism or distilling of lies which is their stock-in-trade as much as did Voltaire.

Another thing the two free-thinkers had in common was miraculous activity. Both of them were not only assiduous in writing books in a disinterested spirit for general readers, but also were as prompt as any Paul to write epistles to disciples, who devoutly preserved them. Biographers tell of Voltaire's twenty letters a day, whereof ten thousand have been printed. Perhaps there is no English author to approach this but Carlyle. Tho both were often merry and fond of fun, Voltaire a wit and Carlyle a humorist, nevertheless they were both prophets rather than scribes—men telling what they saw to be true because they felt they should, and not ordinary entertaining men of letters.

Even when fictioneering, Voltaire was sometimes preaching ; and even when lecturing Carlyle was seldom thinking of how to amuse his audience. He was as earnest as Luther or Knox in the pulpit, or Mahomet or Paul. And that was why he spoke as the spirit moved him after study, and did not merely read his discourses. His earnestness was what distinguished him from other lecturers.

He was always in earnest. Voltaire was equally so when in a passion, but at other times addicted to " society ", rejoicing in its masquerades like a " Mediterranean " man, as befitted a prophet to the fellow-Frenchmen he called tiger-apes. Carlyle could walk alone through the crowd with little effort, like a man from the country through a fashionable ball that was not his concern. Men's limitations sometimes serve them well when they remain sincere.

The same instinct for sincerity which led him to see Mahomet aright had made him choose for the Hero as English King the very Oliver Cromwell who had been so long and so unanimously " damned " that even the sceptical Voltaire was taken in, and supposed that what everybody said must be true, and the man a rogue. The prosperity that palpably attended such a man all his days appeared to Voltaire a striking proof of the most dismal of the conclusions he drew from past events. " The lesson of history is that weakness is punished and big crimes prosper, so that the world is all a scene of robbery, the issue of which is left to ' luck ' [5] or ' fortune '," which he defined as " the necessary connexion of all the events in the universe ."

The sight of Cromwell's prosperous wickedness distressed Voltaire like the Lisbon earthquake. Carlyle did not need to be told his audience did not go with him about Cromwell as they did about Mahomet ; and as soon as the lecture-writing was finished he was to replunge into the Common-wealth papers, and by another successful appeal to facts to vindicate the ways of Nature and reveal old Noll as the best man that had ever been a ruler of England.

[5] *Essai sur les Mœurs*, Chapters 191 and 124.

BOOK XII

TO PAST AND PRESENT

(1840-43)

H

I

THE LONDON LIBRARY

(1840)

A LONGSIDE the writing of *Heroes*, Carlyle was agitating for a London Library, and renewing the social intercourse interrupted in March. Miss Wilson was one of many who were distributing prospectuses for the London Library. Thirlwall was another. Both Carlton and Reform Club members were doing so, admitting the force of James Spedding's argument [1] that, however good their libraries, a club is not the place to read a book in. It was by "energetic aid to establish the London Library" [2] that John Forster became intimate with Carlyle.

Before long hundreds had put down their names as Library subscribers, and it was time to arrange a public meeting "with a Lord in the chair", according to the fashion. So one Wednesday (24-6-40) there was a meeting at the Freemasons' Tavern, "crowded to overflow," said the *Examiner*,[3] with persons "of Literary and political distinction", and after several lords and others had spoken, Mr. Carlyle was received "with loud cheering", and said what was thus reported :—

' It does not become us who are as yet only struggling for existence, who are merely nascent, and have nothing but hopes and a good purpose, to commence by casting any censure on the British Museum. Accordingly we mean no censure by this resolution. We will leave the British Museum standing on its own basis, and be very thankful that such a Library exists in this country. But supposing it to be managed with the most perfect skill and success, even according to the ideal of such an Institution, still I will assert that this other Library of ours is requisite also. In

---

[1] *R. M. Monckton Milnes*, by T. Wemyss Reid, I, pp. 234-5.
[2] *Literary Recollections*, by F. Espinasse, p. 117 ; confirmed by T. C. Letters to John Forster in South Kensington Museum.
[3] *Examiner*, Sunday, 28-6-40, p. 408, etc.

the first place by the very nature of the thing a great quantity of people are excluded altogether from the British Museum as a reading room. Every man engaged in business is occupied during the hours it is kept open ; and innumerable classes of persons find it extremely inconvenient to attend the British Museum Library at all. But granting that they all could go there, I would ask any literary man, any reader of books, any man intimately acquainted with the reading of books, whether he can read them to any purpose in the British Museum ? (Cheers.) A book is a kind of thing that requires a man to be self-collected. He must be alone with it. (Cheers.) A good book is the purest essence of a human soul. How could a man take it into a crowd, with bustle of all sorts going on around him ? *The good of a book is not the facts that can be got out of it, but the kind of resonance that it awakens in our own minds.* (Cheers.) A book may strike out of us a thousand things, may make us know a thousand things which it does not know itself. For this purpose I decidedly say that no man can read a book well with the bustle of three or four hundred people about him. Even for getting the mere facts which a book contains, a man can do more with it in his own apartment, in the solitude of one night, than in a week in such a place as the British Museum. Neither with regard to Circulating Libraries are we bound to utter any kind of censure ; Circulating Libraries are what they can be in the circumstances.

' I believe that if a man had the heroism to collect a body of great books, to get together the cream of the knowledge that exists in the world, and let it be gradually known that he had such a Library, he would find his advantage in it in the long run ; but it would be only in the long run ; he must wait ten or twenty years, perhaps a lifetime ; he must be a kind of martyr. You could not expect a purveyor of Circulating Libraries to be that ! (Cheers and laughter.) The question for such a person to ask is not, " Are you wanting to read a wise book ? " but " Have you got sixpence in your pocket to pay for the reading of *any* book ? " (Laughter.) Consequently he must have an eye to the prurient appetite of the great million, and furnish them with any kind of garbage they will have. The result is melancholy—making bad worse—for every bad book begets an appetite for reading a worse one. (Cheers.) Thus we come to the age of Pinchbeck in Literature, and to falsehoods of all kinds. So leaving all other institutions, the British

Museum and the Circulating Libraries, to stand, I say that a decidedly good Library of good books is a crying want in this great London. How can I be called upon to demonstrate a thing that is as clear as the sun ? London has more men and intellect waiting to be developed than any place in the world ever had assembled. Yet there is no place on the civilized earth so ill supplied with materials for reading for those who are not rich. (Cheers.) I have read an account of a Public Library in Iceland, which the King of Denmark founded there. There is not a peasant in Iceland that cannot bring home books to his hut better than men can in London. Positively it is a kind of disgrace to us, which we ought to assemble and put an end to with all convenient dispatch. The founding of a library is one of the greatest things we can do with regard to results. It is one of the quietest of things ; but there is nothing I know of at bottom more important. Every one able to read a good book becomes a wiser man. He becomes a similar centre of light and order and just insight into the things around him. A collection of good books contains all the nobleness and wisdom of the world before us. Every heroic and victorious soul has left his stamp upon it. A collection of books is the best of all Universities ; for the University only teaches us how to read the book ; you must go to the book itself for what it is. I call it a Church also, which every devout soul may enter—a Church but with no quarrelling, no Church-rates—'

" The remainder of the sentence," says the reporter, " was drowned in cheers and laughter, in the midst of which Mr. Carlyle sat down." [4] An observant hearer [5] said he plainly " thought upon his legs ", but not always aloud, and tried the patience of the audience by long and frequent intervals of pause, tho what he said was felt to be " full of wisdom ". Charles Buller was among those who followed, and

[4] Reprinted in *Carlyle and the London Library*, by Frederic Harrison, pp. 61–72. See also *New Letters of T. Carlyle*, edited by A. Carlyle, I, pp. 198–200, footnote. Both F. Harrison and A. Carlyle assured D. A. W. they took no liberties with the report ; and in his book, p. 69, in a footnote, Mr. Harrison remarks : " The *Examiner* was at this time edited by Albany Fonblanque, Carlyle's friend, and the report was probably seen and corrected in proof by Carlyle." Mr. Froude's report is sheer invention, partly based on a letter written at another time.

[5] *Thomas Carlyle*, by H. J. Nicoll, p. 96, quoting *Chambers' Journal*, 18-2-43.

Mr. Christie said he hoped that all who had come " to hear "
would remain " to pay ". Milnes reminded the meeting that
if Gibbon had not been able to spend £7,000 on books his
great history would never have been written. A Committee
was elected to draw up rules and organize the Library, which
started in a few months with about 500 members.

Applications for the post of Librarian were coming in,
and in the absence of any report of the talks with Christie,
here is a part of a hurried letter to him.[6] The " Cochrane "
named in it was a man of 59, who became the first Librarian,
and did the work well for the dozen years he had still to
live :—

'Chelsea, Thursday Evg.

'DEAR CHRISTIE,—

'There is much in what you say about Cochrane
that seems to me altogether reasonable, well worth considering, and balancing against what is to be said on the
other side.

'He is evidently *older* by ten years than one could have
wished . . . I can well believe that he will not be so
guidable as one of the mere clerk species might be ; the
guidablest of all quadrupeds is a starved cadger's garron
(a poor horse), reduced to skin and bone ; no kicking or
plunging from *him* ; but alas, withal there is no *go* in him !

'What I have known or got to believe of Cochrane is
that he possesses sense, energy, discretion, enterprise, that
his whole life has been a qualifying of himself for the management of such a business, and that now he would undertake
it, sharing the risks along with us, in such a spirit as promises,
were reasonable field granted him, the best results for us.

'He certainly does not *write* in a very oracular manner ;
but . . . elegant writing is not the chief point with us.

'I think it one of the most promising symptoms our
Adventure has ever exhibited, that a solid man, of grave
years, of much acquirement, capability and experience, is
willing to embark his life interest upon it—and make it
either prosper or fail himself to prosper. We should not
lightly throw away such a possibility.

'For the rest I do not so much fight for Cochrane as for
the principle of action involved in choosing him.

'A saving of £50 annually to get a clerk instead of a

---

[6] *Carlyle and the London Library*, by F. Harrison, pp. 25–32.

Manager and Fellow-Adventurer hopefully on mature calculation committed to the scheme, and *bound* to make it succeed, seems to me the deplorablest thrift.

' Lewis [Sir George Cornewall Lewis] says we must feel our way, save our £50, get a subordinate man, and *then* when we have succeeded, appoint some Cochrane over him ! It is like sending out a military expedition for conquest in foreign countries under a *serjeant*, with strict proviso that *when* he has made conquests, we will send a General ! Alas, too clearly, there will never be any General needed.

' I must oppose this sergeant-scheme as altogether unwise, and if there be any general, on not impossible terms, attainable for us . . . for Heaven's sake no Clerk when there is a real Librarian attainable ! Let us all decide upon that.

' My notion of the Librarian's function does not imply that he shall be king over us ; nay that he shall ever quit the address and manner of a *servant* to the Library ; but he will be as a *wise* servant, watchful, diligent, discerning what is what, incessantly endeavouring, *rough-hewing* all things for us ; and, under the guise of a wise servant, *ruling* actually while he serves. Like a Nobleman's Steward, that is in some sort the definition of him. We may make more or not so much approximation to getting such a man. But I am deeply sensible that with no such man we are still hovering among the shallows, a cargo to win or to lose. No enterprise in this world ever prospered without some one man standing to it, not *par amours*, but heart and soul as a business. Lewis says Yes, but Christie will be that man. Dare you undertake so much ? If so, it will very greatly alter my computation ; I shall feel greatly disposed to vote for whom you like ! But fancy a boat propelled now by this man giving it a kick and going his ways, and then by another giving it a kick and going his ways ! There must absolutely be a man with the tiller always in his hand.

' Cochrane writes to me this morning a most despondent response to the letter he has got from you. The endless *hours* (from 8 to 6), etc., etc., strike him altogether dumb. I explain that these are as yet but *suggestions*, that nothing is fixed but the £150; that on the whole he had better still persist in coming up on Saturday, in looking at the business and letting us look at him face to face . . .'

Carlyle agreed to ' do whatever I can ' in selecting books, remarking : ' Our first set of purchases ought to be popular, entertaining, what people will read and *continue to read* (which last narrows the field greatly); that is, to a great extent, the rule for us . . .

' The Lord forgive you for making me scribble all this stuff !

' Come and see me to-morrow, or *soon* at latest. I am, yours always,

' T. CARLYLE.'

As long as the issue about the Librarian was doubtful, Carlyle did not hide that he would go to a vote if needful, saying : " If a man's conviction differ from that of other men, he not only will but should express it." But Cochrane once appointed, unanimously it seems, Carlyle left the rest to others, as he had always said he would, telling Christie : " I am Peter the Hermit, you the Louis VII ; and behold the Crusade, now marches,—Peter retiring to his prayers again." [7]

He continued to take a fatherly interest in the London Library, and occasionally presented to some suitable person a life-member's ticket as a gift. What may need to be told now is the surprising fact that much of the Press was hostile. It seemed dangerous to cheapen reading, as knowledge might foster discontent. Which explains a curious letter of 1840 [8] from James Spedding in the Colonial Office to Carlyle, suggesting to him to write to Forster to get Bulwer, Talfourd and Dickens to give a lead to the Library movement, and confessing : " My prospects of advancement in the [Colonial Office] career which I have undertaken might be seriously injured by taking a forward part in an enterprise of this kind."

[7] Ibid., pp. 79–83.
[8] John Forster Collection, South Kensington Museum.

II

A GLANCE AT MARGARET GORDON

TWICE "in 1840 or so" he met Margaret Gordon in
London—Mrs. Bannerman now. Her husband was an
Aberdeen wine-merchant with money and time to spare,
and so an ideal " Liberal " M.P. When he was in London
they stayed with her stepfather, Dr. Guthrie, Berkeley
Street. Her " dignified carriage and superior air " were
noticeable. She was promenading with her maid in
Piccadilly when she was recognized by Carlyle. A few
months later they met again, on horseback both of them
this time, " in the gate of Hyde Park." He said, " She was
bending a little, tapping her boot in the stirrup with her
riding-whip, when she looked up and saw me," and ''her
eyes (but that was all) said to me (almost) touchingly,
' Yes, yes ; that is you ! ' "

She and her husband were now about half-way through
their fifteen years' political promenade in London. In 1851
he was needing money, and glad to get a job of Colonial
Governor in Prince Edward Island, and then in Newfound-
land, etc. Margaret queened it beautifully everywhere. She
was many years a widow in England, a childless widow, and
religious, evangelical. Her rich half-sister, Dr. Guthrie's
daughter, supplied her with the means to be bountiful, but
tried in vain to induce her to vegetate in comfort in London
or Herefordshire. She devoted herself to her sick or needy
neighbours in Greenwich or Blackheath, and died at eighty.[1]

---

[1] Besides the *Rems. of T. C.* and D. Masson's *Edinburgh Sketches and
Memories*, pp. 257-9, see *Carlyle's First Love, Margaret Gordon, Lady
Bannerman*, by R. C. Archibald, pp. 110, 119–68, etc., and *Carlyle's
First Love* in the *Glasgow Herald*, 6–2–06, by J. Cuthbert Hadden.

III

WHAT NEXT ?

(1840)

AS a seed falls silently, so the founding of the London Library was little heeded. The social event of the season was an Anti-Slavery splutter at Exeter Hall in July, when Dan O'Connell and Prince Albert were both boisterously welcomed, and Caroline Fox, who had gone with the Mills, heard Wilberforce's eloquence, and watched sophist Guizot on the platform nodding approval. She remarked the supercilious looks of Peel, which need no pardon now. Working men in England then might envy the negro slaves. It may have been about this time that Carlyle, talking to Sterling, concluded : " When I look at this, I determine to cast all tolerance to the winds." " My dear fellow," said Sterling, " I had no idea you had any to cast." [1]

The promoters of the Anti-Slavery conferences refused admittance to their platforms to *female* delegates from America because they were females, which brought four of them, "rigid-looking elderly Quakeresses", to complain to Carlyle.

He told his mother how he studied to receive them as well as he could. He is as likely as any other to have advised them to do what in fact they did—hold a meeting " for their own behoof ", but as for joining their " crusade ", he " terribly disappointed" them by his downrightness. " I told them, as usual, that the *green* and *yellow* slaves, grown green with sheer hunger in my own neighbourhood, were far more interesting to me ! I added, moreover, that I myself had been a slave all the days of my life ; and had still a hard battle to fight, at all moments, to get any portion of my own just will made good. In fine, I did not hide from them that I considered their black slaves concern a business lying in *their* parish, not mine."

---

[1] H. M. Pym's *Memories of Old Friends of Caroline Fox*, p. 136.

They might have departed happier if they had discussed the teetotallers in whom he was warmly interested this summer. He told his mother of " a Scotch Bricklayer in this quarter ", saved by teetotallism, and he watched with satisfaction the " great crowds on the Sundays " listening " very considerately " to the speaking of " rough earnest men, reformed drunkards as they profess themselves. The very Irish, poor wretches, are abjuring drink by the million. I say, it is the first *beginning of emancipation* to them. I could almost weep to hear these poor rude workmen zealously calling on their fellow-creatures to abjure the slavery of Gin ! They speak evidently from the heart."

Or the " female delegates " might have been glad to share his interest in Jenny Geddes, the " distinguished female " contemporary of their prophet Fox. For many months Carlyle had been seeking in all directions for credible news of her, explaining to John Forster : [2] " Janet seems to me one of the heroines of this world ; more memorable considerably than Iphigenia or any other of that set. The twirl " of her, the stool she flung, was in short " the *first* stroke " of the Civil War.

He consulted Lockhart also about her in vain (26–10–40), and had to leave " poor Jenny featureless, I am afraid, for ever. Shakespeare's is not the only lost Biography ! Greedy oblivion makes haste to swallow us all ".[3]

The book he put first in his letter to Lockhart was Robert Baillie's *Letters and Journals*, which he had been seeking for two years. But Lockhart could not help him to it, nor Forster, nor David Aitken, Bess Stodart's man, nor anybody till his old friend Thomas Murray came to London this year,[4] and when he called and heard Carlyle was looking for Baillie's book, he was delighted to lend it indefinitely.[5] He had a " noble collection " of books, and as he said in old age, for he lived to be over eighty, after Carlyle left Edinburgh " our feelings remain the same ", tho " our intercourse, even that of an epistolary kind, has been much interrupted". His biographer need not have worried because Carlyle wrote to his brother a letter which should never have been printed, saying " little Murray " was " egoistic, small, vain, a poor

[2] John Forster Collection, South Kensington Museum.
[3] *John Gibson Lockhart*, by Andrew Lang, II, p. 230, etc.
[4] *Autobiography, etc., of T. Murray*, by J. A. Fairley, Dumfries, 1911, with portrait, pp. 15, 28–37, 72–92.
[5] *Early Letters of J. W. Carlyle*, by D. G. Ritchie, p. 297.

grub " with " better instincts ".   " Little " was a word
Carlyle was too fond of applying to anyone shorter than
himself, tho maybe bigger.   The other adjectives are merely
his way of saying of Murray what the biographer himself
puts thus :   " His self-complacency and his sense of his own
importance, [to say nothing of] libations and social
predilections, indicate a successful man of somewhat
bourgeoise type of mind ".   Perhaps neither set of words
was right—the best of Murray may have been his *unconscious*
health.   His portrait shows a strong sagacious face.

The Rev. David Aitken, who supplied Carlyle with many
another book tho unable to find a copy of Baillie's, was also
in London this summer ; and there is a Carlyean reference
to his visit in a letter to another Aitken, a common friend,
a bookseller who used to supply Carlyle with clay pipes: [6]
' David Aitken seemed to be immensely refreshed by the
smell of our smoke, by the sight and sound of our tumult.
It is the way with men !   To him the roaring Strand is
medicine ; to me here, Minto Crags '—a hill in his parish—
' seems not unlike a kind of Heaven.'

Carlyle was resting at home this fall.   He had felt tired
and decided to go nowhere.   He was reading for pleasure, but
not altogether at random, Baxter's *Life* on 19–9–40, and in
general Puritan Histories, Scotch and English.   He liked a
direction to his reading as well as to his walks, and was feeling
at present as he wrote to Sterling, " I fancy I have got to see
into Cromwell for the first time, very lately."   At the same
time he was balancing town and country—which to prefer
for his home—and indulging a favourite daydream of
dwelling in some " cottage by the seashore ".

What led him to recur to such plans was that he was now
feeling free from the immediate need of work and wages
which had brought him to London.   He told Emerson that
getting enough money to live on was the only harmless
result of " all the trumpeting, reviewing, dinner-
invitationing ", which otherwise he tried to ignore.
Reporting to his brother John the receipt of money from
America, he had moralized :—

' I am not likely to be in want of cash for any time visible
yet.   Much cash I feel often would do me little good.   To buy

books, and without any anxiety keep a horse, were perhaps
almost all the benefit of wealth for me here. With an
independent stock of money, I should indeed not continue
here. But before long I shall be spoiled for any other place.

' The rule of heeding no *hearsay* of others, but minding
more and more exclusively what *I* do like or dislike, what is
really important for *me* or not for me, shows many things
in a new light. The whole world may do its uttermost for a
man, and *leave* him altogether poor, insolvent, and only
seeming to be rich. I find in the British Empire astonishingly
little that it would do me essential benefit to have. I hope
a new book is ripening in me ; that were the only blessedness.'

The better to free himself from worry about money and
make sure he would not need to lecture, he was now deciding,
against his wife's advice, to return the mare old Mr. Marshall
gave him last year, because he could not afford twenty-five
shillings a week to keep it. This was in amusing contrast
to Leigh Hunt, whose " affairs took a more favourable
turn this year ", his son reports,[7] whereupon he " was glad
to get away from Chelsea " to Kensington. So this is the
latest date likely for a story attributed to James Hannay [8]
which is worth the telling. In the ' poorer days ' of Carlyle,
when Leigh Hunt was still his neighbour in Chelsea, James
Hannay went ' often ' to see Carlyle and noticed once
' two gold sovereigns lying exposed in a little vase on the
chimney piece. He asked Carlyle what they were for.
Carlyle looked — for him — embarrassed, but gave no
definite answer. "Well now, my dear fellow," said
Mr. Hannay, " neither you nor I are quite in a position to
play ducks and drakes with sovereigns. What *are* these for ? "
" Well," said Carlyle, " the fact is Leigh Hunt likes better
to find them there than that I should give them to him." '

Before sending Citoyenne away, Carlyle determined to
enjoy her company one week more, in a long ride in the
country. The sun was " blazing all the time "—he felt
" roasted " occasionally. He started on a Sunday morning,
2–8–40, a mackintosh before him and a saddle-valise behind,
and his pockets full of maps, cigars, etc. He went to Leatherhead beyond Epsom, where the Bullers were expecting
him, and on the Monday and Tuesday he explored " the

[7] *Correspondence of Leigh Hunt*, edited by his eldest son, II, p. 1.
[8] *The Story of My Life*, by A. J. C. Hare, V, p. 384.

beautiful lanes " and villages around and climbed the hill-
tops, including high Leith Hill. " I struggled to talk with
all manner of peasants and the like," he told his brother,
adding, " they are good people, their life for the most part
more supportable than I have seen it elsewhere." He told
Sterling he had longed for his company—" It is not good
for the riding man to be alone."

On Wednesday morning he left Leatherhead for
Hurstmonceux. He went by Reigate over the uplands,
unhasting, unresting all day, and after sunset was ready to
halt at any " reasonable-looking inn ", but finding none
he went on and on till after ten he reached the Rectory,
and was " welcomed with both hands " by the good Julius
Hare and his women-folk. They were genuine Christians,
and Hare himself ' a good man, tho an archdeacon ', and he
had ' a noble library '.

On the Friday Carlyle departed and at Mayfield saw
St. Dunstan's stithy, and swinging the hammer, made the
anvil ring, and even manipulated the very tongs whereby
the saint is said to have taken the devil by the nose.

He was home by Saturday, his memory filled with pictures
of the Downs and the Weald, the country of Jack Cade and
the Norman Conqueror, as he remembered, the green chalk
hills and the pleasant villages, the good people and the yellow
corn. This was his only outing from London this year. In
a few weeks the continuous dry weather changed to
continuous rain, and instead of going to Scotland he stayed
at home and sent his mother the money he would have
spent on the journey.

He went little into town, unless when he had to go on
business, and told his sister he called on nobody—" they can
come here if they want me." But if they came before two
they could only see his wife, as he was never interrupted,
and in the afternoons he was generally out walking either in
the parks or going across " our old wooden Battersea
Bridge " into the country, where " all is green, musical,
bright ; one feels that it is God's world, this, and not an
infinite Cockneydom of stoor [or dust] and din ". He liked
the look of London best from the outside, when it seemed
really beautiful in the sunshine—a " sea of smoke, with
steeples, domes, gilt crosses, high black architecture
swimming in it ".

In those days one was in " what attempted to pass for
country " as soon as one crossed the river there, and steamers

went " snorting about the river, each with a lantern at its nose " in the evening, while " Chelsea lights burnt many-hued, bright, over the water in the distance—under the great sky of silver, under the great still twilight ".

The evening was the time for those who wanted to find him at home. He declined most invitations, moralizing in his journal, " What are Lords coming to call on one and fill one's head with whims ? They ask you to go among champagne, bright glitter, semi-poisonous excitements. As old Tom White said of whisky, so say I of dinner-popularity, Lords and Lionism—Keep it ; give it to those that like it."

He often finished the day with an evening walk ; and if a caller stayed late escorted him part of the way home.

His wife rejoiced in London, and would not hear of leaving it. *Her* great achievement was to minimize expense, which his simple habits made easy—she needed only a little self-denial. It was with a feeling of victory well-earned that she saw him now subside into the Cromwell books. " I stay here," he told his sister, " because I *am* here, and see not on the whole where I could get forward with my work much better."

IV

CRITICS, WHIGS, AND PUSEYITES

(1840)

NOW that the lecturing had made Carlyle popular, it seemed no longer safe to ignore him. An Oxford Professor, Sewell, was denouncing him in college lectures, saying, " His fame is most rampant, and men are beginning to talk and cant after him in all directions." [1] So Sewell wrote a *Quarterly Review* article against him this year. Carlyle told Emerson it was wonderful, describing Sewell as " an Oxford doctor, one of the chief men among the Pusey-and-Newman Corporation. He finds me ' true, most true '—except when I part from Puseyism, and reckon the shovel-hat to be an old bit of felt ; then I am false, most false. As the Turks say, Allah Akbar ! " [God is great !]

The critic for the Whigs in the *Edinburgh Review* was another Oxford man, Herman Merivale, a Professor of Political Economy on his promotion. On reading what he wrote, " See," said Carlyle to his wife, " we have produced an effect even on Whiggery, awakened an appetite under the ribs of death." " Awakened an indigestion," she answered. He wrote to his brother John :—

' One thing struck me much . . . his theory of Liberal government. He considers Reform to mean a judicious combining of those that have any money to keep down those that have none. " Hunger " among the great mass is *irremediable*, he says. *That the pigs be taught to die without squealing* : there is the sole improvement possible according to him. Did Whiggery ever express itself in a more damnable manner? He and I get our controversy rendered altogether precise in this way.'

To the good Lancashire editor, Thomas Ballantyne, who was earnest " Anti-Corn Law ", Carlyle wrote (8–10–40) :—

---

[1] *Life of F. D. Maurice*, by F. Maurice, I, p. 280.

' I know not what progress the [Anti-Corn Law] cause makes. It seems to me many things between the middle and lower classes will have to be adjusted. And who knows but the blind landlords, at their own extreme peril, are doing a *good service* by *delaying* the Corn-Law Settlement till much else be once a little better settled ? Small thanks to *them* for that ! But all things do, in some sort, work together for good.

' My critic in the *Quarterly* is Sewell, a leading Puseyite. I do not like the Puseyites so ill as you do, I rather like them well. They have many good ideas. This world is a God's world, and must be governed as a " Church ", or else ill-governed. [A] crisis is rapidly drawing on. The Puseyites will contribute their share of good ; the Benthamees and they may well neutralize each other and give us some solid result.

' My reviewer in the *Edinburgh* seemed to me of a much more detestable school than these poor Quarterlies. He writes down this doctrine, that " *hunger* " is perennial, irremediable among the lower classes of men. The pigs' [and so on as before]. ' I had never seen in writing so entirely damnable a statement ; tho it is what all manner of Whigs, and Benthamee Radicals, and other Atheistic men (as our Pusey friends would call them) do constantly act upon without writing it. Good never came from such.'

Then after answering inquiries about German writers and politics and inviting him to call again, he ends, ' I have an immense stock of reading about English Puritanism and Oliver Cromwell laid out for the Winter. Till *we* become Believers and Puritans in our way, no result will be arrived at ! '

When Sterling alluded to Merivale as " your enemy ", he answered :—

' Merivale is no enemy of mine, poor fellow ; but a good stout Sceptical Philosophist and Law Hack, to whom may the gods grant all suitable promotion. I saw the man once, many years ago, in Hayward's rooms, and even argued a little with him and liked him.'

Avoiding controversy, he made no public reply to either critic ; but in a letter to Thomas Spedding (9–11–40), he

gave a " brief portable commentary " on Sewell for private
circulation, and shaped it for fun like an affidavit.[2] The
" tub " at the end is the " tub " of Diogenes.

' T. C. deposes : That he, the said Carlyle, is not, and
never was, in use to make much of Pantheism, or indeed of
any other *theism* or *ism*. That he infinitely prefers *Silence*
on that highest matter to any speech or other utterance by
Liturgy, Ceremony, Painting, Poetry, Surplice, Pitchpipe,
or Hand-organ. That he says sometimes, with Faust in
Goethe, " Who dare *name* HIM ? "—and yet struggles to
pardon the very Calmucks, who pray by means of a rotary
calabash . . .
  ' That, participating in Father Sewell's earnest feelings
about many things, the said Carlyle regards Sewell, morally
considered, as a man of worth ; and Puseyism as a thing of
worth, cheering as a *symptom*, likely to do much good as an
agent—tho whether in revivifying the Church of England or
in more swiftly exploding it, deponent saith not, and indeed
hardly cares.
  ' That Carlyle regards the said Sewell and Puseyism,
intellectually or practically considered, as a Chimera . . .
the shadow of a *shade*—shadow namely, of the right reverend
Father Archbishop Laud, who, little more than a cobweb
even while living, had the head cut off him near two hundred
years ago . . .
  ' That the said Carlyle's pen is very bad, and his time
short. That he persists and is like to persist in hearty goodwill towards Thomas Spedding ; and wishes often he lived,
like him, among the everlasting hills, far from all jargon and
chaff ; and even proposes to do it some day. And farther
the deponent saith not.
  ' Given in our Tub at Chelsea,
        this 9th day of Novr., 1840 years.'

  [2] *Cornhill Magazine*, letters edited by A. Carlyle, May, 1921, pp. 522–3.

V

HOW HUTCHISON STIRLING WAS HELD TO HIS MEDICINE

IN 1840 Carlyle received from James Hutchison Stirling, a 20-year-old medical student in Glasgow, of literary tastes, an elaborate proposal for an association to give an occasional £1,000 prize to a literary man " for the best work " on some subject prescribed. He showed it to John Forster, and told Hutchison Stirling they agreed his plan was " entirely inexecutable " ; and that even if such a society were formed, " the *fallibility* of its decisions would too certainly dissolve it again." He instanced to comfort him the fate of the Society for the Diffusion of Useful Knowledge, lately defunct, and apropos the design to secure to literary men enough to live on, he declared : " If you gave me a true man to breed up, with the heart of a man in him, I should say rather, *let* him be poor." [1]

Hutchison Stirling was convinced and wrote to say so ; and before long reappeared as a producer of prose and verse in search of a verdict. He got a straight one, a reply which was often printed after many years as " Counsels to a Literary Aspirant ". It was not so named by the writer, or written vaguely for an aspirant in general. It was intended for no eyes but the addressee's, who spoke of it gratefully in extreme old age. [2]

' I have read the whole of your prose (and) the poetic MS. in such parts as seemed sufficient. I will, if you still request it, submit the paper to the publisher of *Fraser's Magazine*, the only bookseller I speak to once in six months ; but I think he has no chance to accept it. This is my sincere verdict. A much politer and softer to the ear might easily have been written . . .

[1] *Life of James Hutchison Stirling*, by Amelia H. S., 1912, pp. 49–62.
[2] To D. A. W. verbally.

' You seem to me a young man to whom Nature has given a superior endowment, which you run a considerable risk of *failing* to unfold. Alas, it is so easy to fail. You have in you that generous warmth of heart which is usually, if it be well guided, the mother-soil of all sorts of talent ; but which also, if ill-guided, can run up into miserablest waste and weeds. Your mind is opening in many directions, great ideas or prophecies of ideas announcing themselves to you ; all this is well, and the best. But, as I can discern withal, all this must as yet be kept in, held down with iron rigour, till it fashion and articulate itself . . .

' Grudge not labour, grudge not pain, disappointment, sorrow, or distress of any kind—all is for your good, if you can endeavour and endure. Be of courage ; a man lies in you : but a man is not born the second time, any more than the first, without travail. Your desultory mode of study is a thing you must correct. I fancy I discern in you a certain natural tendency to haste, crudity, semi-articulate diffusion. Stand up against that. It will never do. You must learn the meaning of *silence*—that forgotten knowledge of silence I am always speaking of. Be in no haste to speak yourself. Why be *porous*, incontinent ? Nothing can ferment itself to clearness in a *colander* [or sieve]. Pray that you may be *forced* to hold your tongue. The longer you keep silence the richer will your speech be when it does come.

' Practically my advice were very decidedly that you *kept* by medicine ; that you resolved faithfully to learn it, on all sides of it, and make yourself in actual fact a man that *could heal disease*. I am very serious in this. Pecuniary means need not prove insuperable. If a man bestir himself, what thing *is* insuperable ? Your present wishes, tastes, etc., ought to go for little with you. I would even advise that you resolutely postponed into the unexplored uncertainty of the Future, all concern with literature. As a trade, I will protest against your meddling with it ; describe it as the frightfullest, fatallest, too generally despicablest of all trades now followed under the sun . . . A steady course of professional industry has ever been held the usefullest support for *mind* as well as body : I heartily agree with that. And often have I said, What profession is there equal in true nobleness to medicine ? He that can abolish pain, relieve his fellow mortal from sickness, he is the indisputably usefullest of all men. He is in the right, be in the wrong who may. As a Lord Chancellor, under one's horse-hair wig there might be misgivings ; still more perhaps as a Lord Primate under one's cauliflower ; but if I could heal disease I should say to all men and angels without fear, " En, ecce ! " [behold].

' If literature do unfold itself at length under shelter of such a profession, then let literature be welcome. How many true physicians have turned out to be true speakers ? A man *can* first speak when he has got to *know* something. My decided advice is that you stand resolutely by medicine, determined to find an honest livelihood by medicine and do a man's task in that way.'

Which Hutchison Stirling decided to do. So in a few months more he got his diploma, and soon was busy as a surgeon in South Wales. It was not till 1865 that he published *The Secret of Hegel,* and became famous in his day.[3]

[3] *English Philosophers, etc.,* by James Seth (Dent), 1912, pp. 341–3.

VI

HOW JAMES DODDS WAS HELD TO HIS LAW

IN 1840 Carlyle received a letter from a parson in Dunbar about the parson's cousin, James Dodds, who was eager to begin a " career " in literature with essays on Shakespeare. He was a man of 27 ; had finished four of his five years' apprenticeship on starvation wages in a country lawyer's office near Melrose ; and had resolved to be the " advocate of the poor " as a man of letters. Carlyle replied at length :—

' It is doubtful to me whether the highest conceivable " success " in that course might not be for your cousin an *evil* in place of a blessing. I speak advisedly. There is no madder section of human business than that of periodical literature in England at this day. The meagrest bread-and-water wages at any honest steady occupation, I should say, are preferable for a young man, especially for an ambitious, excitable young man. I mistake much if your cousin were not wise to stick steadfastly by his law, studying of course to perfect and cultivate himself, but leaving all literary glory, etc., etc., to lie in the distance, a possibility which he could do without.'

On reflection, Carlyle recalled that the Rev. David Aitken lived near where Dodds was. He wrote again to make them known to each other, which " friendly office ", wrote Dodds' cousin and biographer, " brought the young clerk and Dr. Aitken together, and led to a lasting friendship between them," of much advantage to young Dodds. He soon was in direct correspondence with Carlyle and known to him face to face. Like Hutchison Stirling, he had the sense to act upon the good advice received, and stuck to the trade he had learned. He prospered. It was not till 1861 that he published the history of the Fifty Years' Struggle of the Scottish Covenanters, whereby he is now remembered.[1]

[1] *Lays of the Covenanters*, by James Dodds, with a Memoir of the Author, by the Rev. J. Dodds, of Dunbar. See also *Early Letters of J. W. Carlyle*, by D. G. Ritchie, p. 296.

Some years after 1840 Sir William Fraser was in Thackeray's company in Germany and remarked to him,— " It must be a fine thing to be a successful author." To which he tells us [2] Thackeray ' grimly ' replied,—" You had better break stones on the road."

[2] Hic et Ubique, by Sir W. F., p. 150.

VII

JOGGING ALONG

(1840)

FROM Germany this September (1840) came the pleasant news that four sets of translations of the songs of Burns had appeared within a year. Carlyle wrote[1] a review of one for the *Examiner*, in which he remarked that there was no version of " A Man's a Man for a' that ", perhaps because such a sentiment might not be acceptable to certain persons in Berlin just then.[2] Through the transmitter of the book[3] he sent to Heintze, the translator, the friendly advice to learn the tunes :—

' Burns always strummed upon the fiddle till he got his head and mind *filled* with the tune (such is his own account), then came the words, the thoughts all singing themselves by that. There is tune in every syllable.'

Then Carlyle presented the German book to a son of the poet, who was in London and occasionally resorted to his house, Major Burns.

Mrs. Carlyle arranged with the publishers about *Heroes*. She was helped by the Mrs. Jameson famous then. For the first edition they got £75, perhaps a hundredth of what he might have made by delivering the lectures in America and elsewhere. Another £75 at the same time for an edition of *Sartor* was welcome. For the five volumes of *Miscellanies* he had received this year £217; and for the summer lecturing over £200; and what had come from America for publication there by the contrivance of

---

[1] Letter of 17-9-40 in the John Forster Collection, in South Kensington Museum. See Examiner, 27-9-40.
[2] *Literary Recollections*, by F. Espinasse, p. 117.
[3] Printed in *Odds and Ends* by John Adams, Chamberlain of Greenock, and reprinted in *Scottish Nights*, 29-2-96, by John Muir, F.S.A., Scotland, to whom D. A. W. is obliged for the information about the gift of the book to Major Burns.

Emerson and Dr. Russell about doubled his total receipts and enabled him to have enough in the bank to feel safe for a few years, and forgetting ways and means to resume his reading on the Commonwealth.

The Commonwealth had long fascinated him and appeared to him now more than ever to have been the greatest epoch of English history. Eighteen years ago he had planned to write about it in the style of Voltaire. Voltaire indeed had seen into what was what better than any of the English yet, declaring Cromwell great as a king, tho wicked and a hypocrite. Carlyle had soon suspected and was now convinced that our historians were all wrong. He saw the greatness of Cromwell as plainly as ever he had seen a proposition in mathematics. " Old Noll " to him was more than Louis XIV was to the Frenchman ; but he found he could make no headway with a readable history, and before October was out confessed to his brother John that he was progressing backwards :—

' That is to say, my interest threatens to decline and die ! It is not tenth part such a subject as the French Revolution ; nor can the art of man ever make such a book out of it. I never read such jumbling, drowsy, endless stupidities : " seventhly and lastly ! " Yet I say to myself a Great Man does lie buried under this waste continent of cinders, and a Great Action : canst thou not *un*bury them, present them visible ? We shall see.'

And in his journal he cursed the bosh that bored him, but he persevered in reading it every day till two, feeling it would be " miserable to be idle ". Tho declining to be lionized, he was steady to old friends, and was often in the houses of such as Rogers and Milnes, Erasmus Darwin and the Wilsons.

Returning from an afternoon walk this fall he found his wife in the back garden, and two men beside her smoking and awaiting him—his old acquaintance Matthew Allen, a doctor who had come to Kirkcaldy to lecture on phrenology and received him as a guest at York long ago, and a neighbour of his who was a stranger to Mrs. Carlyle, the poet Alfred Tennyson. " Allen looked considerably older," wrote Carlyle to his brother John, and he is " speculative, hopeful, earnest-frothy as from the beginning ". The other was a stranger and more minutely described :—

' A fine, large-featured, dim-eyed, bronze-coloured, shaggy headed man is Alfred; dusty, smoky, free and easy '. [At another time he added : ' bright, laughing, hazel eyes ; massive, acquiline face, most massive, yet most delicate ; sallow brown complexion, almost Indian.'] He concluded now :—' swims, outwardly and inwardly, with great composure in an inarticulate element of tranquil chaos and tobacco smoke : great now and then when he does emerge ; a most restful, brotherly, solid-hearted man.'

As FitzGerald remarked, he " took to " Tennyson at once, and does not appear to have attempted to turn him away from poetry. Perhaps no other contemporary poet could boast of so much honour. This very year the much loved Dicky Milnes had put out a book of " Poetry for the People ", and Carlyle advised him to " try prose "—not in private, but at Rogers' breakfast-table ! Milnes was equal to the occasion. He archly pleaded,—" Poetry is so convenient for veiling commonplace ! " while admitting : " It will not be generally read again in these ages." " The honest little heart ! " said Carlyle, recounting this to Emerson, never suspecting irony.

It is likely to have been in reply to something like what he had written to Heintze about Burns, that Carlyle was told that Tennyson had no ear for music. At any rate, according to FitzGerald, he replied : " The man must have music dormant in him, revealing itself in *verse*," and compared his voice to " the sound of a pinewood ".[4]

Writing to Varnhagen von Ense [5] (7–11–40) to thank him for some Memoirs received Carlyle inquired :—

' Did anyone ever write an adequate life of your Frederick the Great ? Is there anywhere a legible life of Luther, so much as an attainable edition of his Tischreden ? ' [Table-talk].

To which Varnhagen generously replied with a *gift* of the books required, and was told, " under penalty of my never again *asking* you about any book, you must not *purchase* for me any more than these." Carlyle proceeded to describe the London Library and the need for it, concluding :

[4] *Memoirs of Tennyson*, by his son, I, p. 77.
[5] *Last Words of Thomas Carlyle*, Longmans, 1892, pp. 201-9.

" Prince Albert is a patron, by his own free offer, and promises ' a stock of German books '. Varnhagen's are already there."

By 16–11–40 Carlyle was confessing to himself :—

' My reading goes on : my stupidity seems to increase with it more and more. I get to see that no history in the strict sense can be made of that unspeakable puddle of a time, all covered up with things entirely obsolete to us—a Golgotha of dead dogs. But some kind of a book can be made.'

Another note before the end of the month reveals how he felt as he read and an opinion often quoted :—

' I struggled through the *Eikon Basilike* yesterday ; one of the paltriest pieces of vapid, shovel-hatted, clear-starched, immaculate falsity and cant I have ever read. It is to me an amazement how any mortal could ever have taken that for a genuine book of King Charles's. It got Parson Gauden a bishopric.'

Hume's wish to believe it the work of the King is now seen to be a palpable prejudice.

On Christmas Day his only company was John Mill, who took a long walk with him. It may have been after they came back to the house that Mill laughingly said someone was " the worst critic in England *but one* ", to avoid declaring him " the worst ", and quoting a French remark : " There's such a press in that direction." He did not stay. He would have to spend the evening with Mrs. Taylor, "his almost infallible counsellor." Mrs. Carlyle knew better than to expect him, and went out to a party somewhere. After Mill went away, Carlyle spent the evening reading Bulstrode Whitelocke.

Soon afterwards his wife was writing to a friend that he had " been sitting for months past in a mess of great dingy folios ", intending to write a *Life of Cromwell*. His journal reveals that in his impatience at failing to make a start, he was balancing London against the country again on the day after Christmas :—

' I feel that the one felicity of my existence is that of *working at my trade*, with or without reward. All life otherwise were a failure to me, a horrid incoherence in which there

was no meaning or result. To work then ! I often long to
be in the country again ; at Puttock again, that I might
work and nothing else but work. Had not my wife opposed,
I should probably have returned thither before now. Unlucky
or lucky ? One never knows. I am a little sicker here, and do
thoroughly dislike the mud, smoke, dirt, and tumult of this
place. Wherein, however, is decidedly a kind of actual
association with my fellow-creatures, *never* granted elsewhere. Solitude would increase, perhaps twofold or more,
my power of working. Shall I go, *carrying* and dragging all
along with *me* into solitude ? Alas ! it is a dreary, desolate
matter, go or stay. My one hope and thought for most part is
that very shortly it will all be over, my very sore existence
ended in the bosom of the Giver of it—at rest somewhere.
Things might be written here which it is considerably better
not to write. As I live, and have long lived, Death and Hades
differ little to me from the earth and life. The human figure
I meet is wild, wondrous, ghastly to me, almost as if it were
a spectre and I a spectre—Taisons [Silence !].

' Oliver Cromwell will not prosper with me at all. I began
reading [again, intending to write] about that subject some
four months ago. I learn almost nothing by reading, yet
cannot as yet heartily begin to write. Nothing on paper yet.
I know not where to begin. It is ungainly in the highest
degree ; yet I am loth to quit it. In our whole English
history there is surely nothing as great. If one can delineate
anything of England, then this thing. Heaven guide me !
Verily one has need of Heaven's guidance.'

VIII

PRIVATE PREACHINGS

(1840–1)

IN 1840 "Society" in London was more than ever "a
hoard" of "bores and bored", because of a fashion,
for which Sydney Smith blamed Hallam, Macaulay and Co.,
of improvizing table-lectures. At the very breakfast-table of
old Rogers once—'unless the kindest of mankind's belied '—
when Sydney Smith himself had kept the company in a
roar of laughter too long, the old man presiding was heard
to mutter, "Nobody can get a word in when *you* are here."[1]
But they were fellows in affliction when Macaulay was there
and drenched poor Smith with his clamour, as a rookery
might a blackbird, and the divine wit said : " I wish I could
write poetry like you, Rogers. I would write an Inferno,
and I would put Macaulay among a number of disputants
and gag him."[1]

One way of escape from boredom is to talk, and two of the
bores Carlyle found hard to bear were geologist Lyell and
Babbage of the calculating machines. Geology had long been
interesting to him, but as he read the books of Lyell he
confessed to his wife, " I seem to hear his uninspired voice
all along, and see the clear leaden twinkle of his small bead
eyes." Babbage was even worse, seeming soured, a man of
many aversions, emitting " hide-bound, wooden irony ",
with his " frog mouth and viper eyes ". " Implacable "
was the word applied to Babbage by young Charles Darwin,
who was happy at home this winter, full of his Beagle
observations and his new theory of coral reefs. About this
time [2] he enjoyed a " funny dinner ", as he called it, at the
house of his brother Erasmus. Both Lyell and Babbage were
there, and feeling full of matter, would have " liked to talk ",
said Charles Darwin, but " Carlyle silenced everyone by
haranguing during the whole dinner on the advantages of

---

[1] *L. and T. of Rev. Sydney Smith*, by S. J. Reid, p. 342.
[2] *Charles Darwin*, by Francis Darwin, pp. 298 and 77.

silence.   After dinner Babbage in his grimmest manner
thanked Carlyle for his very interesting lecture upon
silence.''

This may have been original but it was not new. The
'' Old Philosopher '' of China, Lao-tze, who also tried to
teach the right way of thinking by showing the insignificance
of words in themselves, appeared perplexing even to the
young Confucius, and was mocked by the wits repeating the
epigram :—

> '' ' Who know speak not, who speak know not,'
>   Are words from Lao-tze's lore.
>   What then becomes of Lao-tze's own
>   Ten thousand words or more ? ''

Carlyle was now beginning to talk at large and to be
voted the most entertaining of those who did so. He was
like Sir Walter Scott, telling stories and full of fun. Servants
were often noticed lingering in the room to hear the end of
a story he was telling, or disappearing with their hands on
their mouths to keep from laughing out. It may have been
this winter that Sir Henry Taylor heard him talk of
Cromwell [3] :—

' Insisting in conversation upon the fact that Cromwell
had been throughout his career invariably successful ;
and having with much satisfaction traced the long line of
his successes from the beginning to the end, he added :
'' It is true they got him out of his grave at the Restoration,
and stuck his head up over the gate at Tyburn—but not
till he had quite done with it.'' '

To this winter there is also assigned by editors what
Mazzini is said to have reported in a letter.[4] One evening
he heard another visitor say to Carlyle : '' After all, the first
thing to do is to ensure the happiness of the people.''

He was answered by '' a torrent of invectives, thunder
following on lightning '', till he could stand no more and rose
to go, '' more dead than alive,'' said Mazzini, who added :
'' Mrs. Carlyle, vexed and hurt, accompanied him to the door,

---

[3] Sir Henry Taylor in the *Nineteenth Century Mag.*, June, 1881, p. 1024.
[4] Enrico Nencioni quoted in *The Birth of Modern Italy*, by Jessie
White Mario, pp. 45–7.

murmuring words of apology," which Mazzini could not have heard if he sat listening to this :—

' Carlyle walked up and down the room like a raging lion in a cage, shaking his forest of grey hair. "Happiness! Happiness! The fools ought to be chained up! Man is born to work, not to enjoy! The ideal is within us, the ideal lies in the present moment; work with all your might, and to the best of your abilities. Work, and produce even the least atom. Every kind of work, whether intellectual or manual, is sacred and gives peace to the human soul. Be silent and work—these are the cardinal virtues of humanity. Silence! Yes, only Silence is grand; we live suspended between two silences: the silence of the stars and the silence of the grave. Nations, too, should be silent until genius speaks for them—genius is their voice and interpretation. How great was the silence of the ancient Romans! The Middle Ages too had a solemn silence, which was broken by the sublimest song, human or divine, ever sung—the poem of Dante. These are the true voices of the nations, and when one of them is heard, the nation for which he spoke is a consecrated nation ; it is redeemable even if oppressed, divided, humiliated. Your Italy, oppressed as it is by Austria, is actually a great nation, because Italy has Dante. One day she, too, will be allowed to speak, and will be listened to.

' "The great *blagueurs*" [haranguers or blatherskites in English] "made a loud noise, but renewed nothing, created nothing, exploded like cannon loaded only with powder, and a simple breath of wind swept all their smoke away."

' Then, looking at Mazzini, Carlyle with his imperial, scrutinizing smile, slowly added: "You, you have not succeeded yet, because you have talked too much: the fundamental preparation is wanting!"

' Mazzini answered only with another smile. [He] let Carlyle talk on, not only because he liked to hear, but because he always got his own turn, when he would prove that Dante's message, spoken five hundred years before, was a command to translate thought into action, a command which he was striving to obey and to induce others to obey. Mazzini had an immense interest in listening to and reading Carlyle's utterances.'

He wrote many criticisms and expositions of Carlyle's

works which were paid for, when translated, by English editors and helped to keep his pot boiling. Historians may be right in saying he learned a lot from Carlyle, and in particular learned to "look at facts more analytically than he had been accustomed to do", or in other words to be less dreamy. By and by he used publicly to quote Cromwell as an example to Italy.

IX

MRS. CARLYLE

MRS. CARLYLE rejoiced in London with all her heart, and felt her ambition was fulfilled. Thus she was writing this winter to an old friend, Mrs. Stirling of Dundee, once Susan Hunter (8–1–41) :—

' In my character of Lion's Wife here, I have writing enough to do, by constraint, for disgusting even a Duchess of Orleans—applications from young ladies for autographs ; passionate invitations to dine ; announcements of in-expressible longings to drink tea with me ; all that sort of thing, which, as a provincial girl, I should have regarded perhaps as high promotion, but which at this time of day I regard as very silly and tiresome work ; fritters away my time.'

Her glory was not new—it was great as long ago as 1837, and by now she was accustomed to it. She goes on :—

' Now don't be fancying that I am growing into a " proud Pharisee ! " Not at all ! I have a bad nervous system, keeping me in a state of greater or less physical suffering all days of my life, and that is the most infallible specific against the sin of spiritual pride that I happen to know of.'

Alternate headache and colic and depression that made her long for death were detailed in other letters. She was only in her fortieth year, yet climacteric changes had already begun. She continued for many years to be liable to nervous crises. Her husband had to promise that even if she went entirely mad she would never be sent to any other place, but kept at home beside him. It is the deliberate opinion of the best doctors that few men ever endured better than Carlyle all that a husband may have to suffer from the ailments of a wife.

It was from about this time that she insisted on having a separate bedroom, saying her mother advised it, and she needed it for her sleep. This lasted for the rest of her life. When he put his head into her room in the morning asking, " How did you sleep, dear ? " she used to tell him stories which " no woman could believe ", and one of her best maids said [1] she once ran out of the room lest she might laugh right out when Mrs. Carlyle was describing how she had got up thirty times in one night. It was probably after hearing a succession of such stories that Dr. Carlyle fell out of her favour by telling her candidly : " It cannot be true, for if it were true you would not be alive." Perhaps her husband was not quite so simple as others supposed. It may be because he practised the gospel of silence that nobody ever saw him give any sign of doubting anything his wife said about her health.

There is curious self-revelation in a letter from Mrs. Carlyle to Dr. Chalmers [2] in these years, replying to inquiries about her mother : " I often think, because, perhaps, having no children of my own, I am interested in finding reasons for not regretting it, how little good poor mothers get of their married daughters, whom they have had such a world of plague in bearing, and nursing up, and training, and teaching, until they could shift for themselves." Which shows how kind Nature can be to a childless woman, leaving latent the feelings she did not need to exercise, so that she never suspected that a mother of the right sort wants to " get " no other " good " of married daughters than to know they are well.

[1] To D. A. W.
[2] Found among the papers of Miss Helen Chalmers, daughter of Dr. Chalmers, and printed in the *Liverpool Post*, and supplied to D. A. W. by Robert Cochrane, Edinburgh.

X

LAST SERVICE ON A JURY

(1841)

IN the summer and fall of 1840, Carlyle lost time in attending law-courts on summonses to serve as special jury-
man. He inquired of Charles Buller, " Is there no way out
of it ? " and was told, " You can register yourself as a
dissenting preacher ! "

The first provocation was to be doing nothing but idly
wait. When at last on a jury he saw through the case in an
hour, but had to listen patiently two whole days—a common
judicial experience. What is happily less common was
that it had then to be adjourned unfinished.

Thus, it happened that one Sunday night this winter
Mrs. Carlyle was dining with the F. D. Maurices at Guy's
Hospital, and finding herself sitting next a young barrister,
W. F. Pollock,[1] she entertained him by telling : " Carlyle
has been fearfully troubled by having to serve on a jury.
It is threatening to spoil the Cromwell he is writing. An
official required him, when the case was adjourned, to give
his word of honour that he would come when required. He
answered, ' No, but I offer my word of honour I will not come
back. You may fine me, you may kill me ; but that box
I will not enter alive any more.' Wherefore, to save any
farther annoyance," she cheerily concluded, " I have
burned the last summons sent, and never mentioned it
to him."

Mr. Pollock explained that if the case was partly heard,
his absence would stop the trial and reasonably lead to a
heavy fine. " What can be done now ? " she inquired. She
could remember that it was a patent case about cotton
cards.

This was clue sufficient to Mr. Pollock, who found out
for her the time and the court ; and she comforted herself

---

[1] *Personal Remembrances*, by Sir W. Frederick Pollock, I, pp. 152–7.

for troubling him by the thought that she had spared her
husband " some eight days of the horrors of anticipation ".
She proposed to attend herself and swear him off " on the
ground of incapacity, as no man in his mad state is capable
of seeing into the merits of any case ". As that would not do,
she wrote that he " would go, cursing from the bottom of
his heart the administration of English justice ".

It was in February, 1841.[2] Two Manchester men were
litigating which of them had invented some India-rubber
cotton cards. About £10,000 had already been spent, and
150 witnesses summoned, and two more days were filled by
witnesses and lawyers. By eight o'clock on the night of the
second day, nothing remained but to decide, and eleven of
the jury were ready to give a verdict for the plaintiff, but
one declined to agree. The Judge said they must withdraw
until they were unanimous.

Away they went, Carlyle among them, through passages
and stairs up and down to a little stone cell with twelve old
chairs in it, and one candle but no meat or drink or fire.
Hunger and cold do not sweeten men's tempers. The one
who differed from the others was a thick-set " flat headed "
very powerful fellow, who stalked aside and sat in a corner
with the only candle opening a " yellow-book " or novel to
read, and remarking, " I am one of the firmest-minded men
in England. I know this room pretty well. I have starved
out three juries here already."

He was warmly clad in a waterproof coat, and began to
munch the biscuits and sandwiches wherewith his pockets
were stuffed. In answer to remonstrances he merely
" growled and flashed back looks of deathless determination ".
It seemed likely he would keep them idle, cold, and hungry,
till half past nine in the morning, when they would all be
dismissed and the long trial begin again.

The practice of requiring unanimity is as preposterous
with English juries as with Polish Parliaments. It broke up
Poland, and is a nuisance in our courts. It has continued
too long because it pays the profession, and the judges
sympathize with fellow professionals more than with the
public. However, on this occasion a way of escape was
found.

The other eleven jurymen discussed the dissenter in

[2] The letters of the time are supplemented by various reports of verbal
talk besides Froude's ; e.g. A. G. C. Liddell's *Notes from the Life of an
Ordinary Mortal*, pp. 123-4 ; and Pollock's book in note 1.

On the Monday following (5-4-41) Carlyle and Milnes left London together, with Sir Robert Peel in the same railway carriage, as far as Tamworth. They stopped at Derby and reached Fryston the next day. When Milnes Senior who was sitting smoking rose to welcome " his son's distinguished guest ", he apologized for the cigar in his hand, as smoking was then considered to need an apology.

" Indeed, sir," said Carlyle, " I think that this is about the most sensible occupation which any man could have, and if you don't object, I will just join you in it at once." [3]

Which reminds one of how the old man received Thackeray this year, saying; "Smoke anywhere in this house, even in Mrs. Milnes' drawing-room, only not in Richard's room, for he does not like it." Then said Thackeray to Milnes, Junior : " What a father is thrown away upon you ! " And in departing he told his host : " Your house, sir, combines the freedom of the tavern with the elegance of the chateau." [4]

On the day of arrival Carlyle was praising the prospect from the windows, as they sat smoking their first cigar together, and Milnes Senior sadly " pointed out the single tall chimney of some manufactory on the far horizon, and expressed his regret that it should recently have been erected, and thus spoiled the rustic character of the view."

" Spoiled the view ! " said Carlyle, " why sir, I think that is just the pleasantest feature in the whole bit of scenery. It shows us that somebody is doing something in this part of the world, at any rate."

This delighted Dicky Milnes, who was listening, and he often told it. There were many visitors, and Carlyle had to submit to be lionized, which may be why it was always difficult to bring him back to Fryston. There were many dinner guests, including lords and squires, to whom it was a new sensation to hear the Corn laws called suicidal and dangerous, and bunches of barristers, the glibbest of them Roebuck, called " Tear-'em " in the Commons, and now " as lean, acrid, contentious and loquacious as ever". His pet aversion was the Whigs. He flew at Carlyle several times, and was repulsed to the general entertainment but without distress to anyone. " We parted good friends," Carlyle reported, " with small wish to meet again."

On quieter days, " Richard had to exert himself, but he

---

[3] *R. M. Milnes*, by T. Wemyss Reid, I, pp. 252–60 and 265–8.
[4] Ibid., and *Personal Remembrances*, by Sir F. Pollock, I, p. 177.

was really dexterous, the villain. He pricks into you with
questions, with remarks, with all kinds of fly-tackle to make
you bite—does generally contrive to get you into some sort
of speech. And then his good humour is extreme ; you look
in his face and forgive him all his tricks."

They had a long ride together on the Thursday, but on
Good Friday Carlyle had to ride alone, the rest were at
church. He confided to his wife he hoped to escape the
church on Sunday, too, *"I have even religious scruples about
it—I really begin to have,"* perhaps because Dicky was
incubating his "One Tract More". Milnes had learned
sense from Goethe and Co., not to say Carlyle, and now
preached toleration, but he hankered after divinity, at least
to the extent of wanting to hear Carlyle debating it in
public, which was taboo. The only success in that
direction seems to have been accidental. Somebody at
table spoke of the " Agitator " G. J. Holyoake. Carlyle
said : " That is the man who said there was no God."
Another person chimed in with disparaging remarks, and
was quickly sorry he spoke, for Carlyle confounded him at
once by " some fierce and generous words of vindication ",
which were repeated to Holyoake by the journalist George
Searle Phillips, " January Searle." [5]

Maybe to minimize the table-theology, Carlyle went to
church on Sunday, and explained to Dicky later that the
fat old parson nearly drove him to tears. " The droning
hollowness of the poor old man, droning as out of old ages of
old eternities things unspeakable into things unhearable,
empty as the braying of an ass, was infinitely pathetic."
The like of that was a thing to endure. What he enjoyed
was what he had missed for seven years, the " sight of the
young spring ", which seemed " beautiful or better than
beauty", as he rode or sauntered among Yorkshire fields
and knolls. They were like Annandale, he told his mother,
and " different from London country ".

Milnes and he together inspected, on horseback, the
" smoky spinning town " of Wakefield, and galloped and
trotted in many directions, while the voice of waters and
birds made it easy to bear the chit-chat of Dicky about
Puseyism and Crypto-Catholicism, aristocratic blackguards
and cranks. When he had to speak, Carlyle was plain

[5] *Sixty Years of an Agitator's Life*, by G. J. Holyoake, Ch. XXXVI,
Vol. I, p. 192. He puts it vaguely under 1843, which may have been
when he heard it.

enough about the " foolish, scraggy jargon of Puseyism,
Shovel-hatism and all Isms " that are or ever were, but even
in private that sort of thing was a bore, and perhaps it was
to change the topic that he once asked, " Do you like
Spenser's Fairy Queen ? " and was wittily answered, " Is it
as a public question that you ask me, or as a private
confidential one ? " Which was an ancient Greek reply to
questions about the Gods.

He went to Leeds and spent three days in the house of
James Marshall there, a son of the old Marshall who had
given him Citoyenne. James Marshall's wife was the same
Miss Spring Rice who had been one of the earliest admirers
of Carlyle's lecturing ; and on meeting him at Fryston she
begged him to visit her house too. He always had difficulty
in saying No to a lady.

The fine new mill he inspected on the Saturday, with its
thousands of happy-looking workers, may have been in his
mind's eye later when alluding with praise to the right sort
of mills. He now described it to his wife, and gave her his
impression of the modern English country-house Elysium :—

' I never lived before in such an element of " much ado
about *almost* Nothing " ; life occupied altogether in getting
itself lived ; troops of flunkeys bustling and becking at all
times, the meat-jack creaking and playing all day, and I
think all night, for I used to hear it very early under my
room ; and such champagning, claretting, and witty
conversationing. *Ach Gott* ! I would sooner be a ditcher
than spend *all* my days so. However, we got rather
tolerably through it for these ten days, and I really think
I can report a favourable change in my inner man in spite
of every drawback.

' No wealth should in any case induce me to be concerned
with retinues of flunkeys.' [Then he praised the Marshalls
and Spring Rices and remarked about his Sunday in Leeds] :
' I have shirked the church. I pleaded "conscience". I do
really begin to have scruples ; that is a truth.'

On the Monday he departed for Scotsbrig, and writing
there to Milnes (25–4–41) his cordial thanks and greetings,
let out his joy in the " unwonted blessing " of the silence of
the moors beside him, adding as his news,—" Specks of
snow still checker the blue of Skiddaw and Helvellyn—my
noble friends." He was home in Chelsea on Thursday (6–5–41).

How to write about Cromwell appeared as doubtful as ever, and he felt so much the better of the fresh air he had had that he wanted more of it. The weather was hot, too, and the season at its height. It was from this year that he used to date a change in his habits. Hitherto, his plan had been "*a resolute staying at home*". He now admitted, " I cannot live all the year round in London," and must " fly into the country in summer time, as other Cockneys do ".

An inquiry from the eldest son of the Stracheys he used to know, " on behalf of a lady who was looking for employment as a translator," received reply at once (27–5–41)[6] :—

' I rather fancy the chief difficulty is to *fix on some book* likely to succeed ; there is seldom any offer of a given book to be translated ; or inded if there were, I suppose hundreds are ready for it on bread-and-water terms. Translation I doubt is no very good resource, indeed, literature in any shape, without some express vocation and necessity, is a thing not to be recommended to anyone, to a young lady least of all. My own prosecution of it was entered upon by the sternest compulsion, and has been a life-and-death wrestle all along.'

From Emerson came the news that his *Heroes* had been pirated in New York, and " the New York newspapers print the book in chapters, and you circulate for six cents at the corners of all streets in New York and Boston, gaining in fame what you lose in coin ". The first series of Emerson's Essays also came over in book form ; and to get it republished in England for Emerson's benefit Carlyle wrote for it a preface which gave it a good send-off—the same that made " George Eliot " declare, " This is a world worth abiding in while one man can thus venerate and love another."

It was in June he did that, and in the same month he began the correspondence and friendship with Browning which lasted all his life, by a letter acknowledging the receipt of two volumes of poetry, congratulating him on their failure, and advising him to write in prose.

Mazzini reported a talk at the Carlyles' this June about the elections [7] :—

---

[6] "Reminiscences of Carlyle," by G. Strachey, *New Review*, July, 1893, pp. 17–18.

[7] Letter quoted in *The Birth of Modern Italy*, by J. W. Mario, pp. 48–9.

' £20,000 to £30,000 spent for one election—a nice system, truly, for choosing the representatives of the people. Carlyle and I agreed in this, that Tories and Whigs are the inside and outside of the same coat, and that neither the one nor the other have the will or the power of doing any good; that they would go on butting at each other for some time, and then that the people would send them both to the devil. While we were talking, in came a Tory [old Sterling] of *The Times*. I said to him " Well, are you triumphant ? " " Of course, of course," and thinking me deeply interested, he set himself to prove the absolute certainty of Tory victory. I listened gravely, just then Mrs. Carlyle turned and looked at me, and thinking of our previous conversation, we both burst into laughter. The poor man gazed from one to the other in bewilderment ; we turned the matter off as best we could, and he went away pacified.'

A few days later, Carlyle went by steamer to Newcastle, and spent three or four days at Tynemouth with Harriet Martineau, who reported that he was well and cheerful. He bathed in the sea and watched the election, remarking that there seemed to be only one breed of people from the Humber to the Forth. Then he went on to Scotsbrig, to stay beside his mother till his wife came north. In a long letter he wrote to John Sterling, 14–7–41, there is a glimpse of current theology :—

' The day before leaving town, I met Julius Hare in Burlington Arcade, and spoke a moment with him. A good man, tho an Archdeacon. Does *he* know *Strauss* ? '

He meant Strauss's *Life of Christ*, a translation of which Sterling seems to have been announcing. It was like Carlyle to need to ask of Sterling whether Hare knew Strauss. In conversation with Hare he would taboo the topic, which was the usual rule of behaviour among people of sense in Scotland. He now went on to Sterling about that translation, which was a herald of heterodoxy : ' An ominous thing indeed ! But on the whole a thing we will not grumble at. . . . *Anti*-Straussism is little other than a Cant—properly a despicable trembling sort of Unbelief that there is anything true except shovel-hats, tithe-pigs, and such-like ! Pfui ! Sheer idol-worship in short, and must go about its business the sooner the better.'

XII

GERALDINE JEWSBURY AND GEORGE SAND

(1841)

1840 HAD been remarkable for more than *Heroes and Hero-Worship*. The penny-post began then, a blessing to the public but a pest to public men, like a letting-out of waters. Letters from strangers begging advice were raining on Carlyle as "incessantly" as money-begging letters upon Bulwer-Lytton. Among the swarm of female seekers after sense who buzzed about him for the rest of his life, one of the most memorable to biographers came upon him early—Geraldine Jewsbury. "Some bother in her soul," she said,[1] made her write to Carlyle as a father-confessor, when Christianity became incredible to her. She was a plain-featured little Manchester woman of 29, who had lost her father in 1840 and was keeping house for her brother. She seemed to the simple sage, always off his guard with such as she, "one of the most interesting young women I have seen for years, clear delicate sense and courage looking out of her small sylph-like figure." He drew his wife's attention to her. Mrs. Carlyle was far from sharing her husband's admiration, but did not object as much as he did to Geraldine's enthusiasm for George Sand, and coming north this summer by Liverpool as usual, availed herself gladly of an invitation to stay there in the house of Geraldine's friends, Mr. and Mrs. Paulet, a Swiss with an English wife. On this and many a later occasion, the Paulets' house made her happy by letting her see much of Mrs. Paulet and Geraldine and her uncle and cousins, and yet avoid the Tory politics and church-going which bothered her when living at her uncle's house. She did not fail to impress on her husband how much his new disciple adored George Sand.

Before leaving home Carlyle had been inquiring whether the *Edinburgh Review* wanted an article on French fiction. The editor gladly agreed ; but after reaching Scotsbrig, Carlyle

---

[1] *Literary Recollections*, by F. Espinasse, pp. 132–3.

had to announce : [2] " Arriving here, I find myself disappointed of the house I had counted on occupying till
winter ; not likely to continue here longer than a month,"
and so on. "One of the things that fall to the ground in
consequence is that article."

His silence in public made it seem all the more needful
to be explicit in private to his wife, for her own benefit and
Geraldine's. So he wrote her a letter, wherein he called
Geraldine " an ardent spark of life, struggling and striving
one knows not whitherward ", and added :—

' May the bounteous Heavens be good to her, poor
Geraldine ! I wish she could once get it fairly into her head
that neither woman nor man, nor any kind of creature in
this Universe, was born for the exclusive, or even for the
chief, purpose of falling in love, or being fallen in love with.
Good Heavens ! It is *one* of the purposes most living creatures
are produced for; but except the zoophytes ' [vegetable
animals such as sponges] 'and coral insects of the Pacific
Ocean, I am acquainted with no creature with whom it is
the one or grand object. That object altogether missed,
thwarted, and seized by the Devil, there remains for man,
for woman, and all creatures (except the zoophytes) a very
great number of other objects over which we will still show
fight against the Devil. Ah me ! These are sorry times,
these of ours, for a young woman of genius . . . Recommend me to Geraldine, at any rate, as one who loves her,
and will lament sore if she gain not the victory, if she find
not by-and-by some doctrine better than George-Sandism,
inclusive of George-Sandism, and suppressive of that.'

Then he told how his popularity was suffering because he
was refusing to see anybody, and concluded :—' Adieu,
dear little creature ! sail prosperously. Be not too sick.
Come jumping up when I step upon the deck at Annan Pool.
Kiss Geraldine. I command no more. Yours ever and aye,
'T. CARLYLE.'

" Carlyle read few modern French books," reports
Espinasse,[3] and "spoke contemptuously" of them, despising
their smut as heartily as any decent Chinaman would, or
Muslim. Chateaubriand he called " a man of real sensi-

---

[2] *Correspondence of Macvey Napier*, pp. 348-9.
[3] *Literary Recollections*, by F. Espinasse, pp. 223-4.

bility", but Thiers seemed "a man without a conscience", and Madame Dudevant, alias George Sand, seemed obscene, and Balzac no better. He extended to them Goethe's name for Victor Hugo—the Literature of Desperation.

George Eliot's chosen man, George Henry Lewes, was very " French " in gestures and much else, and in nothing more so than in his admiration of George Sand. He was fond of telling how he once was ushered into the back-garden, where Arthur Helps and Carlyle were walking up and down together, and coming up behind them he was delighted to hear Carlyle say something in praise of George Sand. Indeed, she had many good points. Lewes fell into line and cried, " I am glad to hear you say that, Carlyle." Whereupon, said Lewes, Carlyle changed sides and reviled the lady, for indecency no doubt, to the joy of Helps.[4] On another occasion, Lewes assured Espinasse,[5] he found Carlyle with some of George Sand's books spread out before him, and confessing he had " broken down in an attempt to indite a scathing invective against her and them," which sounds liker a paraphrase than a report. " There is something Goethian about the woman," he added, according to Lewes. What Espinasse himself was surprised to hear Carlyle say once was that she was " a shrewd woman ", quoting Goethe's line:[6] "O the tender hearts, a bungler knows how to touch them ! " To Browning he called her a " sublime High-priestess of Anarchy ", and said he shared his liking for the " melody that runs through that strange ' beautiful incontinent ' soul—a modern Magdalene, with the ' seven devils ' mostly still in her ! "

What was not likely to occur to Lewes was that, before writing on George Sand, Carlyle would feel bound to read all the books she had published, and already she had put out a large part of the 120 volumes that contain her collected works. The meaning of whatever he said to Lewes is likely to have been only this, that he had concluded the result would not be worth the time and work it would take. It would indeed have been like debating with a rookery.

" The only civil thing that I have ever heard him say of the Pope and his obsolete creed," said Espinasse, " was that they might be a sort of barrier against something worse than themselves, George Sandism to wit."

---

[4] *Autobiography of Herbert Spencer*, I, p. 382.
[5] *Literary Recollections*, by F. Espinasse, pp. 223-4.
[6] Venetian epigrams, 78.

XIII

IN SUMMER QUARTERS

(1841)

CARLYLE met his wife on the steamer at Annan as arranged, and drove her on 21-7-41 to her mother's home near Thornhill, thirty miles away. They found the house full of Liverpool Welshes. The only room her mother could give them had a bed so small that sleep was impossible for either. The crowing of the cocks completed their discomfiture. He rose at dawn, about 2 or 3 a.m., and she found that lying diagonally she could just contrive to stretch herself in the bed when he was out of it. Then he went outside and tried to silence the cock, but failed. He harnessed the horse, disturbing nobody, and leaving his wife to make his apologies and explain his sudden departure, drove away towards Dumfries.

The drive down the Nith was better than any opiate. He watched the herons fishing in the river, and in his sister's house in Dumfries had " some hours of sleep " before breakfast, as he wrote and announced to his wife.

A few days later they were together again in their cottage on the shore. She liked it little, and still less his refusal to go about the neighbourhood and enjoy the glory of his fame. " It is not to be a lion," said she, " but to be a tiger." They were living "on the very beach". An American timber ship went down under their windows one day, but " the men were all saved ", he wrote to Emerson; and in accepting an invitation to visit Thomas Spedding at Keswick on the way home, he remarked (12-8-41): " It is long since I have had so interesting a Dialogue with any of my fellow-creatures as with this waste sandy ever-moaning Tide-flood of the Solway. And my friends the Gulls and the Sandlarks, not to say the net Fishers and the two-and-thirty winds of Heaven, bringing cloud-fields and savage wind-music . . . Cockney-dom shrinks all into the size of a worm-eaten walnut."

Four days later he was comforting the editor in Lancashire, Thomas Ballantyne, distressed by the Tory victory at the polls, by telling him, it was " pretty certain the Corn Laws will have to terminate before long ".

They had only four weeks in their cottage by the sea ; and however he enjoyed it, his wife declared to John Forster that she hoped "never to look upon its like again ". Then he took her to her mother's and left her there, and went for a week or two to Scotsbrig. Dating there on 28–8–41, he wrote a long letter to two young Edinburgh students, Dunipace and Espinasse, who had appealed to him for " a solution of the mystery of existence ".[1] To their " surprise " and " delight " they received a spacious answer, telling them frankly : " My curiosity was once as intense as yours, my obstructions perhaps greater," and discussing the books of the German philosophers they had named, and saying Kant was the best. He told them to consult Sir William Hamilton and Mr. Ferrier ; but,—" let it be no disappointment if you do not learn 'what we are'. Metaphysics is but a kind of disease, and the inquiry itself a kind of disease. What we are fit to do is the grand inquiry for us," and that is what " we can always partly know. Your rule in reading for self-culture is to get acquainted with great men and great thinkers ", whom he went on to name. More than forty years afterwards the letter was printed at length by Espinasse. It was typical of many.

[1] *Literary Recollections*, by F. Espinasse, pp. 56–60.

XIV

FREDERICK POLLOCK REPORTS

(1841)

EARLY in September Carlyle went for some days to Thomas Spedding's at Keswick. His wife had also been invited but preferred to stay where she was. At Spedding's he met the same Frederick Pollock who had helped Mrs. Carlyle about the jury summons in February, and had now come north as a " Revising Barrister ", busy upon voters' rolls.

Carlyle came in late to dinner, said Pollock,[1] " having been smoking outside." Isaac Newton was discussed at table. Carlyle remarked, " There was nothing in him, he has done nothing." Pollock says he " ventured " to ask if he knew what Newton had done. Carlyle took no offence but quietly replied, " I have read all that Newton has written."

A day or two later both were of a party that went to the top of Skiddaw, and were thrown together coming down. Carlyle had no respectful remarks upon our politicians, " shams and windbags," from the very top—declaring, " *Burns ought to have been King of England and George III the exciseman.*" But it was on Parliament he was " most severe, and all the apparatus belonging to it. As he knew what I should shortly be doing in the county, he fell foul of revising barristers, and chaffed and laughed at me in the heartiest and absurdest of ways to my great delight and amusement. In the middle of his most trenchant denunciations there would be a twinkle of the eye and a laugh and a sort of quiet mental dig in the ribs."

On Sunday, Carlyle " went to church with the rest. I was next him, and he was very anxious to follow the ritual, having the psalms and lessons and collects and so forth found for him, and was curious and attentive about everything." It is a coincidence that Confucius, too, behaved thus

---

[1] *Personal Remembrances*, by Sir Frederick Pollock, I, pp. 177–80.

in similar circumstances, and insisted it was the right thing to do when it was challenged. It is the politest possible way of showing one is a witness and not a worshipper.

At that time the responses were made by the clerk only; and on the way home Carlyle inquired, " Who is the man that says ' Amen ' ? "

Pollock : " He is supposed to represent the congregation in saying Amen and making the responses, in which it is not very usual for anyone else to support him."

Carlyle : " Do you ever take part in the responses ? "

Pollock : " No, not unless the clerk has a weak voice which seems to want reinforcing."

" This tickled him amazingly," said Pollock, " and he kept bursting out laughing on our way home from church " ; and by-and-by, when Pollock was calling at Cheyne Row, Carlyle's first words were, " Well, have you been reinforcing a weak clerk lately ? "

XV

THE DIVINE RIGHT OF SQUIRES

(1841)

MRS. CARLYLE made her husband take her next to Tynemouth, where they stayed in lodgings beside Harriet Martineau and he bathed in the sea. They went home by rail before the end of September.

His next performance was *Baillie the Covenanter*,[1] an essay making the trial of Strafford, by dint of quotations from onlookers, the most tangible State-trial in English history. No art was needed to make it the most important. It was an episode in a real drama which ended in the execution of Charles Stuart himself, who, on this occasion was sitting with his family and friends " in the eye of all at the back of the throne, but little regarded ".

It was a " sign of the times " that the Press was little interested in the essay as history, while some sentences against the Corn Laws were much quoted and gave a new phrase to politics :—

' They had the *Divine Right of Kings* to settle, these unfortunate ancestors of ours ; shall Charles Stuart and William Laud alone have a soul and conscience in this Nation, or shall others, too, have it ?

' We, their children, have got perhaps a still harder thing to settle : the *Divine Right of Squires*. Did a God make this land of Britain, and give it to us all, that we might live there by honest labour ; or did the Squires make it, and, shut to the voice of any God, open only to a Devil's voice in this matter—decide on giving it to themselves alone ? This is now the sad question and " divine right " we, in this unfortunate century, have got to settle ! For there is no end of settlements ; there will never be an end ; the best

---

[1] *London and Westminster Review*, No. 72, as a review of David Laing's new edition of *Baillie's Letters*, etc. Reprinted in *Miscellanies*.

settlement is but a temporary partial one. Truly, all manner of rights, and adjustments of work and wages do verge into unbearable error, as the Time-flood bears us onward.'

Carlyle explained to Editor Ballantyne that the condition of the working-man depends on more than money-wages—it depends on the constancy of occupation and so on, and 'all this of " Supply and Demand " and so much else, is true only for the time being, and in a very limited sense.' He confessed to John Sterling, too, that he might have to treat further the *Divine Right of Squires*, but said the essay which mentioned it had been written " partly to bring my own hand in", and partly for the sake of David Laing who was editing the new edition of *Baillie's Letters*, and had been obliging to him in his researches. To Forster, begging something for the Foreign Quarterly, he excused himself, saying: " If I get fairly into that Cromwell, I shall have to go on, incessant, as a shot projectile, as a kindled fire, and not stop—under penalty of going out altogether ! " But except concerning Baillie, everything that he wrote about the Commonwealth in 1841 had to be put into the fire.

The plain truth was that he could not settle his mind to it because of what was happening around him. The " Hungry Forties " had begun. 1841–2 was the worst winter for many years, and spring brought no relief. The scarcity became starvation in 1842. He saw the workers being driven into death before his eyes, and he was on fire with pity and indignation.

XVI

THOMAS CHALMERS AND POOR-LAW

IN 1834 the English Commissioners recasting their poor-laws had had nothing but praise for the " admirable practice " in Scotland of not supplementing wages and letting the poor help themselves and each other. But Walpole and Co.'s malt taxes had long ago driven out the cheap and wholesome beer ; and strong drink, the curse of Scotland, was brutalizing and beggaring the people, while immigrants from Ireland offering to do anything for potatoes and salt brought wages down. The land and water were monopolized. In most of the towns the very air was polluted before it reached the poor, while taxes kept the food at famine prices. In 1840 Dr. Alison of Edinburgh published the pamphlet quoted in *Past and Present*, showing that Edinburgh and Glasgow had a higher death-rate than anywhere else in Europe, and that the " higher ranks in Scotland do much less for the relief of poverty than those of any other country".

A Bill for the relief of the poor was the natural result in a reformed House of Commons, but the landowners objecting to assessment were joined by a strange ally. Thomas Chalmers the great divine was against the new proposals, and published a book on the "Sufficiency of the Parochial System without a Poor-rate", etc., etc. He sent a copy to Carlyle with a letter (29–9–41) praising *Chartism*, and begging help for at least an option to return to *Church* relief.

The answer sent without delay (11–10–41) was pleasant reading to Chalmers, but in substance the same as that of his friend Professor Duncan of St. Andrews, that the other parish clergymen were not like Dr. Chalmers. Carlyle added :—

' It seems to me a great truth this fundamental principle of yours that human things cannot stand on selfishness, mechanical utilities, economics, and law-courts ; that if there be not a religious element in the relations of men,' meaning real sympathy and righteousness, ' such relations are miserable and doomed to ruin. The poor and the rich men cannot long live together upon a poor-law! ' [It is only, in short] ' a sad-transitory palliative.

' Alas ! the poor of this country seem to me, in these years, to be fast becoming the miserablest of all types of men. *Black slaves in South Carolina deserve pity enough ; but one pallid Paisley weaver, with the sight of his famishing children round him, with the memory of his decent independent father before him, has probably more wretchedness in his single heart than a hundred Blacks.* Did you observe the late trial at Stockport, in Cheshire, of a human father and human mother for poisoning three of their children to gain successively some £3 8s. from a Burial Society for each of them? A barrister of my acquaintance informs me positively that this case was by no means a solitary one there.'

In short, we will leave any good divine to do his best, but need a poor-law at present, though it were only a "palliative".

In a year or two more the least expected happened. Before the Poor Law Bill was an Act, Dr. Chalmers was no longer a member of the Church of Scotland, but the leader of the great secession from it called the Disruption, in 1843.[1]

---

[1] *Memoirs of Dr. Chalmers*, by William Hanna, IV, pp. 196–201, etc. Italics added.

XVII

STANDING AT EASE

(1841–2)

THE letter written in August to Francis Espinasse and Dunipace in Edinburgh gave them so much delight that when there was a vacancy in the "chair" of History this year, they drew up a memorial requesting the Faculty of Advocates to nominate Carlyle, and in a few days it was "subscribed by upwards of a hundred students attending Edinburgh College." [1] On being told of it, he wrote a letter (17–12–41) which "quashed all that". His wife explained to her mother, who would have rejoiced exceedingly if they had returned to Scotland, that the income of the "chair" was only uncertain fees.

'If he is to make his bread by lecturing, in an uncertain way, why not do it here? Or in America still better, where everyone says he might make thousands of pounds in one year? No, no, we are done with Edinburgh. As for me, I would as soon go back to Craigenputtock as to that poor, proud, formal, "highly respectable" city.'

She added that her husband said to her: "They would not keep me when they had me, and they may try whether they can catch me now."

'To Mr. Dunipace.' Date, about December, 1841.

'MY DEAR SIRS,—

'Accept my kind thanks, you and all your associates, for your zeal to serve me. This invitation of yours, coming on me unexpectedly from scenes once so familiar, now so remote and strange, like the voice of a new generation now risen up there, is almost an affecting thing. I can in some

---

[1] *Literary Recollections*, by F. Espinasse, pp. 61-3.

true sense take it as a voice from young Scotland . . .
Ten years ago such an invitation might perhaps have been
decisive. It is too late now . . .

'I will solicit a continuance of your regards; I will
bid you all be scholars and fellow-labourers of mine in
things true and manly; that so we may still work in real
concert at a distance and scattered asunder, since together
it is not possible for us.'

The letters were kept out of print; but this unusual
" requisition " was known, and about two years later his
old employer, David Brewster, being Principal of St.
Andrews, had the pleasure of offering to Carlyle and making
sure he did not want the Chair of Moral Philosophy, which he
had applied for in 1828. It may be remembered that
Professor Nichol had sounded Carlyle about it in 1839.

Towards the end of December, it may have been on the
very last day of the year (1841), there was a jolly dinner
party at Cheyne Row, where Robert Browning was completely happy and maybe Macready the actor too, and
certainly Macready's friend, Major Burns, a son of the poet
Burns, who sang three of his father's songs, including
" O' a' the airts the wind can blaw", and " John Anderson
my Jo, John, When we were first acquent ". Nobody equal
to the Carlyles, man and wife, was the feeling of the grateful
Browning.[3]

Carlyle was accosted in the street (6–1–42) by an "elderly,
innocent, intelligent-looking gentleman", the clergyman of
the parish; and "replied with all civility", admitting he
was sorry not to know him by face after living seven years
in his parish. They walked together some distance, and
parted with low bows and hopes of becoming better
acquainted,[4] which were fulfilled; and so began his connexion
with the Rectory, which has no history,—it was always
pleasant.

Writing to his mother two days later (8–1–42) [4] Carlyle
told about this as it might please her, and said the newspaper fuss about the Edinburgh Professorship and the
divine right of squires was " not unpleasant, but except for
aiding the sale of one's books, perhaps it is apt to be
unprofitable ".

---

[3] *R. Browning*, by Mrs. S. Orr, p. 134.
[4] *Letters of T. C. to his Youngest Sister*, by C. T. Copeland, pp. 118–22.

' My new book is to be something about that same *Civil War in England* which Baillie was in the midst of ; I think mainly about Cromwell. I am struggling sore to get some hold of it. I tried actual writing at it lately, but found it was too *soon* yet . . . By Heaven's great blessing I am not now urged on by direct need of money. We have arranged ourselves here in what to London people is an inconceivable state of *thrift*, and in our small way are not now tormented with any fear of want whatever for the present. To myself my poverty is really quite a suitable, almost comfortable, arrangement. I often think what should I do if I *were* wealthy. I am perhaps among the freest men in the British Empire at this moment. George Fox was hardly freer in his *suit of leather* than I here ; if to be sure not carrying it quite so far as the *leather*. Jane, too, is quite of my way of thinking in this respect. Truly we have been mercifully dealt with.'

As the mother of Confucius is esteemed the happiest mother in China, so might old Mrs. Carlyle be in Scotland. In the next letter after this, she was told : " Writing of Books, not getting paid for them, appears to be my task in this world," but that rather pleased than pained her, especially as her son went on to say that it was her teaching which had made him superior to wages.

In the Prussian Embassy, Carleton House Terrace, on Saturday, 29-1-42, Bunsen introduced Carlyle to the King of Prussia, along with Arnold of Rugby, Archdeacon Hare, and a crowd of London Germans. It was as free and easy an occasion as the presence of Royalty allowed. A man was playing a new piano he had just bought for the King on commission, to the accompaniment of an organ.[5]

Mr. Bulwer (Lytton) having sent Carlyle a book this year was cordially thanked. He had lost his seat in the Commons, and was esteemed a Radical and Republican as yet, and expected to concentrate upon literature. " I honour much," Carlyle wrote to him (23-2-42),[6] " the unwearied, steadfast perseverance with which you prosecute this painfullest, but also noblest of human callings, almost the summary of all that is left of nobleness in human callings in these poor days. I cordially wish you a long career, and a more and more victorious one." Which shows how seriously Carlyle took Literature.

[5] *A Memoir of Baron Bunsen*, by his Widow, II, pp. 4–7.
[6] *Life of E. Bulwer, Lord Lytton*, by his Grandson, II, p. 39.

His way of working appears in letters this winter about a drama on Strafford, which John Sterling wrote and sent to him. He had himself had a passing thought of the drama as a possible way of doing Cromwell justice ; but found he could not do it. He admitted that Sterling might be right in disregarding him, and remarked :—-

' The inward voice is the prophetic voice of our whole soul and world. All voices from without, and counter-monitions of other men, how prudent and well-meant soever, are in the end but impertinences in comparison.

' Of Dramatic *Art*, tho I have eagerly listened to a Goethe speaking of it, and to several hundreds of other persons, I find that I know yet almost as good as nothing. Indeed, of *Art* generally I can know almost nothing. My first and last secret of *Kunst* (or Art) is to get a thorough *intelligence* of the *fact* to be painted, represented, or, in whatever way set forth ; the *fact*, deep as Hades, high as heaven, and written *so*, as to the visual face of it, on our poor Earth. This once *blazing* within one, if it will ever get to blaze, and bursting to be out, one has to take the whole dexterity of adaptation one is master of or has ever gathered from the four winds, and with tremendous struggling, really frightful struggling, contrive to exhibit it, one way or other ! This is not *Art*, I know well. It is Robinson Crusoe, and not the Master of Woolwich, building a ship. Yet, at bottom, is there any Woolwich builder for *such* kinds of craft ? What *Kunst* had Homer ? What *Kunst* had Shakespeare ? Patient, docile, valiant intelligence, conscious and unconscious, gathered from all winds, of these two things, their own faculty of utterance, and the audience (rude theatre, Ithacan farm-hall, or whatever it was) they had to utter to, add *only* to which, as the soul of the whole, the above-said blazing, radiant insight into the fact, blazing burning interest about it, and we have the whole Art of Shakespeare and Homer.

' Now, my Friend, what I fundamentally object to in *Strafford* is that even such an insight, such an interest, and consequently such a veracity is not there. I object to the fate of Strafford being made to turn on any kind of *quiddity* ; it was a necessity of nature, and till you have shown it as such there is no right *Tragedy* made of it.'

So he suggested to " revise and reconsider almost *all* the

characters. Am not I a modest man ! " In a previous letter
he had exhorted Sterling in the spirit of Horace to let some
poetry " lie till it cool ; then, to it with the file and the rasp.
He that spareth the rasp hateth the Book ". Which helps
to explain the difficulty he found in pleasing himself now,
when writing on the Commonwealth and Cromwell. His
preaching and practice were always tending to be the same.

XVIII

DEATH OF MRS. WELSH

(1842)

ON 25–2–42 Mrs. Welsh died suddenly, and was buried at Crawford beside her father by her brother John Welsh, who had come from Liverpool for the purpose, and did not delay the funeral for Carlyle's arrival, but stayed in the house till he came to receive charge and wind up. Mrs. Carlyle had hurried off on receiving the first alarm, but went no farther than Liverpool on hearing all was over.

In a letter from Carlyle at Thornhill (9–3–42) [1] to Miss Wilson, he said his wife would be home in about a week, with a cousin to nurse her, adding : " Time will bring solacement ; Time alone can . . . All human consolations, philosophies, etc., break futile, like foam, from such a catastrophe." Nevertheless he was copiously comforting his wife by letter, and being overruled by her in the domestic department. She shrieked on paper at his suggestion to keep ' Templand ', the house near Thornhill, and would not even allow him to put some of the furniture in their empty house at Craigenputtock so that they might have it for occasional summer quarters. It was hard enough for her to hold him in London when he had no foothold of his own anywhere else. She would take no risks.

Her alarm was well founded. His enjoyment of life in the country bubbled over in letters at the time, as for example in this to Mill : " It is such a torrid Sahara Whirlpool, that of London ; men's very thoughts cannot meet. Men have no time to think ; they have only time to scheme and work."

There is the humour of reality in the great simplicity of his *Reminiscences* in old age : " I was for trying to keep Templand once, as a summer refuge for us—one of the most picturesque of locations ; but *her* filial heart abhorred the notion ; and I have never seen more than the chimney-tops of Templand since."

---

[1] *Nineteenth Century Mag.*, May, 1921, p. 809.

The income of about £150 a year, which Mrs. Carlyle had relinquished to her mother before her marriage, was now their own, and as he put it, " the *pinch* of Poverty, which had been relaxing latterly, changed itself into a gentle *pressure*, or into a *limit* and little more. We did not change our habits in any point, but the collar round my neck was slackened."

Replying to Lockhart, who had inquired about money matters and said " It would be a fine thing to be independent of booksellers ", he confessed [2] :—

' Our only sure revenue must be Parsimonia, Scotch thrift. Calvinism is Hyper-Stoicism. Abstain and endure— it is the lesson destiny teaches every man throughout this life.

' We growl much about Bookseller-servitude ; worse than Algerine,—and yet at bottom we are but a foolish folk. Consider you, for example, how many of your good things you would perhaps never have taken the trouble to write at all had there been no such servitude ! *Servitude* was a blessing and a great *liberty*, the greatest that could be given a man ! So the shrewd little De Staal [3] found that she had enjoyed the most freedom in the Bastille. As to me ' [it is the same, and in short] ' we are born fools.

' The mountain-tops are a-glow like so many volcanoes : it is poor tarry shepherds burning their heather, to let the grass have a chance. Sirius is glancing blue-bright like a spirit—a comrade of more than twenty years. Penpont smoke cloud and Drumlanrig Castle have alike gone out. In the north is an Aurora—footlights of this great Theatre of a Universe, where you and I are players for an hour. God *is* great ; and all else is verily altogether small.'

The only money matter mentioned to his wife as interesting was that her mother had £189 lying in the bank, and so " was in no money straits at least. Oh Jeannie, what a blessing for us now that we fronted poverty instead of her doing it ! "

He said afterwards he never again saw a spring in the country so well as in these weeks,—which might be because he was so much alone. He used to watch the storms at a distance

---

[2] *Life of J. G. Lockhart*, by A. Lang, II, pp. 233–8.
[3] See for Staal, not Stael, the *New Letters of T. C.*, edited by A. C., I, p. 262.

powdering the hills with snow, and on " one of the stillest Sundays " he sat long by the river-side, and then went sauntering in the woods, " vocal with rooks and pairing birds."

Explaining to his wife in reply to her lamentations that what she needed was work to occupy her, he admitted the difficulty of finding it.   ' The deepest difficulty is the sick sentimentalism we suck in with our whole nourishment.   It is this that makes me so impatient of George Sand, Mazzini, and all that set.   How often have I provokingly argued with you about all that ! I will endeavour not to do so any more. It is not by arguing ' that help can be given, in short.   ' Let us both cry for help to be better for each other, and for all duties in time coming. Articulate prayer is for me not possible, but the equivalent of it remains for ever in the heart and life of man.   I say *let us* pray.   God look down upon us ; guide us, not happily, but *well*, through life. Unite us well with our buried ones according to his will. Amen. My mother sends you her blessing. She was telling me yesterday all about the last parting with her (own) mother . . .   Old scenes sunk forty years in the past can still bring tears into old eyes.'

He seems to have written every day, sending comfort which she needed the more because she had room for " sorrowful reflections ".   " Sympathy is what mortals owe to one another in such a season," he wrote to Thomas Erskine.   " The little birds (left behind) shrink lovingly together when a great falcon has smitten one of them " and snatched it away.

The amiable Mazzini got a nasty surprise. He tried to persuade Mrs. Carlyle that her mother " is not dead, but knows all, and loves more, and watches and waits, intercedes and hovers over her child to help and strengthen her ". He was in earnest himself, too, which reveals him and explains how he was able to see what he sadly confessed, that she did not believe a word of it.[4] She rather despised his simplicity—" he twaddled ", said she,[5] but he was never aware of that.

[4] *The Birth of Modern Italy*, by J. W. Mario, pp. 53–4.
[5] *Literary Recollections*, by F. Espinasse, p. 107.

XIX

THE WAY TO STOP WAR

(1842)

IT seems to have been soon after 1840 that the friendship of Carlyle with Charles Dickens began. A letter Forster quotes [1] may have been of earlier date :—" An Archdeacon with his own venerable lips repeated to me, the other night, a strange profane story of a solemn clergyman who had been administering ghostly consolation to a sick person ; having finished, satisfactorily as he thought, and got out of the room, he hears the sick person ejaculate : ' Well, thank God, Pickwick will be out in ten days anyway ! ' "

What fixed their friendship and set it growing was an important letter to Dickens, written while winding up affairs at Thornhill. It has already borne fruit in legislation, and is still of great significance. Its clearness beguiles us to forget its depth. Perhaps the best commentary upon it is a letter from Carlyle to John Forster,[2] which seems to have been sent with it as a covering letter, and at any rate is dated the same day (26–3–42) :—

' Dickens deserves praise and support : but *the claims of authors seem to me so infinitely beyond what anybody states them at, or what any Congress will hear of, that I can seldom speak of them without getting into banter, or a tone inconveniently loud, which is worse.*[3] Congress will evidently throw out this proposal, and the next, and babble of the thing for many years—and then do it. But we are all right to shorten the years as we can. . .

' Adieu, dear Forster. I must now address myself, if possible in fit dialect, to " the Lord their God, His Grace ".

' Yours ever truly,

' T. CARLYLE.'

[1] Forster's *Charles Dickens*, I, pp. 109 and 313–15.
[2] John Forster papers, South Kensington Museum. London.
[3] Italics added.

The letter to Dickens was of course for immediate publication :—

'. . . We learn by the newspapers that you everywhere in America stir up the question of international copyright, and thereby awaken huge dissonance where all else were triumphant unison for you. I am asked my opinion of the matter, and requested to write it down in words.

' Several years ago, I was one of many English writers, who, under the auspices of Miss Martineau, did already sign a petition to congress praying for an international copyright between the two Nations—which properly are not two Nations, but one ; *indivisible* by parliament, congress, or any kind of human law or diplomacy, being already *united* by Heaven's Act of Parliament, and the everlasting law of Nature and Fact. To that opinion I still adhere, and am like to continue adhering.

' In discussion of the matter, manifold considerations and argumentations will necessarily arise ; which to me are not interesting nor essential. They respect the time and manner in which the thing should be.' In the Bible ' it was thousands of years ago written down, " Thou *shalt not* steal." That thou belongest to a different " Nation " and canst steal without being certainly hanged for it gives thee no permission to steal ! Thou shalt *not* steal at all ! So it is written down. Nay, poor Jeremy Bentham and others step in here, and will demonstrate that it is actually our true convenience and expediency not to steal ; which I do also firmly believe. *For example, if Nations abstained from stealing what need were there of fighting,—with its butcherings and burnings, decidedly the most expensive thing in this world ?* [3] How much more two Nations, which, as I said, are but one Nation ; brother elements of the same great SAXONDOM, to which in all honourable ways be long life ! '

John Forster says, " This brave letter " saved Dickens from many of the nastiest imputations of selfish motives, and he was " very grateful for it ".

That wars are due to international stealing was a novel doctrine then, but as this conclusion from previous history might be established by events since the letter was written, the great discovery, nowhere better put than here, may some day be used. It is only in *practice* that the politicians are rascals. The truth is now so plain that it is not even denied in the Church of England ! A popular Dean in 1923 quoted with approval Ruskin's paraphrase of this bit of Carlyle's teaching: " The first reason for all wars and for the necessity for national defences is that *the majority of persons, high and low, in all European countries, are thieves.*"

The exaggeration of this is Ruskin's, *who would have made the multiplication table seem doubtful if he had written about it.* Confucius was fond of quoting an old saw :—

> " There's none that's fated to be bad,
>   And any can be good ;
> The heart of man is always glad
>   When doing what he should."

The most of us would gladly be truthful and honest, and live above the swamps of lies, where diplomats—and Deans— may delight to dwell ; and that is why humanity can hope to press even politicians into peace, and minimize the public evil-doing.

The idea articulated in the letter to Dickens shines through all the histories of Carlyle, our greatest modern historian—for that is his title to our regard—and indeed it was no novelty there. The idea is as old as Christianity itself in Europe and was the *ideal* of the best of our saints and sages,—that nations should behave to each other as individuals do in any community wherein they have learned aright to live together. In particular they should stop stealing. Meddling in the affairs of other nations is simply wrong. The "international" control of Germany to-day or of China, the English in Egypt or Mesopotamia, the French in Algiers and Tonquin, the Spaniards in Morocco, the Americans in the Philippines, all are merely what St. Augustine called "organised rascality". Our diplomats " love the darkness rather than the light because their deeds are evil ". The war of 1914–18 should surely teach us now that among nations as well as individuals *honesty really is the best policy.* That is as sure as gravitation, whether we believe it or not. The one and only road to "security " and peace is to desist from meddling, and as a nation behave to other nations as these others should behave to us.

XX

THOMAS AIRD

A MAN from Dumfries, who now resorted to Thornhill to enjoy Carlyle's company there, was Thomas Aird, a handsome big Borderer, seven years younger than himself, and curiously like him in circumstances. The son of devout " Seceders " he had early been remarked as swift to learn, and sent at fourteen to Edinburgh University by parents who hoped to see him " wagging his head in a pulpit ". Like Carlyle he sympathized with pious people but outgrew their creed, and fell back upon " the hard granite of natural religion ". He tried to " make a career " in literature, while supporting himself by tutoring and periodical writing. By 1834 he was 32, and had done his tragedy and much else, and been praised by Wilson and printed by Blackwood ; and then in 1835 he accepted an offer like the one Carlyle refused, and went to Dumfries to be a country editor. He was a sincere Conservative, like his friend John Wilson, and idealized his job, declaring " The newspaper is the gospel of God's daily providence working in man's world ". His favourite maxim was " The great soul of the world is just ".[1]

For twenty-eight years after 1835 let him be borne in mind as sending copies of his weekly paper and all else he published to Carlyle in London, and walking and talking with him as often as he came within reach. In Dumfries they used to walk by the riverside, above and below the town. Aird was a naturalist, who sought knowledge of living things by watching them and not by killing them—a disinterested man of science, content to enjoy it. Many a wild bird behaved to him as a friend, and perched on his shoulder or his hand.

[1] See the *Poetical Works of Thomas Aird*, with a Memoir by the Rev. J. Wallace, and a Memoir in the *Pen and Palette* papers for December, 1903, by A. D. Murray.

XXI

THE SISTER OF BURNS AND MANY OTHERS

(1842)

ROBERT CHAMBERS of Edinburgh, who supported
himself by trade and for the sake of his family was
anonymous in writing, had discovered a sister of Robert
Burns at Tranent near there—Mrs. Begg, a poor widow
with two children. He applied to Carlyle for help to them,
and received at once such a letter as he wanted and a guinea
along with it (4–3–42) :—

'MY DEAR SIR,—

'Your Samaritan endeavour on behalf of Burns'
sister is worthy of all praise . . . There can be no possible
objection to your use of my name in the way proposed,
unless it be that a better were easily procurable : Lockhart's,
for example, whom I doubt not I could soon persuade.'[1]

The Duke of Buccleuch was the owner of Templand,
and a difference of opinion arose between him or his lawyers
and Carlyle about a hundred pounds owing by the Duke to
the estate of Mrs. Welsh, a leaseholder. They refused to pay,
and Carlyle wrote to the Duke explaining fully the circumstances out of which the debt arose. He answered curtly
that he did not think the money was due. Carlyle replied
with equal brevity to the effect : " £100 is of importance to
me if not to you. I will do nothing more in the matter ;
but desire you to recollect that you owe me £100." After
some months the Duke sent the money. Nothing else
happened ; and this is told to put an end to rumours.[2]
The Thornhill village historian gives another glimpse of
Carlyle. " During the midday recess " he called upon the

---

[1] "Unpublished Letters of Thomas Carlyle and others to Robert
Chambers," in *Chambers' Journal*, 1900, and the *Glasgow Herald*, 22–5–15,
giving details of a sale at Sotheby's, London, on 17–6–15.
[2] Told by David Masson to D. A. W. on 24–1–03, as what he heard
from Carlyle, correcting country clatter.

tailor Shankland, mentioned in his journal of June, 1832. The " shop " was shut ; but Shankland did not need to be told he was not on business. " Come in, sir," he cried, the " sir " in Scotland not denoting inequality and being then in common use, " Come in, sir,—ye see I'm gey weel employed," and he showed proudly the book he was reading, " one of his own books ", said Shankland afterwards, telling the story. When the time came for parting, Carlyle looked at the book Shankland had been reading, and said, " When I go up to London I'll send you a better printed book than that. You were the first man in Dumfriesshire to appreciate my work." Which Shankland repeated with delight for the rest of his life, in showing to the curious that treasured book.[3]

Shankland was exceptional. Carlyle wrote to his wife in April : ' The babbling inconclusive palaver of the rustic population here, if you have anything to do with them, is altogether beyond a jest to me ; I positively feel it immoral and disgusting.' On the day of the auction at Templand he drove by the Dalveen pass to the graveyard by the Clyde at Crawford, and made sure the new stone was right. There were one or two mistakes of points. He borrowed a hammer and chisel from Mr. Ramage in the adjoining farm of Kirkton and corrected what was wrong, and cleaned the lettering in the old inscriptions. Mr. Ramage used to show the tools as curiosities, and " the hammer and the chisel " became " valued " heirlooms in his family.[4] Across the little river was the farmhouse of Castlemains, where Mrs. Welsh had been born [5] and her forefathers had dwelt for several generations.

Carlyle stayed only another night in Thornhill, preferring to sleep at Scotsbrig and ride to Thornhill when needful in the next two weeks. He wrote to his wife (19–4–42) :—

' It is a wonderful relief to me that I have here got fairly out of the choking sycophant Duke element, which tempted me at every turn to exclaim " May the Devil and his grand-mother fly away with your shabble of a Duke ! " ' [Shabble means a rusty, crooked old sword of no significance. He went on :—] ' What in God's name have I to do with him ?

[3] *Thornhill and its Worthies*, by J. L. Waugh, p. 94.
[4] Article in the *Glasgow Herald*, 29-7-05, by D. MacMillan, " The Carlyles and Crawford."
[5] Ibid., correcting T. C. himself, who supposed she had been born at Caplegill, where she was married.

All the Dukes in creation melted into one Duke were not worth sixpence to me. I declare I could not live there at all in such an accursed, soul-oppressing puddle of a Dukery.'

Departing for home on Wednesday (4–5–42),[6] he stayed two nights at Liverpool, where John Welsh undertook to find subscribers to the fund for Mrs. Begg.[7] On the Thursday Carlyle " went over to Manchester ", as he wrote to Thomas Spedding in Cumberland [6] :—

' The most tragic circumstance I noted there was *want of smoke* ; Manchester was never in my time third-part as clear. What a strange country we are at this hour ! Two thousand men and women assembled the other night before the Provost's door in Paisley, and stood, without tumult, indeed almost in silence ; when questioned as to their purpose, they said they had no money, no food nor fuel, they were Fathers and Mothers, working men and women, and had come out there to see whether they could not be saved alive. The police withdrew to a distance, there were soldiers hard by to have checked any riot. By dint of great efforts the Provost collected a sum which yielded one penny farthing to each, and at sunrise they had gradually dispersed again.'

This haunted Carlyle, and recurs in his letters. Spedding shared his anxieties to the full and begged for London news, remarking [6] :—

' I am not a reader of Judgement, nor could ever discern to my own conviction the design of Providence in the order of this world ; but it is plain at least that man has a perpetual demand upon man for his turn at Nature's table and the means also of making his claim good—whatever persons or things may stand in his way. The ignorance of this on the part of the British Aristocracy seems destined to involve us in some rough weather very shortly.'

To which Carlyle replied : " I suppose the people will revolt, not willing to die like Hindoos, and the Government will order out dragoons. A Chartist Parliament, not far in

---

[6] *Cornhill Mag.*, May, 1921, pp. 530–7. Letters edited by A. Carlyle.
[7] *Letters of T. Carlyle to his Youngest Sister*, by C. T. Copeland, p. 127.

the rear of that, seems likeliest to many. A Chartist
Parliament or any form of Democracy is, with me, equivalent
to Anarchy, and what the Yankees call ' Immortal Smash '."

In short, the thoughts to be soon shaped in *Past and
Present* were keeping him from concentrating on Cromwell
in spite of the strong effort of his will.

On Friday (4–5–42) he went to Rugby as the guest of
Dr. Arnold. On Saturday they drove to Naseby and together
" explored the scene of the great battle very satisfactorily ",
wrote Arnold at the time.[8] Carlyle was home in London that
night, and in telling Thomas Spedding about it,[6] he said
Naseby " *was a most striking place for me* ; *equal to Marathon
or better* ". And yet he could not write about Cromwell in
a way to please himself. He went on trying again and again.
Tho the season was at its height he would not see anybody during working hours, and refused most invitations.
In " the hot blazing days " of this summer he often stayed
indoors till the heat was past, and made long solitary
excursions in the cool of the evening.

Mr. Bain, the biographer of J. S. Mill, gives a glimpse of
him which may be dated this year.[9] It was a habit of
Bain to go to the India House in Leadenhall Street about
4 o'clock, when Mill was leaving, and walk home with
him, and one day he found Carlyle there on the same errand.
They all three ' walked together to the London Library,
Carlyle having the largest share of the talk. I remember only
the conclusion ', says Bain. ' It was as we were entering
St. James's Square that Carlyle was denouncing our religion
and all its accessories. Mill struck in with the remark :
" Now you are just the very man to tell the public your whole
mind upon that subject." Carlyle gave, with his peculiar
grunt, the exclamation, " Ho ! " and added, " It is some one
like Frederick the Great that should do that." '

Carlyle did not forget to speak about the sister of Burns
to Lockhart, who assisted a collection for her in Scotland,
but desired to have no appeal made in England unless
Scotland failed. Carlyle would not wait, but spoke to others.
" Milnes took the fashionables in hand," he wrote to Robert
Chambers. He started collecting himself, and got John
Forster and others to do likewise in the city. Milnes

[8] *Thomas Arnold*, by A. P. Stanley, Chap. X, letter of 19–5–42.
[9] *J. S. Mill*, by A. Bain, pp. 42 and 64 and 190–1.

did best of all in going to Peel, who agreed to give the good widow for her brother's sake an immediate donation of £50 and an annual pension of £20, " with reversion of £10 each to her two daughters if they survived her." A letter from Carlyle to Mrs. Begg announcing this (7-6-42) is now among the treasures of the Burns Cottage Museum, Alloway, Ayr. " The chief agent in this good work," he said, " has been Mr. Milnes, a Yorkshire Member of Parliament ; himself a Poet, and generous-hearted man to whom it is no burden to owe kindness. Properly, however, you do not owe this to anybody but to your own illustrious brother." In sending the news to Scotsbrig he added that Mrs. Begg already had £10 a year from some Scottish charity and would now have £30, besides the £50 and the subscriptions, which soon exceeded £400. Thus Robert Chambers was enabled to settle her and her daughters in a cottage near Ayr, which they preferred, with an income of £60, " just about the happiest sum for them ", wrote Carlyle to Chambers, approving his plans " entirely ". " Work is still useful, necessary ; but no longer tyrannous, treadmill necessity ; they are not dangerously lifted into a new sphere of existence, but rendered easy in the old one." [10] They lived there serenely for many years. The youngest at death was eighty. Their cottage is demolished. They and it have passed away like shadows from the screens.

One evening this summer Carlyle consented to go to the House of Commons to hear Charles Buller speak on the Scotch Church question. Downing Street was letting the Church drift into a smash. But the business was postponed. Carlyle could only watch the members " sitting with their hats on talking to one another, coming and going ", while the Speaker, conspicuous in a wig, was mumbling half-inaudibly, " Say Aye, say No, the Ayes have it," and shoving through sheaves of Bills. Then up rose Peel with a big head and a wrinkle on his cheeks, in a " dark-coloured surtout " with cotton trousers blue-striped.

As Peel began to talk the " humming and bustling " abated to let him be heard, and Carlyle had the pleasure of listening to a politician he could respect.

[10] *Chambers' Journal*, 3-4-42.

XXII

BIRTHDAY PRESENTS

(1842)

IT had been a habit of Mrs. Welsh to give her petted only child a birthday present every year, and this year (14-7-42) Mrs. Carlyle, expecting nothing of that sort any more, was agreeably surprised by one from her husband. Writing next day to her Liverpool cousin Margaret who had also sent her one, she said :—

' It was a good thought in you to send me the little purse, and I feel grateful to you for it. This last birthday was very sad for me, very unlike all former years. Only think of my husband, too, having given me a little present ! he who never attends to such nonsense as birthdays, and who dislikes nothing in the world so much as going into a shop to buy anything, even his own trousers and coats ; so that, to the consternation of Cockney tailors, I am obliged to go about them. Well, he actually risked himself in a jeweller's shop, and bought me a very nice smelling-bottle ! I cannot tell you how *wae* his little gift made me, as well as glad ; it was the first thing of the kind he ever gave to me in his life. In great matters he is always kind and considerate ; but these little attentions, which we women attach so much importance to, he was never in the habit of rendering to anyone . . . And now the desire to replace to me the irreplaceable, makes him as good in little things as he used to be in great.'

In short she rejoiced so much about it that he never again allowed her birthday to pass without a present.

XXIII

THE AMERICAN APOSTLE ALCOTT

(1842)

AMONG this summer's Americans was Amos B. Alcott,
with his long, lean face and figure, a man in his forties,
and more wrinkled than Carlyle, tho younger. He was a
Pestalozzi of " transcendental " Western pattern, who had
taken to lecturing when he had to shut up school, and with
sundry followers was now meditating to practise Emerson's
Gospel of Work by retiring to the country to live by labour
on the land, and avoid such luxuries as flesh for food.
Emerson thought him a " great " and " majestic soul ",
and said he would send him to Carlyle, " to atone by his
great nature for many smaller ones that have craved to
see you."

This was kindly meant, and the new apostle received at
Cheyne Row the welcome bespoken for him and drawled
away with satisfaction. On the second occasion he stayed
all night. He was cheered by his success in converting
Tennyson—for a time. Tennyson abstained from mutton
chops for three whole months before he relapsed into flesh-
eating. Carlyle was less open to such " light ", confessing
to Spedding, " I defended myself with quizzing," and in a
letter to Thomas Erskine describing Alcott as sincere, " but
of the deepest ignorance, and calmly arrogant as an inspired
man may be supposed to be."

On Alcott's third or some later visit to Cheyne Row he
encountered Browning, and was pitilessly chaffed.[1] The
longest argument ends at last, and he rose to go. " When
shall I see you again ? " Carlyle inquired as a dutiful host
should do ; and Alcott drawled a plain reply, " Never,
I guess."

In the letters that passed about him, Emerson said that
Alcott had " more than a prophet's egotism ", which Carlyle
said was " altogether just ".

[1] *R. Browning and A. Domett* (1906), p. 46.

Alcott seemed to him a kind of venerable Don Quixote, whom nobody can even laugh at without loving. But as for his " more than prophetic egotism ", Carlyle remarked : ' Yes ! It is of such material that Thebaid Eremites, Sect-founders, and all manner of cross-grained fanatical monstrosities have fashioned themselves. Sect-founders are a class I do not like. No truly great man, from Jesus Christ downwards, ever founded a Sect—I mean wilfully intended founding one. What a view must a man have of this Universe who thinks " *he* can swallow it all " ; who is not doubly and trebly happy that he can keep it from swallowing him ! On the whole, I sometimes hope we have now done with Fanatics and Agonistic Posture-makers in this poor world : it will be an immense improvement on the Past ; and the " New Ideas ", as Alcott calls them, will prosper greatly the better on that account ! The old gloomy Gothic Cathedrals were good ; but the great blue Dome that hangs over all is better than any Cologne one. On the whole, do not tell the good Alcott a word of all this ; but let him love me as he can, and live on vegetables in peace ; as I, living *partly* on vegetables, will continue to love him ! '

In a few years the apostle was settled peaceably near Boston, more " Emersonian " than ever, lecturing a little and writing, and living to a great age—he did not die till 1888—being beautifully tended by his good daughter Louisa, who produced the popular book called *Little Women,* and seems herself to have been the best of all her father's productions.

XXIV

HOW HE LOST JOHN MILL

MILL and Carlyle had been so intimate that onlookers made many guesses as to how they drifted apart. It is only the details that are doubtful. From year to year they were seeing each other less and less. Acquaintances of both appear to have agreed: " Mrs. Taylor set herself to monopolize Mill as if jealous of any other friendship. She soon separated him from most of his intimates. He ceased to be accessible even to young men seeking such help and advice as he had delighted to give for years before. In spite of Mrs. Carlyle and Mrs. Taylor disliking each other, he clung to Carlyle long after he had let go the rest, and Carlyle in turn was perfectly discreet in avoiding censure of Mill's appropriation of another man's wife. Sterling was a link while he lived, but he was little in London, and long before he died in 1844 they were separated." [1] In 1842 when Carlyle was in Scotland, he was thanking Mill for calling to comfort his wife, and suggesting another call " if he were passing that way ". " But Mrs. Taylor would disapprove of such a thing." [1] And in the July following there was a letter which must have tended to make the separation complete. Mrs. Taylor was ill, and wanted Carlyle to consent to be a trustee for her children under her will ; and Carlyle, in his simplicity and conscious humility, failed to realize that she was not wanting his services as a man of business, but only to be a kind of voucher for her respectability.

' To Mrs. Taylor,
   ' Walton-on-Thames.   CHELSEA.
                            13th July, 1842.

' MY DEAR MRS. TAYLOR,—

     ' What you ask of me is very flattering ; and seemed so small a matter, in regard to " trouble " or the like, that I could not but at once accede to your request when

---

[1] David Masson verbally to D. A. W., reporting what he saw and heard at the time, including the talk of Professor Bain and others.

Mr. Taylor came, that same evening, to enforce it and receive my answer.

' During these two days, however, there have various doubts arisen in me, and, on the whole, a serious, practical question, which I now anew submit to your decision, whether you really ought not to appoint another to that trust ; whether I myself, in justice to all interests, ought not still to decline it !

' The fact is, you have not among all your friends any person possessed of common sense and arrived at years of discretion who is so totally unacquainted with every form of what is called Business ; nor, I think, unlikelier now ever to become acquainted with it. For example, were the matter (as Mr. Taylor assured me this present one could at the utmost only be) that of seeing certain moneys properly invested in Stock, I should not of myself in the least know when it was " properly " done, but must depend altogether upon the judgment of others. *Money* generally is one of my *enemies*— whom I never look at except on compulsion, and then with the strangest *art of oblivion* : if you will believe me, I do not at this moment (nor at any moment except for some half hour after I have looked and rummaged among paper bundles) know, within fractions equal to a fourth or a third of the whole, how much money I myself have—easy as that were to count ! I understand only that I have " money enough for a while to come " ; and so think no more of it. Judge whether you would like your dear children's interests in such a hand ! . . . It is inconceivable that in your circle of friends there should not be many persons with some know-ledge of practical affairs. On the whole, my dear Friend, I will invite you to re-examine the matter, and appoint another ! If there be any real necessity why I in particular should creep out of my snail-shell into so unknown a depart-ment of things, doubt not I will readily creep out, and do my best when out, but if not I pray you, for your own sake and my own, let me continue to lodge there ! . . . I have a notion to come to Walton and speak with you of this matter . . .'

She sent for him, accordingly, and he went to see her. Mill went with him. " It was all very pathetic," said Carlyle long afterwards, " but I had to tell her that she couldn't have made a worse choice, that there was no man less fit to take charge of other people's property, for I could scarcely mind my own, and that if by chance I ever happened to have a hundred pounds of my own, I was altogether at a loss to know what to do with it. And I begged her to ask some-one else, and to let me off, tho I would gladly have served her if I could." [2]

It was like Carlyle not to suspect that she could not put into words " the real necessity why he in particular " was her choice. The facts of her situation were notorious. What made him seem to her a desirable trustee—as good as the whole Bench of Bishops to vouch for her respectability—was his well-known impatience at the sight of married women philandering with strange men. Mrs. Taylor would believe his simplicity now insincere. Even Mill would suppose so, and all the more readily from his intimate knowledge of Carlyle. Here is a private event of this very year.

Mrs. Carlyle reported to her cousin Jeannie : " His wisdom ", whereby she meant her husband, " ' kicked up a rumpus ' for my ' George Sandish excess of humanity ' àpropos of poor Mrs. R. ! " (a married woman who had just eloped from her house with an adulterer.) " My *doctrine* on that whole matter, he would have me to know, was *infamous*—and also my *practice* in making myself the advocate of Whores—it behoved me to reform ! I *cried* like a simpleton, and so made bad worse." [3]

This would not have surprised Mill ; and this sort of thing would make most people agree with Mrs. Taylor in thinking that Carlyle was merely affecting not to see her reason for wanting him. But they would be mistaken. He was merely obtuse. There is something touching in what shows well his sincerity, his lifelong wonder at what he should have otherwise expected, that Mill now drew away from him altogether. In 1873, when Norton reported the news that Mill was dead, Carlyle told the sad story of their friendship and its conclusion, saying :—

' Many a night have I lain awake, thinking what it might be that had come between us, and never could I think of the least thing, for I'd never said a word nor harboured a thought about that man but of affection and kindliness. And many's the time I've thought of writing to him and saying, " John Mill, what is it that parts you and me ! " But that's all over now. Never could I think of the least thing, unless maybe it was this. Godefroi Cavaignac told me of meeting Mill and Mrs. Taylor somewhere in France not

[2] *Letters of C. E. Norton*, I, pp. 495–500.
[3] *J. W. Carlyle : Letters to her Family*, edited by L. Huxley, p. 38.

long before, eating grapes together off one branch, like two love-birds. And his description amused me and I repeated it, without thinking any harm, to a man who was not always to be trusted " (naming him, but Norton, the reporter, suppresses the name), " a man who made trouble with his tongue, and I've thought that he might perhaps have told it to Mill, and that Mill might have fancied that I was making a jest of what was most sacred to him ; but I don't know if that was it, but it was the only thing I could ever think of that could have hurt him.'

As for Mill, during the last thirty years of his life, it was remarked that he seemed to grow " suddenly aged " whenever Carlyle was named.[4]

[4] *Thomas Carlyle*, by Moncure D. Conway, p. 90.

XXV

TO BELGIUM AND BACK

(1842)

THE father of Mrs. James Marshall was the same Spring Rice who was once a Chancellor of the Exchequer, and as Chairman of the Board of Customs was able to make his eldest son a Commissioner of Customs. It was political spoils at any rate, and his son might as well get it as another. The lucky young man, or his sister for him, had obtained from Carlyle this summer a quasi-promise to join him in a three days' cruise to Ostend in a revenue cutter. So on Saturday, 6–8–42, they went to Margate by the river steamer,[1] dined on board their cutter, and landed at Ostend in the morning.

They were to sleep at Ghent, but their train was at four o'clock. Carlyle went alone to the shore to bathe, and not seeing the " jacket and breeches " among his towels in the machine, and not knowing both sexes bathed together, plunged naked, as if in Scotland, into the " most delicious tepid sea ", and was recalled by the machine-man in time to avoid arrest—wherein he was luckier than the two Scandinavian delegates to the Genoa pow-wow in May, 1922, who made the same mistake, and were arrested in the water by the police.[2]

At Bruges (meaning " Bridges ", he guessed, for it stands on many intersecting canals) they had to wait four hours, and explored the town. In the centre of the largest open space grew a straight oak " tree of liberty " planted in 1794, and now affectionately patted by the hand of Carlyle. He admired the Sabbath stillness, not a carriage moving, and the perfect cleanness, smokeless as Salisbury Plain. The cunning kitchen-stoves and warming apparatus burnt little fuel. As he went about in this city of the Bridges,

---

[1] T. C.'s description is printed in *Cornhill Mag.*, October and November, 1922.

[2] Newspapers of 13–5–22.

with its winding streets, broad market-places, and big old buildings, he looked with the mind's eye through the mists of time and saw both city and country to be the result of the work of long-forgotten generations.

' Sand downs and stagnating marshes, producing nothing but heath, sedges, docks, marsh-mallows, and miasmata : so it lay by nature ; but the industry of man, the assiduous unwearied motion of how many spades, pickaxes, hammers, wheel-barrows, mason-trowels, and ten-thousandfold industrial tools have made it—this ! A thing that will grow corn, potherbs, warehouses, Rubens' pictures, churches, and cathedrals. Long before Cæsar's time of swords, the era of spades had ushered itself in and was busy. " Tools and the Man ? " " Arms and the Man " is but a small song in comparison. Honour to you, ye long-forgotten generations, from whom at this moment we have our bread and clothing ; not a delver among you that dug out one shovelful of a marsh drain but was doing us a good turn ! Bruges in the thirteenth century had become the " Venice of the North ", had its ships on every sea ; the most important city in these latitudes was founded in a soil which, as Coleridge with a poor sneer declares, was not of God's making, but of man's. All the more credit to man, Mr. Samuel Taylor ! '

The pretty women of Bruges were admired by the whole party, but not the gentlemen, who " affect to be a kind of mongrel French, and go about in mustachios and sugar-loaf hats—the blockheads ! " [3] Carlyle entered with his companions no less than four of the churches :—

' Enormous high-arched roofs (I suppose not higher than Westminster Abbey, but far more striking to me, for they are actually in *use* here), altar-pieces, carvings, pictures, inscriptions, shrines and votive-tablets, above all, actual human creatures bent in devotion there, mostly women ; all this with the yellow evening sunlight falling down over the new and ancient tombs of the dead—it struck me dumb, and I cared nothing for Rubens or Vandyke canvases while this living painted canvas hung there before me—on the bosom of eternity. The mass was over, but these worshippers, it seemed, still loitered. You could not say from their air that

[3] *R. Monckton Milnes, etc.*, by T. Wemyss Reid, I, p. 281.

they were without devotion—yet they were painful to me :
the fat priests were worse ; I had a kind of hatred of them,
a desire to kick them into the canals unless they ceased that
fooling !   They wore on the streets a black serge or cloth
pelisse exactly like a woman's, some sasheries about their
nasty thick waist, and a narrow scarf of black silk hanging
down right behind from their haunches, sometimes from
the very neck—oftenest very ugly men, and much too fat.
At bottom one cannot *wish* these men kicked into the canals ;
for what would follow were they gone ?   Atheistic
Benthamism, French editorial " rights of man " and *grande
nation*, that is a far worse thing, a far *untruer* thing.   God
pity the generation in which you have to see deluded and
deluding *Simulacra*, Tartuffes, and Semi-Tartuffes ; and to
stay the uplifted foot, and *not* kick them into the canal,
but go away near weeping—in silence ; alone, alone ! '

In writing to Milnes a few days later, he indulged his
friend's delight in divinity by telling him that the
Belgians " still had a remnant of quasi-worship among them
(respectabler than our ' sincere cant '), and crowds of the
nastiest ugly fat priests, whom you could not occasionally
divest yourself of a horrible passing desire to slaughter, and
cure as bacon." ³
It was a sultry noisy night in their hotel in Ghent, and
about five in the morning the clang of St. Michael's great
bell sounded like a gong hanging overhead, and left him only
the consolation to think that perhaps Philip van Artevelde
might have heard the same.   Before breakfast he had seen
the Scheldt and some of the town, including the vegetable
market on a quay, and watched the sabots or wooden
shoes, and discussed them with the innkeeper, who assured
him they made " not bad walking at all ".
After breakfast . . . he went to see churches and noticed
that the votive offerings were " exactly in the old heathen
style, tiny figures of teeth, legs, horses, hands, in mother-of-
pearl, or perhaps in silver or gold—grateful acknowledgments
that by the saint such and such limbs or possessions
had been freed from pain or peril.   Wealthy liberality,
simple-heartedness, and thick darkness of ignorance
strangely looked out upon you as from past ages, here in
your own age ".
In the cathedral he found a " large squadron of priests
and singers busy chaunting a mass for the dead ", and " the

N

sound of them, a loud, not unmelodious bray reverberating from the vast roofs and walls " reminded him that
a traveller's description of the Lama-Liturgy in Thibet said
it was like the mass, as it was " distinguished for its *noise*,
harsh but deep, mournfully impressive ".

In an outer corner of the Cathedral he found two dolls,
the Virgin and Child—" literally they were dolls such as
children have "—before which sat about six women, " not
of the lowest class," applying themselves to prayer, and
while Carlyle stood gazing " speechless ", there :—

' Entered a stunted crooked-looking man, of the most
toilworn, down-pressed aspect, tho still below middle age ;
he had coarse sabots ; leathern straps on him like a chairman
or porter ; his hands hard, crooked, black, the nails nearly
all gone, hardly the eighth of an inch of nail belonging to
each finger—fruit of sore labour all his days, and all his
father's days—the most perfect image of a poor drudge ;
he, poor drudge, put two of his horn-fingers into the holy
water, dabbed it on his brow, and folding the black horn-
hands sank on his knees to pray. The low black head, and
small brow, nailless fingers, face and aspect like the poorest
Irishman—praying to the two dolls there ! '

Carlyle confessed to himself, " L'homme est absurde "
(man is absurd), and moved away, to see the big Town Hall
next, outside and inside, the law-courts sitting and the
police office.　He returned into the streets, which he
remarked were " wonderfully clean ".　He struck into a
narrow obscure street, dirty, ill-paved, where he saw poor
tailors and shoemakers at work, and many women " with
groups of dirty children and an abundance of small dogs ".
The doors were all flung open as it was hot, and in front of
one house, remarkably clean :—

' An *oldish-young* woman sat working lace, with her green
pillow and pattern marked on it, with many pins, which she
shifted according to need, and some fifty or forty slim
little thread-bobbins, which she kept dancing hither and
thither.'

" Dentelle ? " he asked (meaning Lace ?)
" Kann nicht verstahn," she answered, " cannot understand," which he had heard repeatedly already, as " the

lower class is still generally of Dutch dialect, ignorant
of any other ", and French is talked by the bourgeois.
Carlyle considered it " a very miserable thing, this of
an honest Deutsch people struggling to deny its Dutchhood
and become a kind of mongrel Gallic Celts ". However, the
Dutch was sufficiently unlike the German to make conversation difficult immediately, and he watched the lace-
maker in silence, and she made her dog be quiet and seemed
to enjoy being watched. At last he laid a piece of silver on
her pillow and moved away. He soon found himself at the
north-west end of the town, and " an accurate-looking steel-
grey man " answered his inquiries as he looked about, and
presently told him he was an *ancien militaire* (old soldier),
who had fought against the English and the Duke of York
in 1793. " Vous l'avez bien battu," replied Carlyle, " et
enfin c'est ce qu'il a mérité ! Il n'avait que rester chez lui
alors, je pense ! " (You gave him a good beating, and that
was what he deserved—I think he should have stayed at
home.) Whereupon the old soldier squeezed his hand at
parting.

The next building he entered was a church changed into
an excellent hospital. Returning into town after noon
he found himself among a crowd of working people, going
to dinner, clean and decent-looking, many women among
them ; and finding that in the hot weather many labourers
were taking their food in the open air, amid the trees in the
chief square called *Place d'Armes*, he sat down among them
and watched :—

' Their wives or some little boy had brought a jug containing liquor, soup, oftenest beer, or skim-milk, flanked by
black rye-bread and a stewpan of crockery containing
potatoes stewed with meat, eaten ravenously with a pewter
fork. The good wife sat by, seeing her good man eat ; what
he left, before taking to the liquor jug, he carelessly handed
her, and she ate it with much more neatness willingly
enough. They all wiped their mouths ; then tumbled themselves down for a half-hour of deepest ambrosial sleep. All
round this same Place d'Armes, sat, stood, or paraded itself
the flower of the Ghent Donothingism, Dandyism, male and
female. Sumptuous Cafés on this hand and that ; many well-
dressed Frenchified persons,' [but in short, as he had to
confess in the end] ' I did not see a single face as of a truly
superior man in our whole tour.'

They left Ghent about five o'clock, and sailed out of
Ostend in their cutter soon after midnight ; but there was
little wind, and instead of being home by Tuesday they had
to spend the day pleasantly loitering in " a delicious
temperature ", sitting in the shadow of the sails and enjoying
the sight of the clear green sea. It was after dark when they
saw the gas-lights of Margate, and Wednesday (10–8–42)
when they landed at Deptford.

XXVI

CROMWELL INTERRUPTED

(1842)

MRS. CARLYLE joined the Bullers, near Bury St. Edmunds in Suffolk, on the day after he returned. He spent five days recording his impressions, and then resumed his work on Cromwell.

One afternoon in August Richard Owen the naturalist called, and on Sunday, 28-8-42, Carlyle took his brother Dr. John along with him, and they spent two or three hours with Owen in his Museum. "Your friend Owen," Carlyle wrote to Sterling, "is a man of real talent and worth. Hardly twice in London have I met with any who told me a thirtieth part so many things I knew not and wanted to know. It was almost like to make me cry to hear articulate human speech once more, conveying real information to me, not dancing on airy tiptoes, no whence and no whither, as the manner of the Cockney dialect is."

Owen told his wife when the visitors departed that he was glad to find for once an author what he expected, and Carlyle, "as far as I am concerned, much what one could wish." [1]

It was not science that was making concentration on Cromwell hard, but politics. The Manchester insurrection in August worried Carlyle, foreboding "anarchies", he told his wife, "and a secret voice whispers now and then to me, 'Thou, behold, thou too art of it—thou must be of it!'"

Meanwhile the Bullers had driven Mrs. Carlyle to see the fine country house of Lord Calthorpe, beautifully furnished with everything but occupants, and she wrote to her husband telling how Mrs. Buller recalled the Paisley news of May last and said: "Look at this delicious and deserted place, on the one side, and the two thousand people standing all

---

[1] For additions and corrections to Froude, etc., see *Life of Richard Owen*, by his grandson, the Rev. Richard Owen, I, pp. 197-8.

night before the Provost's door, on the other ! And yet you believe that it is a good spirit who rules this world ! "

Carlyle explained to his mother why the poor little Queen was being shot at : " The people are sick of their misgovernment, and the blackguards among them shoot at the poor Queen : as a man that wanted the steeple pulled down might at least fling a stone at the gilt weathercock." [2]

From Wales came a letter from Charles Redwood of Llandough, near Cardiff, begging him to expedite the printing of an essay Redwood had sent to the *Examiner* developing the argument of *Chartism*. " Do not regret if they refuse you—perhaps rejoice rather," replied Carlyle, who had soon to confess : " You are not the first estimable and honest man who, with a sardonic triumph, has announced himself to me as an attorney." Redwood invited a visit ; but Carlyle could not spare the time for a visit to Wales this year. The most he could give to the country was a few days with the Bullers and his wife in Suffolk, and his concern about the rough realities around him may be felt in what he was writing to Emerson just before he went (29-8-42) :—

' You are a kind friend to me, and a precious ; and when I mourn over the impotence of Human Speech, and how each of us, speak or write as he will, has to stand *dumb*, cased up in his own unutterabilities, before his unutterable Brother, I feel always as if Emerson were the man I could soonest *try* to speak with, were I within reach of him ! Well, we must be content. A pen is a pen, and worth something ; though it expresses about as much of a *man's* meaning perhaps as the stamping of a hoof will express of a horse's.

' About Cromwell, one of my grand difficulties I suspect to be that I cannot write *two books at once* ; cannot be in the seventeenth century and in the nineteenth at one and the same moment. For my heart is sick and sore in behalf of my own poor generation ; nay, I feel withal as if the one hope of help for it consisted in the possibility of new Cromwells and new Puritans : thus do the two centuries stand related to me, the seventeenth *worthless* except precisely in so far as it can be made the *nineteenth* ; and yet let anybody try that enterprise !

' Thanks for asking me to write you a word in the *Dial*. I love your *Dial* with a kind of shudder. You seem to me

[2] *Letters of T. C. to his Youngest Sister*, by C. T. Copeland, pp. 125-8.

in danger of dividing yourselves from the fact of this present Universe, in which alone can I find any anchorage, and soaring away after Ideas, Beliefs, Revelations, and such like. I could wish you *returned* into your own poor nineteenth century, its follies and maladies, its blind or half-blind, but gigantic toilings, its laughter and its tears, and trying to evolve in some measure the hidden God-like that lies in *it* ; that seems to me the kind of feat for literary men. Alas, it is so easy to screw one's self up into high and ever higher altitudes of transcendentalism, but whither does it lead ? I dread always, to inanity ! " Stamp ! Stamp ! Stamp ! " Well, I do believe, for one thing, a man has no right to say to his own generation, turning quite away from it, " Be damned ! " It is the whole Past and the whole Future, this same cotton-spinning, dollar-hunting, canting, and shrieking, very wretched generation of ours. Come back into it, I tell you ; and so for the present will " stamp " no more.'

When staying with the Bullers he looked at adjacent Bury St. Edmunds, but was not thinking of writing about it. The farm-labourers around seemed comfortable. One day he saw a chance of making sure and questioned an old man who seemed likely to know and tell. " Do they drink any milk ? " " Milk ? Lord bless you, sir, they never see milk ! They take a little hot water with salt and pepper mixed to soak their bit of bread in, and breakfast on that ! "

That was on the way to Ely, and would be on Tuesday, 6–9–42, when he started on a three days' excursion into Cromwell's country, and rode in sunshine by lanes and cross-roads, through cornfields. The excursion was mainly Mrs. Buller s contrivance to keep Carlyle content " till Charles should arrive ", as she frankly said. When he came near Ely he admired the venerable and majestic cathedral, and made haste to enter it. A country lad emboldened by his example followed him in, and they two alone were there to enjoy the deep solemn music of the organ.

Then he discovered the house where Oliver Cromwell lived, and saw the huge " tithe-barn ", and smoked a pipe, sitting on the stone near the stable which had been Oliver's Horseblock. As he sat among the bagmen in the hotel in the evening he wrote to Sterling, and incidentally made a suggestion for the public use of cathedrals which some future Parliament may yet adopt :—

' I declare it were a good arrangement if they would but keep the music going in all such places, and sweep away the rest of the living lumber ; and leave one alone in these enormous towering spaces, with one's own thoughts and the spirits of the dead ! As the heaving bellows blew, and the yellow sunshine streamed in thro' these high windows, and my footfalls and the poor country lad's were the only sounds from below, I looked aloft, and my eyes filled with very tears to look at all this, and remember beside it (wedded to it now and *reconciled* with it for me) Oliver Cromwell's " Cease your fooling, and come out, Sir ! " In these two antagonisms lie what volumes of meaning ! '

He had a " crumb " of the broken " Horse-block " stone in his pocket as he rode away on Wednesday morning to St. Ives, where he sat and smoked in one of Oliver's fields ; thence to Huntingdon, where his hero was born, and after inspecting the pictures in Cromwell's uncle's house, he rode after supper to Cambridge in a thunderstorm. The Thursday was given to the colleges, and Oliver's picture was seen hanging in Sidney-Sussex college, where Oliver had been enrolled as a student seventeen years of age on the day when Shakespeare died (23–4–1616). Carlyle was back at the Bullers' that night, and used to wonder afterwards at how much he felt at home in Cromwell's country after seeing it so short a time ; but he need not have wondered—it was because he had lived there so much—in mind.

He had seen more than he went out to see on that three days' ride. He had seen " the Workhouse of St. Ives " crowded with strong men idle against their will, and it smouldered in his imagination till he set out the meaning of such a horror in words of flame in the opening pages of *Past and Present*. That would hardly be written before December. When he came home with his wife on Monday (12–9–42) he intended nothing but to continue at Cromwell.

Three days later, 15–9–42, the painter Laurence brought Edward FitzGerald to call, and their talk was about Naseby. FitzGerald's father owned most of the battlefield, and when Carlyle, who seemed " full of Cromwell ",[3] said he had been over it " in company with Dr. Arnold of Rugby, and had sufficiently identified the Ground of the Battle with the contemporaneous accounts of it ", FitzGerald told him he

---

[3] *Letters of Ed. FitzGerald*, edited by W. A. Wright, I, pp. 125–138.

knew the field well and they were mistaken, and had been misled by an Obelisk his father had set up. It was put on "the highest ground of the Field", and was not as they had supposed "the centre-ground of the battle".

Carlyle "was very reluctant to believe that he and Arnold could have been deceived", and said he "could accept no hearsay Tradition or Theory against the Evidence of his own Eyes, etc. However, as FitzGerald was just then going down to Naseby, he might inquire further into the matter".

FitzGerald suggested to him to come himself also; but he thought "it would be too expensive. So", FitzGerald wrote next day, "I have engaged to collect what matter I can for him on the spot."

On reflection Carlyle wrote a letter of instructions (18–9–42), which FitzGerald received before beginning excavations :—

' Profiting by the unexpected fact that *you* are now master of Naseby Battlefield, I have gone over the whole matter once more, probably for the twentieth time; I have copied you my illegible pencil-notes, and re-verified everything.'

These notes were much the same as afterwards appeared in an Appendix to *Cromwell*, and FitzGerald wrote to a friend that his description of the battle was "the best I have seen", and said he had shown "great sagacity in guessing at the localities from the vague descriptions of contemporaries". FitzGerald diligently answered the many questions sent him, and proved that he was right about where "the heat of the battle was", by discovering and reopening a big grave of the Naseby slain, 23–9–42. "The bones [were] nearly all rotted away, except the teeth which are quite good," said he. The nearly ninety-year-old vicar "stood tottering over the verge of the trench", and "two farmers" attended, "one a very solid fellow, who talks like the justices in Shakespeare, the other a Scotchman full of intelligence, who proposed the flesh-soil for manure for turnips."

Encouraging him to persist and "do me and the Genius of history a real favour", Carlyle wrote to FitzGerald among other things (25–9–42) :—

' The opening of that burial heap blazes strangely in my thoughts; these are the very jawbones that were clenched

together in deadly rage, on this very ground, 198 years ago !
It brings the matter home to one, with a strange veracity—
as if for the first time one saw it to be no fable and theory,
but a dire fact. I will beg for a tooth and a bullet ; authenti-
cated by your own eyes and word of honour ! Our Scotch
friend too, making turnip manure of it, he is part of the
Picture. I understand almost all the Netherlands battle-
fields have already given up their bones to British husbandry ;
why not the old English next ? Honour to thrift. If of
5,000 wasted men, you can make a few usable turnips—why,
do it ! '

Confucius might have written that. His contempt for
fighting was at least equal to Carlyle's ; and it is a Chinese
proverb that seeing once is better than hearing a thousand
times.

FitzGerald completed his work in fine perfection, discovering everything discoverable ; and thus commenced
one of the happiest of the many friendships of Carlyle,
extending over the rest of his life. Many a pleasant
evening " dear old Fitz " was to spend in drinking tea that
Mrs. Carlyle made, and many a pipe he smoked with Carlyle
by the fireside, or in fair weather under the cherry-tree in the
garden, talking or hearing talk at random. They differed
enough to be in no danger of monotony.

As for Naseby, they agreed to replace the " blockhead
Obelisk " by a new monument at their joint expense ; but
the estate was sold before they could set up their new stone
souvenir ; and, in spite of their united efforts at various
dates during the next thirty years, stupidity prevailed, and
the new " men of business " prevented it—which may serve
to remind us how little the English heeded then the holiest
of their battle fields—" equal to Marathon or better ". [4]
Voltaire was right, the fights that matter are really few, and
bygones should be bygones ; but all the fights in England
should be forgotten before Naseby.

Not long after Carlyle met FitzGerald, he had a talk with
Allan Cunningham, who seemed as usual, but within a week
sank suddenly dead. As a working mason of genius, he was
a curious contrast to FitzGerald, born into the upper ranks
of rich idlers. Stranger still was a " noble-minded beggar "

---

[4] Besides *Letters of E. F.* in two volumes, and the manuscripts in the
Library of Trin. Coll., Cambridge, reference may be made to *More Letters
of E. F.* (1901), pp. 125–32 ; and T. Wright's *Life of E. F.*, pp. 175–82, etc.

who made his last bow in the house in Cheyne Row in the same September when FitzGerald first appeared there.

Lhotsky was his name, a Pole, whom Mazzini had introduced last winter—an exile. He " spoke nine languages, had travelled extensively in South America, and given his name to a botanical genus ",[5] but was now without bread and clothes. Occasionally seen and helped by Carlyle, he called this September to take leave, as he was quitting England for ever, " being off for Paris ; thence if he failed, to America." To show his gratitude, he now brought "a most priceless Tractate on Death by Starvation in the Metropolis ". A sovereign and a suit of old clothes were given to him ; and Carlyle wrote to his brother (27–9–42) :—

' His silent bow when he left me was beyond any of Macready's ; low, with outstretched arms, expressive at once of gratitude, felicity, despair !—Poor Lhotsky, I read his *Death by Starvation* in spite of its deep sincere tragedy of meaning, with explosions of laughter.'

It was not the way of Carlyle to learn from accidental tractates anything that he could see. He could hardly walk the streets at this time without seeing frightful symptoms of distress, such as he mentioned in a letter to a brother :—

' Here at Chelsea, for the first time, I notice the garden palings torn up this winter and stolen for fuel—a bitter symptom, for the people in general are very honest. Poor creatures.'

The sights he saw and heard reported haunted him, and hindered history-writing. As he told Sterling,—" The two millions of men sitting in poor-law Bastilles " [the name of the workhouses] " seem to ask of every English soul, ' Hast thou no word to say for us ? ' "

There was more than hunger to be cured. In October he wrote to his friend Thomas Erskine, " Evidence " Erskine :—

' I wish all men saw as Emerson does, the everlasting worth, dignity, and blessedness of work. We should then terminate our Fox-hunting, Almacking, Corn-lawing, and a variety of other things ! For myself, I feel daily more and

[5] John Forster Collection, South Kensington Museum, London.

more what a truth there is in that old saying of the monks, *Laborare est orare* [work is worship]. I find really that a man cannot make a pair of shoes rightly unless he do it in a *devout* manner ; that no man is ever paid for his real work, or should *ever* expect or demand angrily to be paid ; that all *work* properly so called is an appeal from the Seen to the *Unseen*—a devout calling upon Higher Powers ; and unless *they* stand by us, it will not be a work, but a quackery.'

In the summer he had seen a Conference of Corn-law Repealers, but felt repelled, and wrote about them to his old mother in the pious phraseology familiar to her :—

' It became painfully clear to me that these poor people too had small chance to do much good. If their Corn-law Repeal were granted them, they would just go on as they had done ; amassing money, fulfilling their desires, their appetites and whims ; living *without* God in the world ; therefore, without sympathy for man in the world ; answering of their brother as Cain did : " Am I my brother's keeper ? " I paid my brother his *wages*, no more can he ask of me ; what more have I to do with him ? These men think, and practically believe, there is no other *reality* but money at all. They are terribly mistaken ; and will learn it by and by.'

He had begun a book on Cromwell in the spring, before Mrs. Welsh died. Yet in October he was soliloquizing with the pen in his journal :—

' I have not got one word to stand upon paper in regard to Oliver. Some hundreds of times I have felt, and scores of times I have said and written, that *Oliver* is an *impossibility* ; yet I am still found at it, without any visible results at all. Remorse, too, for my sinful, disgraceful sloth accompanies me, as it well may. I am, as it were, without a language. Tons of dull books have I read on this matter, and it is still only looming as through thick mists on my eye. There looming, or flaming visible—did it ever flame, which it has never yet been made to do—in what terms am I to set it forth ? I wish often I could write rhyme. A new form from centre to surface, unlike what I find anywhere in myself or others, could alone be appropriate for the indescribable chiaroscuro and waste bewilderment of this subject.'

He could no more rhyme his meaning than an ostrich could fly. Still less could he be in two centuries at once. His perplexity got on his nerves. The young lady next door was " incessantly " inundating his study one forenoon by piano-noises, which made him rise from his desk and walk about violently till at last he took up the poker and gave "two startling blows on the wall ". Tho quiet followed, the writing did not begin. The fact was that he needed a clear conscience before going down among the shades, and forgetting himself among the dead of the sixteen-hundreds, and he could not have that until he felt there was nothing left undone which he could do for the afflicted working people alongside him.

XXVII

AN UNEXPECTED DOCTOR'S CALL

(1842)

ON Monday, 17–10–42, Mrs. Carlyle had put on her hat and shawl to call on Mrs. Buller, when Helen brought her the card of an unexpected caller, her cousin Dr. Hunter of Leeds.[1] She hurried down, as she reported to cousin Jeannie Welsh, who had just departed for Liverpool, and found Dr. Hunter recognizable, but " so altered ! thin, bent, feeble, and in the act of unmuzzling himself from a *respirator*."

" Do not be alarmed, my dear lady ! " he cried. " At least do not alarm yourself *too much* ! I am not so ill as I seem ! " He really believed that himself, and when the first greetings were over, seemed " more concerned " about Mrs. Carlyle's looks than he expected her to be about his. Each thought the other far gone in consumption, and indeed it was only the doctor who was wrong. He told Carlyle that his own spitting of blood was all brought on by over-excitement, and had nothing to do with consumption, " for tho there is a strong consumptive tendency in *this* family," —with a courteous bow towards Mrs. Carlyle—" it all came by old Mr. Welsh's side." He had just come from the Isle of Wight, and was to go to Hastings for the winter, and next winter to Madeira. But " Dear ! Dear ! " he cried, as he looked at Mrs. Carlyle, and put finger and thumb on the hollows of his own cheeks, " Dear ! Dear ! this is not as it should be ! " and he gave his head a great many prophetic shakes, as he looked at her. Then he said to Carlyle, " I am very sorry to see the way your wife is in. I must freely say to you, not merely as her cousin, but as *a medical man*, that you ought to take her abroad and use *any means under Heaven in the way of gratifying her wishes* to get her out of it."

---

[1] *J. W. Carlyle : Letters to her Family*, by L. Huxley, pp. 27–9 and 32.

Reporting to Jeannie, Mrs. Carlyle said her husband " looked monstrous glum " at this — " No wonder " Dr. Hunter " was a well-employed doctor among the women at least, if this be the sort of advice he deals in ! "

" At lowest," the doctor continued cheerfully, addressing his cousin, " I think you should try coming to *me* at Hastings for a month or two—the climate is fit for *weak lungs*. You would have the benefit of my medical advice, and would find Mrs. Hunter *a chatty body!* At all events—I do not say it to alarm you, *but merely in the way of conversation*—if it is necessary for you to leave England next winter, and your husband finds it inconvenient to go with you, need I say that in me you will have *a warm friend and attentive protector,"* in Madeira, he meant.

Mrs. Carlyle reflected that " existence on such terms " would not be worth having, but kept her thoughts to herself, and decided to seek advice from him about a pain in her side, which her brother-in-law Dr. John thought a trifle. Then old Mr. Buller came in with the news that his wife had " gone to the dentist ". So Mrs. Carlyle departed with Dr. Hunter to show him the best way home to his lodgings, and in a day or two she discovered from the doctor's wife that he had soon to die.

XXVIII

MAZZINI AND CAVAIGNAC

(1842)

ONE Friday (21–10–42) Mazzini came radiant to Cheyne Row with interesting news for Mrs. Carlyle, who hastened to pass on the treat to her youngest cousin, Jeannie.[1] A poor Italian had invented a way of regulating a balloon "as perfectly as a steamboat". A Tuscan Duke and Academy of Science had certified his model, which seemed conclusive to Mazzini. For a trifle of two thousand pounds the inventor was willing to sell his secret, and even to wait while Mazzini's "Association" collected the cash, provided Mazzini could find him work to live by in the meantime. "Then," said Mazzini to Mrs. Carlyle, " the power of directing balloons *ours*, all is ours ! "

" You mean that you would invade Italy in balloons ? " she asked. " That *the Association* would descend on the Austrians out of the skies ? "

" Exactly ! And I confess to you—you may think it childish—but there is something of romance, something which flatters my imagination, in the idea of *starting up a nation* in a manner never before heard tell of ! "

" A la bonne heure (Capital !), my Dear ! but if it be decided that we are to begin the war by personating the fallen angels, adieu to *my* share in the expedition."

" Now, why so ? " Mazzini inquired, ' with a look of the most grave astonishment.' " It was just in reference to *you* that I felt the greatest preference to *this means*—to think that you could go without incurring the physical suffering of a sea voyage and all the dangers—what shall I say ?—of being sunk perhaps by a volley of cannon from the shore ! And then there would be something so new and so—what shall I say ?—*suitable* for *you* in descending as it were out of Heaven to redeem a suffering people ! " " All this," wrote Mrs. Carlyle to her cousin, "with eyes flashing hope, faith, and generous self-devotion ! "

[1] *J. W. Carlyle : Letters to her Family*, edited by L. Huxley, p. 34.

There was something motherly in her liking for Mazzini, whereas Cavaignac made her look up. She wrote to her cousin this winter [2] :—

' Perhaps you may think with Cavaignac that (my) being stupid with you is a sign of particular affection. One evening that I was talking to him rather " *wittily* " (as I thought) he said to me *brusquely*, " Spare me your *cleverness, Madame.* Je ne le veux pas—*moi* ! " (*I* do not want it.) " It is not *my pleasure* to rank among those for whom you have to *make minced meat* of yourself!" Regal words, truly! as all his words were ! If that man be not an absolute monarch yet before he die, Nature will have missed her intention with him ! '

At another time, recalling Cavaignac's behaviour when his sister died in 1836, she said [3]:—" Cavaignac, stamping on the floor and repeating his awful 'Ce n'est pas juste—mon Dieu ! ' " (My God, it isn't fair !), " was not a *perfect sufferer*, but was one that I could sympathize with."

[2] Ibid., p. 75.
[3] Ibid., pp. 332–3.

XXIX

WRITING WHAT HE LIKED

(1842–3)

JOHN STERLING proposed to Carlyle to start a new magazine, and in answering (2–11–42) he confessed he had often planned it and would like to be an editor, "were the thing feasible," but he could not think of it now except as a sequel to *Cromwell*.

"Two things as you say, seem very plain : first, that there is at present no preaching in England," and in short great need of it, " and second, that the Printing Press is the chief Pulpit " ; but as for any " Periodical Publication of our own . . . difficulties are many; but the preliminary, desperate difficulty is always with me the question—What *writers* are there ?

"Try to elaborate the scheme in your own head ; make an actual list of writers—especially a list of ' people with funds ', that might be applied to ! I will give it more consideration when you show it me in that shape."

Sterling sent his list without delay, but Carlyle was not delighted with it, consenting only to " have this matter further investigated". One is reminded of Thackeray's " favourite scheme[1] of a weekly paper containing good work," which—"was afterwards carried out by the *Saturday Review*, with some modifications ".

Meanwhile the letters between Sterling and Carlyle in 1842 reveal what may be the most curious of their many differences of opinion. Referring apparently to Carlyle's suggestion in *Heroes* that we might never have heard of Shakespeare as a Poet if he had not been worried out of Warwickshire, Sterling pressed him to retract. He was himself then deep in the writing of dramas, and saw something little short of blasphemy in such a suggestion, and was surprised at the answer (21–11–42) :—

[1] *The Works of W. M. Thackeray with Biographical Introductions*, by his daughter, Anne Ritchie, Vol. V, p. XXXII.

' You ask me to retract . . . It seems a small request !
And yet when I think of Oliver Cromwell, the best King we
ever had, escaping by the merest accident from dying as a
grazier at Ely ; and Martin Luther, by the like from disappearing as a silent Dominican ' (or rather Augustinian) ;
' and when I look at myself, and at other great *un*writing
souls that I have known, and small unweariedly writing
souls that I yet know, it becomes hard for me to retract !
No, my friend, wherever I go or stand, I find the *inarticulate
dust of Poets*, Makers, Inventors, great struggling souls ;
and I say to myself " There have been millions of millions
of Poets, and hundreds of them have been Shakespeares,
perhaps thousands, or a higher ratio, since Adam first
put on fig-breeches ! " That in real sobriety, is my faith.'
And so it was, as Sterling quickly found, for the only result
of his farther persistence was to have it put to him more
strongly, thus : ' It remains part of a very central conviction with myself, which explains many things for me. In
good truth, *the enormous opulence of Life in this old universe
surpasses comprehension.* Gamecocks fight ; but the
million-millionth part of them are never hatched at all ;
they are eaten, by the legion, at breakfast as mere eggs ! . . .
Think, think ! '

While the proposed periodical had to wait for Carlyle till
the *Cromwell* work was finished, he continued unable to
begin *Cromwell*. As late as 9–12–42 he was writing to Miss
Wilson [2] :—

' Oliver remains unutterable ; he is clear, burning before
my heart ; but the means of ever bringing him rightly
before another heart remains invisible, impossible. There is
no use writing *another* dreary vacuity of a " History of
Cromwell " ; we already count them by the score. I feel as
if England had for ever lost her great Oliver. I write much ;
but it goes into the fire.'

Within a week more, his feelings growing warmer and
warmer about the " Condition of England question ", as he
had led the politicians to call it, he became like the friend
of Job who was bursting for utterance and could not hold in
any longer ; and then he began to write with gusto *Past and*

[2] *Nineteenth Century Mag.*, May, 1921, p. 810.

Present—it was like metal long in the furnace and coming out at last with a gush.

He could hardly hide from himself how much he enjoyed the writing of it. On Tuesday, 27–12–42, when he had finished for the day and gone out for his walk, a Member of Parliament called to engage him on the Corn-law Repeal side ; but to all such applications his answer was that he was too well convinced of the folly of the Corn-laws to be useful as a lecturer. To a brother he wrote : " I am already engaged for a far bigger *League* (that of the oppressed poor against the idle rich ; that of God against the Devil)." His wife had a dinner-party that day in consequence of having received from Charles Redwood, " the Welsh attorney," a leg of mutton and a goose. Dr. John Carlyle was there, and Erasmus Darwin and Alfred Tennyson, all in fine form. " Alfred is a right hearty talker ; and one of the powerfullest *smokers* I have ever worked along with in that department," wrote Carlyle. The other two admired the poetry of Alfred, which helped the harmony of the evening.

The life of Carlyle for the next two months was in *Past and Present*, and may be read there. " He works very hard," wrote his wife at the time. " All the forenoons till three or four o'clock, and often in the evenings also." By 23–2–43, he was nearly finished, with little left to do but reading proofs, and he was tired, and writing to Sterling :—

' Work is not possible for me except in a red-hot element which roasts the life out of me.

' It was John Sterling, I think, that first told me my nature was Political ; it is strange enough how, beyond expectation, that oracle is verifying itself.'

Emerson also could have said, " I told you " ; for on sight of *Chartism* he had prophesied (21–4–40) : " The book itself instructed me to look for more. It stands as a pre-liminary word, and you will one day, when the fact itself is riper, write the second lesson ; or those whom you have influenced will."

By the end of February the printers were at work on *Past and Present*, and on 8–3–43 Carlyle was writing serenely to the young lady next door to beg her to keep the piano silent every day till 2 o'clock, declaring he was sure that " a young beautiful female soul, working in the most beautiful element, that of *music*, would not willingly give annoyance to any fellow worker". Her father called at once and everything was arranged agreeably.

Meanwhile Dr. John Carlyle, perhaps in the desperate hope of being heeded before proofs were passed, was voluminously uttering what seemed to Mrs. Carlyle stupid and impertinent criticism of the new book and saying: " I am sure you have formed a wrong judgment of the aristocracy—you have not had the same opportunities which I have had of observing their dispositions and proceedings." ' To which,' the listening wife gleefully wrote to cousin Jeannie, ' Carlyle who had been fretted too long with his *blether* answered—" No ! Perhaps not, Sir—I was never attached to any Nobleman or Noblewoman in capacity of flunkey, or in any menial capacity whatever ! ! " ' [3]

[3] *J. W. Carlyle : Letters to her Family,* edited by L. Huxley, p. 90.

XXX

PAST AND PRESENT

(1843)

P*AST AND PRESENT* was as spontaneous as *Sartor*, and as plain as he could make it. Lockhart wrote to him at once: " Thou hast done a book such as no other living man could do or dream of doing." [1] It was one of the sensations of the spring season of 1843. It was political and also pat—the country was talking politics.

It begins with ' the condition of England '—' some two millions, it is now counted, sit in Workhouses pleasantly so-named because work cannot be done in them ' ; and it describes what he saw in September as if quoting a tourist, ' Passing by the Workhouse of St. Ives in Huntingdonshire on a bright day last autumn.' Then he dwelt on the ' scenes of woe and destitution and desolation ' in Scotland, where hundreds of thousands ' have not yet got even work-houses '. He was as scientific as picturesque, giving in plain words the essence of what could be discovered from ' Factory Inquiries, Agricultural Inquiries, Revenue Returns, Mining-labourer Committees', and Law-reports amplified by lawyers in conversation, and reaching a climax, the horror of which he makes one feel: ' At Stockport Assizes . . . in the autumn of 1841 . . . a Mother and a Father are arraigned and found guilty of poisoning three of their children, to defraud a " burial society " of some £3 8s. due on the death of each child ' ; and the case was typical ! Then he dwelt on the wretchedness of the rich themselves. ' We have sumptuous garnitures for our Life, but have forgotten to *live* in the middle of them.' And restating the Sphinx-riddle of Life, he drove home as no European had ever done before the eternal fundamental right principles—that ' the great soul of the world is *just* ', ' Justice was ordained from the foundation of the world, and will last with the world, and longer,' and what was still

---

[1] *J. G. Lockhart*, by Andrew Lang, II, p. 239.

198

more surprising to the sophisticated savages in power when he wrote, that all alive have a right to work and wages.

' " A fair day's wages for a fair day's work ": it is as just a demand as Governed men ever made of Governing. It is the everlasting right of man.' This is not rhetoric. Carlyle put his philosophy of history all in a nutshell when he added : ' The progress of Human Society consists in the better and better apportioning of wages to work.'

The Manchester Insurrection was superbly vindicated against continental critics, especially for avoiding the waste of violence. Cromwell was glorified and the politicians mocked—their nostrums called ' Morrison's Pills '.—

' For Nature and Fact, not Redtape and Semblance, are to this hour the basis of man's life. The question is asked, not, How do you agree with Downing Street and accredited Semblance ? but, How do you agree with God's Universe and the actual Reality of things ? This Universe *has* its Laws. If we walk according to the Law, the Law-Maker will befriend us ; if not, not. Alas, by no Reform Bill, Ballot-box, Five-point Charter, by no boxes or bills or charters, can you perform this alchemy : " Given a world of Knaves, to produce an Honesty from their united action."

' When an individual is miserable, what does it most of all behove him to do ? All moralists advise : that the man patiently say to himself first of all, Behold, I was not wise enough. Neither with Nations that become miserable is it fundamentally otherwise.'

The conclusion is plain—to avoid mistakes in future, and for that purpose get better leaders. Which naturally leads to the second book—*The Ancient Monk*, Abbot Samson of St. Edmundsbury, a true story of life in England about A.D. 1200, and better than " films " could have shown it, if " films " had been miraculously taken then and preserved. For " films " show little but the outward forms, and the story, as he tells it, shows the spirits of men and makes us feel we know Abbot Samson and the rest, as we know the men in Shakespeare. There was no make-believe : not St. Edmundsbury Abbey rebuilt but the like of Abbot Samson in Downing Street was what he wanted. He used the old chronicle to confound the cash-gospelers and apostles of grab, as David used a stone to kill Goliath. The common-place reply to political complaints was that " the people " should be content, as they were better off than they used to be. Carlyle denies this.

' In no time, since the beginnings of Society, was the lot of those same dumb millions of toilers so entirely unbearable, as it is even in the days now passing over us. It is not to die, or even to die of hunger, that makes a man wretched ; many men have died ; all men must die—the last exit of us all is a Fire-Chariot of Pain. But it is to live miserable, we know not why; to work sore and yet gain nothing ; to be heart-worn, weary, yet isolated, unrelated, girt in with a cold universal *Laissez-faire* ; it is to die slowly all our life long, imprisoned in a deaf, dead Infinite Injustice, as in the accursed iron belly of a Phalaris' Bull ! This is and remains for ever intolerable. Do we wonder at French Revolutions, Chartisms, Revolts of Three Days ? The times are really unexampled.'

The rubbish of Ricardo and Co. was refuted like dead leaves smitten by lightning. The cotton-spinner " Plugson of Undershot " was shown to act in the very spirit of the Pirate Howel Davies, who " dyes the West Indian seas with blood, piles his decks with plunder," or the Red Indian Choctaw hanging up his scalps, and they were contrasted to their disadvantage with " William, the Norman Bastard ".
The feelings of respectable manufacturers and lawyers, deliberately declared by a very serious writer to be no better than pirates or scalp-collecting Red Indians, can be better imagined than described. They scoffed as the animals might have scoffed at the idea permeating the book, but it is now accepted certainty that every community, and even human society in general, is " a living whole " wherein the members have many duties to each other, which could not be measured in cash.
The Ancient Monk was picturesque history, more than equal to Froissart. It makes one of the pleasantest chapters in English Annals. All the rest of *Past and Present* was pitched in the key of a prophet writing to avert a catastrophe, and laying down right principles plainly.
" Society " agreed his politics were shocking. Even Milnes confessed [2] " It would be very dangerous if turned into the vernacular and generally read ". The " unworking aristocracy " were told : ' You did not make the Land of

[2] *R. Monckton Milnes*, by T. Wemyss Reid, I, p. 293.

England', and in short are bound to earn by good government the rents you get. 'There is not an imprisoned worker looking out from those Bastilles but appeals against you' in a way you shall have to heed, and so on, as if joyfully anticipating all that is known to-day as the gospel of Henry George. He did not stop there, however, but shocked the Whigs worse than the Tories by foretelling a ' Property-tax Bill and a still dimmer list of etceteras', meaning the Capital Levy, which really is what was known in England for five hundred years as a subsidy, superseded in 1689 by the National Debt. He gave credit for energy and such qualities to the working aristocracy, typified by the successful manufacturer Plugson, but faithfully explained they were no better than robbers, " Buccaneers and Choctaw Indians," till they worked for something else than selfish profit. Such talk of taxing the rich was blasphemy and treason then ; and " statesmen " meditated on his case. But he had many friends and no personal enemies, and a prosecution of the like of him might influence votes. Besides, his appeal was to the dear-book-buying public, the rich themselves in general, and so he seemed harmless, and escaped the fate of his namesake, the Richard Carlile who was pitilessly jailed for selling the books of Paine.

What also helped to make him safe was that he did not stop at politics. *Past and Present* was the application of the principles of *Sartor* to daily life, upholding the ideal of work without the hope of any reward—beyond subsistence—for the sake of the culture to be got from work. The practical men could not realize that a man of his mental calibre could mean that seriously. Another leading principle of his was the brotherhood of man, requiring us to be ever ready to pity and help each other. Altho that was part of the Christian creed, and may be called science to-day, it seemed a sheer absurdity then ; and he was deemed " eccentric " because he dwelt upon the shame to Edinburgh of leaving a poor widow to be starved and sickened to death, while he praised the noble negro women in Black Dahomey who succoured Mungo Park when he sank down to die—"a horrible White object in the eyes of all." At best the like of that seemed pulpit-palaver, not intended for practice. In the same way his talk about " the Inner Light or Moral Conscience " appeared to be Quakerism, and it was seldom noticed that to him the only " Eternal Bible " was Universal History.

One of the humorous passages was an ancient Muslim parable reshaped.[3] He compared the fashionable ruling classes of England to men changed into apes, " gibbering and chattering very genuine nonsense ; finding the whole Universe now a most indisputable Humbug ! " For the rest of his life he used to allude to them as the " Dead Sea apes ".

The Corn-laws were cursed as both a folly and a crime, in flaming words persuasive to sensible Tories, and it has often been remarked that his prophecy as to the result of repealing them has been fulfilled " to the letter ", a new burst of prosperity and then confusion, to continue till we mend our ways. " Love of men cannot be bought by cash payment ; and without love men cannot endure to be together."

In preaching the Gospel of Work he not only claimed that it was true, but also that it was the oldest of all religions, an "inarticulate, but ineradicable, for ever enduring Gospel". *The essence of education is to teach the habit of work.* His praise of it (B. III, Ch. XI and XII) had the rhythm of passion, the music of Nature, and should be in every school book. Nothing more edifying has ever been printed, and nothing more true, provided the reader defines aright the meaning of " Work ", and knows that it includes the search and discovery of what it is *right* to do. To do what you are told is the method of slaves. Carlyle was fond of saying that the eleventh commandment is—" Don't be bluffed."

In a remarkable chapter on " New Religion " (B. III, Ch. XV) he describes the Chinese ideal of an emperor or republican president, and the right attitude of such a person to various religions, and to the general life of the people. It had to be partly guess work ; but he guessed so happily that his description would have been approved by Confucius himself. Indeed it might be said that the gist of *Past and Present* was the same as the teaching of the Chinese sages— that the business of rulers is first to make the people comfortable, and then to teach them sense, meaning insight into reality and the right principles of behaviour. Assuredly the Chinese would have wondered less than we did at what seemed strangest in this book. There were proposals that seem now inspired, but at the time appeared ridiculous, for the public organization of material work, land and factories, education, emigration, sanitation, and much else. Still

[3] *Koran*, Chapters II and VII. See Sale's Notes.

more a matter-of-course in China and astonishing to the West of the world, was his bold assertion near the end of the superiority of naturally " gifted " men to all others. Genius he declared to be ' " the inspired gift of God ". It is the clearer presence of God Most High in a man. Dim, potential in all men ; in this man it has become clear, actual. I conclude that the Men of Letters too may become an actual Priesthood—so soon as there is nobleness in themselves for that. And, to a certainty, not sooner ! ' The book ends in rational patience and hope.

To-day it is merely literature to many, but it has been repeatedly quoted in the general election of 1923, and in 1843 it was pronounced " the most satisfactory thing Carlyle has done " because of its bearing on immediate politics. As was said at the time,[4] it furnished " material for thought to be wrought up into fresh forms as speeches, leading articles, reviews, etc., by the ' clever men ' and the ' rising men ' of the day—who in Parliament and elsewhere are, to an extent that is quite amusing, gaining a reputation for themselves by expounding Carlyleism into the vulgar tongue ". Disraeli and Tennyson were samples of this ; and perhaps the most sincere of all who might have been so described was Charles Buller, whose speeches on colonization must have been pleasing to his " old teacher ". By-and-by F. Madox Brown seems to have been similarly inspired to paint his famous picture, " Work." [5]

It was like Carlyle to be on his guard against the pride he felt to be besetting him. He wrote in his journal, apropos the reception of this book :—

' A word from F. Maurice in defence of me from some Church of England reviewer is also gratifying. One knows not whether even such things are a benefit—are not a new peril and bewilderment.'

It was only after many years that he heard how the book had brought him a new disciple,[6] John Tyndall, then a young man employed in surveying at Preston. Tyndall witnessed the soldiers there shooting the unarmed and starving men shut out from the idle mills and taking bread from the bakers'

---

[4] Letter of 1843 from J. Arnould, in *R. Browning and A. Domett*, p. 70.
[5] Now in Manchester Municipal Gallery ; see *F. Madox Brown*, by F. M. Hueffer, pp. 195 and 438.
[6] *New Fragments*, by John Tyndall, pp. 348–9 and 392–4.

shops. In the Preston papers he saw reprinted extracts from this book, Carlyle's appeal to the frequenters of Exeter Hall 'to open their eyes to the hunger-stricken, pallid, yellow-coloured " Free Labourers " of Lancashire. In one of these Lancashire weavers, dying of hunger, there is more thought and heart, a greater arithmetical amount of misery and desperation than in whole gangs of Quashees'. Tyndall procured the book and tells us :—

' The first perusal gave me but broken gleams of its scope and aim. I therefore read it a second time, and a third. At each successive reading my grasp of the writer's views became stronger and my vision clearer. But even three readings did not satisfy me. After the last of them, I collected economically some old sheets of foolscap, and wrote out thereupon an analytical summary of every chapter . . .

' It was far from easy reading ; but I found in it strokes of descriptive power unequalled in my experience, and thrills of electric splendour, a morality righteous, a radicalism high, reasonable, and humane.

' Braver or wiser words were never addressed to the aristocracy of England than those addressed to them by Carlyle. Braver or wiser words were never addressed to the Radicalism of England than those uttered by the same strenuous spirit. He saw clearly the iniquity of the Corn Laws, and his condemnation fell upon them, like the stone of Scripture, grinding them to powder. With equal clearness he saw the vanity of expecting political wisdom from intellectual ignorance, however backed by numbers. Hence the pressing need of public education, and an organized system of emigration.'

" But the best of his influence was on the young," concluded Tyndall, in retrospect long afterwards, and Carlyle wrote in his journal :—" I look at the disastrous condition of England with more patience for the present, my conscience no longer reproaching me with any duty that I could do and was neglecting. The book always stood between me and Cromwell."

BOOK XIII

REVEALING CROMWELL

(1843-45)

I

ABOUT SPEAKING AND READING

(1843)

WHILE *Past and Present* was in the press, Carlyle went to the House of Lords (9–3–43) " to hear old Wellington speak ", and said :—

" I found it a fine *aquiline* voice, quite like the face of him ; and got a great lesson out of his speech. I cared nothing about the subject, Lord Ellenborough's " Gates of Somnauth ", and thought the speeches of the others mere ' melodious wind ' ; but Wellington without any eloquence or freedom of utterance, humming and hawing, hitching and haggling for ten or fifteen minutes, made the Duke's opinion completely mine too. I thought of Oliver Cromwell, and have often since said to myself, ' Is not this, to make your opinion mine, the aim of all eloquence, rhetoric, and Demosthenic artillery practice ? ' And what is it good for ? Fools : get a *true* insight and belief of your own as to the matter ; that is the way to get your belief into me, and it is the only way."

He might have been answered that to get a true conviction of our own is the one way to be wise, but in a world of simple persons it is only one of many ways to be persuasive. There is less room for correction in an often printed letter he wrote this month about reading. He was attending a course of lectures on Geology by Lyell in the room in Portman Square, where he was one of a " square-jawed harsh male company of near 200 ", but it was not engrossing. He remembered an unanswered application for advice about what to read, and being now at leisure he sent a long epistle (13–3–43). It was speedily printed, and often reprinted ; and at last he obtained a supply of copies and used to send a copy of it to seekers for advice. So here it is again :—

' DEAR SIR,—

' Some time ago your letter was delivered to me ; I take literally the first free half-hour I have had since to write

207

you a word of answer.　It would give me true satisfaction
could any advice of mine contribute to forward you in your
honourable course of self-improvement;　but a long
experience has taught me that advice can profit but little;
that there is a good reason why " advice is so seldom
followed "—this reason, namely, that it is so seldom, and
can almost never be, rightly given.　No man knows
the state of another;　it is always to some more or less
imaginary man that the wisest and most honest adviser is
speaking.'

This was new in the west.　In Asia it has long been a
proverb that none knows the thoughts or the feelings of
another.　A biographer of Carlyle whose trade was on the
bench for many years in Burma often smiled at English
barristers eagerly denying this, and upheld Burmese witnesses
asserting it.　The letter went on :—

' As to the books which you, whom I know so little of,
should read, there is hardly anything definite which can be
said.　For one thing, you may be strenuously advised to
keep reading.　Any good book, any book that is wiser than
yourself will teach you something—a great many things,
indirectly and directly, if your mind be open to learn.　This
old counsel of Johnson's is also good, and universally
applicable—read the book you do honestly feel a wish and
curiosity to read.　The very wish and curiosity indicate
that you then and there are the person likely to get good of it.
" Our wishes are presentiments of our capabilities " : that
is a noble saying, of deep encouragement to all true men ;
applicable to our wishes and efforts in regard to reading, as
to other things.　Among all the objects that look wonderful
and beautiful to you, follow with fresh hope the one that
looks wonderfullest, beautifullest.　You will gradually by
various trials (which trials see that you make honest, manful
ones, not silly, short, fitful ones) discover what is for you
the wonderfullest, beautifullest ; what is your true element
and province, and be able to abide by that.　True Desire,
the Monition of Nature, is much to be attended to.　But here,
also, you are to discriminate carefully between true desire
and false.　The medical men tell us we should eat what we
truly have an appetite for, but what we only falsely have an
appetite for we should resolutely avoid.　It is very true.
And flimsy, " desultory " readers, who fly from foolish book

to foolish book, and get good of none, and mischief of all—are not these as foolish, unhealthy eaters, who mistake their superficial, false desire after spiceries and confectioneries for the real appetite, of which even they are not destitute, though it lies far deeper, far quieter, after solid nutritive food ? With these illustrations I will recommend Johnson's advice to you.

'Another thing, and only one other, I will say. All books are properly the record of the History of Past Men. What thoughts Past Man had in them ; what actions Past Men did, the summary of all books whatsoever lies there. It is on this ground that the class of books specially named History can be safely recommended as the basis of all study of books ; the preliminary to all right and full understanding of anything we can expect to find in books. Past History—and especially the Past History of one's own Native Country —everybody may be advised to begin with that. Let him study that faithfully ; innumerable inquiries, with due indications, will branch out from it ; he has a broad, beaten highway, from which all the country is more or less visible—there travelling, let him choose where he will dwell.

' Neither let mistakes and wrong directions, of which every man, in his studies and elsewhere, falls into many, discourage you. There is precious instruction to be got by finding that we were wrong. Let a man try faithfully, manfully, to be right ; he will grow daily more and more right. It is at bottom the condition on which all men have to cultivate themselves. Our very walking is an incessant falling ; and a catching of ourselves before we come actually to the pavement ! It is emblematic of all things a man does.

' In conclusion, I will remind you that it is not by books alone, or by books chiefly, that a man becomes in all points a man. Study to do faithfully whatsoever thing in your actual situation, there and now, you find expressly or tacitly laid to your charge,—that is your post; stand in it like a true soldier ; silently devour the many chagrins of it, as all human situations have many ; and be your aim not to quit it without doing all that it, at least, required of you. A man perfects himself by work much more than by reading. They are a growing kind of men that can wisely combine the two things : wisely, valiantly, can do what is laid to their hand in the present sphere, and prepare themselves

P

withal for doing other wider things, if such lie before them.
With many good wishes and encouragements, I remain,
yours sincerely,

'THOMAS CARLYLE.'

This letter deserves the heed that men have paid to it.
Its hints are helpful in more than the choice of books, for
it shows how to seek the right solution of the daily lifelong
problem of what it is right to do, to see what is what, and
without self-deception harmonize our duty and inclination.

II

DEBATE WITH LEIGH HUNT

(1843)

G. L. CRAIK was a journalist and man of letters who had come from Scotland to London before Carlyle,[1] and been a friend of his all along. His house in Cromwell Lane, between Brompton and Kensington, where the Natural History Museum stands to-day [2], was the scene of a talk reported by R. H. Horne in his book *New Spirit of the Age*. It has been often quoted, and " it is true in every detail ", said Craik himself.[1]

' Leigh Hunt and Carlyle were once present among a small party of men. The conversation rested with these two—both first-rate talkers, and the others sat well pleased to listen. Leigh Hunt had said something about the Islands of the Blest, or El Dorado, or the Millennium, and was flowing on in his bright and hopeful way, when Carlyle dropped some heavy tree-trunk across Hunt's pleasant stream, and banked it up with philosophical doubts and objections at every interval of the speaker's joyous progress. But the unmitigated Hunt never ceased his overflowing anticipations, nor the saturnine Carlyle his infinite demurs to these finite flourishings. The listeners laughed and applauded by turns; and had now fairly pitted them against each other . . .

' The contest continued with all that ready wit and philosphy, that mixture of pleasantry and profundity, that extensive knowledge of books and character, with their ready application in argument or illustration, and that perfect ease and good-nature which distinguished each of these men. The opponents were so well matched that it was quite clear the contest would never come to an end. But the night was far advanced, and the party broke up.

---

[1] Told by G. L. Craik to David Masson and by David Masson to D. A. W. on 6–1–97.

[2] Letter from Sir Henry Craik, his nephew, to D. A. W. in 1915.

They all sallied forth and leaving the close room, the candles and the arguments behind them, suddenly found themselves in presence of a most brilliant star-light night. They all looked up. 'Now,' thought Hunt, 'Carlyle's done for! He can have no answer to that!' "There!" shouted Hunt, "look up there, look at that glorious harmony, that sings with infinite voices an eternal song of hope in the soul of man."

'Carlyle looked up. They all remained silent to hear what he would say. They began to think he was silenced at last—he was a mortal man. But out of that silence came a few low-toned words, in a broad Scotch accent. And who on earth could have anticipated what the voice said? "Eh! It's a *sad* sight!" Hunt sat down on a stone step. They all laughed—then looked very thoughtful. Had the finite measured itself with infinity instead of surrendering itself up to the influence? Again they laughed—then bade each other good-night, and betook themselves homeward with slow and serious pace.'

Mr. Horne occasionally visited Carlyle; and when writing his book inquired what he wanted to have told. "Nothing at all," was the answer; and what is still readable there was put together without his connivance; and before it came out, here is what he wrote, soliloquizing with the pen (1843) :—

'What have I to do with their "Spirits of the Age"? To have my "life" surveyed and commented on by all men even wisely is no object with me, but rather the opposite; how much less to have it done *unwisely!* The world has no business with my life; the world will never know my life, if it should write and read a hundred biographies of me. The main facts of it even are known, and are likely to be known, to myself alone of created men. The "goose goddess" which they call "fame". *Ach Gott!*'

This was written for his own eyes only, and has been quite misunderstood. That "the world would never know one's life" was a commonplace to the pious people among whom he was bred. He was articulating in his own way what he had learned from them. "Man is a great deep," said St. Augustine, "and the hairs of his head are easier to be numbered than his feelings and the beatings of his heart."

III

GERALDINE JEWSBURY

GERALDINE JEWSBURY might have been feeling without any piety the same sentiments when *Past and Present* was in proofsheets. She was staying five weeks with the Carlyles at Cheyne Row (6–2–43 to 11–3–43), and fulfilling the worst fears of her hostess. Mrs. Carlyle had hesitated to invite her, as she confessed to her cousin Jeannie, in explaining how it came about. In January she had been lamenting her headaches to her husband, and complaining of loneliness, and in reading to him a letter from Geraldine said she was " after all a good little soul ". What she does not appear to have explained to him was that she and Mrs. Paulet had been finding fault with Geraldine for indecent writing, and the young woman was now repentant. So he said, " You should ask her to come up here for a little while ; it might be of great use to her." Mrs. Carlyle was surprised, and sat staring at him without answering till he said : " Why, you seem doubtful about it. She is very easy to do with, is she not ? And you like her company ? " " Oh, as to the *doing with*, I have no misgivings about *that*, but . . ." " But what ? " " Why, I am afraid that having her beside me from morning till night would be dreadfully wearing ! "

" You had Jeannie beside you from morning to night— what would be the difference ? "

" Jeannie ! Jeannie was not always in a state of emotion ! dropping hot tears on my hands, and watching me and fussing me, as Geraldine does ! "

" Oh, as you like ! only I think it would be a kindness to *the poor lonely girl*—and that her company might be useful to yourself when you have so little of mine."

Mrs. Carlyle " lay awake half that night " considering whether to risk a guest with " a born *spirit of intrigue* ". She told her cousin, bidding her burn the letter, which was never done, " I am not jealous of my husband. I have his habit of preference for me over all other women (and *habits* are much stronger in him than *passions*)," and so on— in short Carlyle was the right sort of man, who takes a wife and then thinks no more of the sex as a sex, but attending

213

to other things becomes, if possible, more serene than Brigham
Young himself on sexual subjects. Wherein he was not
nearly so odd as Geraldine Jewsbury and Mr. Froude supposed.

So Geraldine was invited, and came joyfully, and feeling
like the girl in the song—" I'm now more than twenty, my
time is but small "—she threw herself at several men in
sight, Mazzini, Dr. John Carlyle and Erasmus Darwin,
eligible bachelors all three, but also and most of all at her
hostess's husband, who could not run away from her so
easily as the others when she was in the house. Before the
end of February Mrs. Carlyle was telling her cousin " Of
Carlyle she sees very little, for ever since she came he has sat
upstairs in the evenings as well as in the forenoons . . .
Carlyle made a grand mistake when he held this Geraldine
up to me as something superlative—she is sharp as a meat
axe—but as narrow—there is no *breadth* of character in her,
and no basis of truth: she is ' nothing but just a fluff of
feathers ' ".

It may have been to open his eyes that she risked inviting
Geraldine, and if so she had gained her object by March, when
she was able to announce " Even Carlyle has come to the
conclusion that ' that girl is an incurable fool—and *it is a
mercy for her she is so ill-looking !* ' "

On 12–3–43, the day after Geraldine's departure, Mrs.
Carlyle was describing to her cousin with mockery Geraldine's
" *cant* of sensibility " and readiness to feign and flatter
insincerely. Her tears were always on tap, " but with no
more *real* sorrow in them than there is in drops of rain or in
drops of steam. It must have been from seeing such women
in tears that " in short there is a proverb, ' It's no more
wonder to see a woman weep than to see a goose go barefoot.'

" She is gone," Mrs. Carlyle continued, " and my good
wishes go with her, and abide with her, so long as she keeps
far away ! But never let us try to live under the same roof
again . . . Carlyle seems not a whit less relieved than
myself—altho he had so little of her. He said last night,
' Oh, my dear, what a blessing it is to be able to sit here in
peace without having that dreadful young woman gazing
at me ! ' To be sure, she did *gaze* at him—and try all sorts
of *seductions* on him, but the poor man proved absolutely
unseducible. Even when she took the strong measure
of stretching herself on the hearthrug at his feet and sleeping
there—in the manner of Ruth—all that came of it was a
remark to me afterwards that he ' looked at her face when

she was lying sleeping on the rug and could not help thinking how like she was to an old snap-wife ! ' " (An old woman selling ginger-snaps on a market day at Ecclefechan.)

The lady whom Geraldine visited next for some weeks had also a husband, and the ever-hopeful Geraldine tried him too—alas, in vain ! The husband behaved like Carlyle— " he will not be a moment alone with me," she complained. It was a habit of Geraldine's to be a terror to husbands, her friends admit ; and married women are not likely to blame Mrs. Carlyle for writing to Jeannie in April, " She is ' a vile creature '—and that is the short and long of it." [3]   But that was too severe.   Mrs. Carlyle discovered that the unfortunate Geraldine had recourse to married men only as a makeshift, because the bachelors she selected ran away.   Her servility and flattery that seemed to Mrs. Carlyle shameful were not altogether so, but partly womanly humility.   In an undated letter she sent Mrs. Carlyle [4] she told how she endured her brother's nagging, and concluded :   " ' He that is down need fear no fall, he that is low no pride,' as old John Bunyan says . . . I have a theory that ' the patient Griselda ' was *me* in a previous existence."

Within four months of the reprobation of Geraldine in April, Mrs. Carlyle was telling Jeannie how she was relenting, and when Geraldine returned to London the reconciliation was soon complete [3] :—

' I received her very coldly, but there is no quarrelling with that creature !   Before she had been in five minutes she sat down on the floor at my feet and untied my shoe-strings.   " What are you doing ? " I asked.   " Why my dear, I am merely going to rub your feet—you look starved—I am sure your feet have not got well rubbed since I did it myself last year ! " and all the two days she did not leave off rubbing my feet whether I would or no for a quarter of an hour together.   I never saw her look so well—she actually looked like a *woman*—not as formerly like a little boy in petticoats.   Whether it be her love affair that has developed some new thing in her I cannot say ; but there was now and then a gleam on her face that was *attractive*—I could now fancy a *man* marrying her ! '

[3] Besides other letters, etc., see *J. W. Carlyle : Letters to her Family,* edited by L. Huxley, pp. 61, 82–90, 96–7, 114, 134–5, 243.
[4] Letters *of G. E. Jewsbury to J. W. Carlyle,* by Mrs. Ireland, pp. 94–5.

" The love affair " Mrs. Carlyle had in mind was with a
man called " Q " in these letters. " In a fit of distraction,"
according to Mrs. Carlyle, " Q " took to writing Geraldine
letters of criticism about her improper fiction, and when
she " offered herself to him on paper " he went to Manchester
to look at her, and accepted her proposal and was ready to
complete the transaction. But her brother Frank objected,
and repeatedly wrote to Mrs. Carlyle, entreating her to
interfere, and Geraldine was also writing to her, and so was
the unfortunate " Q ", and Mrs. Paulet, with whom he was
staying. In short, the great question was put before
Mrs. Carlyle as informal arbitrator. " O write to me," said
Geraldine, " *Can* I break off ? For I am *frightened* out of all
love." The answer was plain : " Certainly, only fools marry
for the sheer sake of keeping their promise." In a few weeks
Mrs. Carlyle was able to tell that her advice had been taken.

' The whole affair is blown up—for the present—but I
am greatly mistaken if Geraldine, so soon as she finds the
man takes no further notice of her, do not be at him again—
and he is such a simpleton, poor Q, that anybody with half
Geraldine's art might wheedle him into anything.'

What saved the poor man seems to have been Geraldine's
adoration of a " Mussulman ", *alias* an " Egyptian ", in
whose company she and her brother Frank went off to Paris
for a change. If the guess is right that her hero was
Colonel Selves, the Suleiman Pasha of Lord Houghton's
Monographs, she showed good taste, for Selves was a fine
sample of the officers of Napoleon's army. He had gone to
Egypt after Waterloo and been welcomed by Mehemet Ali,
who employed him in shaping an Egyptian army on
European lines. He lived long in prosperous luxury,
having become a Muslim and married a good Greek slave
he had bought. His private purpose in now coming west had
been to leave a son in France for his education ; but he liked
men and women of letters, and when Geraldine, now a
famous fictioneer, was openly adoring him and sitting on a
footstool at his feet, he responded like a gentleman and
promised to write to her. So for a year or two Mrs. Paulet
and Mrs. Carlyle were often laughing at Geraldine and her
Egyptian, and her frantic excitement whenever a letter
came to her from Egypt. She felt prepared to be one of his
wives—her ignorance of Muslim family life was complete.
The faithful Greek woman who was the mother of his children

for my part I am singularly inaccessible to jealousy, and am
pleased rather that he has found *one* agreeable house to
which he goes regularly—one evening in the week at least—
and then he visits them at their " farm " on Sundays, and
there are flights of charming little notes always coming.
Mrs. Buller in her graceful quizzical way insisted I should
" see a little into the thing with my own eyes ".' So, in
short, she had gone to Mrs. Buller's by appointment one
Monday at seven and seen " the Intellectual Circe " at
leisure, and told Jeannie now : ' Lady Harriet—I liked her
on the whole—she is immensely *large*—might easily have
been one of the *ugliest* women living—but *is* almost beautiful,
simply through the intelligence and cordiality of her
expression—I saw nothing of the impertinence and hauteur
which people impute to her—only a certain *brusquerie* of
manner, which seemed to me to proceed from exuberant
spirits and absence of all affectation. She is unquestionably
very clever—just the *wittiest* woman I have seen—but with
many aristocratic prejudices—a very lovable spoilt child
of Fortune—that a little *whipping*, judiciously administered,
would have made a first-rate woman. We stayed till eleven.
    ' What *she* thought of *me* I should rather like to know—
she took prodigious looks at me from time to time. In the *last*
note to Carlyle inviting him to Addiscombe for next Sunday
she says : " I meditate paying my respects to Mrs. Carlyle—
so soon as I am again making visits—she is a *reality* whom
you have hitherto *quite suppressed*." '

V

THE DISRUPTION OF THE CHURCH OF SCOTLAND

(1843)

CARLYLE remained in London till the end of June. He took lessons in Danish by way of recreation and often breakfasted with Milnes. In Scotland the event of the year was the Disruption of the National Church, an evil deed of the London politicians, which, as an argument for Home Rule, is almost equal to the malt taxes which made whisky the " curse of Scotland ".

Carlyle was aware of how things were drifting, and through March and April, 1843, did all he could for his native country in vain. He was like a passenger in a steamboat who knows of a nasty snag, but cannot make the pilot listen and look and believe it. The old historian Hallam had the ear of ministers and cheerfully gave him an interview. Carlyle explained the calamity impending and how the situation was misunderstood in London, begging him to represent the facts to the ministers. But Hallam could not for a moment believe that clergymen would sacrifice their homes and salaries for anything. Why should not the right of nominating them be bought and sold in Scotland as well as in England ? He listened to Carlyle's prophecies of disruption with the serenity of an ox in the field, and replied at last, " I take no interest in the matter," and let him see he would do nothing.[1] Jeffrey did his best on the bench for justice and common-sense, but was overruled. The Tories were in power and unanimous, like Gadarene swine. Even Sir George Sinclair could not get a hearing—his earnest letter of remonstrance to the minister Aberdeen was useless.[2] The Disruption took place in May (18-5-43), when hundreds of the best of the divines of the Church of Scotland amazed the English by their great renunciation, led by the like of

---

[1] Told by T. C. to David Masson about 1844, and by David Masson to D. A. W. on 24-1-03.
[2] *Memoirs of Sir George Sinclair*, pp. 265-79.

Thomas Chalmers, now 63 years of age, and Henry Duncan, six years older.

When a friend brought young Francis Espinasse to 5 Cheyne Row this year Carlyle had gone to the country, but his wife received them, and Espinasse, who was fresh from Edinburgh, described his reception long afterwards.[3]—

' She talked of Edinburgh, and listened with interest to my account of a procession of some hundreds of ministers and elders of the kirk, through the streets of Edinburgh from their meeting place at the old General Assembly to the Hall of a new one.   Many of the ministers were old men, and all of them had given up their livings and homes for conscience sake, to found a Free Kirk in which the accursed thing patronage should be unknown.   Mrs. Carlyle declared that if she had been there she would have cried.'

[3] *Literary Recollections*, by Francis Espinasse, pp. 64–5.

VI

"ASSOCIATION OF BRITISH AUTHORS"

(1843)

REPLYING to inquiries from a man in Edinburgh this summer about "The British Authors' Society", Carlyle explained that it was "little other than a devout imagination ", adding [1] :—

'I attended once for ten minutes, in a tavern at Charing Cross, a company of some thirty very ugly men, not above three of whom were known to me ; I did admit, in a whisper, in answer to the " Hon. Secretary's " whisper, that the thing Sir L. Bulwer said appeared to have reason in it ; and thereupon, little edified by the physiognomy of the business, I took my hat and glided away without intention to return. About a month ago I formally declined to be a member.

'My decided idea is that " Authors " will associate and become a most stupendous Body Corporate one day ; but it will be, I think, " when they cease to be a canaille " ; nor while they continue one does it seem very possible ! Hunt merely for pudding or praise, we have, like all animals of prey, to do it in a solitary manner. Solitude and hunting are two things that go together. " Authors," it seems to me, are somewhat difficult to lay hold of and define in these days, not all who talk with Printers' Types are authors now ! . . . Success ! Courage, with or without success ! Yours very sincerely,

' T. CARLYLE.'

This illuminates a letter Mrs. Carlyle was writing to her cousin Jeannie on Wednesday, 3–5–43 [2] :—

'My Darling, I was hindered from writing by Robertson— who has been hanging about us of late like a physical malady— time after time he has come here—to bore Carlyle into taking active part in something which he calls *Association of British Authors*. If C. be either out or " engaged " when he comes

---

[1] *Glasgow Herald*, 16–11–1912.
[2] *J. W. Carlyle : Letters to her Family*, edited by L. Huxley, pp. 122–3.

he doggedly sits down to wait for him—three or four hours
it may be—an hour or two makes no difference to him !
And so on Monday he came in at twelve and sat till three—
in spite of all that I could prudently suggest about the risk
he ran of wearing out Carlyle's patience by urging him too
pertinaciously—I knew in fact that C.'s patience had
already reached its *Ultima Thule* (farthest limit), and that
at one word more on the hated subject he would certainly
explode on the unfortunate Blockhead. Accordingly when
C. came down at three and was passing out, *determined* not
to see him, Robertson intercepted him in the lobby and
thrust a paper on him like a bailiff serving a writ. Had you
seen C.'s look !! " *Oh Heavens* ! " And then how he fell to
brushing his hat, saying the while : " Sir ! I have told you
already I will have nothing more to do with that business."
" Why ? " says the other. " Because nobody but a madman
can expect any good out of it under the present circumstances ! " You can imagine ' (the rest in short). ' Robertson
went off in a *red* fury and left Carlyle in a *green* one. It is to
be hoped, however, we have seen the last of him *now*.'

The hope was fulfilled as she meant it, which was not as
we might suppose. The big and handsome laughing
Robertson kept out of the way till Carlyle was in the
country in July, and then resumed calling as if nothing had
happened. He was rather a favourite, in spite of his faults,
and never ceased to be familiar in the house till, after many
years, he *married for his living*, and was " happy ever
after ",[3] but residing out of reach of Cheyne Row.

[3] *Literary Recollections*, by F. Espinasse, p. 129.

VII

DR. FRANCIA, &c.

(1843)

CARLYLE and his brother Dr. John in equal shares gave £500 this summer to their brother Alexander, who was emigrating with his family to America, and soon was prosperously settled in Canada. Whatever it was that turned the thoughts of Carlyle to the West, he was occupied in May and June with an essay for the July number of John Forster's Foreign Quarterly,—*Dr. Francia*. It gives the essence of the recent history of Spanish America. Iturbide, "the Napoleon of Mexico," Bolivar, "the Washington of Colombia," General San Martin, and the great O'Higgins, "Director of Chile,"—all these and their attendants pass before us ; and when "sleek Fatpauncho Usandwonto, sleek aristocratic Donothingism" were ending in riot everywhere, the Gauchos of Paraguay made Dr. Francia dictator (1814), and he organized the force needful to make peace secure, and ruled them prosperously till he died twenty-six years afterwards, 1840, at the age of 83.

A lot of nonsense has been written about this essay by critics who supposed it a plea for despotism. It is not a plea for any "ism", but a picture of reality. Francia was an efficient and honest administrator. The later wars that desolated Paraguay were not peculiar to it, but the kind of thing that was going on all round—a relapse into the folly of fighting from which their Dr. Francia held them back for a quarter of a century. He was not a self-assertive quack of any sort, but an honest man, 57 years of age when made Dictator, and known to the people of Paraguay as their only public man who "would do himself an injury to do a just or true thing ".—

'Who knows but, in unborn centuries, Paragueno men will look back to Francia ! Oliver Cromwell, dead two hundred years ago, does yet speak. The meanings of the one true man, direct from Nature's heart, are endless ! '

VIII

GETTING OUT OF TOWN

(1843)

MRS. CARLYLE was becoming uneasy again at her husband's impatience of London. His brother Dr. John was beside them, and idle, and early in the summer the two brothers went together to inspect where Browning was living—Hatcham in Surrey. " He walked about the place," wrote Browning to a friend,[1] " and talked very wisely and beautifully. He cannot get on for the row and noise " at Chelsea, " and wants to take a cottage with a couple of rooms only, ' for,' said he, ' I can dress my own meals, roast beef and boil tea, do everything for myself.' " To Sterling and others Carlyle wrote to the same effect, and was by no means joking.

Mrs. Carlyle wished her brother-in-law would mind his own business and take a wife himself, and she cast at him many a hint, quoting a ballad Carlyle had enjoyed. One sunny day this summer Carlyle was one of a crowd in a quiet street near Covent Garden, listening to a modern Homer fiddling and singing with great earnestness a song of the history of man, as faithful to the Bible as Milton or Dante, yet poetic like them, and more English in details, showing Adam in Paradise like an English squire :—

" 'E 'ad 'ounds and 'osses for 'unting,
  'E 'ad all things was pleasant in life ;
The all-wise great Creator " (with a deep scrape of the fiddle
" Saw that 'e wanted a wife." (With emphasis on the " 'e ".)

On the last day of June, when he finished *Dr. Francia*, Carlyle wrote to Forster[2] : " I am going off for Wales on Monday " (3–7–43). " I have a sort of half-mad appetite for being left alone, in green places, within sound of the sea ! My wife is to remain here, at least for a week or two."

---

[1] *R. Browning and A. Domett*, pp. 54–5.
[2] John Forster Collection, South Kensington Museum.

His wife refused to take a furnished house in the country
or at the coast. She exhorted him to accept an invitation
from the " honest lawyer " Charles Redwood in Wales, and
was glad to see him go in that direction ; and once she had
him away, made him delay his return because " papering
and painting absolutely needed ", in her opinion, could only
be done in his absence. That was one way of emphasizing
her repeated determination never to quit the house in Cheyne
Row. The noises afflicted her less than her husband, and the
callers, who seemed to him a waste of time, were often a
treat to her. She assured her friend Mrs. Russell at
Thornhill, " I am better in health, however, and do not
dislike London, as Mr. C. does," while she declared to her
husband himself, " London, be it e'er so hot, is ne'er too
hot for me."

He passed through Bath, and, staying at Mrs. Strachey's
house at Bristol for three days, visited Chepstow Castle
for the sake of Henry Marten. If ever he had written of the
English Revolution, as he long intended, and as he did write
of the French, Henry Marten would have been one of the
finest figures. He was the leader of the most advanced of the
Parliamentary parties, and foremost in insisting that Charles
Stuart was a responsible man and not to be treated, like a
Pharaoh or an Egyptian crocodile, as an imaginary
incarnation of divinity. When superstitious sufferers from
the King's Evil found it difficult to get the royal touch which
was to work a miraculous cure, it was Marten who proposed
to satisfy them with a touch of the great seal—a bit of
English humour worthy of Shakespeare. Think of the
unction with which a Lord Chancellor Autolycus would
give the touch !

At the Restoration he was convicted of regicide and
received a life sentence, and was confined in Chepstow Castle,
where he lived to a great age and wrote the couplet Carlyle
was fond of quoting :—

> " Reader, if thou an oft-told tale wilt trust,
> Thou'lt gladly do and suffer what thou must."

On Thursday morning (6–7–43) Carlyle left Bristol in the
steamer for Cardiff, where Charles Redwood was waiting
for him. Redwood was " leaner than himself and about as
tall, rather younger but looking rather older " ; and drove
him to his house near Cowbridge, 12 miles to the west, where

his mother, " an innocent native old Quakeress," had a good dinner ready.

The place was quiet, the weather fine, and the behaviour of Redwood and his mother perfect. They did not show him off or bother him. So he was able to remain much longer than he intended. Daily he had a "divine forenoon" of reading, "lying under shady trees in the most exquisite summer atmosphere." The afternoons were given to exercise and riding to the sea, six miles away, for a bathe.

On Friday, 14th July, Mrs. Carlyle's birthday, a special bottle of wine was produced for the occasion, and they all drank " Many happy years to Jane Carlyle ! " On the Monday following Carlyle took the coach for Carmarthen, to spend a couple of days with Bishop Thirlwall—" a brave man tho a Bishop," he told his sister. He confessed to his wife :—

' I shall certainly not again be lodged so quietly anywhere. I find this Redwood a really excellent man ; honest, true to the heart, I should think. He has been entirely hospitable to me, is sorry I should go, speculates on my coming back, etc. The old mother, too, is very venerable to me.'

Meanwhile Mrs. Carlyle had been happy with " a painter, two carpenters, a paperhanger ", and three others working in the house, while she was writing letters in the garden and receiving many callers. The most interesting was Mrs. Phillips, " Kitty Kirkpatrick," coming to coax her to dine out, and " Oh, my dear, she is anything but good-looking ", wrote Mrs. Carlyle, adding " very sweet, however, and says such flattering things ".

Mrs. Carlyle felt she was more than a wife to her husband— she was his first disciple ; and it was in that capacity that she loved to parade any work she did in the house. She never did much with her hands, and suffered in health from the lack of physical exercise ; but she exulted in showing herself superior to the fine lady species, instead of trying to appear like one of them, as most of the " middle-class " women were doing. Thus on the day her husband was going from Redwood's house to Thirlwall's (17-7-43) she was writing to him :—

' This and the other person drops in and asks if I do not feel lonely. It is odd what notions men seem to have. When

I answered Arthur Helps yesterday, " Why should I feel lonely ? I have plenty to do, and can see human beings whenever I look out at the window," he looked at me as if I had uttered some magnanimity, and said : " Well, really, you are a model of a wife." '

Her female acquaintances made no such mistake. The " sympathy for Mrs. Carlyle " that some took seriously was really insincere. The would-be fashionable ladies pretended to be sorry for her,—needlessly. Even in these her busiest weeks, her main occupation was making clothes and finding situations for young women she was "mothering", Elizabeth and Juliet Mudie, daughters of a man of letters lately deceased, and Miss Bölte, a clever little German Jewess, governess and fictioneer.

IX

DELIGHTFUL DIVINES, &c.

(1843)

ON the way to Carmarthen (17–7–43) Carlyle was watching the people, and remarked that most of the women looked " very hungry and ragged ". They dined at Swansea, and arrived about seven in the evening. Bishop Thirlwall gave him a warm welcome and " plenty of good talk till midnight ".

Before seven in the morning a lackey wakened him to come to prayers " in Laud's Chapel of St. John ", and of course he went and watched the show without compunction. As he afterwards said to the sweet Charlotte Williams-Wynn [1] :—

' I had no right to go to a bishop's house and not conform to his ways. I was particularly struck by no one saying " Good Morning " to his neighbour, when they met in chapel in the morning. It was all very well done, and then, when we met in the drawing-room, came the human greetings and civilities.'

Clergymen unmarried should be on half pay. Even this fine bishop did not keep a wife. His life was in his library, and his voluntary work was rewriting the history of Greece. Carlyle " looked into about a thousand " of his books. The performing chaplain who was the only other inmate of the " Palace " was described to Mrs. Carlyle :—

' Good-humoured, entirely polite, drinks well, eats well, toadies as far as permitted, turned of forty, lean and yellow, has boiled big eyes, a neck, head, and nose giving you a notion of a gigantic human snipe. Is not that a beauty ? '

" You must feel something of a self-constituted impostor in your present location," she answered, but was assured

---

[1] *Memorials of Charlotte Williams-Wynn,* by her sister, p. 59.

he was " very glad " he came, " even at the expense of
sleep." She had provided a novel by Tieck for him to read,
and he found " the admiring bishop possesses a whole
stock" of them. Everything was " precisely the converse "
of the Quaker simplicity he had quitted :—

'It is wholly an element of rigid, decently elegant *forms*
that we live in. Very wholesome for the like of me to dip
for a day or two into that, is it not ? . . . Nothing similar
has ever before fallen in my way, and it was worth seeing
once.' [He did not need to underline the *once*.]
'Do but think of a wretched scarecrow face of Laud
looking down on us in Laud's own house, that once was, as
we sit at meat. And there is much good in all that, I see.
A *perfection of form* which is not without its value. The
bishop himself I find very strangely *swathed* ; on the whole,
right good company.'

They rode together four or five hours every afternoon,
the bishop doing the honours of the countryside, as " the
picturesque " was in fashion. Their ways of riding differed
like their ways of thinking. Carlyle was eager to gallop, and
so was the big horse provided ; but the good bishop would
only move " ecclesiastically " ; and the guest discovered
that whenever he let his horse go he had soon to rein in and
" lie to for his host " ; and Thirlwall, who had tried in vain
to have Milnes and Spedding in the house at the same time,
reported to Milnes [2] : " I mounted him upon a high strong
horse, and we scoured the country together, he with a cigar
in his mouth and expressing much compassion for all mankind, but particularly for the poor inarticulate little Welsh
creatures who could only smile when he asked them the
way,"—while waiting for the bishop to come up, belike.
" The sight of the gates and houses lately demolished by
Rebecca "—the Welsh riots against the tollgates that year—
" did not appear to distress him in the least."
A passing judge and twenty barristers came to dinner one
night, " a dreadful explosion of dullness, champagne and
ennui." The lawyers " filled me with a kind of shudder ",
he reported to his wife. " To think that had I once had
£200 I should perhaps have been that ! " It was to gratify
Thirlwall, who may have wished him to help to entertain
this crowd, that he stayed four nights instead of three ;

---

[2] *R. Monckton Milnes*, by T. Wemyss Reid, I, pp. 302–3.

and they continued friends, and Thirlwall hoped he might fetch Mrs. Carlyle the next time ; but Carlyle was never to come back.   Rousseau has well remarked, " However truthful a man may be, he cannot help lying occasionally when he is a bishop " ; and Carlyle could not but feel that it endangered his esteem for his friend to see him employed in his profession. So he now wrote to his wife : " Peace be with Abergwili," the bishop's place, " and may it be a while before I run across such a mesh of *forms* again, requiring such a curb-bridle on your liberties to observe them rightly ! For what we have received, the Lord make us thankful. Adieu, dearest, adieu—I wish I were with thee. T.C."

On Friday (21–7–43), as Thirlwall wrote to Milnes, " he rolled away with the mail to Gloucester, where, and at Worcester, he is going to look for vestiges of Cromwell." Thirlwall and Carlyle agreed about German novels and much else ; but when he praised " Old Noll " as a saint and more, a saint in practice, and said Naseby was like Marathon, Thirlwall could only shake his head like others at such eccentricity, and may have felt it a *real* kind of blasphemy— blasphemy to the Greeks !

Carlyle thought the siege of Gloucester, in August 1643, which nobody now heeded, a turning point of the civil war. The London shops were shut, and Charles Stuart, with his nephew Rupert " the Robber ", saw nothing but Gloucester to delay the sack of London ; but as soon as the signal fires of the relieving army were seen from Gloucester flaring on Presbury Hill, the gentry and the Germans with Charles Stuart packed their baggage and skedaddled—which now brought the historian out of his way to see Gloucester and look on Presbury Hill top.

He made up arrears of sleep there in spite of bagmen and barristers carousing noisily in the hotel ; and so at parting he was in such visible good humour that the waiter saw it safe to ask and got an extra sixpence, whereon he bowed so low that Carlyle felt like kicking him, and said to himself, " Accursed be the race of flunkeys ! "   But " Boots " beheld that bow, divined the reason of it, and begged and got a second sixpence too, " as they were never to meet more through all eternity."

From Gloucester he went north by train. At Worcester he surveyed the battlefield from Severn bridge.

' It was a most brief survey. A poor labourer whom I

consulted had " heard of such a thing ", and wished to God
" we had another Oliver, sir ; times is dreadful bad ". I
spoke with the poor man awhile ; a shrewd, well-conditioned
fellow ; left a shilling with him, almost the only good
deed I did all day.'

At Liverpool he wrote to his wife on 24th July that,
passing near some Catholic chapel there, and noticing a
great crowd in a yard with flags, white sticks and brass
bands, he stopped and went in and found it to be
Father Mathew distributing the temperance pledge to the
lost sheep of the place—thousands strong, of both sexes—
'a very ragged, lost-looking squadron indeed.'

' Father M. is a broad, solid, most excellent looking man,
with grey hair, mild intelligent eyes, massive, rather
acquiline nose and countenance. The very face of him
attracts you. We saw him " do ", as [Erasmus] Darwin
would say, " an entire batch of teetotallers." I almost cried
to listen to him, and could not but lift my broadbrim at the
end, when he called for God's blessing on the vow these
poor wretches had taken. I have seen nothing so religious
since I set out on my travels as the squalid scene of this
day—nay, nothing properly religious at all ; though I have
been in Laud's chapel and heard daily with damnable
iteration of " the means of grace and the hope of glory "
from that portentous human snipe. Not a bad fellow, either,
poor devil ! But we are in a dreadful mess as to all that ;
and even a strong Bishop Thirlwall constitutes himself
a Macready of Episcopacy as the *best* he can do, and does it
uncommonly well ; and is " a strong-minded man, sir ",
and a right worthy man in his unfortunate kind.'

From Liverpool Carlyle and his brother John went view-
hunting among the mountains of Wales, but rain and mist
soon sent them back, and on 4–8–43 Carlyle left Liverpool
for Scotsbrig.

His wife's letters were good reading. She told of a reference
to *Past and Present* at a dinner-party. Milnes seemed to
know she was overhearing him, and said : " Lord Ashley
is the greatest man alive ; he is the only man that Carlyle
praises in his book."

She also was watching a bishop, Terrot of Edinburgh,
once the professional Episcopalian at Haddington, and an

old acquaintance. He was in town and calling often upon her. She called him " Cuttikins ", Scotch for spats, from the spats which are conspicuous in a bishop's uniform. She wrote :—

' Terrot writes to tell me that he " did not like his reception . . . What did I see to offend me in him ? " he asked with great humility. " He was inclined to suppose that what I objected to in *him* must be want of earnestness ! " But he begged to assure me, etc., etc., in short that he had as much earnestness " as he could bear " ! A letter from a man calling himself Bishop to a woman whom *he* calls infidel, and pleading guilty to her of want of earnestness ! Bah ! I wish I could snort like Cavaignac.'

When the Bishop came again she told him that " warmth of affection cannot be brought about by force of logic ".

" You are right," he answered, " and I do not design to bore you this time." And they parted politely.

But before July was out he was lingering too long again one afternoon, and gave John Sterling a fine opportunity of showing his social " tact ". She reported :—

' John looked at me as much as to say, " Does he bore you ? " and I gave my shoulders a little shrug in the affirmative ; whereupon John jumped to his feet and said in polite undertone, as audible, however, for the bishop as for me, " Well, my good friend, if you cannot keep your engagement with me, I must go by myself—I am too late already." The cool assurance of this speech was inimitable, for I had no engagement in the world with him ; but the bishop, suspecting nothing, sprang to his feet, and was off in a minute, with apologies for having detained me.'

A few days later (9–8–43) she was telling of how John Robertson had taken her to see Father Mathew, now in London, administering the pledge on a space of vacant ground in Commercial Road.

" I dare not be absent for an hour," Father Mathew whispered to her, as she sat beside him. " I think always if some dreadful drunkard were to come, and me away, he might never muster determination perhaps to come again in all his life ; and there would be a man lost."

Next morning she could not feel " normal " till she had written Father Mathew a long letter and sent with it a

copy of *Past and Present*. Her husband wished she had given
something else, as the reference in it to the " stuffed Pope "
might hurt the pious priest ; but Father Mathew was glad
of even such countenance as Mrs. Carlyle could give him,
for he was the target of many enemies in England.   " All
the more " for that reason, Mrs. Carlyle said she was glad
she went, and demonstrated there was no fear of his being
hurt by a story worth repeating :—

' One thing they laugh at him for is, to my thinking,
highly meritorious. Somebody, trying to stir up the crowd
against him, said : " What good can come to you from
that man ?   He is only a Popish monk ! " Whereupon
Father Mathew burst out : " And what do you mean by
saying no good can come from a Popish monk ? Have you
not received just the greatest blessings from Popish monks ?
Have you not received Christianity from a Popish monk ?
The Reformation from a Popish monk—Martin Luther ? "
There was something so delightfully Irish, and liberal at
the same time, in this double view of Luther ! '

X

COUNTRY NEWS AND ECONOMICS

(1843)

AT Scotsbrig Carlyle wrote to FitzGerald, then in Ireland
(16–8–43) : " I do literally nothing." But what he
called " doing nothing " would seem to many hard work,
as he was intently watching realities around him. He was
sending his wife the current country prices and telling her
the latest wages for harvesting at Lockerbie Fair, " lower
than any man ever saw them." It was not that farmers
were growing fat. He thought most of the land was too
highly rented, and described how a well-doing farmer, a
neighbour of his brother James, was being worried into
destitution and death. He roundly declared " it is not fair ".
And here it may be told that James Carlyle was assisted
financially by his elder brothers on several occasions.

Rack-renting was not the only bad result of Land-
ownership Unlimited to be seen this summer. Carlyle's old
friend, the Rev. Henry Duncan, was preaching upon the
sands of the Solway or in a farmer's barn, driven by the
Disruption from the house and church which had been his
home for forty years, and boycotted by the landowners, to
make him go away.

Carlyle went to Thornhill at his wife's request, and visited
her friends and pensioners, and mentioned in writing an old
woman called Jenny Fraser. The Duke (of Buccleuch)
had decided on high that not an inch of ground should be
allowed for a Free Church in that region. No such
church shall there or thereabouts be. ' It is paltry . . . even
if a Duke had made all the land he refuses to concede a few
yards of. Well, but old Jenny Fraser possesses a patch of
ground, about equal to holding a church, and says *she*
will give it. Agents are at work. Go to Jenny, offer her
£10, £20 ; indicate possibilities of perhaps more. Jenny is
deaf as whinstone, though poor nearly as Job. She answers
always, " I got it from the Lord, and I will give it to the

Lord." And there, it seems, the Free Kirk is to be. I had
a mind to go and give Jenny a sovereign myself ; but we
can do it better afterwards. " Duke *versus* Jenny Fraser ! "
It is as ridiculous a conjuncture as has happened lately.
These poor people, living under their Duke in secret spleen
and sham loyalty, are somewhat to be pitied. " The earth's
the Lord's and no' the Duke's," as Charlie Rae said.'

When Carlyle wrote to his wife to send buttons from
London for the clothes that Garthwaite was making for him
at Ecclefechan, their maid Helen " tossed her head with an
air of triumph ", Mrs. Carlyle reported, " and remarked,
' Well, it's a mercy there is *one* thing which the master
fancies is to be got in *London* better than in the country ! ' "

Another perplexity to Helen was that the master's shirts
and drawers were made by his youngest sister, Mrs. Hanning.
It was fifty years after this time that Mrs. Hanning decided
to abate the guesses of commentators and told [1] the reason
why. In 1841 her husband had failed in business and gone
to America, and left her and her children " to shift for themselves ". He sent her no news of himself for many years,
during all which she lived in a house of her own on a regular
allowance from her brothers Tom and John, " from Tom
first of all, and then from John also," said she. She delighted
to make underclothing for them, and when either of them
was on a visit to Scotsbrig she used to come there and bring
her children with her and stay there to help in the current
work, and in particular to watch over their old mother
and prevent her neglecting or over-exerting herself, as she
was prone to do in her excitement, especially when Tom
was in the house.

Before August was out Carlyle was in Dumfries and met
there the Rev. George Gilfillan, a big " lion-faced " divine,
who had been prosperously preaching in Dundee for seven
years, and had safely emerged from a heresy-hunt not long
ago. He was one of the first of the flock of preachers who
found deliverance from doubts in *Sartor* ! ! ! There would be
a twinkle in Aird's eye as he presented the new disciple.
The three men walked together several times. Gilfillan was
full of reverence then, but said afterwards that he found
Carlyle " great, friendly, but on the whole a miserable
comforter ". Which may be explained by what Carlyle
wrote to Emerson apropos an article on Emerson by Gilfillan :

[1] To D. A. W. in Canada.

" The author is a person of great talent, whose position as
a preacher sometimes makes me tremble for him. His being
economically fixed, and spiritually with such germinations
in him, forces me to be very reserved to him." Gilfillan could
not understand that, but his wife did, as if by instinct. She
governed her husband and held him, if not in the " strait
and narrow way " of orthodoxy, at least beyond the reach
of the heresy-hunters.[2]

It was on Friday, 1-9-43, that Carlyle left Dumfries for
Dunbar. He went to Edinburgh by the rumbling heavy
coach at nine o'clock instead of the mail at six, whereby he
was able to please his wife by visiting the grave of her
mother at Crawford on the way.

[2] *George Gilfillan*, by R. A. and E. S. Watson, p. 76, etc., and Gilfillan's
own writings, and statements to D. A. W. by persons who knew him.

XI

EDINBURGH, DUNBAR, &c.

(1843)

A T Edinburgh on Saturday, 2–9–43, the same David
Laing, a Librarian, who had edited the Letters of
Baillie the Covenanter, showed him the books he wanted to
refresh his memory. He went that day to Haddington.[1]
On Sunday, Oliver Cromwell's anniversary, the 3rd
September, he walked to Dunbar and surveyed the battle-
ground and the old Castle. In his 23 miles' walk to and from
it, he noticed at Linton 150 decent Highlanders, " many of
them with Bibles, lying in rows on the green, last remnant
of the old ' highland reapers ' " ; while in many places he
beheld with " rage and sorrow " herds of ' miserable, weak,
restless " wild Irish", their conquerors and successors here.
Between Musselburgh and Dunbar they have made all
thoroughfares a continual Donnybrook. There is not work
for a fourth part of them, wages one shilling a day. They
seemed to subsist on the plunder of turnips and beanfields.
They did not beg ; only asked me now and then for " the
toime, plaise sur ". I almost wondered the Sabbatarian
country did not fling the whole lot into the Forth. I could
not do it myself ; I merely told them " the toime, sur "'.
He then had some days in Edinburgh to see old
acquaintances and look at new. Dining with John Gordon,
he was well pleased to meet the James Dodds whom he had
advised in 1840 to stick to the law for a living. Dodds had
done so, and was now a prosperous law-clerk, married and
living in Edinburgh, with " laughing eyes " at Gordon's
dinner-table, but ever remembering the dreams of his
youth. Not long ago Carlyle had been writing to encourage
him to do so,—" follow your star," he said, and added,—
" to writing you will come at last. A solid man knows how
to combine the ideal with the practical ; to do the *obbligato*

[1] *David Laing*, by G. Goudie, p. 76, etc.

better than another, and combine with it the *volontario*, which others think not of." Dodds was about to come to London and stay there on business, appeals and private bills, and was soon a familiar caller at Cheyne Row.[2]

Mrs. Carlyle's aunts and her mother's servant Betty had their share of Carlyle's time in Edinburgh ; but Jeffrey had most of it. In some ways they agreed now better than of old, and as if by instinct they tabooed the points of difference. Carlyle rejoiced to hear on every hand that " there seldom was a better judge ", and agreed with nearly all the sensible people in Scotland in blessing him because he blamed aloud his stupid colleagues on the Bench, and the still more stupid House of Lords, for delivering the Church of Scotland over to patronage, and causing the Disruption.[3] " Spiritual speldrins " or kippered fish was Carlyle's description of these other judges. He congratulated Jeffrey upon having escaped from his " old London miseries, like a sailor from shipwreck ", so that he was a " lucky man again ". Jeffrey answered some who praised him for growing gentler as he grew older : " It is poor wine that grows sour with age." [4] His house was livelier than usual at present, his daughter Mrs. Empson being there with her husband and children. When once they were all taking their places at dinner, Carlyle remarked, as he looked around : " When I was here before there was a bird . . ."

" Whisht ! Whisht ! " said Mrs. Jeffrey, too late. Jeffrey's face was flushed and his eyes were moist. Few living things were dearer to him than the pet parrot which had died ; and instantly Carlyle divining the truth exclaimed : " Jeffrey, Jeffrey, you're surely not going to cry over that horned beast ! " And they talked of Charles Dickens and others.[5]

From Edinburgh Carlyle went to Kirkcaldy and stayed with the Ferguses. While there his ankle was hurt by a horse he was riding coming down on its nose.[6] On Monday, 11–9–43, Thomas Erskine of Linlathen called for him and drove him to his house beside Dundee, to talk about Cromwell

[2] *Lays of the Covenanters*, by J. Dodds; and *Memoir*, by the Rev. J. Dodds, pp. 56–64.
[3] *Life of Lord Jeffrey*, by Cockburn, I, pp. 387–91.
[4] *Mrs. Grote*, by Lady Eastlake, p. 157.
[5] The reminiscences amplified by Mrs. Carlyle's verbal report to David Masson, repeated by him to D. A. W.
[6] Unpublished letter to E. FitzGerald.

and the condition of the people question. The good
St. Thomas or " Evidence Erskine " had been spending all
his available cash last winter in giving work and wages
to twenty or thirty starving unemployed.[7]

Carlyle came home by steamer from Dundee in the middle
of the month, and writing to FitzGerald (19-9-43) adjourned
their visit to Naseby to a more convenient season.[6] He was
surprised to find himself bilious and tired. No wonder!
He had been thinking of his historical problem everywhere
that he was. The subject had seized him. Yet when home
again among his papers and books he could not begin.

Chelsea was growing noisier, buildings springing up like
weeds; and on the fourth day a young lady next door
inundated his study with sweet sounds which were not
delightful. He told his wife that " there he could neither
think nor live ", and the carpenter prepared an estimate for
a room on the top of the house. But the cost (£120) was too
much to spend till he got a lease. He tried his dressing-
room as a study, but returned to the usual room in a week
or two, by which time the neighbour's piano was hushed
by friendly agreement " till two o'clock ". His wife kept
telling him the same thing as she wrote to her friend
Mrs. Stirling.—"The fact is, the thing he has got to write—
his long projected *Life of Cromwell*—is no joke, and no sort
of room can make it easy, and he has been ever since shifting
about in the saddest way from one room to another, like
a sort of domestic wandering Jew! "

He could not deny she was right, and settled down to
silent wrestling with his task, and soon we find her writing—
" The victim himself looks tolerably composed, ' consuming
his own smoke '." By October he had begun to write, and
then he let nothing stop him. The reviews and newspapers
were still full of *Past and Present*, but Browning, who called,
found him thinking of nothing but Oliver Cromwell.[8]

[7] Letters of Thomas Erskine, II, p. 34.
[8] *R. Browning and A. Domett*, pp. 93 and 98.

XII

THEODORE PARKER AND DAVID WILKIE

(1843)

AMONG the usual shower of Americans this fall—Mrs. Carlyle counted fourteen in a fortnight—there were two in whom she and her husband delighted,—" the best figures of strangers we have had for a long time," wrote Carlyle to Emerson.

One was the Dr. Russell who had been a principal promoter of the sale of the works of Carlyle in America,[1] " courteous, modest, intelligent," he " carries friendliness in his eyes ". The other was the Rev. Theodore Parker, one of the greatest American preachers, a Boston Socrates, with pug nose and bright blue eyes, and, as Carlyle observed, " full of decisive utterance, with humour—and good humour." [2] He had taken to preaching righteousness without any superstition ; and defending himself frankly when attacked, told the people plainly that the Bible miracles had never happened. He called the common Hell-fire Christians " Damnationists ", and attributed sundry moral defects of the white races to their superstition about the blood of Christ. So it is easy to understand why on this occasion when he had to travel for his health, there were prayers being publicly offered in many churches in America that he might never return. Even the " broad " Christian, Maurice, was distressed to see Sterling entertaining such a heretic ; but nobody wondered to see Carlyle rejoicing in him.

About the same time Carlyle was discovering that David Wilkie was a genius, and wishing he had known that sooner when Wilkie was yet alive. He had seen and talked with Wilkie in his studio, but the only pictures he then knew seemed commonplace. He now saw more, and reading Allan

---

[1] *Autobiography of Moncure Conway*, II, p. 104.
[2] *Works of Theodore Parker*, 12 vols., edited by Miss Cobbe ; Weiss's *T. Parker*, I, p. 233, and II, p. 459, etc. ; P. Dean's *T. Parker*, pp. 16 and 128.

Cunningham's Life of the painter, moralized : ' He rebukes me,' meaning—sets me a good example, ' by several of his qualities, by his patience, his submissive, unwearied endeavour in *such* element as he finds—a truly well-doing man. His " card-players" struck me ; genuine life-figures, a great gluttonous substantiality, some glimpse of universal life looking out thro the coarse boor shapes.   Alas ! Poor Wilkie is not here any more.' Reflecting how he himself was stuck in his Cromwell work, Carlyle was calling himself a " Slip-the-labour " in comparison, and felt stimulated by the example of David Wilkie.

XIII

TALK HEARD BY ESPINASSE

(1843)

IN July a friend had brought Francis Espinasse,[1] and Mrs. Carlyle entertained them volubly, for " this was never, in her husband's absence, a silent hostess ". Before the end of the year Espinasse called again by appointment. He was one of the Edinburgh students who wrote to Carlyle in 1841, and was now employed in the British Museum, and living in Chelsea lodgings. With the eye of a librarian he noticed Rushworth, Thurloe, Whitelocke, and other venerable folios of the Commonwealth period prominent among the books in the drawing-room, which was also the workshop. " Mrs. Carlyle received me amiably," he says, but she said little now. " It was with no small awe that I found myself in the presence of the man whom since boyhood I had looked up to," but " I was placed at ease " by his saying that he had found the streets " rather sloppy ", and inquiring about my " occupations and studies ". In the course of the talk that followed, Carlyle complained that when in Scotland this summer he had been " pestered with questions as to who it was that wrote this, that, and the other thing in *Punch* ", and other mere " trivialities of literature ".

Discussing Emerson, he said it was " wonderful how as a lecturer he 'insinuated' himself into his hearers ". He repeated " laughingly " the report of a friend who visited Emerson at Concord, and saw him take his " fretful and tearful " little son in his arms, and caressing him, Emerson said, " I will love the devil out of him."

Asked about the " Lake Poets ", Carlyle called Wordsworth a " dignified preacher and teacher ", but said " he had never given in to the worship " of him. On " Coleridge as a reasoner ", he repeated with glee the verdict of Hazlitt : " No premises, sir, and no conclusion."

---

[1] *Literary Recollections*, by F. Espinasse, pp. 63–73.

243

Something was said about Brougham, by Boswell-Espinasse belike, for tho he lived to do a Life of Voltaire and much else, he never wrote anything better than his reports of Carlyle's talk, which he delighted in drawing out ; and on this occasion he reports that what was said of Brougham :—

' Led Carlyle into a monologue on Brougham's vagaries after he became Chancellor, which he made the text for an emphatic deliverance on the dangers attending gratified ambition, and the duty of a man to remain contented with the position marked out for him, and not to strive for a higher one. It was not unusual for him to wind up a denunciation by discovering some good in the person or thing denounced. " Brougham's promotion of Thirlwall," he said, " would be placed to the credit side of his account. Thirlwall had to resign his tutorship at Cambridge as the result of his plain-spoken pamphlet in support of the admission of Dissenters to the Universities. Whereupon Brougham, then Chancellor, presented him to a living in Yorkshire, which enabled him to finish his *History of Greece*."

' Carlyle spoke sympathetically of the then King of Prussia, Frederick William IV, as placed in a difficult position between the claims of his hereditary kingship and the demands of Prussian Liberalism. On the whole, he was doing the best that could be done under the circumstances, summoning to Berlin men of intellectual distinction.'

Espinasse had soon " lost the awe with which he entered " and was entirely happy. As he rose to go at last, Mrs. Carlyle drew his attention to a portrait of Jean Paul Richter on the wall. He looked at it, and Carlyle remarked significantly,—" His nose is put out of joint,"—which was a perplexity to Boswell-Espinasse till he remembered Carlyle had called Oliver Cromwell " the best fellow I have fallen in with ".

Espinasse was soon coming often to the house in the evenings, and heard Carlyle compare *Sartor* to a stone thrown into a sheet of water : " I see the circle of its influence constantly widening." [2] He also said, " I saw that the French Revolution and German Literature were the cardinal phenomena of the century " ; and at another time, " If it

[2] Ibid., p. 70.

had not been for the French Revolution, I should never have had any hope." It must have been pleasant to Espinasse, as a Frenchman, to suppose, as he did, and he may have been right in supposing, that hopes of good from the French Revolution survived those inspired by German Literature.[3]

[3] Ibid., p. 219.

XIV

HISTORICAL SKETCHES AND CROMWELL

(1843-4)

AS Carlyle had succeeded with a history of the French Revolution, he was trying now to do one of the English; but he could not. The present spurt was the last attempt.

The difficulty was that fashionable fictions had prevailed so long that readers could not now be convinced of the truth without elaborate evidence which it would be tiresome to read. Some descendants of Cromwell in English society then were doing religious penance every year for the "martyrdom" of Charles Stuart, the peculiar "Saint" of the Church of England, and surely suitable for it—a *hereditary* Saint ! ! ! It was only among non-conformist Puritans that the tradition survived that Cromwell was a good man ; and in Scotland there was not even that tradition—for Cromwell had done what no other Englishman had been able to do, he had conquered Scotland, and the insult to the pride of the nation was too much for its piety. The Scotch feared him less than the Irish and hated him more.

In borrowing another book from Mill, who had already lent him many, Carlyle wrote on 9–11–43 :—" I have already tried it successively on ten or twenty different tacks, and been everywhere repelled ; and up to this time I but write and burn, and then write again, very miserably. Were I once into it, the thing would go ! Pity me, and pray for me ; and come to see me soon. Yours ever, as of old, T. CARLYLE."

" The fact is," wrote Carlyle to Sterling on 4–12–43, " I am doomed to write some book about that unblessed Commonwealth, and as yet there will be no book show itself possible. The whole stagnancy of the English genius two hundred years thick lies heavy on me. Dead heroes buried under two centuries of Atheism seem to whimper pitifully ' Deliver us ! Canst thou not deliver us ? ' I have lost four years of

good labour in the business ; and still the more I expend
upon it, it is like throwing good labour after bad. My only
consolation is that I am struggling to be the most conservative
man in England, or one of the most conservative. If the
past time cannot become *melodious*, it must be forgotten,
as good as annihilated ; and we rove like nameless exiles
that *have* no ancestors, whose world began only yesterday . . .
I see almost nobody. I avoid sight rather, and study
to consume my own smoke . . ."

The biography was blocked by the same difficulty as the
history—he had to be too tedious to be convincing. His
wife told Miss Bölte that he said to her one day in utter
simplicity, " Well ! They may twaddle as they like about the
miseries of a bad conscience ; but I should like to know
whether Judas Iscariot was more miserable than Thomas
Carlyle, who never did anything *criminal, so far as he
remembers* ! " This was because he could make no progress
at all.

He had been writing hard for six weeks when, on 18–12–43,
he came down stairs to the dining-room where his wife was
darning his stockings, and laid a great bundle of papers on
the fire. " Waste-paper," she supposed, remembering
thankfully that the chimney had been lately swept ; but
looking up at his face she saw a "grim, concentrated"
self-satisfaction, which let her know he had been burning
what he had been writing for many weeks, which he did not
deny, but said : " I have discovered overnight that I must
take up the damnable thing on quite a new tack." [1]

Two years ago, Thomas Erskine, the most intellectual of
his Christian friends—" St. Thomas " he called him in
distinction from himself as " Sinner Thomas "—had written
to him [2] : " I hope you are proceeding with Oliver's Life.
He was a grand fellow, and full of good English domestic
life, I am persuaded, of which no man could require a better
proof than his calling up one of the maids of his house, whom
he knew to be a Quaker, and telling her that George Fox was
in town, for that he had met him that day. His appointment
of Hale, too, is good. But it is very difficult to collect
specimens of the primary formation of such a man. It would
be pleasant to light on an early or at all events an inner

---

[1] Besides other printed letters, see *Last Words of T. C.*, pp. 290–6, etc.,
for a letter from Mrs. C. to Miss Bölte. An unpublished letter to W. Graham
fixes the date precisely.

[2] *Letters of Thomas Erskine*, II, p. 21.

collection of letters to show what he was before he made the move, or what he *really* was after it." There was no such collection ; but Carlyle had by this time the materials to make one, and he now decided to do so first of all, and set to work at once on the Letters and Speeches of Oliver Cromwell, " with elucidations." It was only after he had finished it, in 1845, that he discovered he had " said his say ". It was not till 8–2–45 that he even settled that this work was to be printed, and not to await the completion of a Life. But immediately he started upon it, in December, 1843, he felt that his difficulties were disappearing and he was making progress.

It was only his unfinished biography that he burned on 18–12–43. Some precious fragments of his unfinished history of the Commonwealth were copied by John Chorley, and published long after he and Chorley were dead as *Historical Sketches*, edited by Alexander Carlyle. Inferior to most of his finished work, they nevertheless make as good reading as can be found in books of English history. There are bits worth libraries of Hallam's and De Lolme's, such as this : " This king's power we said was indefinite, whereby he thinks it infinite. These Commons have an antiquity to go back upon which is also indefinite. Prerogative of Majesty, Privilege of Parliament, these are two indefinites apt to mistake themselves for Infinitudes." The strokes like that are rare, however. There is too much preaching. Yet there are some sketches as good as any in the French Revolution. One seems to see the execution of brave old Walter Raleigh. The tippling, hunting, idle James, selling titles and frowning down the Puritans, killing Raleigh unjustly by cold-blooded legal murder to please the Spaniards, and choosing a Papist wife for the heir of a Protestant country because " there was no Protestant woman of adequate divinity of lineage ", reäppears as if alive among a crowd of contemporaries, from fashionable poisoners and prelates, " little red-faced screechy Doctor " Lauds, and " Knock-kneed, tongue-tied, splay-footed " Charles Stuarts, up to Bible-believing gentry and godly divines, Cervantes and the great Shakespeare himself.

One feels grateful to Chorley as one reads it. The fact that Carlyle was willing to leave such good stuff unpublished reveals his character. He cultivated indifference to money and reputation with amazing success, and feeling " called " to show us Cromwell and his Commonwealth as they were.

he thought of nothing else, and turned away from the subject at once whenever he saw he had done that.

In one way this may have been unfortunate. If he had finished and published these Sketches, as Chorley advised, he might have been better understood. It was presumed that the champion of Cromwell was orthodox, and Evangelicals and Nonconformists were prone to suppose Carlyle must be one of themselves. The Historical Sketches would have revealed him better. The old myth of Heaven and Hell, for example, was venerable to him as it would have been to Confucius, only because it was ' the emblematic expression of a man-like sense of Right and Wrong. A man-like sense, we say, and not beast-like ; for the very beasts and horses know something of "morality", if this be "moral" : To know that on this side lie hay and oats, and on that side lie scourgings and spur-rowels. But to a man, let him understand it or not, his being right or his being wrong is simply the one question. The most flaming Hell he will front composedly, right being with him ; wrong being with him, the Paradise of Houris were a Hell . . . Man, very finite as we see him, is a kind of infinite creature . . . the thrall of this world, or its king. A splendour of Heaven looks through all Nature for him, if he have eyes ; if he have none, it is of course darkness.'

He went on to exalt the sense of Right and Wrong as the one thing that makes us strong, and to " thank the Heavens for Old Romans, Moslems, still more Old Christians, nay Puritans or Modern Christians, ' Believers,' each after his kind, Luthers, Mahomets", and so on. Which explains many a perplexing passage in his writings, where he used the word Believer and cognate words to mean a man who was earnest and sincere, and did only what he thought right ; while in common use the word believer meant a believer in religion, and here and now a Christian. His " Puritanism " also was defined in a way which would have shut him out of the pulpit of any church: "conformity not to human rubrics but to the Maker's own Laws." That was the Puritanism of Carlyle. Thus it is that the *Historical Sketches* elucidate his " elucidations " of the Letters and Speeches of Cromwell.

In about three weeks' time (9–1–44) he was writing cheerily to FitzGerald : ' Surely, if ever I do get this *Book of Cromwell* finished, we will smoke a pipe of triumph over it, and rejoice to remember difficulties undergone ! It is really something like the *sixth* time that I have *burnt* considerable masses of written attempts at commencing the

unwritable ; and to this hour it remains properly uncom-
menced. And it must be commenced and (if God please)
finished . . .

  ' One of the things I have at length got to discern as
doable is the gathering of all Oliver's Letters and Speeches,
and stringing them together according to the order of time.
. . . This I am at present doing : tho this is not what I have
the real difficulty in doing. I have made considerable progress ; time has eaten up most of Oliver's utterances ; but
a fraction still remains ; these I can and will see printed, set
in some kind of order.'

  Then followed details about letters and portraits which he
was hunting with the joy of an antiquary, and in giving the
happy news of a discovery, he reveals himself at work :—

  ' In the British Museum I find the *original* of the Letter
about Naseby, written from Harborough that very night
of the Battle ; I tried hard to find some shiver in the hair-
strokes, some symptom that the man had been bearding
Death all day ; but there is nothing of that sort there ; a
quite composed Letter, the handwriting massive, steadfast,
you would say almost firmer than usual.'

XV

MISS RIGBY SEES CARLYLE

(1844)

IN 1844 Carlyle can be seen in hours of idleness through the eyes of Miss Rigby, a Quarterly Reviewer, in the thirty-fourth year of her age. Tho she had the sweet face and simple faith of an Amelia, she was clever and well read, and could not be looked down upon by Carlyle, for she was as tall as himself. When she went with her mother to live in Edinburgh last year, she was welcomed by both political parties, and pleased by Jeffrey, a " dapper " little man, she said he was, " with splendid eyes, the youngest man of seventy I ever saw," and " the greatest artist " in conversation. John Wilson, old " Christopher North ", declared himself in love with her, and she thought him " a most remarkable man ", and " good and religious as well as witty and poetical . . . it will be a privilege to know more of him ".

She was in London staying with the Murrays at Albemarle Street when, on 27–2–44, Carlyle called with his wife, who was " certainly a more refined half ", said Miss Rigby. She described him : " He is an honest, true man, a character such as he himself can alone describe. He is a kind of Burns in appearance. We quarrelled about Luther, whom he defined as a ' nice man ', and I said he had nothing nice about him."

What a pity Carlyle was not so good and religious as Christopher North ! Miss Rigby must have tried pious topics on him without success. " Like a Christian," she says of him, " he sees the truth, and does not know that it is Scripture ; he would have the will of man converted—what Christian would have more ? " Why cannot you agree with me, man ? *I* cannot see what hinders you. They had to talk of other things.

'5 Cheyne Row, Chelsea, *Feb.* 28, 1844.

' Dear Miss Rigby,—

' I am shocked to discover that in a moment of
enthusiasm I have voluntarily promised what it is not in
my power to perform.

' On my poor shelves there appears nowhere any *Swedish
Grammar*, nothing but a wretched tatter of a *Danish
Grammar*, too ugly for being touched by you ; and this
latter, I begin to see, was what figured in my prophetic
fancy yesterday—the fond illusion of an excuse for seeing
you a second time.

' Such fantasies attend us on our earthly pilgrimage. You
must pity me, and pardon me.

' With many kind wishes, and at least one kind remembrance, I am and remain, Yours most sincerely,

' T. Carlyle.'

On 3rd March Miss Rigby records : " To the Carlyles' in the
evening. Mr. Sterling there, and some others. Carlyle
perfect in his way : that is, a wayward genius, now kindly,
now fretful ; best laugh I ever heard. He has the thinnest
possible surface over his mind ; you can get through it at
once." He has no society veneer at all !—" Talked of
Oliver Cromwell, a favourite hero of his ; also of Fanny
Burney, whom he utterly ridiculed ; of the French Revolution, and of Marie Antoinette, 'the spoilt child of adversity.'
She mended her shoe in prison the night before her execution,
and ' when they had cut off her head she was out of their
hands—the hell-hounds could do no more'. Never felt
myself in more thoroughly intellectual society—such great
knowledge, and such equal originality. Mrs. Carlyle
interested me ; she is lively and clever, and *evidently very
happy*." [1]

Exit Miss Rigby, to return again occasionally in years to
come. We can see her doing so and even dining with the
Carlyles, in one of Mrs. Carlyle's letters to her cousin Jeannie,[2]
wherein she praised Miss Rigby as at once " gigantic " and
"beautiful", and said she had " taken an immense place in
Carlyle's imagination ".

---

[1] *Letters and Journals of Lady Eastlake*, I, pp. 30, 45–6, 64, 116–18.
[2] *J. W. Carlyle : Her Letters to her Family*, edited by L. Huxley, pp. 265–6.

" Besides being a Woman of Genius, she is a world's wonder for *personal* attractions—six feet high ! but so beautifully proportioned that you could not wish her less— with the most magnificent statuesque head, and the grace-fullest manners."

In the fullness of time the new Minerva married a nice little orthodox artist, and, as Lady Eastlake, she decorated the world for many years.

XVI

THE FACTORY ACTS

(1844)

TO Miss Rigby and the rest of her sex Carlyle behaved with a deference which gentlemen might copy. Whatever the colour of their creeds they were safe from disturbance. Among men it was easy to taboo religion; but in politics his politeness to men was limited by plain dealing about practical matters. He talked as freely as if he had large estates! Thus in March this year Lord Eliot, the Chief Secretary for Ireland in Peel's Government, an honest politician and good landlord, was discussing with a number of gentlemen after dinner the duty of the state to the working classes, apropos a pending Factory Bill, which Lord Ashley was trying to mend by reducing from twelve hours to ten the limit of work for women and children in factories. Two years ago the same Lord Ashley had succeeded in passing an Act to stop women being used to drag coal-trucks underground, but in this instance the "House" agreed with the Government that he was now going too far in restricting freedom, and Eliot was astonished when Carlyle said to him: "The Government are absolutely bound either to try whether they can do some good to these people, or to draw them out in line and openly shoot them with grape. That would be a mercy in comparison with doing nothing."

A fair share of the company agreed with him; and tho Ashley was defeated for the time, Carlyle, reporting to his mother, added: "The business is begun, that is the great fact."

XVII

WORDS OF COMFORT, &c.

(1844)

ON 29–3–44 he was writing[1] to comfort William Graham, the Glasgow friend who had been in Philadelphia, and was now distressed by the impending death of a brother there, who could not leave money enough to his family.

' Never lament for the embarrassed young people ; to young strong persons embarrassment is but school exercise ; poverty is often the greatest blessing, tho we poor slaves generally feel sure that it is the one curse—slaves as we are ! As for yourself, my dear friend, I really must enter my protest against this melancholy looking back and bodeful looking forward ; I decidedly bid you give it over! Whatsoever thy hand findeth to *do*, DO that with all thy might, and leave the issues calmly to God. It is man's sole wisdom. Do not dig into the depths of the grave ; they are wisely hidden from us, we know them not. You call yourself very healthy ; but I call all this the extremity of ill-health, unhealthiness of the mind ; drag yourself away from it ! God bless you always ! T. CARLYLE.'

On 28–4–44 he was telling Thomas Spedding he would not come north this year, and added : " My intolerance against the shovelhatted quacks who succeeded poor Oliver, and hung his body on the gallows, and danced round it saying ' Aha, aha ! Glory to Nell Gwynn and the *new* improved Defender ! '—is difficult to repress within just limits." [2]

The confession shows the effort needed to attain the impartiality which has made his statement of the evidence irresistible.

[1] Unpublished letter.
[2] *Cornhill Magazine*, June, 1921, pp. 744–5.

XVIII

FAITH IN DOCTORS

(1844)

ONE April Sunday evening, Mrs. Carlyle found her husband's throat inflamed and induced him to go to bed and leave her alone to entertain some visitors. When they went away, she came up with a mustard plaster for his throat, and he wakened well in the morning. "Almost by main force" Dr. John and she together made him take his breakfast in bed, and John began to prescribe what slops and drugs were needed to complete the cure, but was cut short in " very decided Annandale " :—

' I have a great notion I will follow the direction of Nature in the matter of eating and getting up. If Nature tells me to dine on a chop, it'll be a clever fellow that'll persuade me not to do it.'

This illuminates what he wrote a few weeks later to the Rev. Alexander Scott at Woolwich, once Irving's assistant, who had fallen ill, and been sentenced by the doctors to die of heart disease. Carlyle thus comforted him in a dialect he could understand :—

' Doctors are in no case infallible prophets to me ; my brother, too, says your disease is one they are apt to be mistaken in ; we know nothing yet for certain except even this, that the Eternal does rule in all things ; that all shall be according to His will—and that surely this shall be well. Well and best.' Scott lived till 1866.

XIX

DAVID MASSON SEES CARLYLE

(1844, &c.)

A YOUNG journalist from Aberdeen, David Masson, had
been brought by John Robertson last summer, but
missed Carlyle. He came again about April, 1844, with the
same companion.[1] Mrs. Carlyle was on the sofa with
sewing in her hands, and her husband at a side table writing
a letter. He rose and received them courteously—a tall
lean figure, very erect, in a brownish dressing-gown, with
remarkably red cheeks, like a farmer who lived much in the
open air. He bade them sit down and said he would soon
finish what he was doing. They talked with Mrs. Carlyle
about things in general, and the Plymouth Brethren in
particular. " Do they believe in the Resurrection ? "[2]
asked Robertson.

" Carlyle," she cried, turning towards her husband, " do
the Plymouth Brethren believe in the Resurrection ? "

" O, like winkin'," said he, without looking round till
he had finished his letter, and then he came and joined in the
conversation, taking the lead in it and keeping them
laughing a good deal. He had a Scotch accent which might
have been North country English, clipping the *g* in
" ing " and articulating distinctly. He had none of
the slovenly English paralytic jaw. Perhaps his chief
oddity was giving " true " the liquid sound—" tryu," and
pronouncing " Matthew " without it—" Matha." Unless in
quoting he used no words of Scottish dialect, only " the purest
and most stately English ", and the lilt of his voice was not
like the sing-song echo of the pulpit not uncommon then

---

[1] All that follows is based on what David Masson told D. A. W. in
1896, and between October, 1902, and April, 1903 ; and much of it is in
print in D. M.'s posthumous book, *Memories of London in the Forties*,
pp. 35–85, etc.

[2] " Jesus Christ " in the posthumous book. David Masson seemed
doubtful ; and finally, in 1903, told D. A. W. " Resurrection."

among his countrymen, but a "chant as of a man not
ashamed to let his voice rise and fall" to suit the meaning.
His wife did the same "a little", but his brother had none
of it.   What struck Masson most of all was how Carlyle
looked straight and steadily at you when speaking.[1]

The callers did not leave till after ten, and Carlyle went
with them to the door and said to Masson : " I hope to see
you again as often as you can make it convenient." Masson
was delighted, and was soon resorting to their house, and
heard from Mrs. Carlyle that she and her husband had talked
to each other with some alarm about what might become of
Masson in London with nobody but Robertson to guide him.

He was little over twenty and had come to London to seek
his fortune as a writer or free-lance journalist.   " It was not
long after my first meeting with Carlyle," he reports, "when
I informed him," in reply to what had been his usual
question, "are you writing anything?" that "I had a small
paper on hand which I thought might do for a magazine".
Carlyle wrote a note of introduction there and then to
Mr. Nickisson, proprietor and "substantially" the editor
of *Fraser's Magazine*, "handing it to me to read before he
sealed it," said the ever-grateful Masson, who was really
surprised at its emphasis, for Carlyle had never seen a
scrap of his writing, so far as he knew, and now told Mr.
Nickisson he " would find it to his advantage to have " this
young man among his contributors.   The recommendation
was at once effective.   " On sight of the note, Mr. Nickisson
was graciousness itself, and asked me to leave the paper
for consideration.   In a few days I had a proof," and the
cheque that followed was among his earliest earnings in
London.   " From that day," he said, " *Fraser* was open for
anything I chose to send ; and two subsequent articles of
mine appeared there before the end of the year."   Mrs.
Carlyle used to chaff him on the title of his first, " Emotional
Culture," and one evening she was telling a story about
a child whose name she forgot, and she ended with, " and
the child was called—" " Emotional Culture ! " said her
husband quickly, with a sly look at Masson.

Dr. John Carlyle was now lodging in Brompton thorough-
fare, retired from medical work, and loafing respectably,
almost daily in the Cheyne Row house for an hour or two.
He was " stout and shortish ", says Masson, with " a large

---

[1] On all this, Professor C. E. Norton verbally corroborated Masson.

round face of fair complexion, and hair quite grey already, tho he was five years the junior of his lean and dark-haired brother ".

" When I first knew Carlyle," said Masson, " his work was usually over for the day between two and three o'clock, and he was glad to see callers for a few minutes' talk before he set out for his afternoon walk, but the evening was preferable. If you dropped in about seven, you found Carlyle and his wife at tea with bread and butter, biscuits and jam on the table, and were welcome to join. If you were later, you missed the tea, but had talk as long as you chose to stay, and would be offered a pipe if a smoker. He smoked short clays or cigars when away from home, but in his own house nothing but the old-fashioned long clays. He took a new pipe every day or oftener from a box. The pipe he was using himself stood ready within the fender of the fireplace, and a tin of tobacco on the mantelpiece or the table. When a visitor had filled his pipe and begun to puff, Carlyle would ask, ' Is there breath in it ? ' When the answer was ' No,' he used to pass a long wire through the stem, and hand it back with, ' There, you'll now find breath in it, do you ? ' If not, he gave you another pipe." The wire was kept in an envelope in a handy place. One of the first things Masson noticed was that both he and his wife " were very tidy ".

When Carlyle was himself the only smoker, and some-times as he grew older whether or not, he reclined on the hearthrug while he smoked and sent the puffs up the chimney. This had been begun to please his wife when she objected to tobacco. By 1844 " she was tolerant of what-ever might be his whim ", said Masson, and there could not be a better witness. " Many a time I have seen her fill his pipe and take a preliminary puff or two, and then pass it on to him. Occasionally, when he had filled it he would present the pipe to her for a whiff, ' tendering her the calumet of peace ' he called it." In 1844 Masson saw this several times, and summed up his observations of their private life for many years in saying : " The demeanour of this famous couple to each other was exemplary and loving, with a kind of stately gallantry on Carlyle's part when he turned to his Jane, and on her part the most admiring affection for him in all that he said or did. He sometimes teased her playfully and she was fond of entertaining her friends with sprightly stories of any recent misbehaviour of his ; and on such occasions he would listen most benignantly and approvingly, with the pleased look of a lion whose own lioness was having her turn in the performance."

" If there were several visitors, or one was a stranger, he would go out for his smoke into the back garden, and in summer that was the established smoking-place. There were seats for guests, or they walked on the grass."

In 1844 and 1845 Masson was agreeably surprised to see how serene Carlyle was in the evenings. " He seemed always to have done enough for the day. Tho we often were sitting in the upstairs room which was also his workshop, there was never any litter of books or papers or any sign of pressure ; and if he was reading when you entered, he at once laid his book aside. Invariably when I rose to go after ten, he would say, ' Wait till I put on my shoes, and I'll walk a bit with you.' He would put on an overcoat if the weather required it, but never took an umbrella, and his hat was always a soft felt." They went by various routes and generally separated about Hyde Park corner.

Once in 1844 Masson was invited to dinner, and met at table G. L. Craik and John Forster, both able and willing to be useful to him when he was recommended by Carlyle. What he remembered best was " Carlyle's expertness in carving the mutton, and the excellence of the sherry and of the Cambridge Ale, a present from some admirer. Forster had quite as much of the talk as Carlyle," said Masson, who added : " Carlyle was in the most genial vein of anecdote and miscellaneous talk. Discussing a recent murder by a poor Irish tramp, Carlyle and Forster agreed that one could hardly judge how easily a poor illiterate fellow might resort to murder merely to get out of a scrape."

It seems to have been this summer (1844) that after reaching Hyde Park Corner one night, escorting Masson home, Carlyle strolled with him into the park " to see the starry sky which was specially brilliant that balmy evening ". They found themselves in a solitude. Carlyle talked softly of the sight above them, the mystery, beauty and splendour of the universe, and the infinity within us as well as without : the two infinities he was fond of talking about, the heavens above us, and the sense of right and wrong, which Kant said struck him dumb. On this occasion Carlyle was silent awhile, looking up at the stars, and then he spoke again as if in soliloquy about the jesting too much in fashion among men and women, who should remain awake and earnest in full view of this wonderful and beautiful world, instead of

forgetting it all and giggling thoughtlessly. He ended with
words that remained in Masson's memory for half a century :
" Ah, and I have given in far too much to that myself—
sniggering at things."

Another evening they were taking the riverside road, and
were passing some small shops, when Carlyle said suddenly :
" By the bye, I have a lot of money lying by me at present—
far more than I have any need for ; some of it might be
more useful in your hands than in mine." Masson was
taken aback and stammered his thanks, assuring him he had
money enough at the time, and really did not need it.
" Much better so, much better so," said Carlyle, and changed
the subject when Masson tried to articulate better his
thanks.

One day Carlyle inquired, " Do you know of anyone who
would make searches and copy extracts for me in the Museum
for a moderate weekly wage ? " Masson could think of
nobody at the moment, but afterwards remembered a school-
mate and fellow-student, John Christie, a young doctor
then in money difficulties, in lodgings near Oxford Street,
with a delicate wife and child. " A note from me to Carlyle,"
said Masson, " followed by an interview between Carlyle and
Christie, settled the matter ; and till the conclusion of
Cromwell, Christie acted as Carlyle's factotum in the
Museum " and clerk, and Carlyle assured him, " I could
not have had an abler assistant or a more trustworthy."
Francis Espinasse in the Museum noticed the ' forlorn-
looking young Scotchman whom I observed,' he says,
Carlyle ' treated with considerable delicacy ', and called
" a much-enduring man ".[4]

It was partly to give work to Christie, Carlyle confessed to
FitzGerald this summer, that he made an article out of
some old reports which Christie copied, Suffolk, 1640, and
gave it to Mr. Nickisson for *Fraser's Magazine*, " An Election
to the Long Parliament." When *Cromwell* was finished,
Carlyle kept Christie in sight, and got him regular employment.

In talking to Masson, he seemed to be revealing his own
way of investigating Cromwell. The gist of it all, including
what he said when Masson was working on his *Milton*, was :
" One must follow a line here and then a line there—you
cannot advance while carrying a square in front of you,"

[4] *Literary Recollections*, by F. Espinasse, p. 72.

the two essentials apparently being the need to make quite sure of anything before you feel you know it, and to realize how very little men can really know, and how often after the utmost inquiry, " You never can tell."

Masson used to say Carlyle was fond of a good fire. As they were sitting together at the cosy fireside one evening, Masson broke the silence with : " All things considered, the genius of Shakespeare is nothing less than a miracle."

" Yes, you are right," said Carlyle, and " I remember that ", Masson would add, " because such acquiescence was so rare. If you wanted to hear what could be said for a man, run him down to Carlyle ; and if you praised anyone excessively you might hear mistakes of fact corrected and something said on the other side." Thus once, as became a disciple, he was exalting Goethe, and Carlyle said : " He gave way too much to ' Kunst ' (or Art) and ' Literatur '."

" O Carlyle ! ! ! " ejaculated his wife, but he persisted, saying, " I think so."

In the same way Espinasse, overflowing about Goethe's scientific discoveries, was astounded to be told : " Goethe was too much given to peering into Nature." [5]

By this time nothing in Goethe appealed so much to Carlyle as the fine scheme of education unfolded in *Wilhelm Meister's Travels*, and when Goethe's adoration in old age of a very young lady was mentioned, all he said was, " Poor fellow ! " The make-believe of romanticism had made Carlyle outgrow it soon. Perhaps the most like him of all his recorded remarks on Goethe was what Espinasse heard [6]: " Goethe was the most successful speaker of the century, but I would have been better pleased if he had done something."

[5] Ibid., pp. 221–2.
[6] Ibid., p. 92.

XX

MAZZINI'S LETTERS

(1844)

AS long ago as 1840 Mazzini was writing home that
Carlyle and his wife both loved him like a brother, and
would like to help him.[1] He and Carlyle differed without
ceasing to be friends in 1844 about the Bandiera episode,
which seemed a trifle to Mazzini's admirers, but not to
Carlyle, who cursed what he called "a nest of young
conspirators".

The two Bandieras were brothers and young officers in
the Austrian navy. It seems likely now that they had been
meditating a rebellion and been betrayed, and might have
come to grief altho they had never communicated with
Mazzini ; but that was not known at the time. One of them
did correspond with Mazzini about it, and at the instance of
the Foreign Secretary Aberdeen, Sir James Graham, the
Home Secretary, examined secretly the letters to Mazzini
and his letters in the Post Office, and Aberdeen told what
was in them to the Ambassadors, and the young Bandieras
were soon trapped and shot.

Mazzini laid a trap for the Post Office, and exposed the
trick. Thomas Duncombe was his spokesman in the
Commons, and Home-Secretary Graham, supposing it safe,
took to libelling Mazzini there. Carlyle wrote a letter to
The Times (15-6-44) which went far to set the tune to the
press. " That I call noble," said poor Mazzini, who was
" much touched ", remembering " their late coolness".
Contemporaries declared it " a generous act beyond the
reach of common men ".[2]

' Sir,—In your observations in yesterday's *Times* on the
late disgraceful affair of Mr. Mazzini's letters and the
Secretary of State, you mention that Mr. Mazzini is entirely

---

[1] *Mazzini*, by Bolton King, pp. 84-5 and 103-6.
[2] e.g. *Sixty Years of an Agitator's Life*, by G. J. Holyoake, I, p. 193.

unknown to you, entirely indifferent to you ; and add, very justly, that if he were the most contemptible of mankind it would not affect your argument on the subject.

' It may tend to throw further light on this matter if I now certify you, which I in some sort feel called upon to do, that Mr. Mazzini is not unknown to various competent persons in this country, and that he is very far indeed from being contemptible—none farther, or very few of living men. I have had the honour to know Mr. Mazzini for a series of years ; and, whatever I may think of his practical insight and skill in worldly affairs, I can with great freedom testify to all men that he, if I have ever seen one such, is a man of genius and virtue, a man of sterling veracity, humanity, and nobleness of mind ; one of those rare men, numerable, unfortunately, but as units in this world, who are worthy to be called martyr souls ; who, in silence, piously in their daily life, understand and practice what is meant by that.

' Of Italian democracies and young Italy's sorrows, of extraneous Austrian Emperors in Milan, and poor old chimerical Popes in Bologna, I know nothing, and desire to know nothing ; but this other thing I do know, and can here publicly declare to be a fact, which fact all of us that have occasion to comment on Mr. Mazzini and his affairs may do well to take along with us, as a thing leading towards new clearness, and not towards new additional darkness, regarding him and them.

' Whether the extraneous Austrian Emperor, the miserable old chimera of a Pope, shall maintain themselves in Italy, or be obliged to decamp from Italy, is not a question in the least vital to Englishmen. But it is a question vital to us that sealed letters in an English post office be, as we all fancied they were, respected as things sacred ; that opening of men's letters, a practice near of kin to picking man's pockets, and to other still viler and far fataler forms of scoundrelism, be not resorted to in England, except in cases of the very last extremity. When some new gunpowder plot may be in the wind, some double-dyed high treason or imminent national wreck not avoidable otherwise, then let us open letters—not till then.

' To all Austrian Kaisers and such like, in their time of trouble, let us answer, as our fathers from of old have answered : Not by such means is help here for you. Such means, allied to picking of pockets and viler forms of scoundrelism, are not permitted in this country for your behoof. The Right Hon. Secretary does himself detest such, and even is afraid to employ them. He durst not, it would be dangerous for him ! All British men that might chance to come in view of such a transaction would incline to spurn it, and trample on it, and indignantly ask him what he meant by it ? I am, Sir, your obedient servant,

'THOMAS CARLYLE.'

Mr. Duncombe had an easy victory. Tho Graham made haste to retract and was able to say with truth that he had done " no more than what every Secretary of State did before him " [3] and the letter of the law allowed, he was despised for doing it. Many an evil deed may be legal. It was plainly wrong to help the Austrians to kill Italian patriots, and England fumed with fury at the thought of it. Mazzini had friends and furtherance for the rest of his life, and Graham said on his deathbed that he " would only be remembered as the Home Secretary who opened Mazzini's letters ".[4]

Carlyle told Espinasse [5] that Graham was " a border-riever ", or robber, " disguised as a Minister of State," which seems rough on the Border robbers who acted openly. But Graham was really up to their level, and never peached on his pal, Aberdeen, who escaped the blame he deserved.[6] A few years later " the dice-box of life " went topsy-turvy, and Aberdeen, " a douce, small-headed, sleek and feeble old gentleman," became Prime Minister. When Prince Albert pioposed to him a pension for Carlyle, Aberdeen remembered with a shudder the Mazzini row, and shook his little head, and said that was made impossible by Carlyle's " heterodoxy ".[7]

Wherefore let all be the more thankful now to Carlyle and others, who saved us from the risk of a Russian " Cabinet Noir " (dark office, for opening letters sent by post) ; but what old Wellington was saying was also true, that the French ministers, protesting loudly that they never did such a thing, were lying. It was an old story there. Paris was

---

[3] *Greville Memoirs*, II, p. 249, etc.

[4] *Life and Lets. of Sir James Graham*, by C. S. Parker, I, p. 447, and *Hic et Ubique*, by Sir W. Fraser, p. 287.

[5] *Literary Recollections*, by F. Espinasse, p. 107.

[6] *Life of Disraeli*, by Monypenny, II, pp. 310–11, and other books, including *The Birth of Modern Italy*, by J. W. Mario, p. 68, etc.

[7] Told to T. C. at the time by Sir James Stephen, Under-Secretary for the Colonies.

worse than either Petrograd or London—more wicked, only not so frank. It may have been his French wife who taught the trick of it to Charles Stuart I. Voltaire praises Lord Falkland for refusing to oblige that king in this way. In France Voltaire could not send his MS. by post " because they would copy it ", and he rightly maintains that such wrong-doing under cover of the law is worse than common crime. The letter-picker is as bad as the pocket-picker, and, if safer, all the meaner.

In this case there was more than such meanness to put heat into the curses of Carlyle. Mazzini was a kind of idealist who attracted female sympathy, a dainty little Don Quixote in real life attacking the actual Austrian empire. One is sorry for an " ugly " young Jewess who was plain-spoken and wanted to marry him—he was cruel in letting her see she repelled him—no *loving* woman is ugly. Many women were warmly corresponding with him on one excuse or another. The discovery that Graham and his fellows had been reading all the letters to Mazzini set many female hearts aflame. As " Dicky " Milnes wrote to his father at the time [8] : " A young lady undertook to convert Mazzini to Protestantism and is dreadfully disgusted on Graham having studied all her controversy. Mrs. Carlyle, too, is in a great way at all her letters to him having been over-hauled." It seems likely that Lady Harriet Baring was another sufferer.

Carlyle avenged the women in the very way they wanted, punishing the evil-doers and saying nothing about *them*. From his boyhood he was noticed to be a *woman's man*. The right sort of man is always so. That is how humanity is lifted up, as explained in a students' song describing with scientific precision the ascent of mankind from its humble origin :—

> " We've little to remind us
>   Of savage days like these :
> We left our tails behind us
>   Before we left the trees :
> But all achievements human,
>   And all we have to-day,
> We owe them all to woman,
>   Whate'er the priests may say."

[8] *R. Monckton Milnes*, by T. Wemyss Reid, I, p. 333.

XXI

A DINNER AT ADDISCOMBE

(1844)

CARLYLE agreed to dine with the Barings at Addiscombe (Saturday, 6-7-44), and found the company
" sublime ", " as many as the table would hold," including
old Lady Holland, attended by " an old woman to rub her
legs " as well as a page and her Dr. Allen. Baring and his
wife were radiantly decorating the ends of the table, while
Carlyle, saying little, was watching and rather admiring the
fashionable " art in speech ", avoiding friction.

When Mazzini was named, Stanley reported that
Brougham had been privately telling everybody in the
Lords that Mazzini was a scamp after all, and once " kept
a gaming house ". Lady Holland to Lady Harriet : " Who
is he really, this Mazzini ? " Lady Harriet : " A
Revolutionary man, the head of Young Italy." " Oh, then,
surely they ought to take him up ! " Lady Harriet hinted
no, and that she knew him herself. " What ? " cried
Lady Holland, with wide-open eyes. Lady Harriet added :
" I have actually asked him to come and see me."

Carlyle to Lady Holland : " He is a man well worth
seeing, and not at all specially anxious to be seen." " And
did he not keep a gaming-house ? " " He had never the
faintest shadow of connexion with that side of human
business," said Carlyle. " The proudest person in this
company is not farther above keeping a gaming-house
than Mazzini is."

" That means Byng," said Buller, alluding to " Poodle
Byng ", who was there, " an absurd old curly-headed diner-
out," a superannuated Foreign Office clerk. This caused
an explosion of laughter, and " swallowed up my over-
emphasis ", Carlyle reported to his wife. And a few minutes
later, he and another guest were in a cab which took them
to Piccadilly, sociably smoking, and gave him a clear
Sunday for work on *Cromwell*.

XXII

JAMES BALLANTINE

(1844)

IN the end of 1842 James Ballantine, an Edinburgh house-painter, had received from Carlyle a letter acknowledging his book, the *Gaberlunzie's Wallet*, and bidding him disregard the reviewers. So now in 1844 the successful Ballantine was joyfully sending him his *Miller of Deanhaugh*, and received a letter containing an admonition which, finding its way into print, has been often quoted :—

' You plead with real earnestness for mercy to the poor, for general mercy and generosity from all men towards all men. Which is surely right, and not unwanted at present. By and by, however, I think we shall hear from you withal a more distinct recognition how all men are first, if I may so speak, to show mercy on themselves. Without this preliminary, mercy from others is not possible in general. I desiderate an internal rigour in the heart of your beautiful pity ; like the bony inflexible framework in the beautifulest human body ; such an internal rigour exists everywhere in Nature, physical, spiritual, moral, and without it no virtue can stand on its feet.'

A few months later Mr. Ballantine sent the MS. of a metrical tale. Carlyle showed it to several publishers, who rejected it, whereupon Carlyle advised Ballantine to give up metrical narrative, as the public did not want it, adding : " You could write Scotch songs, I think, to good purpose ; but were wise to go no further in that direction."

Ballantine took the advice, and prospered into old age ; and is now remembered only for songs such as " Castles in the air " and " Ilka blade o' grass keps its ain drap o' dew ".[1]

---

[1] The late Charles Cowie, of Cowie Brothers, Glasgow, supplied the letters, etc., and see the *Glasgow Herald*, 22–1–1910.

XXIII

PARKS AND PUBLIC LOUNGES

(1844)

ON 8–8–44 Carlyle wrote a letter to the Manchester editor, Thomas Ballantyne, who had begged his blessing on public parks :—

'My dear Sir,—I rejoice heartily in the project you have in view, and hope to-day's meeting will be prosperous and productive. On the subject of parks and public places of innocent recreation in large towns I have indeed nothing more to say at present than what I have already said : but I think often enough of it, and trust those whose hands are within reach of such a business will everywhere, the noble part of them, begin doing in it, without more saying than is needful. I do sincerely hope you will get on with it—for the sake of the poor little sickly children, and the dusty, toilsome men, to whom, for a thousand years, generation after generation, it may be a blessing. It were good also if in any Building Acts, or such like, you could silently introduce facilities for having enlargements added to your parks. In the climate of Manchester, too, *there certainly ought to be roofed spaces—large rooms, kept under mild but strict order, into which the poorest man, that would behave himself like a man, might have means of procuring access.* Good Heavens, what benefit might be accomplished would brave men with hearts and heads but bestir themselves a very little !—Yours always truly,

' T. CARLYLE.'

The public lounges here suggested are not started yet.

XXIV

BULWER LYTTON AND TENNYSON

IN 1844 Edward Bulwer, now Bulwer Lytton, came occasionally to Cheyne Row to go walking with Carlyle, and had given him this spring his translation of Schiller's *Poems and Ballads* and his *Life of Schiller*. Carlyle wrote to him : " The grand and truly important writings we have are all biographies, from Homer's *Odyssey* to the Gospel of St. Matthew. I wish we had a hundred such, done in as good a way as this. Many thanks to you, in my own name and that of a multitude of others." [1] In another letter there is a clue to what their talk may have been—a notion of Richter that " Laughter and tears lie very near together ". Carlyle thought so and said that keeping both in action together was the way to avoid ' fanaticism, Rousseauship, etc.'

Not long afterwards Douglas Jerrold was dining at Bulwer Lytton's in the company of Carlyle, and talking about the murder of a woman, then filling the newspapers. Even a tiger is gentle after dinner, and Jerrold did not anticipate contradiction when he declared " capital punishment absurd "; but Carlyle exclaimed : " The wretch ! I would have him trampled to pieces underfoot and buried on the spot." The others did not take sides, and Jerrold dropped his bent little body into a big chair, and tossing back his brown-grey mop of hair with one hand as he lay back with his eyes on the ceiling, merely said : " Cui bono ? Cui bono ? " (What's the use ?) [2]

Jerrold did politics for *Punch*, and before long he was reporting Queen Victoria's reception of Tom Thumb, and describing Carlyle on that occasion as " a plain-mannered thoughtful-looking republican ".[3]

1844 is the likeliest date for what " Dicky " Milnes was fond of telling—to Tennyson himself among others—for

---

[1] *Life of Edward Bulwer, Lord Lytton*, by his grandson, II, pp. 53–60.
[2] Dr. Hutchison Stirling, who told this to D. A. W., was not present, but he was told it all soon afterwards by Douglas Jerrold.
[3] *Douglas Jerrold and Punch*, by Walter Jerrold, p. 132.

the rest of his life [4] : ' " Richard Milnes," said Carlyle one day, withdrawing his pipe from his mouth as they were seated together in Cheyne Row, " when are you going to get that pension for Alfred Tennyson ? " " My dear Carlyle," responded Milnes, " the thing is not so easy as you seem to suppose. What will my constituents say if I do get the pension for Tennyson ? They know nothing about him or his poetry, and they will probably think he is some poor relation of my own, and that the whole affair is a job."

' Solemn and emphatic was Carlyle's response : " Richard Milnes, on the Day of Judgment, when the Lord asks you why you didn't get that pension for Alfred Tennyson, it will not do to lay the blame on your constituents ; it is *you* that will be damned." '

This would be after October, when the idea had first occurred to Carlyle in writing to FitzGerald (26–10–44), and mentioning that Alfred Tennyson had spent a day with them, and " staid with us till late, an unforgettable day. We dismissed him with *Macpherson's Farewell* ", referring to a song that Lockhart called the " grand lyric ", written by Burns to a tune composed by Macpherson himself, who was executed at Banff in 1700. The letter continues :—

' He said of you that you were a man from whom one could accept money ; which was a proud saying ; which you ought to bless Heaven for. It has struck me as a distinctly necessary Act of Legislation, that Alfred should have a pension of £150 a year. They have £1,200 every year to give away. A hundred and fifty to Alfred, I say ; *he* is worth that sum to England ! It should be done and must.'

From FitzGerald Tennyson did take some money ; and Milnes was another friend of his as well aware as Carlyle of Tennyson's urgent need in 1844. For some years there had been a fever of commercial speculation, and Tennyson had caught the infection and put all he had into a get-rich-quick enterprise, which collapsed in 1844, leaving Tennyson owning nothing but a debt not likely to be recovered. The profit from his poetry was negligible as yet. He had friends as well as readers among the ruling classes, and so Carlyle's suggestion was welcomed, and an application was made to

[4] *Richard Monckton Milnes, Lord Houghton*, by T. Wemyss Read, I, pp. 295–7 ; and *Alfred Lord Tennyson*, by his son, I, pp. 220–5.

Sir Robert Peel as Prime Minister for a Civil List Pension of £200 for Tennyson.

It clashed with another application for the same amount for Sheridan Knowles, and, as usual, Peel consulted Milnes, remarking : " I know absolutely nothing either of Mr. Tennyson or of Mr. Knowles." " What ! " said Milnes, " have you never seen the name of Sheridan Knowles on a playbill ? " " No," replied Peel. " And have you never read a poem of Tennyson's ? " " No. Let me see something Tennyson has written."

Milnes sent Tennyson's books, marking *Locksley Hall* and *Ulysses*, with a letter saying that " if the pension were a charitable gift then Sheridan Knowles, infirm and poor, and past his prime, was the proper recipient ; but if it were to be bestowed in the interests of literature, it should be given to Alfred Tennyson ". And to Tennyson it was given ; and tho Knowles received a similar pension three years later, nobody anticipated that at the time. Bulwer Lytton in his *New Timon* denounced the choice and let himself go against Tennyson in the style of Balzac's Parisians, sneering at the " Theban taste " of Peel, who " pensions Tennyson while starves a Knowles ", and speaking of ' Schoolmiss Alfred ' and his

> " Jingling melody of purloined conceits,
> Out-babying Wordsworth and out-glittering Keats."

This was nothing to the abuse Carlyle received without retort from many nameless now ; but Tennyson's feelings prevented him following in practice such an example of the gospel of silence all at once ; and through John Forster [5] he supplied to *Punch* a reply to Bulwer Lytton, " The New Timon and the Poets." He called his opponent a " bandbox ", and " the padded man that wears the stays "—" O Lion, you that made a noise, and shook a mane in papillotes," French for curl-papers—such are the exigencies of rhyme.

> " And what with spites and what with fears,
>   You cannot let a body be :
> It's always ringing in your ears,
> ' They call this man as great as *me* ! '
> What profits now to understand
>   The merits of a spotless shirt—
> A dapper boot—a little hand—
>   If half the little soul is dirt ? "

[5] *Alfred, Lord Tennyson*, by his son, I, p. 245.

CHARLES DICKENS READING AFTER DINNER

In the rooms of John Forster, 1844, from a drawing made at the time there by Daniel Maclise.

[face p. 272.

Carlyle was a friend of both the parties, and did not fail to deprecate such hostilities. In a week the flustered poet was publishing the verses, " Literary Squabbles," which he afterwards republished, and what was better still, he did all he could to suppress as " too bitter " his original lampoon. " Literary Squabbles " is like Tennyson's paraphrase of Carlyle's talk, and if the conclusion is right—

" The noblest answer unto such
Is perfect stillness when they brawl,"—

the practice of Carlyle was better than the best of poetry— " the less said the better." [6]   Both Bulwer Lytton and Tennyson lived to be old men, and they quarrelled no more.

[6] Besides authorities already quoted, see the *Dict. of Nat. Biog.*; *Chambers' Encyclop. of Eng. Lit., etc.*; and *Alfred, Lord Tennyson*, by Arthur Waugh, pp. 81–3; and *Punch*, 1846, where Tennyson signed " Alcibiades ".

XXV

ENJOYING "CROMWELL" UNDER
DIFFICULTIES

(1844–5)

WHAT none of the men of letters then could understand was why Carlyle was dwelling among the dusty paper-masses of the Commonwealth. They saw drudgery in his job, no chance of glory and little hope of gain. The publisher would not risk printing his compilation without a kind of promise of a " Life " to follow, if the " Letters and Speeches " were a failure.[1] Few contemporaries took so much interest in what he was now doing as old Mrs. Strachey,[2] whom he called " the oldest and dearest friend I anywhere have in the world ". She was diligent in getting documents sent him and doing whatever she could to help, and did, indeed, survive to have the pleasure of receiving an " author's copy ". " I am exceedingly busy," he wrote to her in 1844, " fishing up, washing clean, and making legible the letters and speeches of Oliver Cromwell, a heroic man buried in mud and darkness. It seems a kind of duty. I say : ' He *fought* ; thy poor trade is but to *speak* ; speak, then, for him.' Happily this branch of the business is now almost done ; we must then try others, a little more inspiring."

From the end of 1843, when he began the *Letters and Speeches*, his work became enjoyable, and he made rapid progress, keeping " out of the way of all men and things " while the season lasted, and glad to see " the beautiful quality " go away and leave the town quiet for those like him who had work to do. He did not leave London this summer. Young Espinasse, employed in the British Museum, was lodging near him and frequenting his house, and making

---

[1] *Literary Recollections*, by F. Espinasse, pp. 70–5, corroborated.
[2] "Reminiscences of Carlyle," etc., by G. Strachey, *New Review*, July, 1893.

notes for our benefit.[1] " Ill-health has cast a funeral pall over my life," said Carlyle to him now, complaining of want of sleep and headaches, and the reporter says : " I have known him make a characteristic attempt to console himself by remembering that headaches had afflicted some of the greatest of the early German Reformers." But for what he suffered this summer he also blamed the stuffy old reading-room of the Museum, overcrowded and ill-ventilated, and spoke of " the *Museum* headache ". Espinasse used to watch him " stooping as he groped in the confused catalogue, and then filling up the ticket which he called ' the talisman ' ". He astonished the young official by telling him : " All that ought to be incumbent on the reader is to give the name of the book which he wants. It is the duty of the librarian without more ado to find it for him. If you go into a shop to purchase something, you are not expected to indicate to the shopman the whereabouts of the article."

Espinasse did what he could to save him trouble. One night when Espinasse was leaving his house, he received a fragment of manuscript which an Edinburgh gentleman had sent as " an important contribution to Cromwellian history ". Carlyle said he could make nothing of it, and Espinasse soon was able to report it was merely a copy of a passage in one of the accessible Commonwealth newspapers. This led to many more such queries, which it was a pleasure to answer.

The same Robert Chambers, who helped the sister of Burns in 1842, was now the Edinburgh antiquary who enabled Carlyle to leave no doubt about Cromwell's lodging there.[3]

This summer Mrs. Carlyle stayed a while with her uncle in Liverpool, and then with Mrs. Paulet there, but she was home in August when, on " a bright Sunday morning ", a letter came from John Sterling in the Isle of Wight which made her weep, for it was to say he was dying. No hope remained— he was fading away like the snowdrifts in a thaw, and wrote (10–8–44) : " A few words, merely for Remembrance and Farewell. On higher matters there is nothing to say. I tread the common road into the darkness without fear and with hope. Certainty I have none. Towards me it is still more true than towards England that no man has been and done like you. Heaven bless you ! If I can lend a hand when THERE, that will not be wanting. It is all very strange,

[3] *The Story of a Lifetime*, by Lady Priestley, daughter of Robert Chambers, pp. 25–7 ; and *Letters and Speeches of Oliver Cromwell*, Letter LXXVI, Footnote 50.

but not one hundredth part so sad as it seems to the standers-by."

Carlyle sent fitting reply (27–8–44) : " We are journeying towards the Grand Silence ; what lies beyond it man has never known, nor will know : but all brave men have known that it was right GOOD—that the name of it was GOD. *Wir heissen euch hoffen* (We bid you hope). What is right and best for us will full surely be. Tho He slay me, yet will I trust in Him. ' Eterno Amore ' (Eternal Love) ; that is the ultimate significance of this wild clashing whirlwind which is named Life, where the Sons of Adam flicker painfully for an hour."

Of course Carlyle was ready to go and take farewell, but " perhaps I should be but a disturbance ", he wrote, and it seemed better for him not to go. The death of Sterling in September broke a link with Mill, who had lent Carlyle the *Memorials of Whitelocke* and many other books, but had no such enthusiasm for the English Commonwealth as for the French Revolution. " By this time Mrs. Taylor had about monopolized poor Mill," said David Masson.[4] " She had had more trouble in detaching him from Carlyle than from any other of his friends, but she was now succeeding." There was no quarrel. Their friendship was not broken, but it was ceasing.

In September Carlyle went to the Grange, the Hampshire house of Lord Ashburton, the father of his friend Bingham Baring. It was his first visit, and contrived by Mrs. Carlyle, who wanted her husband to be out of the way for a week or two while she was doing her annual house-cleaning. The old Lord Ashburton shared his love of tobacco-smoking, which was considered vulgar then, and they enjoyed each other's company and took long walks together. Carlyle described the house and the guests in a long pencil-letter to his wife, wherein he mentioned the Charles Greville, whose memoirs of politicians and Queen Victoria and her uncles did not begin to be published till 1874. " An old official hack of quality who runs racehorses," was all Carlyle saw in him now.

Carlyle was uneasy at being away from pending work. He did some proof-sheets, and also inspected Winchester, but came home as soon as possible. What he was doing day by day for eleven months to come can be read in *Oliver*

---

[4] Verbally to D. A. W., see Book XII, Chapter XXIV.

Cromwell's Letters and Speeches. A few glimpses of him in hours of relaxation show his spirits rising and himself as well as could be expected under the circumstances.

It seems to have been this winter (1844–5) that FitzGerald told Carlyle : " The more I read of Cromwell, the more I am forced to agree with the verdict of the world about him." Whereupon, according to FitzGerald,[5] " Carlyle only grunted and sent forth a prodigious blast of tobacco smoke. *He smokes indignantly.*"

It was certainly this winter that FitzGerald was spending an evening with him, and found him " looking well ", with nothing to complain about but want of sleep. When they were parting at " the street door—to which he always accompanies you ", said FitzGerald,—there was " an organ playing a polka even so late in the street ", and FitzGerald, who had been feeling dull, was so exhilarated by the outside air that he " polka'd down the pavement ", hoping he was giving something like a shock to Carlyle looking on.

About October 1844,[6] Robert Browning heard Carlyle " croon if not sing " the whole of the Jacobite song, " Charlie is my Darling ", and reported to Miss Barrett his " adoring emphasis " in repeating the " My Darling " of the chorus :—

'Then', Browning went on, 'he said: " How must that notion of ideal wondrous perfection have impressed itself in this old Jacobite's *young Cavalier*—they go to save their land and the *young Cavalier*—when I who care nothing about such a rag of a man, cannot but feel as the Jacobite felt in speaking his words after him." '

A few months later Carlyle was translating and explaining to Browning another old Scotch song, and asked him [6]: " Did you ever try to write a song ? Of all things in the world, *that* I should be proudest to do." Then he defined what he meant by a song, and with an appealing look to his wife, said : " I always say that some day, in spite of Nature and my stars, I shall burst into a song." To Miss Barrett Browning explained that Carlyle meant that " he is not mechanically ' musical', and the music is in the poetry, he holds, and should enwrap the thought as ' an amber drop enwraps the bee '."

---

[5] *Some New Letters by E. FitzGerald*, by F. R. Barton, pp. 101 and 94–5.
[6] *Letters of R. Browning and E. Barrett*, I, pp. 16 and 25–8.

He frankly told Browning that it was the want of music made him feel that Browning's verses were not poetry; and once it is said he called a volume of his " a cartload of stones ".[7]   But nothing abated Browning's zeal to help him.   This very winter Browning was writing [6] in his most tactful way to a gentleman who was withholding a letter of Cromwell, but was persuaded by Browning to let Carlyle use it.

" As a prolegomena to the *Life of Cromwell*," Browning had heard Carlyle saying,[8] " I am going to publish the *Letters and Speeches* with notes.   If I can get people to read *them*, I will be saved much trouble in telling them whether they have judged wisely of Cromwell or no."

Browning was surprised to see that he " himself seems to entertain a boundless admiration for the man.   I never remember him more delightful.   The intensity of his radicalism too is exquisite ".

[7] *The Story of My Life*, by A. J. C. Hare, VI, p. 96.
[8] *R. Browning and A. Domitt*, p. 111.

XXVI

AN EVENING WITH CHARLES DICKENS

(1844)

DICKENS had been living in Italy of late, and wrote the *Chimes* there ; but he came home for a few days to read it to his friends after dinner. He had written to John Forster in advance that Carlyle was " indispensable ", and his wife too ; but, Mrs. Carlyle being laid up with one of her influenzas, the " select few " whom Forster had dining at his rooms in Lincoln's Inn Fields on Monday, 2–12–44, were merely men.   This occasion, said Forster in 1872,[1] " was the germ of those readings to larger audiences by which the world knew him in his later life.   All are now dead who were present, excepting only Mr. Carlyle and myself.   Among those Maclise ' made a note of it ' in pencil.   The reader may be assured (with allowance for caricature to which I may claim to be the chief victim) that in the grave attention of Carlyle, the eager interest of Stanfield and Maclise, the keen look of poor Laman Blanchard, Fox's rapt solemnity, Jerrold's skyward gaze, and the tears of Harness and Dyce, the characteristic points of the scene are sufficiently rendered.

" When I expressed to Dickens my grief that he had had so tempestuous a journey for such brief enjoyment, he wrote from Paris : ' I would not recall an inch of the way to or from you, if it had been twenty times as long and twenty thousand times as wintry.   It was worth any travel— anything ! ' "

---

[1] *Charles Dickens*, by John Forster, II, pp. 149–50.

XXVII

JEFFREY'S GOOD STORY

(1845)

O N 13–4–45, when Mrs. Carlyle was re-reading *Sartor*, in walked D'Orsay, as superlative a dandy as ever, tho decked in darker shades than five years ago, " in compliment to his five more years," she supposed, remarking his " slightly enlarged figure and slightly worn complexion ", and admiring the consummate skill of his dress and decoration—" only one fold of gold chain round his neck, tucked together right on the centre of his spacious breast with one magnificent turquoise ".

Jeffrey came in equally unexpected before D'Orsay departed. " What a difference ! The prince of critics and the prince of dandies. How washed out the beautiful dandiacal face looked beside that little clever old man's ! " whose penetrating eyes seemed brighter than ever at seventy-two. He now delighted the dandy as well as Mrs. Carlyle with a real good thing, quite new. Lord Brougham had been saying to him that so-and-so " would never get into aristocratic society ; first, because his manners were bad, and secondly," said Brougham, " because there is such a want of truth (!) in him. In aristocratic society there is such a quick tact for detecting everything unveracious that no man who is not true can ever get on in it ! " " Indeed ! " said Jeffrey, " I am delighted to hear you give such a character of the upper classes ; I thought they had been more tolerant." " Oh," said Brougham, " I assure you it is the fact ; any man who is deficient in veracity immediately gets tabooed in the aristocratic circles." And our recording angel, Mrs. Carlyle, knowing Brougham to be untruthful, concluded : " The force of impudence could no further go."

XXVIII

A ·NIGHT WITH PADDY AND WHAT FOLLOWED

(1845)

ON Saturday, 26–4–45, Frederick Lucas brought three young Irishmen to Carlyle's, " hot and hot live Irishmen," wrote Mrs. Carlyle, with " the brogue rather exquisite ", and brimming over with " repale ". Lucas was an English Quaker who had turned Catholic, and started the *Tablet* in London as a Catholic paper—a lawyer, but a journalist by trade. One of his companions was the same, Charles Gavan Duffy, editor of the Dublin *Nation*, and writer of Irish songs. The other two were lawyers only, John O'Hagan and Pigot. All three had come to London to dine at an Inn of Court to qualify for call to the Bar.[1]

Mrs. Carlyle cheerfully poured out tea for them, and sided with them when they remonstrated, " almost with tears in their eyes," against the Irish lady quoted in *Chartism* about her countrymen : " A finer people never lived ; only they have two faults, they do generally lie and steal."

Mrs. Carlyle won the hearts of the visitors by bantering her husband on his style and his opinions; and Pigot, a handsome, romantic-looking pale-faced youth, after looking at Carlyle and listening to him attentively for an hour, said : " Now I am assured you are not in your heart so unjust to Ireland as your writings lead one to suppose ; and so I will confess, for the purpose of retracting it, the strong feeling of repulsion with which I have come to you to-night."

" Then why in the name of goodness did you come ? " asked Mrs. Carlyle, which was awkward for a moment, but only for a moment—the nimble Irish terriers were soon barking at something else. David Masson was there, but saw he should efface himself, and went away early, but it

---

[1] Besides the Carlyle correspondence, see for this Chapter *Conversations with Carlyle*, by Sir C. Gavan Duffy, pp. 1 to 8.

may have been on this occasion that he admired Carlyle's
dexterity in parrying debate upon the kind of tortures in
Hell, by pitying the Devil and saying, " If the Devil had
my stomach to chew with, I could not wish him worse,
poor fellow ! " [2]

" In general," said Masson, " Carlyle loathed argument,
and would meet contradiction by sudden silence or changing
the subject.　But on this occasion he was plainly enjoying
the talk," tho he would not be serious about the Devil.
Lucas and the other three were unanimous against the
" intolerance " of the Scotch ; and Carlyle " took up the
cudgels " for his countrymen, instead of telling, as he might
have done, how he had stood up for the emancipation of the
Catholics in 1829 against his neighbours.　" How could
they do otherwise ? " he now inquired, " If one sees one's
fellow-creature following a damnable error, by continuing
in which the Devil is sure to get him at last and roast him
in eternal fire and brimstone, are you to let him go towards
such consummation ?　Or are you not rather to use all
means to save him ? "

A surprising conclusion might have been reached if the
eager debators had been allowed to answer this, but women
have no patience with Socratic methods.　" A nice prospect
for you ! " said Mrs. Carlyle to Lucas, " to be roasted in fire
and brimstone ! "　" For all of us," said he, laughing good-
naturedly, " we are all Catholics."

She pointed to her husband and said to Lucas, " Thomas
tells me not to be afraid of Hell—there's no such place ".[3]
Lucas gravely replied, "I think all his principles lead
logically to a belief in Hell."　" In a certain sense, that is
true," said Carlyle, but left Lucas bewildered by saying no
more.　Hell was very real to poor Lucas and the Irish then,
but a side issue on this occasion.　It was the Irish character
and history they were discussing, and these young men were
showering upon him " circumstantial details " of Irish
affairs, in the hope of persuading him to be their advocate
" before England and the world ".　When they had said
their say, Mrs. Carlyle turned the talk to gossip, saying to
Duffy—" Tennyson does not tell his own story in *Locksley*

---

[2] Told to D. A. W. by David Masson, 16–12–96.
[3] Sir C. Gavan Duffy to D. A. W. at Nice, 20–4–97 ; and see the *Life
of Frederick Lucas, M.P.*, by Edward Lucas, I, pp. 207, 208, etc.　Edward
Lucas was not present on this occasion, and Duffy had a vivid recollection
of it.

Hall as some suppose. He is unmarried and unlikely to marry, as no woman could live in the atmosphere of tobacco smoke which he makes about him."

They did not depart till late, and Duffy, who became one of the best of Carlyle's Boswells, said they all were very greatly impressed : " They did not accept his specific opinions on almost any question, but his constant advocacy of veracity, integrity and valour, touched the most generous of their sympathies, and his theory that under the divine government of the world right and might are identical, as right infallibly became might in the end, was very welcome to men struggling against enormous odds for justice." " It was not a mere theory, but a strong conviction," admitted Duffy afterwards,[4] " and one began to share it as one listened to him."

From that day forward, Duffy sent his *Nation* regularly to Carlyle, and proudly reports that Carlyle read it constantly and had it " sent after him, wherever he went, from time to time throwing out friendly suggestions how the work might be more effectually done ". In a few weeks (12–5–45) he was writing : " Justice to Ireland—the whole English nation except the quacks and knaves does honestly wish you that. Do not believe the contrary, for it is not true ; the believing it to *be* true may give rise to miserable mistakes yet, at which one's imagination shudders.

" Well, when poor old Ireland has succeeded again in making a man of insight and generous valour, ought I not to pray and hope that he may shine as a light instead of blazing as a firebrand, to his own waste and his country's ! Poor old Ireland, every man of that kind she produces it is like another stake set upon the great Rouge-et-Noir of the Destinies ; ' Shall I win with thee, or shall I lose thee too— blazing off upon me as the others have done ? ' She tries again, as with her last guinea. May the Gods grant her a good issue ! "

After reading more of the *Nation* he wrote again in sending *Past and Present* to Duffy : " I wish all Ireland would listen to you more and more. The thing you intrinsically mean is what all good Irishmen and all good men must mean ; let *it* come quickly, and continue for ever."[5] " True Thomas "

---

[4] Verbally to D. A. W.
[5] To see how well this praise was deserved, see *My Life in Two Hemi- spheres*, by Sir C. Gavan Duffy, I, pp. 63 to 73, etc.

was what these " Young Irelanders " were soon calling Carlyle in their private letters.[6]

More than fifty years afterwards, Gavan Duffy wrote of their friendship with him : " We agreed in few opinions except in the duty of living for ends which are not selfish or sordid ; but his talk was as stimulating as the morning breezes in an Alpine valley." [7]

[6] Ibid., I, p. 138.
[7] Ibid., I, p. 77.

XXIX

WHILE FINISHING "CROMWELL"

(1845)

ONE Friday evening (2–5–45) there was "a pleasant dinner-party" at the house of the ex-police-magistrate Wedgwood, whom Carlyle esteemed. Mazzini was there as well as the two Carlyles, and happily also Emma Darwin, who used her pen next morning to tell [1] :—

'Mazzini was clever and just in an amusing dispute with "Thomas" about music. T. C. could see nothing in Beethoven's Sonatas—"It told nothing." It was like a great quantity of stones tumbled down for a building, and "it might have been as well left in the quarry". He insisted on Mazzini telling him what he gained by hearing music, and when Mazzini said inspiration and elevation, Carlyle said something not respectful of Beethoven, and Mazzini ended with : "Dieu vous pardonne." It was very amusing. George Sand's novels entered also into this dispute, and then C. was right and Mazzini on the wrong side.'

Mrs. Carlyle had no patience with her husband's resurrection of Puritan piety, and told her intimate, Mrs. Russell of Thornhill, that she was looking forward to the end of it—"and then my husband will return to a consciousness of his daily life, and I shall have peace from the turmoils of the Commonwealth. For, if Carlyle thinks of nothing else but his Book while he is writing it, one always has this consolation, that he is the first to forget it when it is written."

In June he bought a horse and resumed his riding. In July he was assorting the heaps of borrowed books and planning to return them. Thus came to pass a last flicker of friendship between him and Mill. He wrote on 4th or 5th July, 1845 :—

[1] Emma Darwin, *A Century of Family Letters*, II, p. 95.

' Dear Mill,—

' I have had for a long time a *Whitelocke* of yours, which is now got much marked with Notes of mine, generally unintelligible to everybody else. I lately fell in with a nice clean copy of the Book ; if you have not some *pretium affectionis* [or fancy value] attached to your own (as is possible) I will give you this instead ; and bring it up some evening to you.

' My hurry and confusion for these many months past have been extreme ; but I hope to be thro' this present enterprise in some six weeks now ; and I sometimes think I shall then quit *Cromwell* and these Puritan Lumber-books for good. Yours ever truly,

' T. Carlyle.'

The answer came from the India House, 7–7–45 :—

' My dear Carlyle,—

' I have no *pretium affectionis* nor any other kind of *pretium* [value] attached to the *Whitelocke*, and I should think it money wasted on your part to provide me with another, for which I shall probably never have any use. " The tools to him who can use them ", and it would be a real pleasure to me if you would keep the *Whitelocke* with your annotations, and come to me some evening *without*, instead of *with*, another to replace it. Yours ever,

' J. S. Mill.'

In July Mrs. Carlyle made her husband take her to see Taglioni dancing, and she was indignant at the fashionable adoration of such indecency, which may have been why her husband repeated to her something he heard. Two London mechanics were standing at a printshop window, and one said to the other in his hearing, in a jaunty, knowing tone— " Ha ! *Tag-li-oni* ! Bit of fascination there ! " " Poor Taglioni," wrote Carlyle on reflection, " was elastic as india-rubber, but as meaningless too, pour soul."

Soon after seeing Taglioni, Mrs. Carlyle went on a visit to her uncle John in Liverpool. Her two vexations there were Tory prejudice, the common politics of rich merchants, and formal church attendance, to escape which her habit was either to keep her bed on Sunday, or go to the church of James Martineau, the Unitarian. She was attracted by the news that Martineau was quoting Carlyle from the pulpit in a friendly way.

On 31–7–45 she was writing to her husband what is plainly a good echo of their confidential talk: "Yesterday evening came a young N., in black, returned from the funeral of his only sister, a promising girl of sixteen, the poor mother's chief comfort. I recollected when Mrs. N., then Agnes L., consulted me whether she ought to marry J. N. Where were all these young N.'s then—the lad who sat there so sad, the girl just (dead) ? Had Agnes L. lived true to the memory of her first love, would these existences have been for ever suppressed by her act ? If her act could have suppressed them, what pretension have they to call themselves immortal, eternal ? What comfort is there in thinking of the young girl just laid in her grave ? ' My dear, you really ought not to go on with that sort of thing—all that questioning leads to nothing. We know nothing about it, and cannot know, and what better should we be if we did ? ' ' All very true, Mr. Carlyle, but—' at least one cannot accept such solution on the authority of others, even of the wisest—one must have worked it out for oneself. And the working of it out is a sore business, very sore ; especially with ' a body apt to fall into holes '."

The Welshes went to Scotland in August, and then Mrs. Carlyle went to stay with the Paulets, and soon was joined by Geraldine Jewsbury, " very amusing and good-humoured, does all the ' wits ' of the party. You would find our talk amusing." When James Martineau was present, it was serious and satisfactory too. Mrs. Carlyle thought Martineau " very near kicking his foot through " theology. Her husband replied (18–8–45) :—

' I begin almost to pity poor J. M. The lot of so many poor men, doomed to twaddle all their lives in Socinian jargon, and look at this divine Universe through distracted, despicable Jew-Greek spectacles, and a whole Monmouth St. of " Old Clo ", seems to me very sad.'

Inspired by this she said to Martineau, " You had better cut Unitarianism, and come over to us." " Who is it that you mean by *us* ? " " Carlyle." " He sighed and shook his head," wrote she, " and said something about a man being bound to remain in the sphere appointed to him till he was fairly drawn out of it by his conscience."

Whereupon she was admonished by return of post : " Do not seduce poor J. M. from his Unitarian manger, poor

fellow ! I do not in the least want proselytes. Ach Gott !
No ! What is the use of them ? And for himself it might
cut off the very staff of bread. Let him hang on there till
the rope of itself gives way with him."

Early in August Carlyle had " finished copying the last
letter of Oliver's", which left only the last chapter to be
written—the Death of the Protector. On 26–8–45 he wrote
to his wife—" I have this moment *ended* Oliver ; hang it !
He is ended, thrums and all. I have nothing more to write
on the subject, only mountains of wreck to burn. Not (any
more) up to the chin in paper clippings and chaotic litter,
hatefuller to me than most. I *am* to have a swept floor
again."

He joined her at the Paulets' a few days later, and stayed
a week.[2] She was resolute to go no farther north, and so he
went on by the Annan steamer, enjoying at the start the
sight of the " Vanity Fair of Liverpool, tents on the sands,
swings and whirligigs", but rather enduring than enjoying
the rest of the voyage, for the smells on board, and the bad
ventilation, made him feel like another Jonah in a " greasy
whale's belly". But he was not allowed to be lonely, for he
was instantly recognized by a fellow-passenger, " big
Thomson the cattle-dealer," who had called upon him at
Cheyne Row eleven years ago, a Falstaff in face and figure,
with a great gift of familiarity, proclaiming who Carlyle
was " to the ship's company in general", so that he " had
the strangest addresses, free and easy as in the Age of Gold ".
Early in the morning they were at Annan, and a few hours
later Carlyle was at Scotsbrig, and walking with his frail old
mother on the silent moor, where the only sound was his
mother's voice, as she told of pleasant letters from his wife.
The seas and hills lay beautiful all round, and " the sun and
sky were bright as silver ". The whole thing seemed to him
like a pleasant picture, " or a dream."

The proofs of *Cromwell* gave him no great trouble. His
mother enjoyed his company about two months. On fine
days he went driving with her to Annan or as far as Dumfries.
In talking to Aird at Dumfries one day about a book by
Gilfillan, he said he " magnifies trifles too much by over-
heated enthusiasm ", a hint which Aird passed on as true,
and Gilfillan himself was fond of quoting some comfort

---

[2] For Mr. Froude's imaginary " angry letter ", see A. Carlyle's *New
Letters and Memorials of J. W. C.*, I, pp. 171–2.

against critics which Carlyle gave him : " If they receive it ill, write you the second better, so much better as to shame them." [3]

For his own behoof Carlyle was reading at large at Scots-brig, becoming curious about the Prussians, whom he called a " kind of German-English ", and particularly enjoying two books by Preuss on Frederick the Great, which Varn-hagen von Ense had sent him some time before. He told Von Ense that they awakened in him " the liveliest curiosity to know more and ever more about that king. Certainly if there is a Hero for an Epic in these ages—and why not ?— then this is he ! But he remains still very dark to me. I should like to know much more ", so please consult Preuss if needful, and " send me a few names of likely books on the subject ".[4]

" If I had any turn for travelling," Carlyle wrote to his wife, " I should go to Berlin and make acquaintance with him and his people. They are both of them very strange. Alas, what is the meaning of Literature ? 'German Literature' should have given us some melodious image of this greatest German Man. German Literature too is but a smallish matter . . .

" What next ? We shall see by and by. My appetite for writing is considerably modified ; but I have no other trade—why should I wish any other ? I will stick by my trade ; and say a thing or two yet, if I live ! . . . Total idleness does not answer me long."

In a letter to his brother in Canada, he told of the crowds of Irish come to dig and make the new Caledonian Railway, and he described the ominous potato disease he saw beside him, and read about in Holland and Germany, as well as in England and Ireland.

---

[3] *George Gilfillan*, by R. A. and E. S. Watson, pp. 134, 176, etc., and George Gilfillan's own writings.
[4] *Last Words of T. C.*, Longmans, Green & Co., pp. 240–2.

XXX

MRS. CARLYLE AND LADY HARRIET

(1845)

MRS. CARLYLE was now seeing the last of old Sterling, and a good deal of Lady Harriet Baring, afterwards Ashburton. "Dicky" Milnes contrived to bring the women together again for an hour one Sunday (28–9–45), and Mrs. Carlyle wrote to her husband at Scotsbrig: "I daresay, in spite of Mrs. Buller's prediction, we shall get on very well together; altho I can see that the lady has a genius for *ruling* while I have a genius for—*not being ruled.*"

One item of their gossip had been Peel giving Tennyson a pension of £200 a year. Lady Harriet: "He wants to marry; must have a woman to live beside; would *prefer a lady*, but cannot afford one; and so must marry a maid servant." Mrs. Henry Taylor: "I am about to write him on behalf of our housemaid, who is quite a superior character in her way." As Dr. Johnson said, "The insolence of wealth will out."

They talked of books. Lady Harriet was "all agog" about the memoirs of Blanco White, an Irish R.C. priest of Spanish training, who was interesting because he had outgrown his creed and taken Church of England "orders" and become a "Protestant Champion"! But then he outgrew the thirty-nine articles also, and was called at last a rationalist Thomas-à-Kempis. He is still remembered for a fine sonnet on Night, which Coleridge praised ecstatically. "Mysterious Night, when our first parents knew thee . . ." at first—on their honeymoon night in the Garden of Eden, he means—they thought the world was coming to an end; but as soon as they had leisure to look round, a night or two later, the darkness disclosed the stars to them, which proves the possibility of immortality. So be content to die—"If Light conceals so much, wherefore not Life?" You never can tell, so wait and see—an old, old story; but the talk on Blanco White would clear the air and let the women see each other's religious footing.

Lady Harriet and Mrs. Carlyle now fell into a violent friendship. They had much in common, perhaps too much ; both witty, perhaps too witty ; accustomed to win admiration by talking, and prone to let themselves go, and feel like Juvenal's lady that whatever she wills must be right, because she wills it. As an American Missionary lady once told a judge in Burma, " Heaven approves of women."

On reading his wife's report, Carlyle responded :—

' There is nothing to hinder you, in spite of Mrs. Buller's prediction, to get on very well there. The Lady Harriet has a genius for ruling. Well ! did you ever see any lady that had *not* some slight touch of a genius that way, my Goodikin ? I know a lady—but I will say nothing, lest I bring mischief about my ears—nay, she is very obedient, too, that little lady I allude to, and has a genius for being ruled withal. Heaven bless her always ! Not a bad little dame at all. She and I did aye very weel together ; and, " 'tweel, it was not every one that could have done with her." '

He soon was writing cautions from Scotsbrig against too extensive a promise from his wife to winter with Lady Harriet at Bay House in Hampshire. " Indeed," he wrote (4–10–45), " as Mr. Croaker says,[1] I wish we may be all as well at the end of that business as at the beginning ! "

To which she answered, " Bah ! " and settled to take him with her from the middle of November to stay six weeks there. She knew he would be resting then at any rate. He came home in a week or two, and on the last day of October was writing from Chelsea to his mother that the potatoes were short all over Europe :—

' The present fever of trade is nearly certain to break down soon into deep confusion, so that one may fear a bad winter for the poor, a sad thing to look forward to. They are best off, I think, who have least to do with that brutal Chase for money which afflicts me wherever I go in this country. " Give me neither poverty nor riches, feed me with food convenient for me." '[2]

His *Oliver Cromwell* was published in November.

---

[1] Goldsmith's Mr. Croaker in *The Good-Natured Man*.
[2] C. T. Copeland's *Letters of T. C. to His Youngest Sister*, 1899, p. 183.

XXXI

"OLIVER CROMWELL'S LETTERS AND SPEECHES"

(1845)

OLIVER CROMWELL'S Letters and Speeches had an immediate success surprising to author and publisher; and beyond its author's hopes it soon appeared plainly to be a great event in history, the unveiling of the greatest Englishman who ever ruled and led us. It was like sunshine appearing after the darkness of many ages.

There had been an Alfred long ago, and in humbler places an occasional Abbot Samson had made life bearable ; but so vile in general had been our " dogs in office " that, after the Restoration, it was easy for Clarendon and Co. to persuade us that the great Oliver had been a selfish ambitious man and a humbug—like one of themselves. It was the worst they could say of him, and the only thing they could think. It came to them like winking. Men like to look down—it may be a habit we inherit from our arboreal ancestors. There is no doubt about the pleasure ; and the habit could only be the stronger the more one knew of history. It is true of other people besides the Turks that in general they no more deserve a history than the tigers or wolves.

So it was without fear of contradiction that Pope had written of " Cromwell, damned to everlasting fame". Even Voltaire had been taken in, and moralizing over Cromwell's prosperity combined with wickedness, laid down as true the most dismal lesson of history, that it is weakness which is punished and big crimes prosper, making the whole world a place of robbery ruled by " Fortune ".

1845 was the year of Benjamin Disraeli's *Sybil*, wherein he lifted up afresh for adoration the royal martyr, the " virtuous and able monarch ", Charles Stuart I, who " laid down his heroic life " for " the Church " and " the Poor " ! [1]

---

[1] *Life of Disraeli*, by Monypenny, II, pp. 268–9.

the highest ideals of Christians and Confucians. His likeness should be in every school ; but when that is done, the children should be told of how he championed free-thinking and free-speaking, and how little he had in common with the politicians familiar in history, slippery cheats and domineering duffers, and whatever blend of force and fraud they use, as conscienceless as cats. " Old Noll " was a man of conscience to his finger tips, successful in war, yet a scrupulous lover of peace; disinterested, just and merciful; controlling his fighting men, and not even dismissing the " Rump " till the gentlemen of the " Rump " had become a public nuisance. Far from defying the opinions of good men, he was continually conciliating them, and made his country peaceful and prosperous.

In 1856 Carlyle was to receive from John Forster the proofs of a review of Guizot's *History of the English Republic and Cromwell*, and made some confidential pencil jottings there worth quoting now.[7] He had thought highly of the beginning of the History, but now he detested Guizot as a fellow who posed as a religious man and yet, to keep his place in politics, sank so low as to abet the royal rascal Louis Philippe in his wholesale corruption ; and as Carlyle read about Guizot's notion that Cromwell mixed statecraft with religion, he called the ultra-respectable French states-man a " Sophist " and even a " galvanized dead dog ", and his book " a dirty French pamphlet ". Forster having quoted Guizot as saying that Cromwell desired to found a dynasty, Carlyle retorted : " It is false that he ever wanted to found a dynasty. His notion was—and that very loose—a dynasty like the Hebrew Judges." Forster agreed to this.

Poor Guizot ! Men have to judge of others by themselves. Wisdom and Goodness seem dodging to dodgers. Perhaps the reason why Carlyle was able to divine and prove the superlative sincerity of Cromwell was that he was a sincere man himself, and in his own father had long known, familiarly and yet with reverence, a real Christian of the same sort as Oliver Cromwell. His old mother in Annandale dwelt with delight on the Letters and Speeches of Cromwell, but skipped her son's " elucidations "—they were needless to her.

Soon after the publication of the *Letters and Speeches*, he wrote to Thomas Erskine, the good Christian friend who had first thought of the value of such a collection : " One thing

[7] *Literary Recollections*, by F. Espinasse, pp. 84–6.

I do recognize with much satisfaction, that the general verdict of our poor loose public seems to be that Oliver *was* a genuine man, and if so, surely to them a very surprising one. It will do them much good, poor bewildered blockheads, to understand that no great man was ever other ; that this notion of theirs about ' Machiavellism ', ' Policy ', and so forth, is on the whole what one might call blasphemous —a real doctrine of Devils."

" Jesuitry " he called it in another letter soon after this (same to same), describing " Jesuitry " as " the blackest, most godless spot in history . . . a solemn wedding in God's name of truth and falsehood—as if the two were now one flesh and could not subsist apart ! " His hatred of such humbug made him rejoice in the success of his book " as one other symptom of the rapidly deepening seriousness of the public mind ".

' The conviction seems to be pretty unanimous that this is actually the history of Oliver ; that the former histories of him have been extraordinary mistakes—very fallacious histories—as of a man walking about for two centuries in a universal masked ball (of hypocrites and their hypocrisies spoken and done), with a mask upon him, this man, which no cunningest artist could get off. They tried it now this way, now that ; still the mask was felt to remain ; the mask would not come off. At length a lucky thought strikes us. The man *is in his natural face.* That is the mask of this one ! Of all which I am heartily glad. In fact, it often strikes me as the fellest virulence of all the misery that lies upon us in these distracted generations, this blackest form of *incredulity* we have all fallen into, that great men, too, were paltry shuffling Jesuits, as we ourselves are, and meant nothing true in their work, or mainly meant lies and hunger in their work, even as we ourselves do. There will never be anything but an *enchanted* world till that baleful phantasm of the pit be chased thither again and very sternly bidden abide there.'

Talking to Espinasse about the same time, " Carlyle said that if Cromwell had nominated as his successor his capable younger son, Henry, who was governing Ireland for him when he died, the Protectorate might have been firmly established, and thus the pernicious restoration of the Stuarts been averted." Many more talks may best be

summed up in his own words to the Edinburgh students
in 1866 :—

' That Protectorate of Cromwell's appears to me to have
been the most salutary thing in the modern history of
England. If Oliver Cromwell had continued it out, I don't
know what it would have come to. It would have got
corrupted probably in other hands, and could not have gone
on ; but there was perfect truth in it while he ruled over it.'

Tho Carlyle had shared the surprise of his wife and
publisher at the success of his *Cromwell*, and admitted he
thought it " heavy ", he always ' predicted it would be
" the most lasting of all his books " ', said Espinasse, who
added : ' It was the only work of his of which one heard
him hint that its execution did not fall far short of his
ideal.' [8]   As he wrote to his mother at the time, " In all
probability this is the usefullest business I shall ever get to
do in the world ; rescuing the memory of a Noble Man from
disfigurement, and presenting him again to a world that
stands much in need of the like of him."

Its success has continued and in every sense been complete,
so complete that we can hardly realize to-day how great it
was. The condemnation of Cromwell had seemed unanimous
for nearly two hundred years. For example, the book of
history most highly praised by Sir Walter Scott was Lodge's
Portraits. It " exhibits before our eyes our ' fathers as they
lived ' ", he wrote to its publisher.[9]   Lodge was conscientiously conventional, and here is how he begins his
biography of Cromwell :—

' It may seem strange that the character of this
remarkable person should have been suffered to find its own
level in unbiassed judgment ; that no flowery Whig pen has
yet attempted to varnish it with eulogies ; nay, that even
the fierceness of democracy has not furnished a single
champion to bedaub it with coarse and plain-spoken praise.
. . . The cause is the absence of any one positive virtue in
the man, as well as of any form of that generosity, real or
affected, which too frequently serves to lessen the deformity
of wickedness. . . . The anxiety, perhaps more amiable

---

[8] Ibid., p. 75.
[9] Lockhart's *Sir Walter Scott*, X, p. 98 ; and for the letter Vol. I of
Lodge's eight volumes, in later editions.

than prudent, of a descendant has of late put forth a large cento of quotations, under the title of " Memoirs ", etc. ; but they are urged merely in negative apology, and aim only at relieving his memory somewhat of certain charges, without making a single effort to adorn it by bringing forward any redeeming merit . . .' and so on.   The narrative sticks to this like a demonstration in Euclid to the theorem.   Thus, for example, near the end : ' The bodily health of Cromwell gradually declined.   His cruelty increased with his fears,' and in short ' the last public acts of his life were the erection of one more of those infamous tribunals ', which readers should curse like Robespierre's.[10]

Nobody writes such stuff to-day.   Biographers and historians agree that " Old Noll " was a man of the right sort ; and Dryasdust in many a new embodiment is eager to hide his old mistakes and pretends to improve on Carlyle's performance, and modestly demands our praise for correcting a comma or two.   Anybody can go to America—after Columbus has shown the way.

There is another matter whereof we may need to be reminded in days when the American republic appears reactionary.   The idol-worship of Royal persons was made impossible to English readers after 1845, and Disraeli's attempt in that year to whitewash the cruel coward James Stuart of 1688 seemed like a joke.   It is needless to repeat here the whole of the humorous and yet conclusive commentary on the Death Warrant signed by Cromwell and others for the execution of Charles Stuart, the father of that James :—

' No modern reader can conceive the then atrocity . . . First, after long reading in the old dead Pamphlets, does one see the magnitude of it.   Alas, in these irreverent times of ours, if all the Kings of Europe were cut in pieces at one swoop, and flung in heaps in St. Margaret's Churchyard on the same day, the emotion would, in strict arithmetical truth, be small in comparison . . . This action of the English Regicides did in effect strike a damp like death through the heart of Flunkyism universally in this world. Whereof Flunkyism, Cant, Cloth-worship has gone about sick ever since ; and is now at length very rapidly dying.'

[10] Lodge's *Portraits*, V, pp. 75–92.

John Morley thought differently in 1900;[11] but what Americans call the " Cascade of Kings " at the end of the last royal row, the Willie-and-Nicky war, confirms Carlyle. " Old Noll " was always a hero in the West. Massachusetts even sheltered the Regicides who went there after the Restoration. Since 1845 the ideal of an American President is to be like Oliver Cromwell, and now that his statue is set up beside the Houses of Parliament in Westminster, it may be hoped that the habits of hypocrisy and lying may become less fashionable among our own politicians. If so the literary critics may be wrong, and Carlyle's own feeling right. His " Elucidations " of the *Letters and Speeches* may be the least of his writings as literature ; but his revelation of the sincerity of Oliver Cromwell may be his greatest work.

[11] *Oliver Cromwell*, by John Morley, pp. 285-6.

BOOK XIV

RELAXING

(1845-46)

I

DR. JOHN IS STARTED ON DANTE

(1845)

ABOUT the beginning of November 1845 seems to be the date of what Carlyle told Mr. Symington in 1869.[1]

'Walking in Rotten Row he told me how his brother John had amassed in Italy an enormous amount of Dante material (for) a prose translation. For long Carlyle had unsuccessfully urged his brother to set about it ; but urge and progue as he would, he could not get him to begin. So he bethought him of the man who was driving pigs to Killarney, and who told his friend to hush and speak low, for the pigs thought he wanted them to go the other way.' This Carlyle ' told with animation, standing still and acting it, saying :—

" *That* was how I got John to begin his translation. One day, said I : ' John, man, if I were in your shoes, I would get quit of that Dante business, which hangs about your neck like a dead albatross. Cast it away from you and give up all thought of ever translating Dante. If you had been a young man you might have looked forward to overtaking it ; but now you are *too old*. Read and enjoy yourself, and bother your head no more about Dante ! ' The steel struck fire as intended. John exclaimed : ' ME *too old* ! I'm nothing of the kind ! ' and set to work, and produced one of the very best translations of Dante to be found anywhere." '

Which illuminates what was perplexing Espinasse, who reports [2] : ' While the poor doctor was labouring hard at Dante, Carlyle rather pooh-poohed his zeal as expended on an " obsolete " theme.'

Dr. John was lodging beside them this winter, and a constant visitor. " He looks on love as a disease of the

---

[1] *Personal Reminiscences of C.*, by A. J. Symington, pp. 112–14.
[2] *Literary Recollections*, by F. Espinasse, pp. 109–10.

nerves," said Mrs. Carlyle to Espinasse. He and his brother discussed and differed about the elective principle, and John, "a logic-chopper from his infancy" his brother called him, stood up against denunciations of voting, and spoke with admiration of how official medical posts were better filled in Paris by the suffrages of medical men than in London by outsiders.

' Like his brother,' said Espinasse, summing him up, ' he loved thoroughness of knowledge and despised superficiality.' But they differed like Don Quixote and Sancho Panza. Carlyle was never weary of saying " when one is not working one ought not to be happy; one ought to be very unhappy, *seeking* out work." John agreed in words, but could always be happy doing nothing or as near it as possible.

Which appeared in this very Dante translation. The Comedy Divine of Dante is in three parts—Hell, Purgatory, and Paradise. By the end of 1848 John was sending out his *Hell* " by way of experiment ", he said in his Preface. What Symington was told was true—it remains one of the best translations in English. The 1899 edition was the seventh, and it is still selling, as Carlyle told him it would (28–12–48). But the immediate result being unsatisfactory, Dr. John disregarded his brother's urging, as when he wrote on 28–2–50 : ' Do not grudge trouble for the *Purgatorio* ; I tell you always it will last a very long while.' John could not be set going another time. He left *Purgatory* and *Paradise* to be translated by Posterity, if ever Posterity wanted them ; and loafed at leisure well-content to the end of his long life As he was fond of saying to Mrs. (Thomas) Carlyle, " There is no use at all in rebelling against Providence." His professional advice to his brother Tom was equally sound. He confided to Espinasse,—" I preach cheerfulness to him."

II

DR. CHALMERS CONVERTED ABOUT CROMWELL

(1845)

IN November David Masson went north, and on 22–11–45 was breakfasting with Thomas Chalmers at Edinburgh, and heard him say : " I have just got Carlyle's *Cromwell*, but not yet begun to read it. What's his drift ? " He was told, and went on : " So he has taken to whitewashing Cromwell ! Well, it won't do." Chalmers talked at length about the Commonwealth, showing he shared the current prejudices. One of his remarks was : " Baxter tells us that Cromwell kept a very disorderly house."

A fortnight later Masson was breakfasting with him again, and found him ' in ecstasies about Cromwell,' saying, " I wish they had made him King. As for the Scotch, they showed what I have found among them myself—a great deal of capernoitedness " (obstinacy). He approved of everything Carlyle had written except a few interpolations in the speeches, concluding with strange earnestness, as if in a sudden soliloquy :—

" That laddie has looked with a most intelligent eye on the peculiarities of Calvinism, and yet—, and yet—, and yet—" (the voice rising and the sentence left expressively unfinished).[1]

Masson was puzzled at Carlyle being called a " laddie ", but it was easy to explain. Chalmers had never seen Carlyle since the winter holidays of 1820–21. So in his mind's eye Carlyle was still the young friend of his young assistant, Irving.

---

[1] Told to D. A. W. by David Masson in March, 1896.

III

CARLYLE'S TEMPTATION

(1845)

EDWARD FITZGERALD was soon a favourite of Carlyle, but Mrs. Carlyle did not " get to like him " till 1849.[1] He had often come to their house before then, alone or with Thackeray,[2] but Carlyle and he had what Mrs. Carlyle considered the bad habit of adjourning to smoke together in the garden or in a little room on the second floor at the back of the house, a " dressing-room " of Carlyle, which in 1843 had been tried as a study by way of a refuge from piano noises, and remained an occasional smoking room for intimates. While Carlyle was still busy on the *Letters and Speeches*, FitzGerald described [3] how they sat there with ' the window open, and looked out on nursery gardens, their almond trees in blossom, and beyond, bare walls of houses, and over these, roofs and chimneys, and here and there a steeple, *and (the) whole (of) London crowned with darkness gathering behind like the illimitable resources of a dream*. I tried to persuade him to leave the accursed den, and he wished — but — but — perhaps he *didn't* wish on the whole . . .

' London is very hateful to me. I am sure a great City is a deadly Plague ; worse than the illness so called that came to ravage it. I tried to persuade Carlyle to leave his filthy Chelsea, *but he says his wife likes London.*'

One does not swop horses while crossing a stream, and till the *Letters and Speeches* were finished, Carlyle said no more about leaving London. On 14–11–45 he was writing to Thomas Aird,[4] the editor at Dumfries, who had applied to him to get notice in the reviews for a book by the

---

[1] *J. W. Carlyle : Letters to her Family*, edited by L. Huxley, p. 333.
[2] Ibid., pp. 102 and 333.
[3] *Letters of Edward FitzGerald*, Macmillan, 1894, I, pp. 157-9. (Italics added.)
[4] Memoir in the *Poetical Works of Thomas Aird*, by J. Wallace, p. XXXV.

Rev. George Gilfillan, which Carlyle did. But what is interesting now in his letters to Aird and Lockhart [5] about Gilfillan is only what he says about London : " Chelsea, the old address, will always find us " and " this, in spite of its fogs, is the Paradise of ' men at large ', this big Babylon of ours ".

Next day he went with his wife to Alverstoke on the shore near Portsmouth, to spend six weeks with the Barings there, as Mrs. Carlyle and Lady Harriet had arranged. On 7–12–45 he was writing to John Forster [6] :—

' We are leading a peculiar life here on these mild coasts ; kind elegant people ; the beautifullest December weather I ever saw ; a beautiful House, beautiful sea, and Isle of Wight with its ships and towns; all very "beautiful"; but amounting to the most perfect state of *Donothingism* ! That is the drawback . . . I suppose one's conscience will send one home before long. As for me, I am totally annihilated ; good for nothing at all but smoking tobacco, and sitting silent on the shingle amid the furze-bushes here. Good-bye, dear Forster. Yours ever truly,
' T. CARLYLE.'

But he was not sitting on the shingle all the time. There was a ride almost every day and music in the evenings, to say nothing of talk continually. One could let oneself go after dinner, which was what Monckton Milnes may have been meaning when he said, " Out of the abundance of the mouth the heart speaketh." There was general rejoicing now in the Barings' house at the news of which they had early intimation that Peel had decided to abolish the Corn-laws ; and maybe it was Carlyle's warm approval of this that made him take Peel's side when Milnes, his friend and fellow-guest, was complaining that Peel had unfairly passed him over—he should have had some office. The biographer of Milnes [7] has quoted his note-book to show that in private Carlyle gave him ' probably the best advice that was ever given to any man under such circumstances', namely: " It seems to me that the chief thing for you to do as regards Peel is to look clearly into yourself, and try and find out what it was that prevented him promoting you as you seem to have deserved."

[5] *J. G. Lockhart*, by Andrew Lang, II, pp. 241–2.
[6] Unpublished Letter.
[7] *R. Monckton Milnes*, L.H., by T. Wemyss Reid, I, p. 437.

In company, however, when Milnes was babbling, he was chaffed. " The only office you are fit for," Carlyle told him,[8] after commending Peel's " judgment and penetration "— " is that of ' Perpetual President of the Heaven and Hell Amalgamation Society '." He meant that Milnes was too easy-going, tolerant of evil-doing, but was easily answered by hints about not interfering in the clergy's business, as if he had been referring to post-obit places. In fact, and this was what made the fun, Carlyle was more English than the English in tabooing theology.

While thus he was resting after labour and beholding every day the beautiful sea, changing but aye the same, he remembered FitzGerald's words, and was almost persuaded that he should cease to live in London. His wife discovered with alarm, as she said,[9] that ' Alverstoke awakened all his enthusiasm again for country life—and horror of London. He talked of building a house on the shore—but there was a hideous man who went about shooting—without his nose— and after encountering him some twenty times, Carlyle discovered that it would be impossible for him to live where he would be liable to meet that man '. He spoke of Scotland —" Perhaps poor old Annandale would be the best place after all." His wife derided such speculations, but began to be uneasy about them. Nothing would persuade her to prolong their visit. She felt she could not get him home too soon to keep him out of temptation. Her love for London was the only cause of friction there ever was between them, and she needed all her tact to keep him there.

[8] *Autobiography of Henry Taylor*, I, p. 331.
[9] *Mrs. Carlyle : Letters to her Family*, edited by L. Huxley, p. 262.

IV

TIPS FOR BIOGRAPHERS

(1845)

THE Rev. Alexander Scott was better now, and meditating a Life of Dante. He applied for advice, and Carlyle bestowed it (5–12–45) copiously and without reserve, which makes it interesting, tho Scott's book was never written. As for " artificial helps to remembrance ", Carlyle had tried them with little benefit :—

' Can you not begin straightway to write ? There is no end of inquiring. . . . You ask me how I proceed in taking notes. I would very gladly tell you all my methods if I had any ; but really I have as it were none. I go into the business with all the intelligence, patience, silence, and other gifts and virtues that I have ; find that ten times or a hundred times as many could be profitably expended there, and still prove insufficient ; and as for plan, I find that every new business requires as it were a new scheme of operations, which among infinite bungling and plunging unfolds itself at intervals (very scantily, after all) as I get along. The great thing is, not to stop and break down ; to know that *virtue* is very indispensable, that one must not stop because new and ever new drafts upon one's virtue must be honoured ! But as to the special point of taking Excerpts, I rather avoid *writing* beyond the very minimum ; mark in pencil the very smallest indication that will direct me to the thing again, and on the whole try to keep the whole matter simmering in the *living* mind and memory rather than laid up in paper bundles or otherwise laid up in the inert way. For this certainly turns out to be a truth. Only what you at last *have living* in your own memory and heart is worth putting down to be printed.'

V

LADY HARRIET AND OTHERS

(1845)

IT is often said that you never can know people till you
have lived with them. By the first week in December,
Mrs. Carlyle had seen a good deal of Lady Harriet Baring,
her hostess, and wrote to her cousin Jeannie [1] :—

' I am still alive and experiencing, as Darwin wished for
me at parting, "as few *disagreeablenesses* as could reasonably
be expected." Lady Harriet is as kind as possible, and has
not done, said, or looked a single thing to justify the
character for haughtiness and caprice which she bears—in
fact a woman more perfectly regardless of *rank* I never
happened to see. *Strength* is what she goes upon ; a *weak*
Prince of the blood she would treat with undisguised scorn,
and would behave herself quite *sisterly* towards a *strong*
street sweeper. In fact, she is a *grand* woman, every inch
of her—and *not* a coquette the least in the world. She is not
well employed—but floats along on the top of things in a
rather *ignis fatuus* sort of way . . .

' There is no talk of going home—but I *must* go—*alone* if
necessary, when the Paulets return to London. Now that
I am fairly settled into the thing I feel no haste to encounter
London winter—if the sea *be* " somewhat chilly " it is at
least very *clean* to look out upon. . . . And really there is as
little of burdensome *state* here as can possibly be made to do
—not so much *dressing* as *you* have to transact in Maryland
Street—rational hours—and no strain on one's wits—for
Lady Harriet *does* all the wit herself ; and nobody " feels
that it is his duty " to amuse—if it lie in his way to do so
well and good—but things will go on briskly enough
without him.'

Pleading one excuse or another, and taking her husband

---

[1] *J. W. Carlyle : Her Letters to her Family*, by L. Huxley, pp. 258–9.

with her, Mrs. Carlyle went home before the end of the year, and on 30–12–45 was writing to Thornhill :—

'DEAREST MRS. RUSSELL,—
    ' We are just returned from Hampshire . . . worn out with " strenuous idleness " . . . I wonder why so many people wish for high positions and great wealth when it is such an " open secret " what all that amounts to—merely to emancipating people from all the practical difficulties which might teach them the facts of things and sympathy with their fellow-creatures. This Lady Harriet Baring is the cleverest woman I ever saw ; she is full of energy and sincerity, and has, I am sure, an excellent heart ; yet so perverted has she been by her high position that I question if in her whole life she has done as much for her fellow-creatures as my mother in one year, or whether she will ever be anything other than the most amusing and most graceful woman of her time. The sight of such a woman should make one content with one's own trials, even when they feel hard ! '

    Mrs. Carlyle recurred to the Lady Harriet on 19–1–46, in telling Jeannie[2] of her husband's schemes to escape from London. ' He now says he would like to go to Prussia for a while !—I wish I might know what is to become of me ! —*that* is *all* I pretend to—a modest request !—but with such uncertain views of the future there is no getting any use of the present. Lady Harriet asks in her last letter " Will I come to Rome next winter ? " and *she* always *means* every least syllable she says.'
    Which at least reveals an uncommon feature of that lady's character, and goes far to explain Carlyle's esteem.
    Ever since her mother died Mrs. Carlyle had been remorsefully remembering some of her mother's ways, which she had not understood at the time. As she had explained to Jeannie[3] : ' Often I used to feel vexed at my mother for spending so much of the little she had upon others, and getting so few comforts and pleasures out of it for herself—fool that I was, I made that a reproach to her which was her goodness, her wisdom. Oh, I am very thankful now that she followed the thought of her own generous heart instead

---

[2] Ibid., p. 262.
[3] Ibid., p. 36.

of my mistaken counsels ! She made herself *loved* as a benefactor . . . All that she *enjoyed* is useless to her now ; but all that she *gave* belongs to another sphere—its fruits remain for ever and ever.'

Mrs. Carlyle " brought forth fruits of repentance ", by continuing to pay the kind little pensions and annual presents her mother used to give. She also more and more became herself a good Samaritan with the minimum of fuss, befriending all in need whom she could see and reach, and letters remain to show how she took pains to avoid mistakes, and make her help effectual, not merely questioning a poor woman her husband noticed in his walks and indicated to her, but sifting what was told her, and acting accordingly.[4] She "had a kindly disposition", Espinasse testifies,[5] " and often ' did good '," especially to " those in whom she took a personal interest ".

[4] Ibid., pp. 71–3.
[5] *Literary Recollections*, by F. Espinasse, p. 105.

VI

TIPS FOR HISTORIANS, &c.

(1846)

ACCORDING to Espinasse,[1] Carlyle returned home at the end of 1845, apparently rested and ready for more work. ' From (his) conversation at this time, I inferred that he was looking for a theme to the England of the eleventh century and William the Conqueror. He came with his brother John to the Library of the British Museum, and carefully inspected there the engraved reproduction of the Bayeux Tapestry, Anglo-Norman history in needlework, the handiwork undoubtedly of a contemporary of the Conquest. In the rude but genuine scenes, from Harold taking leave of the Confessor before starting for Normandy, to the battle of Hastings, there was (what) delighted Carlyle. He had long thought the figure of the Conqueror distorted by historians. Under Harold, Carlyle thought, England would have lapsed into anarchy. The rebellion of Harold's brother Tostig, supported by a Danish invasion, prefigured a series of rebellions and invasions. In the rule of the Conqueror Carlyle saw a great deal more than ruthlessness, and he looked on William and his Normans as the true makers of the greatness of England. His keen interest in the Conquest had apparently been first aroused by Thierry's History,' meaning the *Conquest of England*, Thierry's masterpiece.

' Carlyle could not believe that the England fashioned by William was the result of nothing better than the Norman cruelty and rapacity, with pictures of which Thierry's pages teemed. Such a notion was entirely false, and had produced, he thought, practically mischievous conceptions of the course of human affairs. I heard him maintain that the acceptance of Thierry's theory of the Norman Conquest had contributed to produce the cruelties then recently perpetrated by the French in Algeria!'

[1] *Literary Recollections*, by F. Espinasse, pp. 79–81.

In the first week of 1846, Carlyle was sadly remarking in his London walks : " Many poor creatures are already on the streets with a look of pinching hunger in their faces. Ah me ! " There still survives a letter from him about this time,[2] sending two pounds to a man in Dumfries who was in need. He was told that potatoes were " four for three half-pence ". It began to seem possible there might be famine even in England. Yet the " landed " Tories were loud against Peel, and the Duke of Norfolk, according to historians,[3] " went about recommending a curry powder of his own device as a charm against hunger." In spite of such a noble invention, the corn taxes were going to be abolished !

In every country in Europe the potatoes were a failure, and many were hungry ; but only in Ireland was there a government so heedless of the people that other food was allowed to be exported to pay the rents, while men, women and children perished in thousands of sheer starvation. While O'Connell and his tail were busy contriving how to get the best prices possible for their votes in the political crises impending, Carlyle gave some of his time this winter to reading Young Ireland's *Nation*, and corresponding with Gavan Duffy, who in turn was gladly helping him to make perfect the Irish names, etc., in his *Cromwell*, the second edition of which occupied the first half of 1846.

[2] Unpublished letter.
[3] *History of our own Times*, by J. McCarthy, I, p. 290.

VII

CROMWELL AGAIN

(1846)

THE success of his book made many persons send him letters of Cromwell not known before. The Duke of Manchester brought his share of such treasures with his own hands.[1] To weld the new material into the old was far from easy. Carlyle said he had " to unhoop his tub which already held water and to insert new staves ". It needed " one's most exquisite talent, as of shoe-cobbling, really, that kind of talent carried to a high pitch ".

His wife had been only too glad to get out of " the Cromwell atmosphere ", she said, and was far from rejoicing at any return of it. She thought the English " a singular people " to give the *Letters and Speeches* " such a cordial reception ", while comparatively indifferent to " a book so interesting as *Past and Present* ". But to Carlyle himself the new edition " was a labour of love ", said Espinasse— he was so glad to see his countrymen thinking as he did about his hero. " Once more " his talk was of Cromwell.

' I can see him now in an old brown dressing-gown, seated on a footstool on the hearthrug, close to the fireplace in the little parlour, sending most deftly up the chimney whiffs from a long clay pipe. I can hear him, between the whiffs, in the strongest possible of Scotch accents, contrasting Cromwell and his Puritans with contemporary English politicians, and the multitudes whom they were leading by the nose.

' Mrs. Carlyle with head bent and one hand covering her face, listening in silence ' awhile, interrupted ' fierce denunciations with : " Don't be angry with Mr. Espinasse, *he* is not to blame," or " My dear, your tea is getting quite cold ; that is the way with reformers ".' Then perhaps he would stop and ' break into a hearty laugh at his own vehemence '.

---

[1] *Literary Recollections*, by F. Espinasse, pp. 74, 81–8, 122, 228–9, for this chapter.

Admitting " the wisest man should rule ", Espinasse would ask : " How is the wisest to be discovered ? " He was answered :—

" First of all we have to discover the need for the supremacy of Wisdom, together with the utter futility of our present method of choosing our Governors by counting votes at the polling booth." 'I ventured to hint,' says Espinasse :—" Even were the wisest man discovered he would not be immortal, and there might be a difficulty about the succession." To this, he says, ' Carlyle replied in rather an irate tone : " That is the sort of twaddle that used to be poured into me when I was young," and proceeded to speak of the good government enjoyed by the world under the five great Roman emperors,' Nerva, Trajan, Hadrian, and the Antonines. Gibbon in his third chapter calls this the " most happy and prosperous period in the history of the world ", and as Espinasse seems to have been reminded, they " succeeded each other by adoption ". It may have been an afterthought of his, that the last of the five appointed as successor " his vile son Commodus ". At any rate when Espinasse spoke " of the stoical grandeur of the Meditations of Antoninus ", Carlyle cut him short with, " The unreading Germans came in and put an end to all that sentimentality," which puzzled Espinasse more than ever, as the *Meditations* were quoted as a motto for the *French Revolution*.

Carlyle's idea, of course, was that hereditary succession to public office was absurd and wrong, an idea which the teaching of Confucius had made political orthodoxy in China for milleniums. To Cromwell's Independents it would seem a matter of course.

Among the British Museum collections which Carlyle had been consulting, was a " vast mass of pamphlets " dated from 1640 to 1660, collected by a contemporary, and well arranged in order of time with a written catalogue. " The mere titles " of them, he said, " often very quaint, would be more amusing than most books " to-day. As much of the " unknown history " of the period was buried in these pamphlets, Carlyle memorialized the governing " Trustees " to print the catalogue, setting forth that by a proper exploration of them the England of those years might be " restored to life " yet. " Even the age of Elizabeth is irrecoverable " now, he said ; but there still was time for " the genius of the English people " to work out a Crom-

welliad. In France " the Michelets and the Mignets " were
set to such work in the archives. If Espinasse, who was
shown the memorial, but kept no copy, and who was then a
Museum official, is right in guessing that it may be still
among their records, the Trustees should print it without
delay, as a set-off to what happened at the time. " Old
Hallam " was the Trustee to whom the rest said ditto in
research, and tho he gave Carlyle an interview, he declined
to be interested, and nothing happened. Carlyle allowed
himself to hope for awhile that he might get " a few faithful
men " as volunteers to join him in exploring fully these and
similar papers; but had to give it up.

In the second edition of his *Cromwell*, 1846, the new
Cromwell letters were carefully incorporated, and Espinasse
mentions that, ' with a conscientious thoughtfulness too
rare among successful editors, he printed the new letters
and elucidations in a detached supplement for the benefit
of possessors of the first edition.'

When by-and-by John Forster was seeking a new subject
to write upon, Carlyle advised a Life of Strafford, the greatest
man on the royalist side, which showed impartiality. So far
was he from undervaluing the talents of contemporaries,
that he often talked in the hearing of Espinasse of ' the
talent wasted on current literature little better than
" intellectual prostitution ", men " blazing themselves out in
newspapers " who might produce something noble '.

Espinasse dwells upon the tippling hand-to-mouth habits
of contemporary men-of-letters ; but that was not at all
Carlyle's way of talking. The best guess of Espinasse is
that he meant his British Museum sifting of old pamphlets
to be a beginning of that ' " organization of literature " which
he sometimes dreamt of ' and much wanted.

' When I first knew Carlyle,' he says, ' he took a
melancholy view of literature as of most things. Writing [if]
not commonplace would not find an audience. " There are
no people of any culture in England." " No man in England
can get himself developed." ' That was what seemed to
distress him in the lot of his fellow-writers, and ' he said :
" They have no homes ", and still worse, " They have no faith."
Young men of talent possessing any earnestness, were being
driven into Radicalism. " I hope they will go on rebelling
until they get something to do," ' [2] said Carlyle. But ' after the
success of *Cromwell*, he took a more hopeful view of the
prospects of serious literature like his own. " You get," he
said, " an audience at last." '

[2] Italics added.

VIII

AN INTERRUPTION TO DINNER

(1846)

IT may have been early in 1846 that Carlyle and his wife were sitting at dinner together one day, and Helen brought in a card from a caller at the door, remarking, "It is an American." "Tell him we are at dinner," said Carlyle. She returned and said, " I've told him, but he still wishes to speak to you." " Tell him again," said Carlyle. She again returned and said, " He still wishes to speak to you," inquiring, " Shall I show him upstairs ? " The room upstairs was hardly a drawing-room yet, a library and workshop mainly. " Then show him in here," said Carlyle.

He rose to his feet as the stranger entered, and without leaving his place at the table asked, " What do you wish with me ? " " O, Mr. Carlyle, I just wished to ask you a single question." " Ask it, what is it ? " " It is just this, I wish to ask you, Mr. Carlyle, if you can tell me what was the relationship that existed between Goethe and the mother of Goethe's son ? "

In a few sentences Carlyle explained how Goethe's informal union had become a legal marriage many years after the son was born. " Is that all you wish to know ? " he concluded. " Yes, Mr. Carlyle, that is all." " Then, good-day, sir." " Good-day, sir," said the stranger ; and when he departed Mrs. Carlyle ejaculated, " I wonder at your patience with him," and was answered " I saw that he was one of those unfortunate beings whom the Creator for his own wise purposes has sent into the world without any modesty".[1]

[1] Told by David Masson to D. A. W., 3–3–96. He had heard Mrs. Carlyle tell the story many times, and once in the presence of T. C.

IX

MRS. CARLYLE ESCAPES FROM "CROMWELL"

(1846)

IT was when Carlyle was putting into final shape his *Oliver Cromwell* that he gladly passed an evening in the company of Richard Cobden, the advocate of free-trade. He saw the fine character of Cobden at once, and heard from him something to repeat to aristocratic acquaintances. What he said to Baring and others may be guessed from what he wrote to Edward FitzGerald,[1] that unless they abolished the corn-laws, " he and the huge ready-money Cotton-men will fling them on their back and wrench the power from their hands forever and a day ! I believe it ; and do not want to see such an issue," added Carlyle.

Meanwhile his wife escaped from the boredom of Cromwell by a headlong friendship with Baring's wife, Lady Harriet. Both were of the " dangerous age ". Each of them had been rather spoiled by a devoted husband who fooled her to the top of her bent, and what Milnes said of Lady Harriet [2] was equally true of Mrs. Carlyle—she " preferred the society of men " to women in general. She was " kind and even affectionate" to children, and to girls and young women in particular, so that one of them said,[3] " I never count the days " at her house, " I only know that it is morning when I come and night when I go away." But Lady Harriet, being childless, " shrank from the sympathies of family life," said Milnes, " and avoided topics that might suggest useless regrets. Nearly the whole of her female companions were in the same domestic position as herself." The Barings had come to town early in the year, and now Lady Harriet's carriage used to come for Mrs. Carlyle after seven, and fetch her home between ten and eleven, which gave them more than two hours together to talk or play.

---

[1] MS. in the Library of Trinity College, Cambridge.
[2] *Monographs by R. M. Milnes*, Lord Houghton, pp. 247–51.
[3] Apparently Blanche Stanley, Lady Airlie.

Geraldine Jewsbury was immensely interested, and eagerly questioned Mrs. Carlyle about her,[4] but she was held aloof as a gossip, and cherished a grievance in consequence.

Lady Harriet had little love for London or the dreary dinners then in fashion, remarking once : " If I am to go into London society, and sit for hours by Lord (Fitznoodle), all I say is, I shall be carried out." Considering how enviable her lot appeared to the climbers on the social treadmill, there is the humour of reality in her reply to a suggestion from someone, perhaps her anxious husband : " You say it is a fine day and wish me to go out. How can I go out ? Ordering one's carriage and waiting for it and getting into it, that is not going out. *If I were a shopkeeper's wife, I would go out when and where and how I pleased.*" She used to say sincerely : " It is dreadful for me to have no domestic duties. I always envy the German women. I am a ' cuisinière incomprise '." (A cook misunderstood.)

No wonder she and Mrs. Carlyle rushed into intimacy rather rashly. ' Lady Harriet is returned,' wrote Mrs. Carlyle to her cousin Jeannie, ' and seems disposed to keep up our country intimacy—she sends her carriage often for me in the evenings and sends me back—treats me in all respects with *a consideration* for which I cannot but be grateful to her. She never *says* to anyone that she likes them, she goes upon *the silent system* as to all the thoughts of her *heart*—it is only the thoughts of her *head* that she gives one the benefit of—and so she has never *said* what one could call a *kind* word to *me*, but she proves by all her behaviour that she is rather fond of me, the mere fact of her having *kissed* me at parting and meeting again proves more affection for me than twenty reams of protestations from a Geraldine would do—for her ladyship is *sincere* to death—and would think much less of boxing the ears of a person indifferent to her than of kissing her ! For my part I *love* her now as much as I *admired* her in the beginning. She is the only woman of *genius* I have found amongst all our pretenders to it. I only wish I had got to know her twenty years ago when I was better capable of enjoying the advantages of such an acquaintance—the " getting on in society" part of it looks to me often enough a practical irony at this time of day rather than a good fortune to thank my stars for.

[4] *Letters of G. E. Jewsbury to J. W. Carlyle*, by Mrs. Ireland, pp. 188, 196, etc.

' You would be amused to see the increase of charm I have for the smaller gentry since Lady Harriet took me up ! I could not help answering a *kind* note I had from Lady Monteagle the other day *after a twelve months' silence*—in a tone of very *frank sarcasm.*' [5]

But—there is always a *but*—Mrs. Carlyle was far from well. On 10–3–46 she was telling Jeannie : " For ten days I was nearly out of my wits with want of sleep. Four nights in one week I never once closed my eyes, and *henbane* even in large quantities of no more use to me than cold water. The consequence was such a state of nervous excitation as nobody ever saw me in before—Carlyle declares me to have been ' quite mad ' for half an hour—and I can well believe him. I have for a long while back been dreadfully haunted with the apprehension of going *mad* some day, and I am only too thankful to have got off with ' half an hour ' of it thus far. For the last week I have been sleeping and *dead stupid.* Oh ! the blessedness of *stupidity* at times !

' On the 20th (March) I am going with Lady Harriet to Addiscombe '—their country house near Croydon—' for a month, and that will be good for me, I suppose.'

So she and Lady Harriet were together at Addiscombe for a month, Carlyle coming out for the week-ends, as well as Baring and Buller. Occasionally Buller and he rode out together. It had been an intimacy between Buller and Baring which led to Baring's acquaintance with Carlyle, and while Baring merely tolerated most of his wife's friends and she his, Buller and Carlyle were exceptional in being welcome to both. Peel may have been another of the same. At any rate, Milnes quotes the lady as saying once : " Public men in England are so fenced in by the cactus-hedge of petty conventionality, which they call practical life, that everything good and humane is invisible to them. Add to this the absence of humour, and you see all their wretchedness. I have never known but two men above this—Buller and Peel."

Even at Addiscombe Mrs. Carlyle complained to her husband of want of sleep, " pitted against Chaos " all night, with a result that upset her, for it led him into the very temptation she wanted to keep him out of, and he renewed a suggestion she hated. " I really wish you could find an eligible house somewhere, out under the quiet sky, removed

[5] *J. W. Carlyle : Letters to her Family*, by L. Huxley, pp. 267–70.

Y

fairly from these tumults and loud-braying discords of every
kind, which it is really growing horrible and miserable to
me to spend the remainder of my days among. 'Like living
in a mad-house,' as the lady says. Truly so, and one has
nothing to do with it either."

This was dated 8–4–46, when the work remaining in hand
at Cheyne Row was little but the proof-sheets of the new
edition of Cromwell. So a quiet time of rest appeared in
prospect for Carlyle, and FitzGerald's advice to "leave
your filthy Chelsea" recurred to mind, and the ever-
beautiful sea beside which he dwelt last winter. He hankered
more than ever for a house out of town. No wonder he echoed
the lady's words, "like living in a mad-house," as the never-
ending city noises, permeating everywhere, seemed louder
than ever now when he was at leisure to listen. His wife's
health, too, would be the better for country life. It had been
for her sake that they first went to Craigenputtock. He had
come to London reluctantly to get work there ; but now he
could afford to leave it—why not ? From year to year the
rumble was growing worse, and beautiful quiet Chelsea
was becoming merely a bit of the town.

"Like living in a mad-house" indeed ! Lady Harriet
meant only to sympathize. She had not and maybe never
had a suspicion of Mrs. Carlyle's recurring struggle to keep
her husband in Cheyne Row. If now Mrs. Carlyle acted
as she sometimes did—quoted aloud and derided what her
husband had written, and the other woman, off her guard,
supported the mere man sufficiently to alarm her, then the
fat would be in the fire. At any rate that is the likeliest
reason why Mrs. Carlyle came home declaring that they must
break with the Barings for ever at once. Mrs. Taylor, she
was doubtless aware, had cut short Mill's attendance on that
intellectual Circe,[6] and she wanted to do the same with
Carlyle. But she could not. He was insubordinate. He would
only agree to withdraw from the Barings by degrees and
without any quarrel ; and long before the withdrawal was
complete Mrs. Carlyle did not want it.

Two days after coming home she was writing to her
husband's sister in Dumfries, Mrs. Aitken *alias* " Jane the
lesser ". 'I am just returned from an aristocratic visit of
a month's duration, with the mind of me all churned into
froth, out of which, alas, no butter is to be expected !

---

[6] *J. S. Mill*, by A. Bain, pp. 166–7, footnote.

Yes, "gey idle o' wark" have I been for the last month. Seeing "how they ack" in the upper places does not give me any discontent with the place I am born to, quite the contrary. I, for one solitary individual—as Carlyle says—could not be other than perfectly miserable in idleness, world without end ; and for a grand lady it seems somehow impossible, whatever may be her talents and "good intentions", to be other than idle to death. Even children do not find them in occupation and duties.' They leave their children to others, in short.

At the same time she was writing at length to her Liverpool cousin, Jeannie (22-4-46) [7]: 'My visit to Addiscombe went off quite well. Her Ladyship was, as usual, without caprices or any sort of questionabilities for me . . . *Ach Gott* ! if I had not such an eternal hundredweight of leaden thoughts on my heart I might live *pleasantly* as other people do, but once for all, life is *not pleasant* for me, and the best I see in it is that it does not last very long.'

Writing to Jeannie's sister Helen, a few weeks later,[7] she said : ' The more I see of aristocratic life, the more I wonder how people can keep themselves alive in it—and *sane* ! Lady Harriet especially, who is the woman of largest intellect I have ever seen—how *she* can reconcile herself to a life which is, after all, a mere dramatic representation, fills me with astonishment . . . A poor woman has enough of serious occupation, we in *our* sphere have also something given us to *do* . . . But a great lady—should she take the notion to put away Great-lady-things and lead a rational useful life, how is she to set about it ? How extricate herself from the imposed *do-nothingness* of her *position* ? As Lady Harriet herself once said to me, "One would have to begin by quarrelling with all one's husband's relations and one's own "—a beginning rather questionable !

'The Cromwell-turmoil is subsiding. "*Thanks*, God!" and now I hope we shall really be done with that man ! What is to come next, Heaven knows. We have been inquiring all about for houses in the country. Sometimes in desperately bilious days Carlyle speaks of returning to Scotland and living *there* " in seclusion for his few remaining years ". This perpetual talk of moving takes away all one's pleasure (such as it was) in Chelsea—I feel myself no longer in a *home* but in a *tent* to be struck any day that the commanding officer is sufficiently bilious . . .

[7] *J. W. Carlyle : Letters to her Family*, edited by L. Huxley, pp. 273-8.

' The most important thing that has *happened* to me since my return has been the gift of a splendid Indian scarf (from Lady Harriet) almost " *too* splendid *for anything* ". But I was greatly pleased with it because of its being the facsimile of one she had got for herself. She rails at *sentiment* and never puts any into her *words*, but it peeps out often enough in her *actions*. She would not put an *affectionate* sentence in her letters for the world, but she will put *violets*—leaves of the *flowers one likes*—sometimes sends me envelopes by post containing nothing else ! ! What a contrast I often think betwixt that woman and Geraldine ! the opposite poles of woman-nature ! . . . Ever your own, ' JANE CARLYLE.'

X

TENNYSON ON IMMORTALITY

(1846)

MANY callers at Cheyne Row were old acquaintances from Scotland. There was a "very jolly" evening when Henry Inglis came. He inquired about a recent party of American visitors. "They did nothing," said Carlyle, "but spit my fire out."[1] Free spitting was "good form" in America till within living memory, and a Speaker of the House of Representatives would spit at large to make new members feel at home.

In April, 1846, Carlyle told Browning of an American who was commissioned by some learned body of his countrymen to ask him two questions, one about Goethe's domestic arrangements, and the other—"What is your opinion as to a future state ? "[2]

That was a question beginning to be asked in England, too, after *Oliver Cromwell* had appeared ; and Alfred Tennyson was as curious as any. Tennyson was very touchy about this. The best Irish bull reported in his talk was—he cried, " I'll shake my fist in God's almighty face and say it isn't fair, if I find there is no immortality." Such were his sentiments assuredly. Excusing once a deliberate suicide by chloroform after a good dinner, he said, " That is what I should do if I thought there was no future life."[3]

On 3–5–46 FitzGerald called at Tennyson's London lodgings and found Carlyle already there, and reported to his friend Barton at the time[4] : ' They two discussed the merits of this world and the next till I wished myself out of *this*, at any rate. Carlyle gets more wild, savage and unreasonable every day ; and I do believe will turn mad. " What is the use of ever so many rows of stupid, fetid

---

[1] Told to D. A. W. by his widow, Mrs. Henry Inglis.
[2] *Letters of R. Browning and E. B. Browning*, II, p. 98.
[3] *Alfred, Lord Tennyson*, by his son, II, p. 35.
[4] *Some New Letters of E. FitzGerald*, by F. R. Barton, pp. 123-4.

animals in cauliflower wigs—and clean lawn sleeves—
calling themselves Bishops—Bishops I say of the Devil—
not of God—obscene creatures, parading between men's
eyes and the eternal light of Heaven," etc., etc. This, with
much abstruser nonconformity for two whole hours ! '

This is the best clue to the date of some words which are
otherwise undated, and which were repeated by Tennyson
to Thackeray's daughter Anne,[5] who was a favourite of
his. He described how he had been giving tongue as usual
on his favourite topic of the certainty of life for men after
death, while Carlyle and FitzGerald were smoking quietly
in his company. When he finished, FitzGerald was silent.
For half a century " good form " in England had required
that gentlemen should either say they believed in
immortality or else be silent. So Tennyson felt pretty safe,
and did not want an answer ; but instead of the hoped-for
" grunt " of acquiescence, Carlyle let out between the puffs
some words that must have made a deep impression, for
Tennyson's report to Miss Thackeray is the same in effect as
what he told his son in extreme old age.[6]

" Eh ! Old Jewish rags ! Ye must clear your mind of
all that ! Why should we expect a hereafter ? Your
traveller comes to an inn and he takes his bed. It's only for
one night, and another takes it after him."

" Your traveller comes to his inn," said Tennyson, " and
lies down in his bed almost with the certainty that he will
go on his journey rejoicing next morning."

Carlyle made no reply but " a grunt ", smoking in silence,
which was like him ; and when he went away FitzGerald
said to Tennyson, " You had him there " ; " Which proves,"
said Tennyson to Miss Thackeray, " how dangerous an
illustration is." Of course, it is not a demonstration ; but
it is curious that the same figure of speech which Carlyle
may have read in Addison's *Spectator*, is in FitzGerald's
Omar Khayyam, which was not published till 1859, long after
any likely date for this chat.

> " Think, in this battered Caravanserai (or inn),
> Whose Portals are alternate Night and Day,
> How Sultan after Sultan with his Pomp
> Abode his destined Hour, and went his way."

[5] *Letters of Anne Thackeray Ritchie*, edited by her daughter, p. 231.
[6] *Alfred, Lord Tennyson*, by his son, II, p. 410. As Miss Thackeray
said she made her note at once, she is followed in details.

It is a beautiful figure of speech, which is in the Bible and in Chinese scriptures, and used by *both* the believers in immortality and those who are able to look open-eyed at the dark.   In the Far East it has been a proverb for millenniums that " we are such stuff as dreams ".

Carlyle tabooed the topic, endeavouring to follow the example of Confucius, whom he quoted in this connexion,[7] but Tennyson on this occasion made him speak.   It is part of the gospel of silence that nothing need be said when nothing can be known.   So—Silence !   Hush !   Look at the dark as much as you like, it rests the eyes, and it has other uses, which you may miss if you start chattering to keep your courage up.   Silence !   Hush !

This explains why in the fullness of time Carlyle interred his wife in silence, and why it was that he left such orders that a service over his corpse in Westminster Abbey was refused and he was buried himself in silence.

[7] *Literary Recollections,* by F. Espinasse, p. 196.

XI

RICHARD OWEN'S REPORT

(1846)

ABOUT the beginning of May, 1846, Carlyle was at the
Museum of the College of Surgeons.[1] He had gone
to see a copy procured by Richard Owen, who presided there,
of the portrait of Oliver Cromwell at Florence. It had
been painted from life, and was " in quite a different style "
from the one Carlyle already had. " He greatly admired our
picture," wrote Owen in his diary, " and studied it
attentively. It is curious how like his books Carlyle's conversation is. He grew very eloquent when telling us of the
way in which he was plagued by people who would insist
upon sending him their books. Young ladies especially
often wanted his opinion on their poetry. ' I hate poetry,'
he said comically."

" Do you hate Horne's ' Orion ' ? " asked Owen.

" Ah," he said, " Horne's a clever man," which was a neat
evasion of the question. The portrait done, " we walked
about in the museum," wrote Owen, " looking chiefly at
fossils."

---

[1] *Life of Richard Owen*, by the Rev. R. Owen, I, p. 283.

XII

TALKS WITH BROWNING

(1846)

ROBERT BROWNING was courting Elizabeth Barrett this summer, and found reports of Carlyle's talk good to use in his love-letters [1] :—

' Carlyle was saying he understood why the Romans confined acting to their slaves. It was no employment for a free man to amuse people, and be bound to do it,' and suppress ' other faculties tending to other results on an audience than amusement. Our amusers, writers of fun, concocters of comic pieces ' were in short not well employed.

' Carlyle thinks modern Italy's abasement a direct judgment from God. Here was a nation amid which arose men who *could* doubt and examine the new problems of the Reformation. If they had chosen, they were able to trim the balance at intervals, and throw overboard the accumulations of falsehood. Other nations around them were less favoured. The other nations had to fumble and grope, laboriously doing it for themselves. Now was the time for the acumen of the Bembos, the Bentivoglios, and so forth, and these and their like one and all turn away and decline the trouble, saying in effect : " These things may be true or not, meanwhile let us go on verse-making, painting, music-scoring." To this the whole nation accedes, glad to be saved bother. Upon which God " bids the Germans go in and possess them ; pluck their fruits and feel their sun, after their own hard work." Carlyle said the *sense* of this between two huge pipe-whiffs the other afternoon,' wrote Browning, and this might be how Carlyle used to " justify the ways of God to man " in answer to Mazzini.

---

[1] *Letters of R. Browning and E. B. Barrett (Browning)*, I, p. 457 ; II, pp. 238, 277, etc.

XIII

SIR ROBERT PEEL

(1846)

SIR JABESH WINDBAG of *Past and Present* was nobody in particular but a type, and less like Peel than other politicians, for Peel was now abolishing the Corn Laws and so becoming a saviour of society of the right sort, that is, a man averting violence by doing right. So Carlyle sent a copy of his *Oliver Cromwell* with this letter to Peel :—

'CHELSEA, 18*th June*, 1846.

' SIR,—Will you be pleased to accept from a very private citizen of the community this copy of a book which he has been occupied in putting together, while you, our most conspicuous citizen, were victoriously labouring in quite other work ? Labour, so far as it is true, and sanctionable by the Supreme Worker and World Founder, may claim brotherhood with labour. The great work and the little are alike definable as an extricating of the true from its imprisonment among the false ; a victorious evoking of order and fact from disorder and semblance of fact. In any case, citizens who feel grateful to a citizen are permitted and enjoined to testify that feeling each in such manner as he can. Let this poor labour of mine be a small testimony of that sort to a late great and valiant labour of yours, and claim reception as such.

' The book, should you ever find leisure to read and master it, may perhaps have interest for you—may perhaps, who knows ? have admonition, exhortation, in various ways instruction and encouragement, for yet other labours which England, in a voiceless but most impressive manner, still expects and demands of you. The authentic words and actings of the noblest governor England ever had may well have interest for all governors of England ; may well be, as all Scripture is, as all genuine words and actings are, " profitable "—profitable for reproof, for correction, and for edifying and strengthening withal. *Hansard's Debates* are not a kind of literature I have been familiar with ; nor, indeed, is the arena they proceed from much more than a distress to me in these days. Loud-sounding clamour and rhetorical vocables grounded not on fact, nor even on belief of fact, one knows from of old whither all that and what depends on it is bound. But by-and-by, as I believe, all England will say what already many a one begins to feel, that whatever were the spoken unveracities of Parliament, and they are many on all hands, lamentable to gods and men, here has a great veracity been *done* in Parliament, considerably our greatest for many years past—a strenuous, courageous, and needful thing, to which all of us that so see it are bound to give our loyal recognition and furtherance as we can.—I have the honour to be, Sir, your obliged fellow-citizen and obedient servant, T. CARLYLE.'

The reply was :—

'WHITEHALL, *June* 22, 1846.

' SIR,—Whatever may have been the pressure of my public engagements, it has not been so overwhelming as to prevent me from being familiar with your exertions in another department of labour, as incessant and severe as that which I have undergone.

' I am the better enabled, therefore, to appreciate the value of your favourable opinion ; and to thank you not out of mere courtesy, but very sincerely for the volumes which you have sent for my acceptance ; most interesting as throwing a new light upon a very important chapter of our history ; and gratifying to me as a token of your personal esteem.—I have the honour to be, sir, your obedient servant, ROBERT PEEL.'

XIV

MRS. CARLYLE GROWS WORSE

(1846)

GERALDINE JEWSBURY was writing to Mrs. Carlyle in June (22–6–46) [1] congratulating her that she would soon be at Seaforth, the house of the Paulets near Liverpool. "It is an instinct of nature, as well as friendship, that moves you to go to Seaforth"—which was true, for the "great heat of London" was making the sea-breezes of Liverpool attractive. "Women are very silly creatures!" Espinasse heard Carlyle say about this time,[2] as he 'protested against his wife's admiration of George Sand'. She was fretful and sickly, and feeling the heat so much that at last she felt she must go north without him. She had been hoping for his company; but the proofs were still unfinished. So on Saturday, 4–7–46,[3] he saw her safe away in a train for Liverpool, where Paulet and his wife were awaiting her on the platform. She posted a newspaper as a sign of safe arrival; but it miscarried. When nothing came on the Monday, he supposed she was giving him a dose of silence for not breaking with the Barings as she had wanted him to do.

He wrote complaining (6–7–46) : 'I hope it is not any accident or illness that robs me of a note this morning.' In short, let us try to see what is right and do it. 'On coming home on Saturday I sate down to my work. Yesterday (Sunday) I suppose you fancied me happy at Addiscombe. Alas! I was in no humour for anything of that laughing nature. I sate digging all day in the rubbish heaps. Adieu, dearest—for that is, and if madness prevail not may for ever be, your authentic title. Be quiet; do not doubt of me—do not yield to the enemy of us all, and may God bless thee always.—T. C.'

---

[1] *Letters of J. E. Jewsbury to J. W. Carlyle*, edited by Mrs. Ireland, pp. 209–10.

[2] *Literary Recollections*, by F. Espinasse, p. 103.

[3] The date 2–7–46, p. 365 of Vol. I, Froude's *Letters and Memorials of J. W. C.*, is wrong. See A. Carlyle's *New Letters and Memorials of J. W. C.*, I, pp. 186–97, for this and many more important corrections.

She was in the act of writing to him as he was writing to her ; and next morning he knew all was well, and wrote : ' Chelsea, July 7.   Thousand thanks, dear Goody, for thy good little letter !   It has lifted a mountain from my poor inner man . . .'   And a few days later he sent off in good time her annual birthday present.

Meanwhile, she was receiving two long letters from Mazzini, from which it appears she had written to him.   Her letters have not been kept.   From what he wrote we learn she had sent him a " few words ", and that somehow she had said her life " proves an empty thing ".   Now Mazzini was in the thick of his conspiracies against the Austrians ; and it is absurd to imagine without evidence that Mrs. Carlyle was bothering him by seeking his advice because her husband was insubordinate about the Barings, who are not named in these letters.   Her " few words " were most likely to let Mazzini know she had gone north, and spare him a needless call, which he says in these letters he had meant to pay that Saturday (4–7–46), and for the rest what she wrote would naturally be a continuation of conversations he quotes in his letters.

The loss of parents is common ; but they both felt it more than usual ; which was inspiring him to try again to recall her to the ancient dreams of other worlds, where all is made right that so puzzles us here.   He was quite aware she had dropped the hopes he was holding on to, for he wrote, " We have a different conception of life, and are condemned here down to walk on two parallels."   Nevertheless, he pleads : " You believe in God.   Don't you think, after all, that this life is nothing but an ephemeral trial ; and that He will shelter you at the journey's end under the wide wing of his paternal love ?   You had, have, tho invisible to the eyes of the body, your mother, your father, too.   Can't you commune with them ?   *Can you, in a word, love them less because they are far from sight ?*   I have often thought that the arrangement by which loved and loving beings are to pass through death is nothing but the last experiment appointed by God to human love " ; and so on.

" I am carrying a burden even heavier than you " was one of the things he said, and added : " But by dint of repeating to myself that there is no happiness under the moon, that life is a self-sacrifice meant for some higher and happier thing . . . I have mustered up strength to go on till I reach the grave ; for which the hour is fast approaching."

If Mrs. Carlyle's letters had been kept, we might find she
had rather been showing sympathy than craving it, for
Espinasse says [4] that her admiration for Mazzini was then
at its highest. She never shared his politics, and wrote to
her cousin Jeannie, who knew him, that he was born to
" make a martyr of himself ".[5] But she liked him none the
less for his Quixotic absurdity, and many other good women
then were feeling like her impelled to help so beautiful a
spirit—Lady Harriet Baring one of them. But perhaps no
other was so like a sister to him as Mrs. Carlyle. This year,
a few months before the summer letters, she was writing to
Jeannie about him [5]: " Mazzini does not go mad, but I do not
know whether it would not be better for him if he could ;
these long many years of failed hopes and destroyed illusions
seem to be taking effect on him—not on his health, or sanity,
but on his *temper*—he is grown so *captious* and *silently
irritable* that one knows not what to make of him." In short,
he was the last man in the world to bother about her squabble
with her husband, because he would not quarrel with the
Barings ; but there was nothing surprising in the circumstance that her short note, which she wrote to save him a
needless call, was answered by a gush of words imploring
her to help him to keep his spirits up by sharing his hopes
of eternal life.

There is nobody to blame, and nothing, only something to
smile at and much to pity, in Mrs. Carlyle's occasional
nervous crises. Take this letter to her husband at this very
time as a sample.

' SEAFORTH HOUSE, *Tuesday*, 14*th July*, 1846.

' Oh, my dear husband, fortune has played me such a
cruel trick this day ! But it is all right now ; and I do not
even feel any resentment against Fortune for the suffocating
misery of the last two hours. I know always, even when I
seem to you most exacting, that whatever happens to me is
nothing like so bad as I deserve. But you shall hear all how
it was.

' Yesterday, in coming back from the Post Office, my head
took to aching. I made a bad wakeful night of it, tormenting
myself with the fear that *he* will not write to me to-day
either.

---

[4] *Literary Recollections*, by F. Espinasse, pp. 106, 107.
[5] *J. W. Carlyle : Letters to her Family*, edited by L. Huxley, pp. 129,
334, 261, and compare pp. 183, 196, etc.

' At ten, the post hour, I slipped away myself to the Post Office, but was *detected* by Betsy (Paulet) and Geraldine (Jewsbury), who insisted on putting on their bonnets and accompanying me. I could well have dispensed with the attention ; however, I trusted there would be a letter, and their presence would only hinder me reading it for a little. And *two* were handed out, which I stretched *my* hand to receive. Both for Betsy ! None for *me*, the Post Mistress averred !

' Not a line from you on my birthday—on the fifth day ! I did not burst out crying—did not faint—did not *do* anything absurd, so far as I know ; but I walked back again without speaking a word, and with such a tumult of wretchedness in my heart as you who know me can conceive. And then I shut myself in my own room to fancy everything that was most tormenting. Were you finally so out of patience with me that you have resolved to write no more at all ? Had you gone to Addiscombe and found no leisure there to remember my existence ? Were you taken ill, so ill that you *could* not write ? That last idea made me mad to get off to the railway and back to London. Oh, mercy ! What a two hours I had of it ! And just when I was at my wit's end, I heard Julia crying out through the house: "Mrs. Carlyle ! Mrs. Carlyle ! are you there ? Here is a letter for you ! " And so there was, after all ! The Post Mistress had over-looked it, and given it to Robert when he went afterwards, not knowing that we had been. I wonder what *Loveletter* was ever received with such thankfulness ! Oh, my dear, I am not fit for living in the world with this organization. I am as much broken to pieces by that little accident as if I had come through an attack of cholera or typhus fever. I cannot even steady my hand to write decently. But I felt an irresistible need of thanking you by return of post. Yes, I have kissed the dear little card-case. And now I will lie down awhile and try to get some sleep—at least to quieten myself. I will try to believe—O why cannot I believe it once for all—that with all my faults and follies, I am " dearer to you than any earthly creature."—Your own JANE CARLYLE.'

The fact was that she was much depressed by bodily weakness and also by drugs which she had been taking to bring sleep. While she was writing this letter, her husband was responding to her religious questionings better than

Mazzini was able to do : 'As for the Redeemer, yes, "the Redeemer liveth": he is no Jew or man, or image of a man or Jew, or Surplice or old Creed; but the Unnameable Maker of us, voiceless, formless within our own Soul—whose voice *is* every noble and genuine impulse of our Souls; *he* is yet there in us and around us, and *we* are there : no Abbess, Eremite (Hermit), or fanatic whatever, had *more* than we have; how much less had most of them.'

On the following day she wrote : " One may go a far way in Scepticism—disbelieve in God and Devil, in Virtue and Vice, in Love, in one's own Soul, never to speak of Time and Space, Progress of the Species, Rights of Woman—only *not* in Death ! The most outrageous Sceptic—even I after two nights without sleep—cannot go ahead against *that*." To which her husband answered by return of post : " Death is indeed very indisputable; but *Life*, too, Life, I should think is not less so, and that is our present concern. Compose thy poor soul; and *know well* that to the wise no sorrow is in vain, no sorrow is not precious. God be with thee."

XV

MRS. CARLYLE GROWS BETTER

[1846]

ON 18–7–46 Carlyle was writing a letter to his wife :
'I was at the Barings' last night, saw Buller, etc.
I do not go to Addiscombe to-day nor to-morrow, nor,
indeed, for an indefinite, perhaps infinite time to come.
To the lady, I have, of course, told nothing, except that you
are very unwell. But she seems to have discerned pretty
clearly for herself that our intercourse is to be carried on
under different conditions henceforth, or probably to cease
altogether before long ; to which arrangement she gives
signs of being ready to conform with fully more indifference
than I expected ; with no unkindness at all ; but with no
discernible regret either ; on the whole, with the most
perfect politeness and graceful conformity to destiny, such
as becomes all people—such as I, too, am ready for, if it
come to that. That perversity of Fate, too, I can adopt or
accept, as I have had to do a few in my time. An opening
is left for my meeting them about Carlisle or Edinburgh
on their Scotch tour ; but it seems to be with little
expectation on either side that it will take effect. We shall
endeavour to see what the real monition of the matter is
when the time arrives.'

Such self-denial as this brings its own reward. Through the
eyes of the Rev. W. H. Brookfield, writing to his wife this
very day [1] (18–7–46), we can see how happy Carlyle could be :—

' I hurried to a Committee at London Library. Present :
Milman, Bunsen, Forster, Milnes, Lewis, somebody else
and Carlyle. There was lots of fun, Carlyle being the chief
lever who upraised it all directly or indirectly. It was very
amusing.' A likely guess is that the fun would be over the
books they were selecting.

---

[1] *Mrs Brookfield and Her Circle*, I, p. 187.

337   z

Four days later Carlyle was reporting again to " the woman that owned him " :—

' I took leave of the Barings last night. All is handsome and clear there, and nothing is wrong ; except *your* and my ill-genius may still force it to be so a little. To the lady I " said " simply nothing ; and her altered manner, I suppose, might proceed altogether from the evident chagrin and depression of mine. Was that unnatural in me ? In fact, I myself was heartily weary of a relation grown so sad, and in my mind almost repented that it had ever been. But you may take it as a certainty, if you like, that there is no unkindness or injustice harboured to you there ; and if you choose to write a little word of news to Lady Harriet, as to how you are and what things you are amidst, I do believe it would be a real and very welcome kindness to her.'

He followed the letter in a few days (23-7-46) ; and stayed a fortnight with her at the Paulets'. She did not wish to go farther north, as her nearest relatives were the Welshes beside her there, in Liverpool. So he went on alone (6-8-46) to Scotsbrig. The farmhouse noises seemed louder than usual and his sleep was broken because his wife was not writing to him, apparently because she resented his promise to meet the Barings at Carlisle and be their guide through Dumfriesshire. He hoped the bad weather might make them change their plans, but when they came on as arranged he went to meet them, writing to his wife as he started (14-8-46) :—

' No word from you yet ; not the scrape of a pen this morning either. It is not right, my poor dear Jeannie ! It is not just nor according to *fact* ; and it deeply distresses and disturbs me who had no need of disturbance or distress otherwise, if all were well known to thee. But it is best that I suffer it with little commentary. To thee, also, I will believe it is no luxury. Silence is better than most speech in the case. This, however, I will say and repeat : " The annals of insanity contain nothing madder than ' jealousy ' directed against such a journey as I have before me to-day." Believed or not, that is verily a fact. Oh, my Jeannie ! My own true Jeannie ! Bravest little life-companion, hitherto, into what courses are we tending ? God assist us both, and keep us free of frightful Niagaras and temptations of Satan. I am, indeed, very miserable. My mother asks: " No word from Jane, yet ? " And, in spite of her astonishment, I am obliged to answer " *None* ".'

He had been sending many reminders. Mrs. Paulet, too, was worried about the " wild looks " of her visitor, and told her so, declaring she had " liver-complaint " and looked like " Nodes after he had taken poison ", or " Marianne before her brain fever ", or " old Nannie in her last illness ! " " Like the Devil and his Grandmother ! " thought Mrs. Carlyle, and went to Manchester on a visit to Geraldine Jewsbury at the time when Carlyle was with the Barings, escorting them through "a deluge the like of Noah's", as Lady Harriet wrote to Mrs. Carlyle. By 20–8–46 the Barings were at Hamilton and Carlyle again at Scotsbrig, where a letter from his wife was awaiting him, to explain how faultless she had been :—

17th August, 1846.

' My dear husband, I am very grieved at all this uneasiness you have had for want of letters. To punish you was as far as possible from my thoughts. Often as I have pained you, first and last, I *never* caused you *intentional* pain, as far as I remember, and cannot fancy that I should ever be so " far left to myself " as to do that.

' I did not answer your first letter to Seaforth by return of post because I was feeling myself really *frightfully* ill, and *could* not have written at the moment without saying so ; and I did not wish to make you anxious about me—more anxious that you already were.' So in short she had come to Manchester on a visit to Geraldine, and was thankful she had come, for Geraldine had diverted her and given her sleep by the best of all soporifics, healthy fatigue, taking her through many Manchester workshops, and showing her a few of Manchester's best men. Whether by happy accident or unusual " skill ", the benefit she did was palpable, and Mrs. Carlyle " never forgot Geraldine " for it, said her grateful husband twenty years afterwards.

Lady Harriet in parting from Carlyle gave him a letter for her : ' The only check to our felicity has been the missing you ; and more, the accounts he gave of the little permanent good Seaforth had as yet done you when he left you . . . You are very, very foolish to go on without some trial, at least, of advice and remedies. I *am sure* your headaches could be very much mitigated ; and coughs and all sorts of derangements will come upon neglect . . . I hope that you are really bettering ere this ; and that we shall improve and take still further care of you in November at Alverstoke. You must spend that dreary month with us there, where I hope we shall be fixed by the end of October.'

By 23–8–46 Mrs. Carlyle was able to reassure her husband by a long narrative letter, saying : ' I long to tell you all I have seen and done ; but it would fill a volume ; and must lie over till we meet.'

Then she told of seeing ' all sorts of factories ', as well as Bamford the radical, Whitworth the inventor, and Dilberoglue ' a young Greek merchant, an admirer of yours.'

' My dear Goody,' her husband answered (26–8–46), ' I had thy letter at last. Many thanks for it and do not keep me waiting so long again. No news could be welcomer,' and so on. ' God be thanked you are better ; and now tell me that you eat a little food at breakfast as well as dinner, and I will compose myself till we meet.'

She was to go to her uncle's for a few days and then home. Perhaps the most remarkable new acquaintance she made this summer was the Boston actress, Charlotte Cushman, with whom she made a lasting friendship. Miss Cushman was a big, healthy woman, with a comely square face, an ideal mother's face ; but as she never had children of her own, she was all the more prompt to mother stage-struck girls who came her way, and one of those she helped became Mrs. Dilberoglue. She was spending a few days at the house of the Dilberoglues in 1846, when a lady came to see her whom we know. Charlotte Cushman writes [2] :—

' On Sunday Mrs. Carlyle came at one o'clock and stayed till eight. And such a day I have not known ! Clever, witty, calm, cool, unsmiling, unsparing, a *raconteuse* unparalleled, a manner inimitable, a behaviour scrupulous, and a power invincible—a combination rare and strange exists in that plain, keen, unattractive, and yet unescapable woman ! O, I must tell you of that day, for I cannot write it ! After she left, of course, we talked *her* until the small hours of the morning.'

[2] *Charlotte S. Cushman : her Letters, etc.*, by E. Stebbins, pp. 84–5, etc.

BOOK   XV

LOOKING   ROUND

(1846-48)

I

IRELAND, &c.

(1846)

AMONG the children at Scotsbrig when Carlyle was there in August, was his niece, Margaret Hanning, eight years old. " Uncle Tom always had trouble in his stomach," said she,[1] " and generally took his food alone when the rest had finished, his commonest dinner being chicken and bread pudding with brandy sauce. When I got a share of the bread pudding he left over, I used to think it the nicest thing in the world to eat. I asked my mother one day : ' Do you think uncle Tom will leave any pudding ? ' I was merely considering whether to run out or remain inside a while. He overheard me, and called out, ' It's extremely probable I will, Margaret ' ; and always after that he left some pudding for us."

He might often have been seen with a pipe in his mouth at the waterfall near by, or listening to talk in the village ; but he was also riding and walking much, observing the black fields of rotten potatoes, and the navvies making the railways, and their drunken pandemoniums on pay-days. He arranged to return by Dublin in order to see " Young Ireland ". On Wednesday, 2–9–46, when Mrs. Carlyle went straight home, he was as far as Dumfries on his roundabout way. He went to look at Craigenputtock, partly on business, but mainly as a schoolboy might go to take a look at something he wants but cannot get. He never made any attempt to raise the rent of Craigenputtock farm, tho the farmer was soon allowed to occupy their old house, long empty ; and the parish minister, who counted him as a " heritor ", described him as particularly liberal in his contributions for the schools.

By Friday he was in Ayr, beholding the " Twa Brigs " and other souvenirs of Burns. From Ardrossan that night he took steamer to Belfast, and thence on Saturday, 5–9–46, he went by coach to Drogheda, remarking on the way the Portadown Bridge of the 1641 massacre, and the stink of

---

[1] Said by her (Mrs. Leslie she was then) to D. A. W. in her own house, Comely Bank Farm, near Oakville, Canada, 28–9–95.

rotten potatoes in the fields.   A young man from Dublin
was sitting next him, and entertained him merrily, naming
places they passed, and smiling assent when Carlyle was
pointing to bad fences and saying: "What is the use of
fencing at all if this is the way of it ?   Leave one gap in
your field, it is quite the same surely as if you had never put
a thorn in it at all."   At Drogheda, Duffy and Mitchel were
waiting for him, but missed him by the fault of the postmaster.   They had left a letter in the Post Office and Carlyle
applied for it, but the postmaster overlooked it and said
there was none, and insisted, "None, I tell you!"   So
Carlyle took train to Dublin, and from his hotel roamed
"far and wide about the broad pavements", watching
Dublin's Saturday night.

Next day he went to Duffy's country lodgings at
Dundrum, where Duffy joined him at night, entreating him
to make a complaint against the postmaster ; but he would
not, saying: "He was an angry old fool, but misanthropic,
not dishonest."

At Duffy's lodgings, and in Dublin at the house of the
big blonde Ulsterman, John Mitchel, he made acquaintance
with "humorous Carleton" and the rest of "Young
Ireland".   They took him to Conciliation Hall where Dan
O'Connell was performing "in his green cap" complete.
There had been scarcity all winter in Ireland, and now with
the failure of this year's potatoes, starvation was at hand,
and Dan was manœuvring at the instance of place-hunters
to kick "Young Ireland" out of the National Association,
so as to do his deals with the Whigs in convenient darkness.
As part of the bargain, he was advising the people to let
the grain and cattle be exported as usual, altho the potatoes
were rotten and there was nothing else to eat.   In no other
country of Europe was such a thing allowed.   It caused
many deaths and made England hateful.   With heartless
impudence Dan was declaiming, "We may get more from
England than we send there," [2] ignoring the numerous
deaths in the interval of men, women and children.   "Rents
must be paid," said the newspapers, and Dan was doing
his best to get the people to "die without squealing".
That was why Conciliation Hall seemed hateful to Carlyle,
as he stood among a group of non-members listening to
Dan "haranguing his beggarly squad".

[2] *My Life in Two Hemispheres*, by Sir Charles Gavan Duffy, I, p. 196,
and generally, pp. 135–210.

The place itself was 'like a decent Methodist chapel', wrote Carlyle by-and-by, ' but its audience very sparse, very bad, and blackguard-looking. The speech—on potato rot (most serious of topics)—had not one word of sincerity, not to speak of wisdom, in it. Every sentence seemed to you a lie, and even to know that it was a detected lie.'

A low voice close at his ear whispered with an Irish accent, " Did you ever hear such damned nonsense in all your life ? " He recognized his Belfast-Drogheda coach companion, and cordially agreed with him. He wrote to Edward FitzGerald that Daniel was " the hugest *palpable* Humbug I had ever set eyes on ",[3] and told his brother that the *most* disgusting sight in Ireland was O'Connell in Conciliation Hall, and added—" He is sinking, I think ; that is a good symptom."

Another thing that comforted him was the new Act which " signified to the landlords that *they* would have to assess themselves " and stop starvation. He could sympathize with the impatience of Mitchel, but did his best to teach him prudence, saying at last, " You'll probably be hanged, tho they cannot hang the immortal part of you."

Before the end of the week, on his last day there, he was conveyed by Duffy and Mitchel through beautiful scenery to Bray, where they dined and sat talking till the hour of departure, and these two were in the crowd on the pier as he waved adieu from the moving steamer. Next morning he and his luggage were set down at the door of Mr. Welsh's house in Maryland Street, Liverpool. To avoid disturbing the sleeping household, he sat smoking upon his luggage with Oriental patience. The maids were up, however, and discovered him before the first cigar was done. He was home a fortnight after his wife, and by 22–9–46 he was writing to FitzGerald [3] that his wife was much better, and as for himself :—' In the whole course of my journeyings, I could find no place half as quiet for me as Chelsea, with an empty London behind it, now is.' His wife hoped he would always feel so. She sometimes complained that he might want her to read aloud to him *her* letters ; but she would have felt ill-treated indeed if he had ever hesitated to let her read his. It is likely that this remark to FitzGerald was intended to reassure her.

[3] *Some New Letters of Edward FitzGerald*, by F. R. Barton, pp. 131–2.

II

MARGARET FULLER HAS TO LISTEN

(1846)

LEWES once confided to Holyoake[1] that tho he " had few rivals " in holding the ear of a company, he " found one " when " invited by W. J. Fox to meet Margaret Fuller. Carlyle was another guest that night. Fox, Carlyle, and Lewes were famous talkers ; but when Margaret Fuller took her turn, they were all silenced, and—their turn came no more ". The gentle Thomas Cooper also met her at Fox's,[2] and " felt only a modified pleasure in her company. She talked in a nasal tone, and lifted up her head to shout, so as to be heard by all in the room ",—as overbearing as Macaulay. She had been the miracle of Boston drawing-rooms, this thickset and plain-faced woman. " Seldom," said her friends,[3] and then only " as a special grace ", did she treat anyone as an equal.

After editing *The Dial* to the admiration of many, she was on the staff of Greeley's *Tribune* when a wealthy Mr. Spring engaged her to come to Europe as a polyglot companion to his family. She felt in need of more experience. America was too small for her. As she often confessed to her friends, " I now know all the people worth knowing in America, and I find no intellect comparable to my own."[3] So Lowell wrote of her [4] :—

> " Here comes Miranda. Zeus ! Where shall I flee to ?
> She has such a penchant for bothering me, too !
> She always keeps asking if I don't observe a
> Particular likeness 'twixt her and Minerva."

[1] G. J. Holyoake's *Sixty Years of an Agitator's Life*, I, p. 244.
[2] *The Life of Thomas Cooper*, written by himself, p. 312.
[3] *Memoirs of Margaret Fuller Ossoli*, II, pp. 5, 1 ; III, pp. 95–104 ; II, pp. 3 and 14, etc.
[4] *Margaret Fuller*, by J. W. Howe (Allen & Co.), p. 31. The quotation is from Lowell's *Fable for Critics*.

" Mr. Carlyle came to see me at once," she reported to Emerson,[3] " and appointed an evening to be passed at their house."

7th October, 1846, was the date, and Margaret came with several other globe-trotters, and appeared herself an agreeable surprise, " a strange lilting lean old maid, not half such a bore as I expected," Carlyle confessed to Emerson, while she wrote to Emerson about him :—

' I was quite carried away with the rich flow of his discourse ; and the hearty noble earnestness of his personal bearing brought back the charm which once was upon his writing before I wearied of it. I admired his Scotch—his way of singing his great full sentences, so that each one was like the stanza of a narrative ballad. He let me talk now and then enough to free my lungs and change my position, so that I did not get tired. That evening he talked of the present state of things in England, giving light witty sketches of the men of the day, fanatics and others, and some sweet homely stories he told of things he had known of the Scotch peasantry. Of you (Emerson) he spoke with hearty kindness, and told, with beautiful feeling, a story of some poor farmer or artizan in the country, who on Sundays lays aside the cark and care of that dirty English world, and sits reading the Essays and looking upon the sea.

' I left him that night intending to go very often to his house. I assure you there never was anything so witty as Carlyle's description of . . . It was enough to kill one with laughing. I, on my side, contributed a story to his fund of anecdote on this subject, and it was fully appreciated. Carlyle is worth a thousand of you for that ; he is not ashamed to laugh when he is amused, but goes on in a cordial human fashion.'

In short, he seemed at first worthy of her highest praise : " He appreciates me." [3] To honour Emerson's letter he did all he could to show her whoever she wanted to see. As one of these was John Mill, Carlyle set out for the India House to invite him to come to dine and meet her ; but, as he afterwards told Norton [5] : " Before I got there I met him coming along the street, and he received me like the very incarnation of the east wind, and refused my invitation peremptorily." Which dates the conclusion of their social intercourse—there never was any quarrel.

[5] *Letters of C. E. Norton*, I, p. 499.

There is nobody indispensable even for a dinner-party.
The table was filled with others, and Margaret reported :—

' The second time I met him Carlyle had a dinner-party,
and there was present there a witty, French, flippant, sort
of man (George Henry Lewes), author of a *History of
Philosophy*, and now writing a Life of Goethe. He told
stories admirably, and was allowed sometimes to interrupt
Carlyle a little, of which one was glad, for that night he
grew wearisome to me.

' For a couple of hours he was talking about poetry.
Tennyson wrote verse because the schoolmasters had
taught him that it was great to do so, and had thus,
unfortunately, been turned from the true path for a man.
Burns had, in like manner, been turned from his vocation.
Shakespeare had not the good sense to see that it would
have been better to write straight on in prose ; and such
nonsense, which, though amusing at first, he ran to death
after a while.

' The most amusing part is always when he comes back to
some refrain, as in the French Revolution of the *sea-green*.
In this instance, it was Petrarch and *Laura*, the last word
pronounced with his ineffable sarcasm of drawl. Although
he said this over fifty times, I could not ever help laughing
when *Laura* would come ; Carlyle running his chin out
when he spoke it, and his eyes glancing till they looked like
the eyes and beak of a bird of prey. Poor Laura ! Lucky
for her that her poet had already got her safely canonized
beyond the reach of this Teufelsdröckh vulture ! ' (Poor
Margaret Fuller, rather ! She had lisped in Latin, and
always supposed she *should* admire the sentimental slush
of Petrarch about another man's wife. How she would
have screamed against him if he had been a contemporary
American ! She continued candidly) :—

' The worst of hearing Carlyle is that you cannot interrupt
him haranguing. If you get a chance to remonstrate a
moment, he raises his voice and bears you down. True, he
does you no injustice, and with his admirable penetration
sees the disclaimer in your mind, so that you are not morally
delinquent ; but it is not pleasant to be unable to utter it.
The latter part of the evening, however, he paid us for this
by a series of sketches, in his finest style of railing and
raillery, of modern French literature, not one of them,
perhaps, perfectly just, but all drawn with the finest, boldest

strokes, and, from his point of view, masterly. All were depreciating, except that of Béranger. Of him he spoke with perfect justice, because with hearty sympathy.

'After this they went to stay at Lord Ashburton's, and I only saw them once more, when they came to pass an evening with us. Unluckily Mazzini was with us, whose society, when he was there alone, I enjoyed more than any. He is a beauteous and pure music ; also, he is a dear friend of Mrs. C., but his being there gave the conversation a turn to "progress" and ideal subjects, and Carlyle was fluent on all our "rose-water imbecilities". We all felt distant from him, and Mazzini, after some vain efforts to remonstrate, became very sad. Mrs. C. said to me : "These are but opinions to Carlyle ; but to Mazzini, who has given his all, and helped to bring his friends to the scaffold in pursuit of such subjects, it is a matter of life and death." '

It did not occur to the women that Carlyle may have been as much in earnest as Mazzini, and feeling bound to say what he could to open the eyes of his friend to save him and others from the waste of martyrdom. The next bit of Margaret's report is unintended caricature :—

'All Carlyle's talk that evening was a defence of mere force—success the test of right. If people would not behave well, put collars round their necks ; find a hero, and let them be his slaves, etc. It was very Titanic, and anti-celestial' (and, addressed to a self-assertive woman, listening against her will, it was also very funny ; but she had no suspicion of that, and went on) :—
'I wish the last evening had been more melodious. However, I bid Carlyle farewell with feelings of the warmest respect and admiration. We cannot feel otherwise to a great and noble nature, whether it harmonize with our own or not. I never appreciated the work he has done till I saw England. I could not. You must stand in the shadow of that mountain of shams to know how hard it is to cast light across it. Honour to Carlyle ! *Hoch !* '

Which is not the less creditable to Margaret because it may have cost her an effort. It may have been on the same night that Margaret perorated picturesquely, to the admiration of all her listeners but one,—" I accept the Universe ! "

" Gad, you'd better ! " said Carlyle, which may explain
what she wrote at Paris in December, 1846 :—

' Accustomed to the infinite wit and exuberant richness
of his writings, his talk is still an amazement scarcely to be
faced with steady eyes. He does not converse ; only
harangues. This is not in the least from unwillingness to
allow freedom to others. On the contrary, no man would
more enjoy a manly resistance to his thought. But it is the
impulse of a mind accustomed to follow out its own impulse
as the hawk its prey, and which knows not how to stop
in the chase. Carlyle, indeed, is arrogant and overbearing ;
but in his arrogance there is no littleness—no self-love. It is
the heroic arrogance of some old Scandinavian conqueror ;
it is his nature, and the untameable impulse that has given
him power to crush the dragons. You do not love him
perhaps, nor revere ; and perhaps, also, he would only
laugh at you if you did ; but you like him heartily, and like
to see him the powerful smith, the Siegfried, melting all
the old iron in his furnace till it glows to a sunset red, and
burns you, if you senselessly go too near. He seems to me
quite isolated—lonely as the desert—*yet never* was a man
more fitted to prize a man, could he find one to match
his mood. He finds them, but only in the past.
' He sings, rather than talks. He pours upon you a kind
of satirical, heroical, critical poem, with regular cadences . . .
For the highest kinds of poetry he has no sense. His talk
on that subject is delightfully and gorgeously absurd. He
sometimes stops a minute to laugh at it himself, then begins
again with fresh vigour. His talk, like his books, is full of
pictures ; his critical strokes masterly. He is a large subject.
I cannot speak more or wiselier of him now.'

She wrote to her newspaper about him ; and a long letter
to Emerson, too, who thought she had given the best
description he had had of Carlyle's discourse. He sent
the newspaper to Carlyle, who, replying soon, had to speak
about a volume of Emerson's poetry, and reiterated his
opinions with deliberate candour which may not seem so
absurd to-day as at the time of writing :—

' It is my fixed opinion that we are all at sea as to what is
called Poetry, Art, etc., in these times ; labouring under
a dreadful incubus of Tradition, and mere " Cant heaped

balefully on us up to the very Zenith ", as men, in nearly all other provinces of their life, except perhaps the railway province, do now labor and stagger ; in a word, that Goethe-and-Schiller's *Kunst* has far more brotherhood with Pusey-and-Newman's *Shovelhattery*, and other like Phenomena, than it is aware of ! I am more serious in this than you suppose.'

As for " the good Miss Fuller ", he thought she flattered him. Both he and his wife had liked her :—

' Since she went I have been reading some of her papers in a new Book, greatly superior to all I knew before ; in fact, the undeniable utterances of a true heroic mind ; unique among the Writing Women ; rare enough among the writing Men. She is very narrow, sometimes ; but she is truly high ; honor to Margaret, and more and more good-speed to her.'

It only remains to be added that Margaret speedily found at Rome a young friend of Mazzini, Ossoli, willing to marry her. He was an excellent listener. She became a happy wife and mother, and was busy in the hospital while her husband fought on the walls for Mazzini's republic. Ossoli's brothers were soldiers of the Pope. The French took Rome, and Margaret planned a *History of the Late Italian Revolution,* invoking and receiving at once the help of Carlyle with the booksellers. He wrote to Emerson : " She has a beautiful enthusiasm ; and is, perhaps, in the right stage of insight for doing that piece of business well." But Mazzini and his men missed their Homer, if such she could have been. In a few months more, she and her husband and child were drowned together in shipwreck on the shores of America.

III

JEALOUS WIVES

(1846)

"C. SHOULD have had a 'strong-minded woman' for wife," wrote Mrs. Carlyle to her cousin this fall,[1] 'with a perfectly sound liver, plenty of *solid fat*, and mirth and good humour world without end: men do best with their opposites. *I* am too like himself in some things, especially as to the state of our livers, and so we aggravate one another's tendencies to despair! But there is no altering of all that now—nothing to be done but make the best of it—which I candidly confess I am far from doing. I do *try*, however, to the best of my humble ability . . . Every morning I take the shower bath—quite cold—and three pailfuls of it. Then I eat all I can and drink *bottled porter*, and I *walk* six or seven miles in the day on an average! I also try to be neither *solitary* nor *idle.*"

This is also the likeliest date for what may have been the most exciting domestic news she ever sent to her Liverpool cousins. The wife of John Sterling's brother, Captain Anthony, had gone mad, her monomania being that her husband was in love with Mrs. Carlyle, and ruining himself in giving her presents. Mrs. Anthony Sterling fell into a frenzy and flung the poker at her husband because Mrs. Carlyle, in her ignorance, called to inquire for her! She was not unique. There was another married lady jealous of Mrs. Carlyle and behaving absurdly, tho not yet flourishing a poker; whereat Carlyle was making merry at his wife's expense, speaking of these events as "the judgment come upon you", and greeting her with the honourable title of "*Destroyer-of-the-peace-of-families*" in place of the usual "Jane" or "My Dear". One morning he suddenly exclaimed: "Just to look at you there, looking as if butter would not melt in your mouth, and think of the profligate life you lead!"[2]

---

[1] *J. W. Carlyle: Letters to her Family*, by L. Huxley, p. 282.
[2] Ibid., pp. 285-7, 312-13, 319, 322.

" It is *very* absurd ! " said Mrs. Carlyle to her cousin ; but perpaps the woman is right who has suggested [3] that " he was only retaliating ", and quoted the vivid words of Caroline Fox :—

' She plays all manner of tricks on her husband, telling wonderful stories of him in his presence, founded almost solely on her bright imagination ; he, poor man, panting for an opportunity to stuff in a negation. They are a **very** happy pair.'

It is pleasant to add that Mrs. Anthony Sterling's delusion about Mrs. Carlyle departed with the frenzy that caused it.

[3] *The Carlyles' Married Life*, by Elizabeth Garrett Bell, *Cornhill*, July, 1924, p. 67.

Aa

THACKERAY AND HIS DAUGHTERS

(1846)

THACKERAY'S *Cornhill to Cairo* came out not long before *Oliver Cromwell's Letters,* and when finishing it Thackeray lived secluded in the inn at the end of Cheyne Row. The first intimation the Carlyles had of his return from the free trip round the Mediterranean which the steamer company had given him, was " a note which the pot-boy brought over " from the inn " for the loan of a Bible ".[1] Mrs. Carlyle and her husband would have been less disappointed with *Cornhill to Cairo* if they had seen what Thackeray wrote to his mother after their Bible had enabled him to refresh his memory :—

' I am guarded with Jerusalem, not wishing to offend the public by a needless exhibition of heterodoxy, nor daring to be a hypocrite. I have been reading lots of books—Old Testament, Church histories, travels. I find there was a sect in the early Church who denounced the Old Testament; and get into such a rage myself when reading all that murder and crime which the name of the Almighty is blasphemously made to sanction, that I don't care to trust myself to write.'

Cornhill to Cairo remains one of the best of globe-trotters' books, like the *Innocents Abroad* ; but in speaking of it about 1846, Carlyle remarked to Charles Buller that for Thackeray to accept a free berth from the steamer company on this voyage, was like " a blind fiddler going to and fro on a penny ferry-boat in Scotland, and playing tunes to the passengers for halfpence ".[2] Charles Buller repeated this to Thackeray, who came and complained and was answered frankly by Carlyle : " It is undoubtedly my opinion that, out of respect for yourself and your profession, a man like you ought not to have gone fiddling for halfpence or otherwise in any steamboat under the sky."

[1] *Works of W. M. Thackeray with Biographical Introductions,* by his Daughter, Anne Ritchie, Vol. V, p. XLII.
[2] *Conversations with Carlyle,* by Sir Charles Gavan Duffy, pp. 76-7.

This made Thackeray angry : but in no wise affected the pleasant relations between his little daughters and Mrs. Carlyle. By 1846 he was writing *Vanity Fair* and making a home for his two little girls in Young Street, near the S.W. corner of Kensington Gardens ; and 1846 would be when they first came to Cheyne Row. Let Anne, the elder of them, tell the rest [3] :—

' There is one part of London whither we used often to go as children : Cheyne Row, where Mr. Carlyle and Mrs. Carlyle lived. (Their) house is one of the first things I can remember when we came to London. Its stillness, its dimness, its panelled walls, its carved banisters, and the quiet garden behind, where at intervals in the brickwork lay the tobacco pipes all ready for use : (and) little Nero, the doggie, barking.
' In the dining-room stood that enchanting screen '— which Mrs. Carlyle had made—' covered with pictures, drawings, prints, fashions, portraits without end, which my father liked so much ; upstairs was '—the library or work-shop, which by-and-by became—' the panelled drawing-room with its windows to the Row, and the portrait of Oliver Cromwell hanging opposite the windows. But best of all, there was Mrs. Carlyle herself, a living picture. Gainsborough should have been alive to paint her ; slim, bright, dark-eyed, upright, in her place. She looked like one of the grand ladies our father used sometimes to take us to call upon. She used to be handsomely dressed in velvet and point lace. She sat there at leisure, and prepared for conversation. She was not familiar, but cordial, dignified, and interested in every-thing as she sat installed in her corner of the sofa, by one of the little tables covered with nicknacks of silver and mother-of-pearl.
' Almost the first time we ever went to see her we had walked to Chelsea through the snow, and across those lanes which have now become South Kensington, and when we arrived, numb and chilled and tired, we found her in the dining-room below, standing before the fire, two delicious hot cups of chocolate all ready prepared for us, with saucers placed upon the top. " I thought ye would be frozen," said she ; and the hot chocolate became a sort of institution. Again and again she has sat by, benevolent and spirited, superintending our wintry feasts, inviting our confidences, confiding in us to a certain degree.

[3] Chapters from some Memoirs by Anne Thackeray Ritchie, pp. 134–7.

' As children we did not have much of Carlyle's company ;
if he came in and sat down, we went away ; but the sense
of his presence overhead distinctly added to our enjoyment
so long as he remained upstairs.'

Then comes what can best be understood by recalling
that these young girls had no mother to counsel them at
the dangerous age they were approaching. ' Many of her
admonitions and friendly warnings have remained in my
memory. Once, looking expressively at me with her dark
eyes, she began to speak of self-control. " We have all,"
she said, " a great deal more power over our minds than it is
at all the fashion to allow, and an infinity of resource and
ability to use it. There was a time in my own life when I felt
that unless I strove against the feelings with all my might
I should be crazed outright. I passed through that time
safely ; I was able to fight it out and not let myself go.
People *can* help themselves, that I am convinced of, and
that fact is not nearly enough dwelt upon." ' This would
refer to an early period of life.

As the years went by like clouds, and the girls became
interested in the great business of match-making, she used
to tell them true stories ' which have since come into print ',
said our recording angel. ' She was never weary of dis-
coursing on " Carlyle ", of his genius, his dyspepsia, (or) of
quoting his sayings,' and her habitual advice was : " If you
wish for a quiet life, never you marry a dyspeptic man of
genius." '

Tho Thackeray was always delighted in dinner-table
debates to meet Carlyle's denunciations of men and things
with disconcerting jests,[4] they never quarrelled, and their
family friendship never abated. In old age Mrs. Carlyle
used to take Anne with her in her daily drives, and doubtless
some of her talk then about nearly going mad referred to
her own nervous crises in the forties. It was natural and
kind to speak of that to Anne Thackeray, whose own mother
had long been under restraint for insanity following puerperal
fever.[5] It was equally natural for Mrs. Carlyle to speak of it
to almost nobody else, and least of all to one she considered
an incurable gossip—Geraldine Jewsbury. Geraldine was
left to imagine, and she imagined much.

[4] *Literary Recollections*, by F. Espinasse, pp. 215–16.
[5] *Letters of Anne Thackeray Ritchie*, edited by her daughter, pp. 12, 13,
124, and 188.

Carlyle told Gavan Duffy [2] that Thackeray had " far more literary ability than Dickens, but one could not fail to perceive that he had no convictions, after all, except that a man ought to be a gentleman, and ought not to be a snob. The chief skill he possessed was making wonderful likenesses with pen and ink, struck off without premeditation, and which he could not afterwards improve. Jane had some of these in letters from him, where the illustrations were produced apparently as spontaneously as the letter ".

Carlyle thought that dining out in London society made Thackeray less sincere, and once he said to Espinasse,[4] " Thackeray is like Wilson of Edinburgh" (Christopher North), " he has no convictions." He ' preferred Dickens, who always treated him with deference', according to Espinasse, who adds that it was on sight of *Vanity Fair* that Carlyle said, " Thackeray is a man of much more judgment than Dickens." But he spoke of the relief which he found on turning from Thackeray's terrible cynicism to the cheerful geniality of Dickens.

V

THE GRANGE

(1846)

L ADY HARRIET BARING found she could not be in her
own house at Alverstoke by the end of October ; but
had no difficulty in persuading Mrs. Carlyle to fetch her
husband to the Grange instead, the home of Lady Harriet's
father-in-law, the first Lord Ashburton, who was now over
seventy, and wanted her to help to entertain the usual
autumn crowd of visitors. The Grange was the " country
house " or palace which had been sold by the Henry
Drummond of this history,[1] when in 1817 he set out with
his wife for the Holy Land. It was not far from Winchester,
and has often been described. Mrs. Carlyle's first impressions were in a letter to her cousin on 30–10–46, after she
had been two days there [2] :—

' DEAREST BABBIE,—

' I have no prospect of being able to write you a
deliberate letter. Tho I have not a room merely, but a
suite of rooms all to myself, still my soul is in a state of
hurry-scurry, which makes *deliberate* writing quite impossible.
The very look of this bedroom with its immense dimensions,
its vaulted and carved ceiling, its princely magnificence of
every sort, makes me ill at ease—I feel to have got out of my
latitude—as much as if I were hanging on to the horns of the
moon ! And then the recollection of all the idle restless
people under the same roof with me—whose idleness and
restlessness are so contagious ! . . .

' Besides Lady Harriet and Mr. Baring, there are some
dozen visitors, the Marchioness of Bath, Lord Ashburton's
eldest daughter, with two tiny ladyships and their French
governess—old Rogers—an Honble. Mr. Byng—a beautiful
Miss Dalton—a rich Mr. Portal, etc., etc. In all *my* life

---

[1] *Carlyle T.* " T. F. R.," Book IX, Chap. II, pp. 243–4.
[2] *J. W. Carlyle : Letters to her Family*, edited by L. Huxley, pp. 288–90.

I never drew my breath in such a racket! Some of the
people go to-morrow and then others will come. It is the
ruling Principle of the Host and Hostess to keep the house
always full. *We* shall remain till the end of next week. The
Ashburtons one and all of them are excellent people—very
homely—and very kind—they make me as much at home as
it is possible for a *fish* to be in the *air*. Lady H. also continues *kind* to me after her fashion . . .

' But it were more amusing for you to hear something of
the Place and People than of *my* feelings towards them. The
Place is like, not one, but a conglomerate of Greek Temples
set down in a magnificent wooded Park some five miles in
length. The inside is magnificent to death—the ceilings all
painted in fresco—some dozen public rooms on the ground
floor all hung with magnificent paintings—and fitted up like
rooms in an Arabian Nights' entertainment—but the finest
part of it is the entrance hall and staircases—which present
a view of columns, frescos and carved wood and Turkey carpet
—that one might guess at a quarter of a mile long !

' In the Hall which indeed resembles a church, Lord A.
reads prayers every morning to a numerous congregation,
consisting of men and women-servants ranged on opposite
sides, and his own wife and daughters kneeling beside him.
The *effect*, as seen from the *gallery above*, is very pretty ! ! but
I did not meddle with it personally further than looking
over the balustrade—and I saw old Rogers this morning
doing the same. They are very *good* in the religious sense
of the word, the whole family of them—except of course
Lady Harriet—who *goes* on nothing of that sort—but they
are not bigoted, and let one hold one's own opinions.

' They have had their own trials, poor people—a favourite
daughter, the beauty and genius of the family—when grown
to womanhood was burnt to death in Italy some years ago—
and the Marquis of Bath *drank* himself to death—this poor
lady now here has still such a suffering, patient look! And
this morning she was maintaining against me the Beauty
and Holiness of *marriage*, even in these days ! ! ! Every
mortal woman I fancy is born to be made miserable through
one cause or another.—Ever your affectionate, J. C.'

Old Rogers, eighty-three years of age, was at the Grange
as long as the Carlyles, and displeased Carlyle by his
frivolity—' hovering over the rim of deep eternities with
nothing but light babble, fatuity, vanity, and the frostiest

London wit in his mouth. Sometimes I felt as if I could throttle him, the poor old wretch ! but then suddenly I reflected, "it is but for two days more." Pity the sorrows of a poor old man ! '

This cannot be quite intelligible without knowing what the cheery old man was saying. He was quite capable of presuming on old age's privileges to chaff Carlyle ! A healthy old man of eighty-three might feel his work was behind him, and that he had less cause to worry than when younger ; and surely to be alive and healthy at such an age is Nature's own certificate of good behaviour.

By 7–11–46 Mrs. Carlyle was announcing to her cousins in Liverpool her safe return home, and perhaps replying to some question from that commercial city in telling that the Ashburtons had eighty thousand pounds a year. She had arranged with Lady Harriet to stay a month with her after the Christmas holidays, and so one of her cousins was to come to Cheyne Row for six weeks without more delay, which of course she did.

VI

THE SICK MAID

(1846)

CARLYLE was reading at large, and all went well till about 20–11–46, when Helen Mitchell was succeeded by a new girl. She was a " handsome, cultivated-looking Edinburgh girl, filled with the consciousness of free grace ", instilled into her by Mrs. Carlyle's Edinburgh aunts, simple old women with nothing to do, who had " taken to religion " to kill time, as an old servant said, " and might have taken to worse." The woman of their choice had been in a house where she was one of eight servants, but, having seven cousins in London, she was willing to get her fare to London paid by agreeing to serve Mrs. Carlyle for six months.

She seemed to Mrs. Carlyle to be in terror of spoiling her hands, and unwilling to learn what she did not know of the work of a " general " ; but in fact, as a doctor noticed, and said at once, she was suffering from green sickness, which was spoken of as a vice ! Instead of explaining that it was a symptom of real sickness, and might mean serious disease, the doctor talked of beating her. At least, so said Mrs. Carlyle, who might have known better if she had been well herself, but in this instance saw nothing but the depravity of human nature and misled her husband.

Every woman who ever worked with Mrs. Carlyle knew she was hopelessly irregular in her house work ; and under ordinary circumstances, the new girl might have muddled along unnoticed for her six months ; but unfortunately there was a woman visitor in the house, Helen Welsh from Liverpool, which made Mrs. Carlyle feel on her mettle. So she set to work to challenge her cousin's admiration and teach the new maid ; and in a day or two caught one of the eight annual influenzas, which Harriet Martineau said she indulged in, and of course collapsed immediately and took to bed, leaving her cousin to attend to her and everything else—which Miss Welsh did very well. But by what his wife said, Carlyle was led to believe that the maid had made her mistress ill by laziness and selfishness ; and irritated perhaps by her self-complacency he told her, " You would have got more real education if you had been left to paddle through the gutters with your neglected fellow-brats, by whom you would have been trampled out of the world if you had behaved no better than now."

Apparently nobody whispered sickness to him, and he seems to have spoken to her more cruelly than he ever spoke to any other woman, for she was the victim of a story Mrs. Carlyle was fond of telling, and Lady Harriet of repeating.[1] ' The Carlyles had a maid who was untidy, useless in all ways, but " abounding in grace " and in consequent censure of everyone above or below her, and of everything she couldn't understand. Carlyle ended a long apostrophe one day as she was bringing in the dinner, with : " And this I can tell you, that if you don't carry the dishes straight, so as not to spill the gravy, so far from being tolerated in Heaven, you won't be even tolerated on earth." I often feel as if I were spilling that gravy,' concluded the witty lady.

The girl was equal to the occasion. She had told Mrs. Carlyle plainly, " I will never slave myself for anybody's pleasure," and on Saturday night, a fortnight after arrival, perhaps the day of the admonition about the gravy, she sent up word to her mistress that she must be let go next day, Sunday tho it was, and if not, she said,—" I will take fits and be laid up in your house a whole year, as happened to me once before in a place where the work was too hard."

" Go then, in the Devil's name," said Carlyle, according to his wife. His own report is that he bade her disappear straightway and never let him see her again. He consoled his wife, who was in bed upstairs and wanted to make the girl stay another fortnight, by saying that they should be " glad to be rid of such a lump of selfish, dishonest fatuity on any terms ".

As for repaying the two guineas advanced, the girl had given Mrs. Carlyle the conclusive answer, " I have no money " ; and she departed delighted, taking her master at his word, and came back next day in the best of spirits with a friend to remove her box, and reported, to Mrs. Carlyle's aunts apparently, that she had been obliged to leave them because they " received company on the Sabbath ".

[1] G. S. Venables, Fortnightly Review, May, 1883, p. 629.

Carlyle said she was the worst specimen of Scotch
character he ever saw, which was true, of course, but
perhaps he did not see right. Mrs. Carlyle said that the
handsome girl would come upon the streets; but she never
did. She died, poor soul, in a year or two, and mutely
appeals to us without a name for a kinder judgment—
illustrating the fallibility of the wisest men in comprehending
women.

Her place was filled, and Miss Welsh went home, and
Mrs. Carlyle, who was well aware that *cold* was most of her
own illness, prepared thankfully to winter for a month or so
at Alverstoke again, as she and Lady Harriet had arranged.

VII

CARLYLE SURPRISES HIS WIFE

(1846)

CARLYLE'S aversion to shopping was well known to his wife, and this December she said to him [1]:— " Promise me without knowing what it is that you'll do what I ask. The thing is easy and rational," she added. He promised and was told—" Then you're not to give me anything on New Year's Day." He laughed very much, and repeated that he would not. But he bought her on Christmas Eve a cloak she needed, and " when he came in on Christmas morning to ask how I was, he cunningly slipt it down on the chair at the bottom of my bed ".

About the middle of the day, Mrs. Carlyle who had had influenza for three weeks, was putting on her clothes, and sadly recalling the warm things her mother used to send her at that season. Then she saw for the first time on the chair " a new dressing-gown like the former ones ", and she said : " I stood staring at the thing uncertain if I were going mad and merely *fancying to see it*," till " I laid hold of it and found it was a woman's cloak—and then I understood the whole matter." She said she told him " *it could be worn* " to comfort him, because he said he had bought it " *by gas light* and felt quite desperate about it when he saw it in the morning ". And she told her cousin: " It is a wonderful cloak for *him* to have bought—warm and not *very* ugly—and a good shape." She disliked the colour, but for a man's buying it was well enough.

[1] *J. W. Carlyle: Letters to her Family*, by L. Huxley, pp. 291-2.

VIII

MRS. BÖLTE AND CARLYLE

(1846–7)

"FOR God's sake stop Mme. Bölte," wrote Thackeray once to Mrs. Carlyle, unable to think her a Miss, when she was seeking only a situation for herself. When she had a nice young man to help she was uncontrollable. It might be this winter that David Masson, familiar enough in the house to seem to her negligible, was witness to a scene she made.[1] He and Mrs. Carlyle were all eyes and ears, but felt as impotent as if looking at Niagara.

She had brought a translation of the Nibelungen Lied by a young gentleman, a friend of hers ; and her business was to get from Carlyle a certificate that would ensure acceptance by a publisher. It was plain enough Carlyle believed the work did not deserve it. She would take no hint, and heeded not plain No. The pages of the MS. were turned over. Carlyle glanced at it again politely, and pointing to the name Gunter, asked : "Is that the confectioner?" She ignored the chaffing question, and said severely : "You've only to look at it and write ten words, Mr. Carlyle," and grimly awaited his reluctant reply, "No, I will not." "Don't say that. YOU MUST ! ! ! You see . . ." and then she rattled on at length and finished with another appeal that had to be answered : "I really cannot." "Now, Mr. Carlyle, he is quite a nice young fellow, and it is so much to him, and he says . . ." and then she told his merits and his sayings with the prolixity of a leading counsel paid by the day for spouting words. She ended at last, on an expectant note. "No, no," said he again.

"Mr. Carlyle, Mr. Carlyle—if I go down on my knees to you here and now—won't you do it? Won't you, now?"

"No, I won't." Miss Bölte, indignantly : "Mr. Carlyle, there are a great many pleasant things in the world *you* know nothing about."

[1] Told by David Masson to D. A. W., 5–11–1902.

By this time it was late, and Masson rose to go. " Wait till I put my boots on," said Carlyle, and they went out together, and in a quiet street they passed a house all lighted up and full of guests, the music audible outside, and dancing visible. " Some people making merry," said Carlyle genially.

" Ah, Mr. Carlyle," said Masson, " there are a great many pleasant things in the world *you* know nothing about," a sally answered by a hearty laugh.

The little squall with Miss Bölte left no bitterness. She was now " fat and *almost* contented ", a fictioneer successful with the German public as well as a prosperous governess. She was fond of telling about " a fine lady " who possessed the works of Carlyle, and said she liked them in many respects, and always took his part in public ; but " there is one thing about him deeply to be deplored ". Miss Bölte : " What ? " " Why, you know, on certain subjects Mr. Carlyle thinks for himself, and that is so very wrong ! "

On another occasion Miss Bölte complained of a critic in the *Athenæum* who had been finding fault with her descriptions of London Society.[2] " Oh," said Carlyle, con-soling her, " the man who wrote the article is probably in debt to his landlady, and with very forlorn outlooks." What tickled the listeners was that they knew (tho Carlyle did not) that the writer complained of was ' the opulent John Chorley ' familiar to them all. They were good-natured enough to enjoy the joke in silence, and allow her all the comfort Carlyle could give her.

[2] *Literary Recollections*, by F. Espinasse, pp. 233–4.

IX

A GOOD STORY

(1847)

MRS. CARLYLE took some weeks to make up her mind to accept Lady Harriet's invitations to Alverstoke. She was unwilling to risk sickness in another's house ; but Lady Harriet was persevering and coaxing, and at last, as Mrs. Carlyle wrote to her cousin,[1] she started, and sleeping in the train, arrived at Alverstoke, where a carriage was waiting for her, " hardly so tired as I have been on getting up from the sofa of late weeks to make tea . . . When Lady H. likes to *manage* me she is always able to do so—she can *wind* me about as she pleases," and on this occasion Lady H. had abundance of leisure.

" I will not go to town till the 1st of March," said Lady Harriet to Mrs. Carlyle on her arrival in the latter half of January, " and I really do hope that now you are here you'll stay, and let Mr. Carlyle go back by himself if he wishes it—he might really spare you a while for your good." So they stayed about five weeks. Mrs. Carlyle had her favourite chess unlimited with a lady in the neighbourhood of kindred tastes, and was going about as well as possible by the middle of February. Charles Buller and " Dicky " Milnes occasionally came down, and Mr. Baring himself came regularly every week-end. Carlyle was reading at large, but passing much of his time alone on the seashore or in the country lanes, reflecting, as he wrote to his mother, " what a stupendous thing is this human life that we live, in many cases, as if it were of no consequence ! When I think of those old dear ones that are with God, and how we shall all soon be there ourselves, I have no word to say."

Indoors the women talked and talked and " worked " for bazaars, Mrs. Carlyle for one of Mazzini's, the lady who played chess for " a Scotch bazaar ", and a Lady Joscelin, who lived near them, for " an Irish bazaar ". " Lady

---

[1] *J. W. Carlyle : Letters to her Family*, by J. Huxley, pp. 293-5.

Joscelin, you may remember," Mrs. Carlyle wrote,[2] " is that daughter of Lady Palmerston who had Count Giuliano for Father. She has been over almost every day." One day when she was not there Lady Harriet told a tit-bit from the London talk about her mother. Mr. Bancroft had just come to London as American ambassador, and his wife was perhaps the only woman in society who did not know that Palmerston was the Lady's second husband, but generally understood to be the real father of the sons she bore while yet the wife of his predecessor and colleague, Lord Cowper. As Foreign Secretary in the new Whig cabinet, Palmerston had now to entertain ambassadors, and so it happened at his table that when once his wife said, " Sons generally resemble the mother much more than the father," Mrs. Bancroft was there and answered her, " Well, I am quite astonished that your Ladyship does not see the most wonderful likeness in your second son to Lord Palmerston ! " Perplexed at Lady Palmerston's reception of this, she exclaimed to someone, " Is it not strange that Lady Palmerston sees no likeness in her second son to his father ? " When the boy came in with the dessert and approached Mrs. Bancroft, she put her hand on his head, and looking affectionately at Palmerston she cried : " Ah, my lord, no one need ask who is this young gentleman's papa ! "

Carlyle himself repeated the story as he heard it, and might have added tho he never did the favourite quotation of Sir Walter Scott on such occasions :—

> " I know not how the truth may be,
> I tell the tale that was told to me."

---

[2] Ibid., pp. 297–8 ; and see *Conversations with Carlyle*, by Sir C. Gavan Duffy, pp. 217–18.

X

THE REPEAL THAT IRELAND NEEDS

(1847)

A FEW days before he went to Alverstoke, Carlyle had been writing to FitzGerald[1] that he "never thought of Bunyan. Rhadamanthus would be a much likelier subject, precisely the fellow for me! The world's main want is a Rhadamanthus. Such an all-pervading life-element of cant, in which all men and institutions live—truly it were well worth while to rend it asunder, to burn it up with Heaven's lightning if one could, and send *it* back to the Devil in the shape of stinking gas, which it is! If not in Heaven's fire, then in Hellfire, all that accursed twaddle *will*, one day, be burnt up ; of that I am at all times sure enough ! "

The most " supportable " reading he could recommend was Acta Sanctorum, or Lives of the Saints, upwards of fifty folios edited " really well " by the Jesuits, in the course of the last 150 years, and other monkish histories with a preface by Selden, the honest lawyer in our civil wars. But the key to his prayers for fire to purify our politics was in the events of the day, for he added : " Ireland is a perpetual misery to me ; lies like a kind of nightmare on my thoughts . . . Certainly men ought to subscribe—those that have pity for their starving fellow-creatures, what *less* can they do than give a little money ? "

At Alverstoke he was studying the *Nation*, which Gavan Duffy had been sending him regularly from Dublin, and the Roman Catholic *Tablet* of poor Frederick Lucas, and soon after he came home to Chelsea he wrote to Gavan Duffy,[2] (1–3–47) and sent him a paper he had that day received from the writer of it, Forster, a young man he liked, ' the son of a Quaker ', the same W. E. Forster afterwards conspicuous as an honest politician.—

' The Quakers some months ago made a special sub-

---

[1] 12–1–47. FitzGerald MS. in Trinity College, Cambridge.
[2] *Conversations with Carlyle*, by Sir C. Gavan Duffy, pp. 24–8.

scription for Ireland, and decided on seeing their money
laid out. Forster's father and self were of the deputation
for that end, and this is the report. Read it, I say, and enjoy
five minutes of a Sabbath-feeling—not too frequent in
these times . . .

'The aspect of Ireland is beyond words at present. Your
Irish governing class are now actually brought to the Bar,
arraigned of *mis*governing this Ireland, and no combination
of men can save them from their sentence: to govern it
better, or to disappear and die. The Skibbereen peasant
dies at once in a few days; but his landlord will have to
perish by inches, through long years of disquieting tumult,
dark violence, and infatuation under yet undeveloped
forms; and *him* . . . nobody will pity! And then our
Scotch landlords, and also our English, come in their turn
to the Bar—not much less guilty, if much more fortunate—
fortunate in this, that we have already *another* aristocracy
(that of wealth) which does actually guide and govern the
people, to such extent at least as that they do not by wholesale die of hunger. That you in Ireland, except in Ulster,
altogether want this, and have nothing *but* landlords, seems
to me the fearful peculiarity of Ireland. To render Ireland
habitable for capitalists, if not for heroes; to invite capital,
and industrial governors and guidance, what other salvation
can one see for Ireland?

'You must tell Mitchel that I read with ever greater pain
those wild articles of his, which, so much do I love in them
otherwise, often make me very sad . . . Mitchel may depend
on it, it is not repeal from England, but repeal *from the
Devil*, that will save Ireland. Ireland cannot *lift anchor*
and sail away. We are married to Ireland by the ground-
plan of this world—a thick-skinned labouring man to a
drunken ill-tongued wife, and dreadful family quarrels
have ensued! . . . "Young Ireland" ought to understand
that it is to them that the sense of veracity of England looks,
not to the O'Connell party.' He concluded by praising the
words of some priests meeting at Cloyne, near Cork, and
reported in 'the *Tablet* of yesterday', as 'the first rational
utterance of the human voice I have yet heard in that wide
howl of misery and folly which makes the heart sick! May
all true Irishmen join with them. Adieu.'

Witnesses report his talk this year foretelling revolutions
in Europe soon. Here is something in his next letter to

Gavan Duffy (15–3–47)[3]:—'*The world, mainly a wretched world of imposture from zenith to nadir, seems as if threatening to fall rapidly to pieces in huge ruin about one's ears. How to demean oneself in these new circumstances is rather a question. We shall see. Bocca stretta occhi sciolti.*' " Mouth shut, eyes open," an improved version of the good advice which Sir Henry Wotton gave John Milton going abroad—i pensieri stretti, ed il viso sciolto, thoughts close and face frank. Carlyle of course was thinking of Duffy's danger and Mitchel's.

While these letters were passing much of Ireland was " one silent vast dissolution ". For countless thousands in Skibbereen and elsewhere there was nothing to do but die. Few rational reading men in Europe were unmoved. The very Turks were sending subscriptions.

[3] Ibid., pp. 28–30. Italics added.

XI

THE RICHEST AUTHOR IN BRITAIN

(1847)

IN 1847 Carlyle received from publishers £800; in 1846, £100; in 1845, £700. "Amid the huge fluctuations" he guessed his income at not less than £150, about £200 or £300. Craigenputtock brought in another £150; and his wife earned his admiration and gratitude by saying nothing to him about Craigenputtock, and making £300 a year cover all expenses, which meant a balance in the bank always growing, and no worry at all about ways and means. This enabled them both to be liberal in gifts, and explains what he wrote to his mother in March, 1847 :—

' My poor books bring me in a little money now to fill the meal barrel every year, and the wealth of all the Bank of England is daily a smaller and smaller object to me; indeed it is long since (it became) well near no object at all, which is perhaps a very good definition of being extremely *rich*, the "richest author in Britain" at present. I read books. Indeed, one's busiest time is often when altogether silent.'

Regarding the size of house an author needed, Thackeray was writing to his mother [1]: ' Tom Carlyle lives in perfect dignity in a little £40 house at Chelsea, with a snuffy Scotch maid to open the door, and the best company in England ringing at it. It is only the second or third chop great folk who care about show.'

About this time Carlyle was one of several men of letters who joined in a complaint against Mr. Panizzi's management of the British Museum. A Parliamentary investigation was granted, and many reforms effected. Panizzi's spite against Carlyle did less harm than might have been expected. His subordinates and colleagues were unanimously attentive, and even proud to serve him, and fellow readers boasted of courteous attentions received from him.[2]

[1] 1848. Biographical edition of Thackeray, by Mrs. Ritchie, Vol. II, p. XXXIII.
[2] *Thomas Carlyle*, by W. H. Wylie, pp. 212–15.

In March, 1847, Carlyle was writing to his sister, Mrs. Aitken, in Dumfries, who had reported for sale a house in the country which might suit him.—'We must not think of it at present,' he wrote. ' London is the home of *Freedom* for the like of me. In good truth, no king in all the earth is so royal as any poor thinking man can here be, with an independent heart in his body, and barely money in his pocket to pay his way. All manner of princes, dukes and drakes go by him like as many phantasms ; he, in his rusty coat, alone has meaning, the only king ; a king with *one* subject ! ' This was pleasant reading to his wife, and he often spoke like this to anyone abusing London. He would praise the pavements as fine for walking upon—" no country roads to equal them," and in this connexion he was fond of quoting the poem which keeps green the memory of the truthful ambassador, Henry Wotton[3] :—

> " How happy is he born and taught
> That serveth not another's will ;
> Whose armour is his honest thought
> And simple truth his utmost skill ! . . .

> " This man is freed from servile bands
> Of hope to rise, or fear to fall ;
> *Lord of himself,* tho not of lands ;
> And having nothing, yet hath all."

[3] David Masson and others, verbally to D. A. W.

XII

MILNES AND CARLYLE

(1847)

IT would be about the end of April this season that one of Milnes' successes in drawing out Carlyle found a good reporter, for it was on 2-5-47 that Bishop Wilberforce was writing[1] :—

' I dined the other day in company with Carlyle. He was very great. Monckton Milnes drew him out. Milnes began the young man's cant of the present day of the barbarity and wickedness of capital punishment, that, after all, we could not be sure others were wicked, etc. Carlyle broke out on him with "None of your Heaven and Hell amalgamation companies for me. We *do* know what is wickedness. *I* know wicked men ; men whom I *would not live with* ; men whom under some conceivable circumstances I should kill or they should kill me. No, Milnes, there's no truth or greatness in all that. It's just poor miserable littleness. There was far more greatness in the way of your old German fathers who, when they found one of those wicked men, dragged him to a peat bog, and thrust him in and said, "*There*, go in *there*. There is the place for all such as thee."'

The reference is to the *Germany* of Tacitus, chapter xii : ' In the council of the tribe, accusations may be made and capital charges. They make a distinction in punishments according to the crimes. They hang on trees the traitors and deserters ; while those who are dastards in war or abominable in body they thrust into filth and marsh and put a hurdle over them. The meaning of the distinction is that crimes of the first sort should be exposed when punished, whereas the other sort should be buried out of sight. Lighter offences are punished in proportion by fines,' . . . including even homicide.

[1] *Life of Samuel Wilberforce, Bishop,* by A. R. Ashwell, I, pp. 399–400.

XIII

THOMAS CHALMERS AND OTHERS

(1847)

WHILE Carlyle was reconciling himself to London, Lady Harriet was recognizing that to keep him in her circle she had to conciliate his wife ; and she did it. She had to be in Paris this spring, as her mother lived there and was ill and needed her ; but before the season was in full swing in the summer she was awhile at Addiscombe, and had Mrs. Carlyle out for several days (3 to 8–5–47) to go sauntering and driving with her.

The best of London was its convenience for callers. Jeffrey was with them as usual this year, as " brisk " as ever, " the same old man," and also one who had not called before, Thomas Chalmers, the great divine. " It was a pathetic meeting," wrote Carlyle on 21–5–47, recalling 1820. " The good old man is grown white-headed, but is otherwise wonderfully little altered—grave, deliberate, very gentle, full of real kindliness, and sensible even to honest mirth."

He tabooed the sordid business that had brought him to London, the infinite meanness of landowners in Scotland refusing sites for churches. He preferred to talk about painter Wilkie, who had been an intimate of his in youth. " Painters' language," he said, " was stinted and difficult." Thus Wilkie had told him he had been long at a loss about how to show that the sorrowful woman with her children in the picture of the *Rent Day* was a widow, till one morning in the Strand he met an artisan family going on excursion, and noticed in some hand or pocket the visible house-key. " That will do ! " thought Wilkie, and prettily introduced the house-key as coral in the baby's mouth. " We were most cordial and coalescing, and he very complimentary and pleasant," said Chalmers. " His talk was not at all Carlylish, plain and manly, good ordinary common-sense, with a deal of hearty laughing on both sides."

" What a wonderful old man Chalmers is ! " said Carlyle to a visitor soon afterwards. " He has all the buoyancy of youth. When so many of us are wringing our hands in helpless despair over the vileness and wretchedness of the large towns, there goes the old man, shovel in hand, down into the dirtiest puddles of the West Port of Edinburgh, cleans them out, and fills the sewers with living waters. It's a beautiful sight."[1]

When the old man died a few weeks later he wrote to his mother, " I believe there is not in all Scotland, or all Europe, any such Christian priest left."

He talked as he wrote ; and it was a natural mistake of the Dundee divine, the Rev. George Gilfillan, who called on 30-5-47, soon after the death of Chalmers,[2] to continue supposing Carlyle a Christian ; but in writing on 12-6-47 to the "Saint" Thomas Erskine, of Linlathen, near Dundee, Carlyle had been explicit enough.

' One is warned by Nature herself not to " sit down by the side of sad thoughts", as my friend Oliver has it, and dwell voluntarily with what is sorrowful and painful. Yet at the same time one has to say for oneself—at least, I have—that all the *good* I ever got came to me rather in the shape of sorrow ; that there is nothing noble or godlike in this world but has in it something of " infinite sadness ", very different, indeed, from what the current moral philosophies represent it to us ; and surely it is good for a man to be *driven* into looking at this great universe with his own eyes and trying to adjust himself truly there. By the helps and traditions of others he never will adjust himself : others are but offering him their miserable spyglasses : Puseyite, Presbyterian, Free Kirk, old Jew, old Greek, middle-age Italian, imperfect, not to say distorted, semi-opaque, wholly opaque, and altogether melancholy and rejectable spyglasses, one and all, if one has *eyes* left. On me, too, the pressure of these things falls very heavy : indeed, I often feel the loneliest of all the sons of Adam ; and, in the jargon of poor grimacing men, it is as if one listened to the jabbering of spectres—not a cheerful situation at all while it lasts. In fact, I am quite *idle* so far as the outer hand goes at present. Silent, not from having nothing, but from having infinitely too much to say . . .'

---

[1] What is here and does not come from Carlyle papers is from *Thomas Chalmers*, by A. J. S. (pub. Guthrie, Ardrossan, and Houlston & Sons, London), p. 163.

[2] *George Gilfillan*, by R. A. and E. S. Watson, p. 77.

' The great soul of this world is *Just*. With a voice as soft as the harmony of spheres, yet stronger, sterner, than all thunders, this message does now and then reach us through the hollow jargon of things. This great fact we live in, and were made by. It is " a noble Spartan *Mother* " to all of us that dare be sons to it. Courage ! we must not quit our shields ; we must return home *upon* our shields, having fought in the battle till we died.'

The reference is to a Spartan mother's alleged advice to her son about his shield,—" With it, my son, or upon it ! "

For " No Surrender " was the ancient Spartan ideal, two thousand years before Ulster articulated it again at the siege of Londonderry in 1689. Carlyle applied it to the things of the mind, and would have " No Surrender " to falsehoods of any fashion.

XIV

A CHAMPION OF RASCALITY

(1847)

ABOUT the end of May Geraldine Jewsbury came for two or three weeks, which dates, as in the end of May or first-half of June, a thing worth telling, reported by a Boswell who never intended to Boswellize.

Robert Scott Skirving was a boy in Haddington, bird-nesting, when he saw Mrs. Carlyle sitting on her father's grave in 1833. In 1847 he would be in his twenties, and he had been in Italy and seen something of the world when he came to call one afternoon at Cheyne Row, and was entertaining Mrs. Carlyle and Miss Jewsbury when Carlyle entered "in a flowered dressing-gown and a pipe a foot long". His report of what followed is hostile. He praised Disraeli, and was contradicted, and fired up in defence of Disraeli, saying : " You cannot deny that he is a great speaker, if not a great novelist." He says Carlyle replied to him.—

" Young man, I hope you will live to get sense, and learn that words are no good at all ; it is deeds and deeds only." This was caricature, of course. What Carlyle made plain was that he objected to Disraeli as a liar and a conscious humbug ; and Mr. Skirving boldly undertook to defend that kind of character !

" You do not agree with one of the wisest of the Greeks, Mr. Carlyle ! " he cried, and triumphantly quoted from the Philoctetes of Sophocles the passage where Odysseus justifies rascality when it is needful for success. The young son of Achilles had said he would rather do right and fail than succeed by evil ways, and Odysseus replied to him (Mr. Skirving used to say he quoted these very words to Carlyle) :—

> " Son of a noble sire ! I too in youth
> Had a slow tongue and an impatient arm ;
> But now, time-tried, I see in words, not deeds,
> The universal ruler of mankind."

Thus did Odysseus, and Mr. Skirving after him, talk like a prehistoric Jesuit, concealing the true issue, whether fraud was right, and pretending that that depended on whether words or deeds were the more important. In the play the young man is at first misled, and is persuaded to practise fraud, but then feels it is wrong, and repents in time and makes reparation, and the artful dodger Odysseus, the model of Skirving, " making liars of the gods to shelter himself behind them," is disregarded and discredited.[1] The meaning of the play had been missed by Skirving, who may have read it as a " scholar" does, missing the meaning of the writer, and mindful only of phrases and verbal gibberish. To score over him would have been easy enough ; but Carlyle was not thinking of scoring—he was reprobating rascality. " I see what you are now," he thundered, according to Skirving, " a damned impudent whelp of an Edinburgh advocate."

This was a mistaken inference—he was not an advocate at all ; and may be believed when he adds that Carlyle became more kindly after this, went with him to the door, and held his hand some time at parting ; and when he afterwards met Mrs. Carlyle in Scotland, she said what he took for an apology for the treatment he had met; but apparently he never had the sense to see that he deserved it.[2]

[1] Jebb's translation, *Tragedies of Sophocles*, pp. 329, 360, 367-76.
[2] *Early Letters of J. W. Carlyle*, edited by D. G. Ritchie, pp. 315-16.

XV

MACAULAY AND CARLYLE

(1847)

1847 MAY have been the date of a breakfast party in London reported by handsome Venables, when Macaulay ran down Henry Cromwell, the best of the Protector's sons. Mrs. Hutchinson in her *Memoirs* had said that he and his brother-in-law Claypole "were two deboshed ungodly cavaliers", and Macaulay denounced Henry Cromwell accordingly.

Carlyle maintained "the charge was unjust" and the man "an able and upright statesman". A hot debate then followed. Macaulay came out like a river in flood, 'but I observed,' said Venables,[1] 'that Carlyle referred to many contemporary authorities, while Lord Macaulay, at the end of every rhetorical period, invariably reverted to Mrs. Hutchinson and her deboshed cavalier.

' " I have read," Carlyle once answered, not without impatience, " all that that shrill female ever wrote, and I can assert that she knew nothing of Henry Cromwell. I have read every existing letter which he wrote, and all that is written about him, and know that he was not a deboshed cavalier." '

Distinguishing Carlyle from Macaulay, Venables explains that Carlyle 'was always ready to recognize in his turn any happy remark or appropriate anecdote, and he had the great merit of being a hearty laugher'. Thus there was a story 'which I think he had heard from Mr. Tennyson' and repeated many times 'with bursts of unextinguishable laughter. Some Scotch gentlemen in the good old times had a three days' bout of steady drinking. Late on the third day one of the party, pointing to another, said to his neighbour : "The laird looks unco gash" (very ghastly). "Gash!" was the answer. "He may well look gash, as he has been dead these two days." Nothing had been said of it so as not to spoil the party !

[1] "Carlyle in Society and at Home," G. S. Venables, *Fortnightly Rev.*, May, 1883, p. 632.

'I heard the story for the last time as we came away from a house where we had been dining,' said Venables, 'and Carlyle must have surprised his fellow-passengers in a Chelsea omnibus which he entered before he had done laughing.'

A greater contrast to the sleek genteel Macaulay cannot be imagined. What always happened in their table debates was that Carlyle, refusing to be brow-beaten, contradicted whenever needful briefly but forcibly, after which Macaulay continued as before, irrepressible as a shower of rain. They never were rude to each other, nor assailed each other personally in public or in private. Their most typical collision was a while after this. Macaulay was perorating the shibboleths of political economy, the wages fund, supply and demand, Devil take the hindmost, governments *cannot* organize labour, workers *must* be exploited for the interest of employers, and so on, these rules he was proclaiming as eternal dogmas, as sure as gravitation. Carlyle challenged them all as dogmas, and insisted on the *necessity* of organizing labour. When he went home he described Macaulay in his notebook : 'Very good-natured man . . . in official mail of proof. Stood my impatient fire-explosions with much patience, merely hissing a little steam up . . . All that was in him now gone to the tongue ; a squat, thick-set, low-browed, short, grizzled little man of fifty. These be thy Gods, O Israel !'

When once Espinasse praised Macaulay, he said [2] Carlyle turned on him 'rather fiercely' and declared: "Macaulay has never said anything not entirely commonplace," but then he added : "He is a very brilliant fellow. Flow on, thou shining river ! "

[2] *Literary Recollections*, by F. Espinasse, p. 216.

XVI

THE DUKE OF SAXE-WEIMAR

(1847)

THE reigning Duke of Saxe-Weimar, grandson of Goethe's Duke, was in London with his family on a visit to Queen Victoria in June, 1847, and the secretary of the Grand Duchess, James Marshall, a " curious little German-Irish-Scotchman ", the same who made Weimar for many years a pleasant place to English visitors, came to call on Carlyle with a letter of introduction, and a message from his mistress that she would like Carlyle to call upon her " in her wing of the Palace ". The invitation was " politely declined ". Then the Duke sent an offer to call, which was accepted, and drove up in an open carriage about four o'clock on the last Sunday of June.

Mrs. Carlyle had put her maid-of-all-work, Ann, into her best gown and gone to Mrs. Buller's to be out of the way, and, in common with the rest of Cheyne Row, Ann admired the fine clothes of the two flunkies, and afterwards described them thus : " Genteel dress—plain black coats, blue breeches, and white silk stockings—gold garters."

Ann opened the door and ushered the Duke into the dining-room on the ground floor, from which Carlyle had just escaped upstairs with an American visitor, whom he had to dismiss with apologies, and according to Mrs. Carlyle, reporting Ann no doubt, " the American loitered, and seemed to think it strange that *he* should not be invited to assist at the interview."

The Duke was accompanied by Secretary Marshall and a whiskered chamberlain, Baron Something, a most awe-struck looking man, " officially awe-struck." They were standing when Carlyle came in, and the Duke " apologised for intruding on his retired habits ", and was answered : " I am glad to see the grandson of Goethe's friend and protector." The Duke looked round the room and said that he "could fancy himself at home in Weimar here, so many reminiscences of Goethe and Germany ". He went about looking at the various portraits of Goethe, and was greatly pleased by a very fine one of Frederick the Wise, who stood by Luther at the Diet of Worms. It was an engraving of Albert Dürer's, a present from John Ruskin. The Duke at last sat on the sofa and *invited* Carlyle to be seated, and for over an hour they talked together. Carlyle told his wife that he was a young man of about twenty-four, 'straight as a rush' and 'very handsome', 'with beautiful blue eyes' and 'the most dignified German' he had ever seen, 'very much the gentleman as one might expect', yet 'not without honest sense and faculty'. He invited Carlyle to Weimar, promising to show him various things if he came, and undertaking at once to send him a scarce book they had been discussing.

"Why is German literature not more studied in England ? " was one of his questions.   "Because of our sulky radical temper," replied Carlyle.[1]

"Do not forget me. Come and see us yonder," said the Duke as he went away.

---

[1] *Literary Recollections,* by F. Espinasse, pp. 219–20, for this detail. The rest is from letters, etc., and see T. C.'s essay *The Prinzenraub,* and *J. W. Carlyle : her Letters to her Family,* by L. Huxley, pp. 301–2.

XVII

THE PROFESSION OF LETTERS

(1847)

ON 23-6-47 Carlyle was writing to Browning in Italy, congratulating him on his marriage and bespeaking a kind reception for Margaret Fuller. He let fall some remarks on their trade [1] :—

'We seem to me a people so enthralled and buried under bondage to the Hearsays and the Cants and the Grimaces, as no people ever were before. Literally so. From the top of our Metropolitan Cathedral to the sill of our lowest cobbler's shop, it is like one general *somnambulism*, most strange, most miserable—most damnable! Surely men " of genius " are commissioned under pain of death to throw their whole " genius " into the remedy ; into the battle against this! And they spend their time in traditionary rope-dancings, and talk about " Art ", and show proudly their salary,' and in short boast of being Artists. ' Surely I am against all that, and the length to which it goes, and the depth and height of it, and the fruit it bears (to Irish Sanspotatoes visibly, and to nobler men less visibly but still *more* fatally), has become frightfully apparent to me. A mighty harvest indeed ; and the labourers few or none. O for a thousand sharp sickles in as many strong right hands ! And I, poor devil, have but one rough sickle, and a hand that will soon be weary! . . .'

'Dickens writes a *Dombey and Son*, Thackeray a *Vanity Fair* ; not *reapers* they, either of them! In fact, the business of the rope-dancing goes to a great height . . .'

Perhaps there was here some kind of reference to the touching words attributed to Jesus, and more like real history than most of the Gospels :—

'When he saw the multitudes, he was moved with compassion on them, because they fainted, and were scattered

[1] *Letters of Carlyle to Mill, Sterling, and Browning*, edited by Alexander Carlyle, pp. 281–4.

abroad, as sheep having no shepherd. Then saith he unto his disciples, "The harvest truly is plenteous, but the labourers are few : pray ye therefore the Lord of the harvest that he will send forth labourers into his harvest." '

About the same time a stranger writing from Manchester inquired the economic prospects of the new " profession " of letters, and received a reply often printed. Carlyle had come to the same conclusion as the Quakers and Socrates, who " called those who took money for their discourses their own enslavers ".

'CHELSEA, *July* 1847.

'MY DEAR SIR,—Unluckily it is not possible to answer your main inquiry. The incomes of literary men even of a high reputation vary, according as the men work for popularity by itself, or for other objects, from £4,000 a year to perhaps £200 or lower. Add to which that all such incomes are uncertain, fluctuating on the wildest chance, and that not one literary man in the hundred ever becomes popular or successful at all. You perceive it is like asking what may be the income of a man that shall decide to live by gambling. No answer to be given. Reporters to the daily papers, whose industry is the humblest of all real or *un*-servile kinds in literature, receive, as I have heard, about £200 a year. Perhaps, all things considered, a man of sense, reduced to live by writing, would decide that in the economical respect these men's position was actually the best. By quitting reality again, and taking to some popular department of literary *rope-dancing*, a person of real tough-ness and assiduity, not ashamed to feel himself a slave, but able even to think himself *free* and a king in rope-dancing *well paid*, contrives, with moderate talent otherwise, if he be really tough and assiduous, to gain sometimes con-siderable wages ; in other cases dies of heartbreak, drinking and starvation. That really is his economic position, so far as I have seen it. But for a man really intent to do *a man's work* in literature in these times, I should say that even with the highest talent he might have to be fed oftentimes like Elijah, by the ravens ; and if his talent, though real, was not very high, he might easily see himself cut off from wages altogether ; all men saying to him, " The thing you have to offer us is, in the supply and demand market, worth nothing whatever." Such a man as that latter, if he could live at all, I should account him lucky.

' This, my generous young friend, this is the sad No answer I have to give you—a sad but a true one. The advice I ground on it you already discover—Not by any means to quit the solid paths of practical business for these inane froth oceans which, however gas-lighted they may be, are essentially what I have called them somewhere, base as Fleet Ditch, the mother of dead dogs. Surely it is better for a man to *work* out his God-given faculty than merely to speak it out, even in the most Augustan times. Surely of all places in this planet where the gods do most need a working man of genius is Manchester, a place sunk in sordid darkness of every kind except the glitter of gold, and which, if it were once irradiated, might become one of the beautifullest things this sun has ever seen.

' Believe me yours, with real good will, kinder than it looks.—T. CARLYLE.'

He said the same to Espinasse about the same time.[2] Espinasse had been worried out of his British Museum employment by Panizzi, and was thinking of " literature " for a living, but was admonished, " You may lead a wild Ishmaelitish life as a man of letters." It seemed better to want to " guide the people onward from day to day ". So Espinasse decided to seek work as a journalist, and Carlyle introduced him to John Forster and John Robertson that they might help him ; and when he found a place in Manchester, Carlyle encouraged him to be content there, saying Manchester was " perhaps one of the best soils in this era ". When Espinasse pleaded ignorance of politics, Carlyle approved of his ' waiting a little before meddling with them ', but said, " Politics are the grandest of all things." This puzzled Espinasse, who never saw as Emerson did that what was meant was not the politics of the politicians, or any other kind of hocus-pocus, but the right principles of action in public affairs, and in short what Aristotle and the ancients meant by Politics.

[2] *Literary Recollections*, by F. Espinasse, pp. 113 and 132, and his private talk to D. A. W. in the Charterhouse, in his old age.

XVIII

IN VACATION

(1847)

ON Friday, 6–8–47, Carlyle and his wife went together
to Matlock, or, as she expressed it, " we started on
*The Pursuit of the Picturesque under Difficulties—*the first
time in our married lives that we ever figured as declared
tourists." On the Sunday morning he took a long walk to
Cromford, and saw Arkwright's mills, ' one of them the
first erected mill in England, and consequently the Mother
of all Mills.' He found the ' *luke-warm* springs ' of Matlock
' pleasant enough to swim in ', but good for nothing as
medicine, ' except as the imagination may be solaced by
them,' and was glad to see W. E. Forster from Yorkshire
arrive on Friday, 13–8–47, to be their guide.

On Saturday they were at Buxton, ' among bare green
hills,' and here is Forster's report in a letter (16 & 17–8–47)
to his " Aunt Charles " [1] :—

' We had one rich scene. Determined to see Buxton
properly, we drove to a first-class hotel in the Crescent—
a stylish, comfortless temple of *ennui*, inhabited by old
maids, and worn-out half-pay roués, and peaked-up parsons,
a species of walking white neck-cloths, altogether a race of
men the most opposite to Carlylean that can be conceived.
Well, down we went to the table-d'hôte, self at the bottom
as last comer, C. and his wife on one side of me, and a tall,
starched, gentlemanly Irish parson on my left. For a time
all went on easily, till at last Carlyle began to converse
with parson, then to argue with him on Ireland, then to lose
thought of all argument or table-d'hôte and to declaim.
How they did stare. All other speech was hushed ; some
looked aghast, others admiring. Of course, they none of
them had ever heard or seen any approach to such a monster.
We remained *incog.* the whole time, spite of all the schemes

[1] *W. E. Foster,* by T. Wemyss Reid, chap. vii, pp. 115-20.

of the guests, and the entreaties of the waiter to book
our names, and my proposal to Mrs. C. to save our
expenses by showing him at so much a head.'

Carlyle saw something at Buxton worth telling his
mother :—

'Among the sights was that of a lone old woman living
literally like a rabbit, burrowed under ground. This was
near Buxton, a sight worth remembering. There are huge
quarries of lime there ; the rubbish, ashes of the kilns, etc.,
when many years exposed to the weather, hardens into real
stone, and is then a kind of rocky moleheap of large
dimensions, with grass on the top. The natives then scrape
out the inside, and make a cottage of the upper crust !
There are five or six such huts in that place, and used to be
more. This poor old woman and her hut, were all as tidy as
a new pin, whitewashed, scoured, etc. ; a most sensible,
haughty, and even dignified old woman, had been born there,
had lost father, mother, husband, son there, and was drinking
her poor tea there in dignified solitude when we came, no
company with her but a cat, and no wish to have any, she
said, " till the Lord was pleased to take her to those she had
lost." An elder sister, upwards of fourscore, inhabiting with
some children and grandchildren a similar cave not far
off, had just fallen into the fire and been burnt to death two
days before. None of us, I think, will ever forget that poor
old woman, with her little teapot, her neat *mutch* and black
ribbon, her lean hook nose and black old eyes as sharp as
eagles. We left a shilling with her and great respect, and
came our way.'

The next stage was Tideswell, where Carlyle was hoping
to find in the Birth Register of the Parish an entry of
James Brindley in 1716 ; but it was not there. Then on
they went to " the most enormous Cavern in the world ",
Peak Cavern now, and of old " Devil's i' Peak." Some rope-
spinners had set up their wheels in the high-vaulted entrance.
One of them was an eminent Methodist preacher. Forster
wrote to his " Aunt Charles " on the Monday :—

' I find Mrs. C. like a girl in her delight at new scenes and
situations, and the master uncommonly good-humoured
and accommodating. They have both much real heart and

genial kindness. It's little notion of a Sunday they have, but last evening I deluded them into a Methody meeting-house, for which I did catch it afterwards. It was a sad failure, a local preacher full of fluent cant, or rather a pair of them, praying at one another with all sorts of disgusting contortions, a burlesque of prayer. He was furious afterwards, declaring that their belief, if any, was in " a heaven of lubber-land ", " a paradise of Burton ale and greasy cakes ", and declared that little more would have roused him to protest that it would be well " if they would forthwith cast off this rotten blanket, and step forth in their naked skin "—said rotten blanket being the Methody garment of the religious idea.

' Of course, he constantly utters shocks to all one's ideas and principles, sacred and profane ; but it is no use arguing with him, as he takes no notice of argument.'

In 1860 the " blind preacher " from America, the Rev. Mr. Milburn, was smoking with Carlyle in the back garden at Chelsea, and happening to mention he was a Methodist, heard what he thus reported.[2]

' We've a queer place in this country called the Derbyshire Peaks ; and I was there some years ago for a part of the summer, and went on Sunday to the Methodist chapel, and a man got up and preached with extraordinary fluency and vehemence, and I was astonished at his eloquence. And they told me that he was a nail-maker ; that he wrought six days in the week with his own hands for his daily bread, and preached upon the seventh without charge. And when he had ended another man came forward and prayed ; and I was greatly moved by the unction of his prayer. And they told me that he was a rope-maker, and that he toiled as the other.

' But the sum and end of all the fluency and vehemence of the sermon, and of all the fervour of the prayer, was : " Lord, save us from Hell ! " And I went away musing, sick at heart, saying to myself : " My good fellows, why all this bother and noise ? If it be God's will, why not go and be damned in quiet, and say never a word about it. And I, for one, would think far better of you." So it seemed to me

[2] *Thomas Carlyle*, by A. H. Guernsey (1880), pp. 16–17. Mr. Guernsey, reporting Milburn, wrote " the Lord's day ", but the balance of evidence is that T. C. said " Sunday ".

that your Methodists made cowards ; and I would have no
more to do with their praying and their preaching.'   As if
they had been the only Christians afraid of Hell !

It was a natural mistake of the good blind preacher to
suppose that Carlyle used to frequent the Methodist chapels.
He never did.   And if he had believed in Hell as his
father believed, he would have had more sympathy with
shuddering sinners.

On Monday, 16–8–47, they quitted Derbyshire and went
by Sheffield and Leeds to Forster's house, between Leeds
and Bradford.   One day they were all three coming
home from Bradford, Carlyle on horseback and Forster
driving Mrs. Carlyle in his gig, the mare in the gig
began to pull, and Forster had to wind the reins round
both his hands.   After many a long pull and strong pull,
she fairly galloped away at the sound of Carlyle's horse
overtaking them.   A strap gave way, the shafts broke,
and the gig fell forward.   Mrs. Carlyle had turned round and
" embraced the gig ", and just rolled out and was not hurt.
But Forster was standing up to get purchase to pull, and so
he was shot out and sprained his ankle.   They were glad it
was no worse.

Mrs. Carlyle wrote to Mrs. Jameson soon after arrival :
' I never enjoyed a visit so much before ; and so far as I can
dive into the secret of my contentment, it lies in the
fact of there being no *women* in the house, except servants !
So that I have as fine a time of it as Beauty in the castle
of the Beast !

> " Speak thy wishes, speak thy will,
> Swift obedience meets thee still."

' The only time I have been reminded that I live in a con-
ditional world, was when pitched out of a gig ; but except
bringing me back to what Carlyle calls " the fact of things ",
even this did not harm ; I have felt rather better for the
tumble.'

She was so plainly improving in the country air and quiet
that they stayed for two or three weeks instead of days,
to the delight of Forster.   As Milnes was a neighbour,
Carlyle wrote to him (19–8–47) [3] :—

---

[3] *R. M. Milnes, L.F.*, by T. Wemyss Reid, I, pp. 386–7.

' DEAR MILNES,—Are you at present in these parts ? If you are at Fryston I will give you a meeting any day at any spot near mid-distance, and hold with you a solemn conference of more than an hour . . . '

They met accordingly, and went on together to the house of Milnes, and next day Milnes rode back with him and spent a day and night at Forster's, who wrote to Barclay Fox the day he departed :—

' Monckton Milnes came yesterday, and left this morning— a pleasant companionable little man, well fed and fattening, with some small remnant of poetry in his eyes and nowhere else ; delighting in paradoxes, but good-humoured ones ; defending all manner of people and principles in order to provoke Carlyle to abuse them, in which laudable enterprise he must have succeeded to his heart's content, and for a time we had a most amusing evening, reminding me of a naughty boy rubbing a fierce cat's tail backwards, and getting in between furious growls and fiery sparks. He managed to avoid the threatened scratches.'

This was the likeliest time and place for some words often quoted. The education controversy was waxing furious then, and Carlyle was fiercely impatient of the opposition of the churches to education, and said " among other characteristic things, that the man who had mastered the forty-seventh proposition in Euclid stood nearer to God than he had ever done before ".[4]

There was now little for the English to do about slavery ; but that made anti-slavery patter all the more popular. It may have been now that Milnes heard Carlyle say about it,[5] " An industrious man seeing a great strong man perfectly idle—a squatting, pumpkin-eating black—has the best right to make a slave of him and make him work at something."

" Forster had the greatest admiration for Carlyle," says his biographer, " but still a keener admiration for Mrs. Carlyle," of whom he once said : " She was one of those few women to whom a man could talk all day, or listen all day, with equal pleasure." Which helped to make her enjoy the visit.

[4] *Thomas Carlyle*, by W. H. Wylie, p. 63.
[5] *R. M. Milnes, L.H.*, by T. Wemyss Reid, II, p. 480.

On 3–9–47 Carlyle was reporting his wife to be " much amended and fully in her average state of health." She was also wanting now to go home, and confided to Mrs. Jameson : " While he is visiting his relations, I project a great household earthquake at Chelsea." On 6–9–47 he parted from her at the railway station at Leeds, and went himself to Manchester, while Forster wrote to his " aunt " :—

' The Carlyles left me this morning. His holiness and I have got on remarkably well these last few days, quite lovingly, and before leaving to-day he actually committed some pretty speeches to the effect that they had " reason to be thankful for three pleasant peaceful weeks ", " a sabbath in the mountains ", etc., to which I purred forth gratitude for their visit, and so we parted.

' I miss them much. He is a most delightful companion, (with) a rich store of hearty, genial, social kindness, and his eccentric humour striking laughter out of everyday occurrences. Nor, when I got accustomed to it, did I find his will by any means inconvenient. With tact one gets one's own way quite sufficiently with him.

' If Carlyle's companionship has had any mental effect upon me, it has been to give me a greater desire and possibly an increased power to discern the real " meanings of things ", to go straight to the truth wherever its hiding-place, and sometimes his words, not so much by their purport as by their tone and spirit, sounded through me like the blast of a trumpet, stirring up all my powers to the battle of life.

' Another effect has been to make me desire to sift my faith, to get yet firmer foothold, to strengthen my convictions so that I may be able to meet him or his likes, not with a mere logical opinion, but with a living faith . . . Quakerism wants universality, and somehow is hardly, to use one of Carlyle's best expressions, altogether " conformable with the everlasting laws of God written on our nature ".'

XIX

IN MANCHESTER, &c.

(1847)

ESPINASSE was now a journalist in Manchester, and met Carlyle at the Railway Station and piloted him through ' the streets and suburban highways ' [1] to the home of the Jewsburys, where Carlyle was to stay. On the way they talked much ' of France and the French '. Tho Espinasse had been educated in Edinburgh, he never forgot he was a Frenchman. Carlyle began about the Paris news, the murder there on 17-8-47 of the Duchess of Praslin by her husband, who was detected and poisoned himself to avoid a trial. Carlyle had just written to his mother about it—" that frightful murder excels in atrocity and infernal quality all that we have heard of for a long time. France, especially in the upper classes of it, is said by everybody to be in a shocking state of unprincipled depravity ; and new commotions are expected in it very confidently when once Louis Philippe has ended his cunning work in this world. The Lady was in London some years ago, when her father was Ambassador, and many persons knew her there." What Espinasse remembered was that Carlyle was ' greatly moved ' by the tragedy. Louis Philippe and his minister Guizot were exasperating the people by their repressions and their ' scandalous intrigues ' about the Spanish marriages, and the ' infamous corruption ' of civil and military officials. " France is on the verge of another insurrectionary convulsion," concluded he, with an emphasis remembered because the prophecy was so soon fulfilled.

Miss Jewsbury made the most of her opportunity and Espinasse has treasured many bits of the talk of Carlyle at her house or elsewhere in her company. He was ' full of Arkwright ', says Espinasse, and ' hinted that having then no literary enterprise on hand, he thought of settling in

---

[1] *Literary Recollections*, by F. Espinasse, pp. 145-55, for this and other quotations in this chapter.

our neighbourhood, and writing a life of Arkwright with appropriate comments '. That would have been a way of escaping from London, at any rate ; but he never did that. The Manchester folk were agreeably surprised to discover how much he knew about them. He was familiar with Edward Baines' *History of the Cotton Manufacture* and Dr. Aikin's *History of the Country forty miles round Manchester.* He said Brindley and Arkwright were " the two heroes of English Industrialism in the eighteenth century, and the Duke of Bridgewater, the founder of British canal navigation, worth almost all the English dukes put together". When, by and by, he was urging John Chorley to write a history of Lancashire, he told him : " There is not a bigger baby born of Time in these last centuries."

What most of all surprised the Manchester people was Carlyle's familiarity with *Tim Bobbin*, a humorous book in Lancashire dialect, and its author, John Collier. He ' dilated genially on Collier's speedy return to his little cottage and cheerful semi-idyllic poverty, after having been tempted away to Yorkshire to enter the well-paid service of some magnate of the woollen trade '.

He visited various mills and factories. One to which Espinasse accompanied him was Sir James Whitworth's. He said : " Whitworth puts me in mind of Thomas Watts of the British Museum. He has a face like a watch." Whitworth interested him in a new invention, ' a knitting machine, which imitated so exactly the movements of the feminine fingers, with their final jerk,' that Carlyle in watching it ' burst into a hearty laugh '. When taking refreshments Carlyle entertained Whitworth with the story of how Dr. Francia, the Dictator of Paraguay, bade the sentry make a " poor Shoemaker " walk under the gallows, to frighten him, as a punishment for spoiling the state's leather, whereby he was led to make belts better than were ever known in Paraguay, and so became Beltmaker-General. The story is told gravely in one of the books reviewed in the article *Dr. Francia*, and Carlyle was fond of quoting it, but Espinasse is surely mistaken in supposing Carlyle did not see it was a practical joke, and as he wrote in the essay, maybe ' in part poetic '.

As Carlyle had said " There is good in Bright ", he was taken to Rochdale, where John's brother Jacob received him and showed him his modern mill. The afternoon and evening were spent pleasantly at his house, and Carlyle '*launched into facts and figures to show how unjustly the Exchequer mulcted the poor, onwards from the old widow smoking her pipe of enormously-taxed tobacco*'.

Discussing the new parliament, he mentioned with 'grim satisfaction the rejection of " flowery rhetoricians " ', meaning Macaulay at Edinburgh, 'whose procedure in the Corn Law controversy had displeased the Anti-Corn Law leaguers. He laughed heartily at the statement that the extension of manufacturing round Rochdale had driven from it all but a solitary survivor of the squirearchy, substituting the mill for the manor-house. A report of some sayings and doings of a local High Church cleric led Carlyle to say with considerable emphasis that, if the Church of England went on quietly in the old ways, it might last for a long time, but that it would soon be sent about its business if it asserted sacerdotal pretensions.'

John Bright came to the drawing-room after dinner, 'with his cock nose and pugnacious eyes and Barclay-Fox-Quaker collar,' and harmony became controversy when somebody—Carlyle blamed Espinasse afterwards, but he protests it was not he, and it may have been Editor Ballantyne or Editor Ireland—began to draw out the visitor. " Abolition of Capital Punishment " seemed sublime to the Quaker ladies, and they cackled in chorus about Negro slavery. It was the English fashion then to praise ourselves as better than other people, especially the Americans, because we had paid for emancipation; and Carlyle declared it a bad thing which had ruined the West Indies. He was going on what he had heard from men who had first-hand knowledge,[2] Dumfriesshire Scots and Stephen and Taylor of the Colonial Office, John Sterling and others. John Bright triumphantly relied on statistics which showed an increase of exports—which was not convincing. Once begun to contradict each other, they could not stop. When Bright expatiated on the good that the railways had done to manufactures, Carlyle replied that much of the quiet industry of the country had been dislocated, giving as an instance a watchmaker in Dumfries ; and even when Bright was praising the benefits of education Carlyle could not agree altogether. He told of the sagacity and knowledge of his own uneducated father, " tho he could not tell you of the bitter ale consumed in the City of Prophets "—a hit at

[2] Espinasse does not mention this, but it is quite sure.

Thackeray's *Cornhill to Cairo*.   In walking home with
Espinasse, Carlyle ' spoke regretfully of his vehemence '.

' At the little parties which the Jewsburys gave,' says
Espinasse, ' Carlyle was always genial, pleasantly con-
versable, never vehement. Miss Jewsbury declared that there
was " a sort of Devil-may-care air about him which she had
never seen before ".   Samuel Bamford, the author of
Passages in the Life of a Radical, was at one time a hand-
loom weaver. He was a great admirer of Carlyle, and Carlyle
had a great regard for " the brave Bamford ",' as he calls
him in letters to John Forster. ' The two met more than once
at the Jewsburys,' and had much friendly talk. Bamford
was a genuine Radical but was looked askance at, because
all along, before, during and after the Chartist agitation, he
had steadily raised his voice against physical force or
violence.'   Which alone goes far to confirm the belief of
Espinasse that it was Carlyle's recommendation which led
Lockhart to notice the *Passages* very favourably in the Tory
Quarterly Review, and Lord Ashburton to send the author a
present of £100.

' A discussion on the relative claims of Sheridan Knowles
and Leigh Hunt to a pension, he cut short by saying—
" Pension them both."   Hunt had received his Civil List
Pension of £200 in June this year,[3] and Carlyle had helped
him to get it by a plain-spoken unpublished argument,
" Memoranda concerning Mr. Leigh Hunt." [4] But he said
nothing of that now.

Obedient to his wife, Carlyle made the acquaintance at
the Jewsburys' of a Greek merchant in Manchester, Stavros
Dilberoglue, who earned a place in this history by giving
Mrs. Carlyle the pet dog she named Nero. Remarking
Dilberoglue's long neck, ' Carlyle compared him to a crane
that had alighted on our shores and would one day wing
his way to his distant home.'

A Scotchman at the Jewsburys' sang a plaintive new
song, " There's nae covenant noo," intending to please
Carlyle, and seeming praiseworthy to Espinasse, who tells
us it was a lament over the passing away of the old creed ;
' but when it was finished Carlyle shook his head, and
hinted that the emotion was '—not genuine, in short. Of
Emerson, whom they were expecting to see soon in

---

[3] *Leigh Hunt*, by C. Monkhouse, p. 219.
[4] *On the Choice of Books*, by T. Carlyle, with a new life of the author,
by J. C. Hotten, pp. 35–8.

Manchester, 'he spoke without enthusiasm—"a flowing poetic man."'

His mother was expecting him at Scotsbrig, and he did not stay many days; but he was very pleased with his Manchester visit, and when urged to remain a little longer settled the matter in a way usual with him in such cases, tossing up a penny, and the result of the toss decided him to depart. Missing the first train by which he intended to travel, he was bitterly self-reproachful,' and amused Espinasse without intending it by exclaiming : " If my wife had been here, this would not have happened."

'Soon after arriving' at Scotsbrig, 'he wrote Miss Jewsbury one of those beautiful letters in the inditing of which none could equal him, encouraging her to make the home over which she presided the socially intellectual centre so much needed in Manchester.'

Before he went away he had been heard to "doubt" how far the work of merely " spinning clothes " was desirable occupation for great masses of human beings, "without strong counteracting influences " ; but by-and-by in talking to Espinasse, looking back on all he had seen in Lancashire, he said in conclusion : " They would do very well down there if the factory-inspectors did their duty."

The work he saw needing to be done by factory inspectors appears from a letter to his wife soon after reaching Scotsbrig (13–9–47) :—

' Oh the fetid, fuzzy, ill-ventilated mills ! And in Sharp's smithy do you remember the poor " grinders " sitting underground in a damp dark place, some dozen of them, over their screeching stone cylinders, from every cylinder a sheet of yellow *fire* issuing, the principal light of the place ? And the men, I was told, and they themselves knew it, and " did not mind it ", were all or mostly *killed* before their time, their lungs being ruined by the metal and stone dust ! These poor fellows, in their paper caps with their roaring grindstones, and their yellow *oriflammes* of fire, all grinding themselves so quietly to death, will never go out of my memory.'

" Did not mind it," it was said. They could not but mind it ; only—they saw no escape, nothing to do but die. In a sense that awaits us all ; but it is wrong to shorten life, except in relief of pain. The factory inspectors were needed to keep the conditions of work in harmony with the laws of health.

XX

AT HOME

(1847)

FROM Scotsbrig Carlyle wrote to Edward FitzGerald on 14-9-47,[1] and in anticipation of much he had to tell by word of mouth, said he had found Derbyshire ' really interesting ; and above all things a cleanly, diligent, well-doing population, in whom, as in a living Bank of England, one could trace the funded virtues of many generations of humble good men ; but no man had ever heard of Brindley ', the engineer.

Soon after Mrs. Carlyle began " earthquaking " she took to bed, being bilious and feverish. But Dr. John Carlyle came twice a day and did everything needful, tho he was " prohibited " from letting Carlyle know of the illness till it was over, and as soon as possible Lady Harriet carried her off for several days to Addiscombe. So her husband was told by her that his absence had been " the greatest possible comfort ", as the women wanted the house all to themselves.

A letter he was writing to his brother in Canada (2-10-47) shows Scotsbrig farm on a Saturday night. He and his mother were in the east room upstairs, with a bright fire, he at one table writing to his brother in Canada, and she at another writing a little note to go along with his letter, the first time she had tried to write for a year past, he told his brother. " Jenny and her bairns," his youngest sister, Mrs. Hanning, were " scouring up things " in the other end of the house, while from the ground floor below came the sound of farm work more and more subdued as the night wore on. The harvest had been " quite over, a fortnight ago ", and now :—

> " The toil-worn cotter frae his labour goes,
> This night his weekly moil is at an end,
> Collects his spades, his mattocks, and his hoes,
> Hoping the morn in ease and rest to spend."

[1] From the FitzGerald MSS. in the Library of Trinity College, Cambridge.

XXI

EMERSON IN ENGLAND

(1847)

ABOUT a week later Carlyle moved south and stayed some days at Keswick to see his friend Thomas Spedding, who had been ill. By 13-10-47 Carlyle was home, and nine days later Emerson landed at Liverpool for a lecturing tour, and was met by an invitation from Carlyle " irresistible as gravitation ", said Emerson.[1]

' The door was opened,' he wrote, ' by Jane Carlyle at ten at night, Monday (25-10-47), and the man himself was behind her with a lamp in the hall,' and saying, " Well, here we are, shovelled together again." Emerson was soon confessing to his journal, ' They were very little changed from their old selves of fourteen years ago.'
They sat up late. The next day Carlyle conducted him to Hyde Park and the Palaces, the National Gallery and the Strand, ' melting all Westminster and London into his talk and laughter.' There was plenty to look at for as many days as Emerson could stay. Breakfast was at nine. " Carlyle is very prone to sleep till ten or eleven if he has no company," said his wife severely. ' C. and his wife live on beautiful terms,' wrote Emerson, summing up his observations on this visit. ' Their ways are very engaging.'

Tho Emerson was familiar with Carlyle's writings, he was surprised at his ' real vigour and range ' of thought, which he declared could not be realized without close contact. Carlyle was ' more extraordinary ' in talking than in writing, ' his guiding genius ' being his ' perception of the sole importance of truth and justice ; and he, too, says that there is properly no religion in England '. He ' has a huge respect for the Duke of Wellington as *the only Englishman in the Aristocracy who will have nothing to do with any manner of lie* '.

[1] *Correspondence of T. Carlyle and R. W. Emerson*, II, pp. 144–52 ; and Ireland's *R. W. Emerson*, pp. 156–8 ; Cabot's, pp. 119–24 ; and see also the Lives by Garnett and Holmes, and Emerson's *Journal*.

He 'reprimanded' the American depreciation of the
British Isles, and was 'quite contemptuous' of the gabble
about " Art ", German, English and American. He ' has a
hairy strength which makes his literary vocation a mere
chance, and what seems very contemptible to him. I could
think only of an enormous trip-hammer with an Æolian
attachment ', wrote Emerson, as if flinging the pen down
in despair of describing an uncommon reality no formula
could cover.

From a rough draft of his, here are some jottings, worth
more as evidence than elaborate records :—

' His sneers and scoffs are thrown in every direction. He
breaks every sentence with a scoffing laugh—" windbag,"
" monkey," " donkey," " bladder " ; and let him describe
whom he will, it is always " poor fellow ".

' I said : " What a fine fellow are you, to bespatter the
whole world with this oil of vitriol."

' " No man," he replied, " speaks truth to me."

' I said : " See what a crowd of friends listen to you and
admire you."

' " Yes, they come to hear me, and they read what I
write ; but not one of them has the smallest intention of
doing these things." '

Emerson reported to a friend in America ² : " Carlyle takes
Cromwell sadly to heart. When I told him that he must not
expect that people as old as I could look at Cromwell as he
did, he turned quite fiercely upon me." Which made
Emerson say to Espinasse, on returning to his lecturing
headquarters at Manchester after this visit, " Carlyle's
heart is as large as the world, but he is growing morbid."
But the irritation soon disappeared, and even in the midst of
it he was " lost in wonder at the vividness of Carlyle's
conversation, more marvellous than his books ", and
" like sculpture ".³

He told Espinasse that ' Carlyle had advised him to try
some historical subject, his reply being that he had no genius
for history. Referring to Carlyle's vehement denunciations
of authorship,' meaning authorship by trade, the profession
of letters, Emerson ' said : " If Mr. Carlyle can show me any

² Cabot's *Emerson*, II, pp. 132–3.
³ *Literary Recollections*, by F. Espinasse, pp. 156–60.

MRS. CARLYLE

From a drawing by Samuel Lawrence, purchased by John Sterling, and presented by his grand-daughter, Frances Sterling, to the Carlyle House, Cheyne Row.

[face p. 400.

better employment than literature, I shall be happy to betake myself to it." '

A young Manchester vegetarian, having written a " mystical book " or two, was admired by Emerson, who had hopes of his " future "—so many vegetarians in America being prophets ; whereas Carlyle, when pressed by Bozzy Espinasse, had only " contemptuous wonder ".[3]   The matter-of-fact opinion was right, of course.   Whatever the witty Bernard Shaw may say, there is no necessary connexion between potatoes and apocalyptic visions—unless the potatoes are distilled.

XXII

SQUIRE PAPERS, &c.

(1847)

ONE of the pleasures of this November was reading John Forster's *Goldsmith*. Carlyle was fond of Forster's company, and writing to him (18–11–47) [1] declared his book 'An artistic picture of the eighteenth century, and a moral discourse on it, both in one '.

Before the month was out Carlyle had sent to *Fraser's Magazine* the Squire Papers, thirty-five Cromwell letters discovered this year, whereon there hangs a tale. In January Carlyle had received a letter from a stranger, William Squire of Yarmouth, announcing Cromwell letters in his possession, and in June FitzGerald obliged Carlyle by calling on Squire and hearing his story at full length. He reported Squire to be ' a wholesome, well-grown, florid, clear-eyed, open-browed man ' of about 38, who said that his ancestor, Samuel Squire, had been one of Cromwell's Ironsides and risen to be an ' auditor,' or adjutant, and left behind him a voluminous journal and thirty-five letters of Cromwell, mostly of 1642 and 1643. Squire's kindred had been partly Roundhead, partly Royalist; and William Squire felt it a duty to do nothing to awake anew the old animosities. The upshot was that he copied the Cromwell letters for Carlyle, and then distressed Carlyle by burning the journal and the original Cromwell manuscripts.

FitzGerald,[2] and by and by (1849) Carlyle himself, and many another who saw and heard William Squire, believed the man to be honest ; but, of course, by burning the originals he had made the copies doubtful In the absence of

---

[1] From the Carlyle letters among the John Forster MSS. in South Kensington Museum ; partly printed in the *New Letters of T. Carlyle*, edited by Alexander Carlyle, II, pp. 51–2.

[2] *Life of Edward FitzGerald*, by T. Wright, I, pp. 220–1. See also *Letters of E. FitzGerald*, MacMillan, 1894, I, pp. 231–2.

any sufficient motive for forgery, all the likelihoods are in favour of authenticity ; but when Carlyle published them the floodgates of Macaulay's pedantry were opened, and many dinner-parties bored by preposterous voluble expert demonstrations recalling the proverb of the law-courts : " The three grades of liars are liars, damned liars, and experts."

Carlyle declined debate about trifles, stated his opinion, and left the matter.[3] As he thought the letters genuine he included them and his article of December, 1847, in an appendix to later editions ; but they are all insignificant and not worth discussing. Some recent editors omit them. The only thing interesting about them is that in spite of all Macaulay could do, he could not draw Carlyle into controversy.

He was more successful with others. In dining out this winter Emerson heard old Hallam maintaining that the Squire letters were genuine, and being flooded out by Macaulay's cocksure declamation, quoting words in the letters not current till later, and so on, and so on, the sort of scholastic sophistry by which it is often possible to prove anything required—and Emerson complained : " The tiresome controversy lasted during the whole dinner." [4]

The newspapers were vacant at the moment and a fight is attractive. So there was plenty of stuff in them about Squire and his papers—the clap-trap of Macaulay reverberating far. Carlyle compared the debaters to dogs in a village barking when aroused by someone flinging a potsherd into the street. " Whaf-thaf ? Bow-wow ? " It went on till the revolutions of 1848 provided more interesting matter.

Writing to a sister at Christmas (1847), Carlyle told how he was working steadily, tho he had nothing particular as yet " on the stithy " to hammer at ; and he mentioned as good news that ' Nothing hurries me from without ; nothing. I have grown absolutely to care not about " fame "; and for the rest, I have money to buy meal and broadcloth with.'

The morbid self-consciousness that haunted him gives the delicious humour of reality to a letter he sent on the last day of December, 1847, to the Ragged School Society of

---

[3] See appendix to Vol. II of *Letters and Speeches of O. Cromwell*, 1846, and many later editions.

[4] Ireland's *Emerson*, pp. 170–1.

Dumfries.[5] He approved their aims and methods, and concluded : " One other wish I will utter, that you have virtue given you to follow that invaluable precept, let not thy left hand know what thy right hand doeth ! A precept very difficult to follow in your peculiar circumstances "— needing subscriptions—" but one which all men in all circumstances can in some measure follow, and which no man departs from without fatal damage to his enterprise."

[5] Letter still preserved in the office of the " Dumfries and Maxwelltown Industrial School ". Printed in the *Scotsman*, 20-4-1918.

CHAPTER XXIII

AN OFFER FROM ROTHSCHILD

IN 1847 London city elected L. N. Rothschild as its M.P.
When he honestly said he was unwilling to take oath
" on the true faith of a Christian ", the other M.P.s wanted
to waive the superannuated formality, but the Lords
repeatedly refused to let them. So 1847 or later is the date
for what Froude says that Carlyle told him—and it is a
pleasure to be able to quote Froude without correction.

When one of the Jew Bills was pending, Rothschild
'wrote to ask him to write a pamphlet in its favour, and
intimated that he might name any sum which he liked to
ask as payment.' " I had to tell him it couldn't be," said
Carlyle, " But I observed that I could not conceive why he
and his friends, who were supposed to be looking out for
the coming of Shiloh," or the Messiah, " should be seeking
seats in a Gentile legislature." Rothschild, in replying,
" seemed to think the coming of Shiloh was very dubious,
and that meanwhile, etc. . . ."

It was a generation afterwards that Froude heard this
confidentially. Carlyle told nobody at the time, remarking
only to his mother : " For the ' Jew Bill ' I would not give
half a snuff of tobacco, for or against. We will leave that to
fight its own battle." Rothschild had to be content with the
help of the sleek Delanes and the other regular clergy of the
Press, the natural champions of injured innocents with
plenty of money.

XXIV

SIR HARRY VERNEY

(1847–8)

IT seems to have been this winter (1847–8) that Thomas Cooper, the "moral force Chartist", saw Carlyle at tea at the house of Sir Harry Verney. Verney was an evangelical Christian of broad sympathies, ex-soldier and attaché, and for the last fifteen years M.P. for Buckingham, which he represented for over fifty years. In politics he supported Peel abolishing Corn Laws and Shaftesbury struggling to diminish "sweating", and in many ways was an ornament to the House ; but he is mainly notable now as the ideal country gentleman. On succeeding to an estate he had devoted himself to reclaiming land, repairing cottages, welcoming railways, founding Agricultural societies, and dispensing justice on the bench in a style that "raised the tone of Quarter Sessions ".[1]

According to a letter from Cooper to G. J. Holyoake,[2] Carlyle on this occasion 'boldly denounced abuses and *laissez-faire* according to his wont. He declared roundly that the enactment of the Charter is at hand—tho he does not believe it will result in immediate benefit to the people. " Profitable employment for the people is what we want," he says, and says justly. We entered largely into that all-important subject, and Sir Harry Verney eagerly and pointedly inquired what working men propose in that direction for themselves. I gave him some account of Minter Morgan's plans, of Fourierism and communism, and, at his desire, have promised to send him a list of books unfolding what those plans and systems are.' So Holyoake was asked to help to compile the list.

[1] Portrait said to be in Aylesbury Infirmary. See *Dict. of Nat. Biog. Art.* Verney, Sir H.
[2] *Life and Letters of G. J. Holyoake,* by Joseph McCabe, I, pp. 127–8.

XXV

"EXODUS FROM HOUNDSDITCH"

(1848)

THE Carlyles intended to spend five or six weeks at Alverstoke this winter ; but about 7–1–48 the day before they were to start and after their portmanteaus were all packed, Mrs. Carlyle discovered she had a sore throat, and next day she was suffering from one of her annual influenzas. Her husband went on alone on 12–1–48,[1] expecting her to follow soon.

Another guest who was in the Barings' house at the same time was his friend, Henry Taylor,[2] Colonial Office clerk and man of letters, who wrote to Miss Fenwick (22–1–48) : ' We have had Carlyle here all the time. His conversation is as bright as ever, and as striking in its imaginative effects. But guidance there is none to be got from him ; nor any illumination, save that of storm-lights. But I suppose one cannot see anything so rich and strange as his mind is without gaining by it in some unconscious way, as well as finding pleasure and pain in it. It is fruitful of both.'

Writing to Aubrey de Vere he was even more uncomplimentary to the other visitors, tho they included Milnes, fresh from Spain : ' None interesting,' writes Taylor, ' except Carlyle, who from time to time threw his blue lights across the conversation, strange and brilliant.' Describing the talk of Carlyle in general terms, Taylor says ' the iconoclast ' predominated in his conversation, and ' the idolater ' in his writings.

It was now a time of economic confusion and much unemployment. So it is easy to guess at what was most disturbing to Taylor in the talk of Carlyle, who never missed an opportunity of emphasizing his conviction that it was the business of government to organize labour and find work.

[1] Carlyle Letters in John Forster MSS., S. Kensington Museum, London.
[2] *Autobiography of Henry Taylor*, I, pp. 325–30.

Corresponding with his friend Thomas Spedding this year about the French attempts at the organization of labour, Carlyle remarked : [3] ' I find hitherto scarcely any human soul that will admit the possibility of thus dealing with Pauperism ; and no official soul that does not shriek with horror at the bare mention of it. Alas, alas, the light giggling humour of almost all official and other men, in these days, makes me for one very serious ! '

In a letter of 18–1–48 his wife told him the neatest thing that Espinasse ever wrote. ' Little Espinasse ' was seeing and hearing a great deal of Emerson in Manchester, and liking him " much better than he did ", he reported. Mrs. Carlyle wrote to him that Emerson had no ideas (except mad ones), that he had not got out of Carlyle. To which Espinasse answered : " But pray, Mrs. Carlyle, who has ? "

Carlyle came home in ten days or so, when it was clear his wife was not to join him. The most noteworthy of those who had called upon her in his absence were Sir Harry and Lady Verney, 19–1–48, whose visit she had reported to him : ' Ann putting in her head with the look of a person who had good news to tell, informed me, " I thought the gentleman looked nice, and that you would like to have him come up." And so he did look " nice "—ten years younger than when I saw him last ; and lively. I have heard no such hearty laughing as he laughed since *you* went away. " Pray, Mrs. Carlyle, will you tell us what we are to believe about these letters of Cromwell ? " ' In short the Squire papers supplied the fun on this occasion.

Dr. John Carlyle was the doctor in attendance, and having practically no other patient, he was able to give her as much of his time as she wanted, reading to her by the hour, and helping to entertain the callers. Plenty of good company was an agreeable part of his cure.

The only worry she had had was about a new work of fiction by Geraldine Jewsbury, who had become popular by sexual writing and now was naturally going farther. From Mrs. Carlyle's letters to John Forster [4] it appears that tho Carlyle had stopped his wife's proof-correcting, yet it was Mrs. Carlyle herself who, without waiting to refer to

[3] *Letters*, edited by A. Carlyle, *Cornhill Mag.*, June, 1921, p. 750.
[4] See *Letters and Memorials of J. W. Carlyle*, by J. A. Froude, II, pp. 19 and 30–1, and *New Letters and MS. of J. W. C.*, by A. Carlyle, I, pp. 238 and 242.

him, decided in his absence, on sight of the work, that
' this is perfectly disgusting for a young Englishwoman to
write. I would not have such stuff *dedicated to me* as she
proposed for any number of guineas. But I am done with
counselling her—her tendency towards the unmentionable
is too strong for *me* to stay it.'

Carlyle was now facing the problem, what to do next ?
Reduced to—what to write about ? it still was far from
simple. He took to soliloquizing in his journal (9–2–48) :—

' For above two years now I have been as good as totally
idle, composedly lying *fallow* . . . . Art, etc., has all gone
down with me, like ice too thin on a muddy pond. I do not
believe in " Art "—nay I do believe it to be one of the
deadliest *cants* ; swallowing it, too, its hecatombs of souls.

' At Alverstoke in January last for the third time now. . .
Have seen a good deal of the higher ranks—plenty of lords,
politicians, fine ladies, etc. Certainly a new *topdressing*
for me that, nor attainable either without peril. Let me see
if any growth will come of it, and what. The most striking
conclusion to me is, how like all men of all ranks in England
(and doubtless in every land) are to one another. Our
aristocracy, I rather take it, are the best, or as good as any
class we have ; but their position is fatally awry. Their
whole breeding and way of life is to go " gracefully idle "—
most tragically so ; and which of them can mend it ? . . .

' Schemes of books (to be now set about ?) " *Exodus
from Houndsditch* ",' (meaning from Christian and Jewish
superstition in every shape, Houndsditch being the old
name of the part of London frequented by Jews who dealt
in old clothes).

' That, alas ! is *impossible* as yet, tho it is the gist of all
writings and wise books, I sometimes think—the goal to
be wisely aimed at as the first of all for us. Out of
Houndsditch, indeed ! Ah, were we but out, and had our
own along with us ! But they that come out hitherto come
in a state of brutal nakedness, scandalous mutilation ; and
impartial bystanders say sorrowfully, " Return rather, it is
better even to return."

' *Ireland : Spiritual Sketches.* Begin with St. Colm. ;
end with the *rakes of Mallow.* Had I more knowledge of
Ireland, I could make something of it in that form.

' " Life of John Sterling." I really must draw up some
statement on that subject—some picture of a gifted soul

whom I knew and who was my friend. Might not many things withal be *taught* in the course of such a delineation ? '

Archdeacon Hare's *Life of Sterling* had come out in January and started religious strife ; and Captain Anthony Sterling was imploring Carlyle to place his brother in a true light. Emerson and Carlyle talked over the matter, and agreed that " Sterling was too considerable a man to be set up as a ' theological cockshy '," and that either Emerson or Carlyle must tell the truth about him. This explains Carlyle's delay—he paused to let Emerson begin, if he liked, remarking in his journal :—

' The ancient mythologies and religions were merely religious readings of the History of Antiquity, genial apprehensions, and genial (that is, always *divine*) representations of the events of earthly life, such as occur yet, only that we have no geniality to take them up, nothing but stupidity to take them up with . . .

' All sorrows are included in that ' (stupidity), ' the fountain of degradation for the modern man, who is thereby reduced to baseness in every department of his existence, and remains hopelessly captive and caitiff till the nightmare be lifted off him. Oh, ye Colleges of Ancient Art, Modern Art, High Art ! Oh, ye Priest Sanhedrins ! ye Modern Colleges, Royal Academies, ye Greek Nightmares, and still worse Hebrew Nightmares, that press out the soul of poor England and poor Europe, when will you take flight, and let us have a little breath, think you ? *Exodus from Houndsditch*, I believe, is the first beginning of such deliverance.'

Carlyle tabooed theology ; but his doing so was often eloquent, when all sorts of men were talking and writing about it, and the highest judges in the land and solemn statesmen were debating it volubly, with all the sham seriousness of the augurs, etc., of pagan Rome. A niece of Carlyle has described [5] how when she was in his house on a visit, he told her on arrival the way to every church and chapel within reach, and took pains to make her see and feel she was free to go wherever she liked ; but he was not going to any himself, " and somehow," said she, " I soon forgot all about church and chapel while I was living there." One of the amusing things about the life of Carlyle is how often he was working at the *Exodus from Houndsditch* without being aware of it.

[5] To D. A. W.

INDEX

Printed in Great Britain by Stephen Austin & Sons, Ltd., Hertford.